Taking SIDES

Clashing Views on Controversial Social Issues

Ninth Edition

Edited, Selected, and with Introductions by

Kurt Finsterbusch
University of Maryland

and
George McKenna
City College, City University of New York

Dushkin Publishing Group/Brown & Benchmark Publishers
A Times Mirror Higher Education Group Company

To Karl, Tina, Rachelle, and Craig, who are venturing forth on the sea of life to find their destiny while giving richly to people along the way.

Photo Acknowledgments

Part 1   Digital Stock
Part 2   UN PHOTO 148 578/John Isaac
Part 3   UN PHOTO 155551/R. Vogel
Part 4   UN PHOTO 150,094/Yutaka Nagata
Part 5   DPG/B&B
Part 6   UN PHOTO 153429/John Isaac

Cover Art Acknowledgment

Charles Vitelli

Manufactured in the United States of America

Ninth Edition

10 9 8 7 6 5 4 3 2 1

Library of Congress Cataloging-in-Publication Data

Main entry under title:
   Taking sides: clashing views on controversial social issues/edited, selected, and with introductions by Kurt Finsterbusch and George McKenna.—9th ed.
   Includes bibliographical references and index.
   1. Social behavior. 2. Social problems. I. Finsterbusch, Kurt, *comp.* II. McKenna, George,
comp.

302
0-697-31295-X   95-83865

 Printed on Recycled Paper

PREFACE

The English word *fanatic* is derived from the Latin *fanum*, meaning temple. It refers to the kind of madmen often seen in the precincts of temples in ancient times, the kind presumed to be possessed by deities or demons. The term first came into English usage during the seventeenth century, when it was used to describe religious zealots. Soon after, its meaning was broadened to include a political and social context. We have come to associate the term *fanatic* with a person who acts as if his or her views were inspired, a person utterly incapable of appreciating opposing points of view. The nineteenth-century English novelist George Eliot put it precisely: "I call a man fanatical when... he... becomes unjust and unsympathetic to men who are out of his own track." A fanatic may hear but is unable to listen. Confronted with those who disagree, a fanatic immediately vilifies opponents.

Most of us would avoid the company of fanatics, but who among us is not tempted to caricature opponents instead of listening to them? Who does not put certain topics off limits for discussion? Who does not grasp at euphemisms to avoid facing inconvenient facts? Who has not, in George Eliot's language, sometimes been "unjust and unsympathetic" to those on a different track? Who is not, at least in certain very sensitive areas, a *little* fanatical? The counterweight to fanaticism is open discussion. The difficult issues that trouble us as a society have at least two sides, and we lose as a society if we hear only one side. At the individual level, the answer to fanaticism is listening. And that is the underlying purpose of this book: to encourage its readers to listen to opposing points of view.

This book contains 40 selections presented in a pro and con format. A total of 20 different controversial social issues are debated. The sociologists, political scientists, economists, and social critics whose views are debated here make their cases vigorously. In order to effectively read each selection, analyze the points raised, and debate the basic assumptions and values of each position, or, in other words, in order to think critically about what you are reading, you will first have to give each side a sympathetic hearing. John Stuart Mill, the nineteenth-century British philosopher, noted that the majority is not doing the minority a favor by listening to its views; it is doing *itself* a favor. By listening to contrasting points of view, we strengthen our own. In some cases we change our viewpoints completely. But in most cases, we either incorporate some elements of the opposing view—thus making our own richer—or else learn how to answer the objections to our viewpoints. Either way, we gain from the experience.

Organization of the book   Each issue has an issue *introduction*, which sets the stage for the debate as it is argued in the YES and NO selections. Each issue

i

concludes with a *postscript* that makes some final observations and points the way to other questions related to the issue. In reading the issue and forming your own opinions you should not feel confined to adopt one or the other of the positions presented. There are positions in between the given views or totally outside them, and the *suggestions for further reading* that appear in each issue postscript should help you find resources to continue your study of the subject. At the back of the book is a listing of all the *contributors to this volume*, which will give you information on the social scientists whose views are debated here.

Changes to this edition   This new edition has been significantly updated. This edition represents a considerable revision. There are nine completely new issues: *Is the Moral Decline of America a Myth?* (Issue 1); *Does the News Media Have a Liberal Bias?* (Issue 2); *Is There a Date Rape Crisis in Society?* (Issue 5); *Should Society Be More Accepting of Homosexuality?* (Issue 6); *Are the Poor Responsible for Their Poverty?* (Issue 9); *Should Affirmative Action Policies Be Discontinued?* (Issue 10); *Is Choice a Panacea for the Ills of Public Education?* (Issue 15); *Does Population and Economic Growth Threaten Humanity?* (Issue 19); and *Are Standards of Living in the United States Improving?* (Issue 20). Of the issues retained from the previous edition, three have been changed so completely that we consider them to be new: *Is Feminism a Harmful Ideology?* (Issue 4); *Should Traditional Families Be Preserved?* (Issue 7); and *Does Welfare Do More Harm Than Good?* (Issue 14). In addition, either the YES or the NO selection has been replaced in three issues to bring the debates up to date: *Does Third World Immigration Threaten America's Cultural Unity?* (Issue 3); *Is Government Dominated by Big Business?* (Issue 12); and *Is Incapacitation the Answer to the Crime Problem?* (Issue 18). In all, there are 26 new selections. The issues that were dropped from the previous edition were done so on the recommendation of professors who let us know what worked and what could be improved. Wherever appropriate, new introductions and postscripts have been provided.

A word to the instructor   An *Instructor's Manual With Test Questions* (multiple-choice and essay) is available through the publisher for the instructor using *Taking Sides* in the classroom. A general guidebook, *Using Taking Sides in the Classroom*, which discusses methods and techniques for integrating the pro-con approach into any classroom setting, is also available.

Acknowledgments   We received many helpful comments and suggestions from our friends and readers across the United States and Canada. Their suggestions have markedly enhanced the quality of this edition of *Taking Sides* and are reflected in the new issues and the updated selections.

Our thanks go to those who responded with suggestions for this edition:

Kathy H. Edwards
Marshall University

Donald F. Anspach
University of Southern Maine

Joanne Ardovini-Brooker
Western Michigan University

Charles E. Butler
University of Oklahoma

David L. Carlson
Concordia College

Vibha Chandra
Santa Clara University

Darrell J. Cook
Benedictine College

W. Edward Folts
Appalachian State University

Jack Franklin
University of Houston

Hugo A. Freund
Drexel University

Willie Hamilton
Mount San Jacinto College

Dean R. Hoge
Catholic University

Terry Huffman
Taylor University

Karen Jennison
University of Northern
 Colorado

Andrew Kampiziones
Florence–Darlington
 Technical College

Lane Kenworthy
Rochester Institute of
 Technology

Kenneth C. Land
Duke University

James M. Makepeace
College of St. Benedict

Robert D. Manning
American University

Harold W. Moses
Bethune Cookman College

Ronald J. Oard
Mount St. Mary's College

Jane A. Penney
Eastfield College

Adrian Rapp
North Harris College

John A. Reilly
Columbia–Greene
 Community College

Judy Rosenthal
Pennsylvania State
 University–Du Bois

Charles Seidel
Mansfield University

Bhavani Sitaraman
University of Alabama–
Huntsville

Carole H. Stumbaugh
Georgia State University

William Thompson
East Texas State University

Johannes Van Vugt
St. Mary's College of
 California

We also wish to acknowledge the encouragement and support given to this project over the years by Rick Connelly, former president and publisher of the Dushkin Publishing Group, Inc. We are grateful as well to Mimi Egan, publisher for the Taking Sides series. Finally, we thank our families for their patience and understanding during the period in which we prepared this book.

Kurt Finsterbusch
University of Maryland

George McKenna
City College, City University of New York

CONTENTS IN BRIEF

PART 1   CULTURE AND VALUES   1

Issue 1.   Is the Moral Decline of America a Myth?   2

Issue 2.   Does the News Media Have a Liberal Bias?   18

Issue 3.   Does Third World Immigration Threaten America's Cultural Unity?   36

PART 2   SEX ROLES, GENDER, AND THE FAMILY   57

Issue 4.   Is Feminism a Harmful Ideology?   58

Issue 5.   Is There a Date Rape Crisis in Society?   80

Issue 6.   Should Society Be More Accepting of Homosexuality?   96

Issue 7.   Should Traditional Families Be Preserved?   112

PART 3   STRATIFICATION AND INEQUALITY   129

Issue 8.   Is Economic Inequality Beneficial to Society?   130

Issue 9.   Are the Poor Responsible for Their Poverty?   156

Issue 10.   Should Affirmative Action Policies Be Discontinued?   172

Issue 11.   Do Social and Mental Pathologies Largely Account for Homelessness?   190

PART 4   POLITICAL ECONOMY   209

Issue 12.   Is Government Dominated by Big Business?   210

Issue 13.   Should Government Intervene in a Capitalist Economy?   230

Issue 14.   Does Welfare Do More Harm Than Good?   248

Issue 15.   Is Choice a Panacea for the Ills of Public Education?   266

PART 5   CRIME AND SOCIAL CONTROL   281

Issue 16.   Is Street Crime More Harmful Than White-Collar Crime?   282

Issue 17.   Should Drugs Be Legalized?   300

Issue 18.   Is Incapacitation the Answer to the Crime Problem?   320

PART 6   THE FUTURE: POPULATION/ ENVIRONMENT/SOCIETY   341

Issue 19.   Does Population and Economic Growth Threaten Humanity?   342

Issue 20.   Are Standards of Living in the United States Improving?   362

CONTENTS

Preface   i

Introduction: Debating Social Issues   xiv

PART 1   *CULTURE AND VALUES*   1

ISSUE 1.   Is the Moral Decline of America a Myth?   2
YES: Everett C. Ladd, from "The Myth of Moral Decline," *The Responsive Community*   4
NO: James Patterson and Peter Kim, from "The Decline and Fall: An Alarmed Perspective," *The Responsive Community*   13

Everett C. Ladd, president of the Roper Center for Public Opinion, argues that the evidence shows that the moral decline thesis is a myth. Businessmen and community volunteers James Patterson and Peter Kim maintain that America is in moral decline and that its central institutions are suffering.

ISSUE 2.   Does the News Media Have a Liberal Bias?   18
YES: H. Joachim Maitre, from "The Tilt to the News: How American Journalism Has Swerved from the Ideal of Objectivity," *The World and I*   20
NO: Martin A. Lee and Norman Solomon, from *Unreliable Sources: A Guide to Detecting Bias in News Media*   27

Journalism professor H. Joachim Maitre argues that news reporters are liberals who allow their political views to seep into their reporting. Media critics Martin A. Lee and Norman Solomon argue that media bias in reporting is toward the conservative status quo.

ISSUE 3.   Does Third World Immigration Threaten America's Cultural Unity?   36
YES: Peter Brimelow, from *Alien Nation: Common Sense About America's Immigration Disaster*   38
NO: Francis Fukuyama, from "Immigrants and Family Values," *Commentary*   44

Peter Brimelow, a writer and senior editor of *Forbes* and *National Review*, asserts that immigrants from non-European countries are steadily breaking down cultural unity in the United States. Francis Fukuyama, a former deputy director of the U.S. State Department's policy planning staff, argues that today's immigrants may actually strengthen America's cultural foundations because they share many of America's traditional values.

PART 2   SEX ROLES, GENDER, AND THE FAMILY   57

ISSUE 4.   Is Feminism a Harmful Ideology?   58
YES: **Robert Sheaffer,** from "Feminism, the Noble Lie," *Free Inquiry*   60
NO: **William H. Chafe,** from *The Paradox of Change: American Women in the Twentieth Century*   67

Robert Sheaffer, a consulting editor for *Skeptical Inquirer*, argues that feminists are attempting to impose an inappropriate equality on men and women that conflicts with basic biological differences between the genders. William H. Chafe, a professor at Duke University, maintains that the vast improvements that women have made and the obvious need to end continuing discrimination demonstrate the value of feminism.

ISSUE 5.   Is There a Date Rape Crisis in Society?   80
YES: **Robin Warshaw,** from *I Never Called It Rape: The* Ms. *Report on Recognizing, Fighting, and Surviving Date and Acquaintance Rape*   82
NO: **Katie Roiphe,** from "Date Rape's Other Victim," *The New York Times Magazine*   88

Journalist Robin Warshaw presents evidence indicating that a high percentage of college women are victims of date rape, though few report the crime to authorities. Author Katie Roiphe challenges the statistics about date rape and criticizes those who contend that there is a date rape crisis for undermining the autonomy of women.

ISSUE 6.   Should Society Be More Accepting of Homosexuality?   96
YES: **Richard D. Mohr,** from *A More Perfect Union: Why Straight America Must Stand Up for Gay Rights*   98
NO: **Carl F. Horowitz,** from "Homosexuality's Legal Revolution," *The Freeman*   105

Philosophy professor Richard D. Mohr argues that homosexuality is neither immoral nor unnatural and that homosexuals should have the same rights as heterosexuals. Carl F. Horowitz, a policy analyst at the Heritage Foundation, argues that legal acceptance of homosexuality has already gone too far.

ISSUE 7.   Should Traditional Families Be Preserved?   112

YES: **David Popenoe,** from "The American Family Crisis," *National Forum: The Phi Kappa Phi Journal*   114

NO: **Judith Stacey,** from "Dan Quayle's Revenge: The New Family Values Crusaders," *The Nation*   121

Sociologist David Popenoe contends that the traditional family's societal functions have declined dramatically in the last several decades, with very adverse effects on children. Sociologist Judith Stacey argues that high-conflict marriages are more harmful to children than low-conflict divorces and that single-parent families are roughly as good for children as two-parent families when income and self-esteem are the same.

PART 3   STRATIFICATION AND INEQUALITY   129

ISSUE 8.   Is Economic Inequality Beneficial to Society?   130

YES: **George Gilder,** from *Wealth and Poverty*   132

NO: **William Ryan,** from *Equality*   144

Social critic George Gilder argues that the American political economy provides many incentives for people to get ahead and make money and that, as a result, all classes of people benefit. Professor of psychology William Ryan contends that income inequalities in America are immoral because they vastly exceed differences of merit and result in tremendous hardship for the poor.

ISSUE 9.   Are the Poor Responsible for Their Poverty?   156

YES: **Edward Banfield,** from *The Unheavenly City*   158

NO: **Jonathan Kozol,** from "Poverty's Children: Growing Up in the South Bronx," *The Progressive*   163

Sociologist Edward Banfield asserts that a cultural outlook that is unique to the poor tends to keep them in poverty. Author Jonathan Kozol argues that structural conditions and personal tragedies create poverty independent of any culture of the poor.

ISSUE 10.   Should Affirmative Action Policies Be Discontinued?   172

YES: **Arch Puddington,** from "What to Do About Affirmative Action," *Commentary*   174

NO: **Roger Wilkins,** from "The Case for Affirmative Action: Racism
Has Its Privileges," *The Nation*   **180**

Policy analyst Arch Puddington argues that Americans support antidiscrim-
ination laws but strongly oppose racial preference policies. Professor of history Roger Wilkins argues that racism and discrimination are still virulent
and that the right kind of affirmative action will benefit whites as well as
blacks.

**ISSUE 11. Do Social and Mental Pathologies Largely Account for
Homelessness?**   **190**

YES: **Myron Magnet,** from *The Dream and the Nightmare: The Sixties'
Legacy to the Underclass*   **192**

NO: **Jonathan Kozol,** from *Rachel and Her Children: Homeless Families
in America*   **199**

Essayist Myron Magnet argues that the vast majority of the permanently
homeless consist of pathological individuals taking advantage of public shelters and other state-run charities. Social commentator Jonathan Kozol maintains that homelessness is the result of the lack of affordable housing and an
economic downturn that has forced the poor into the streets.

PART 4   POLITICAL ECONOMY   **209**

ISSUE 12. Is Government Dominated by Big Business?   **210**

YES: **John C. Berg,** from *Unequal Struggle: Class, Gender, Race, and
Power in the U.S. Congress*   **212**

NO: **Jeffrey M. Berry,** from "Citizen Groups and the Changing
Nature of Interest Group Politics in America," *The Annals of the
American Academy of Political and Social Science*   **220**

John C. Berg, a professor at Suffolk University, argues that the U.S. government takes care of the interests of big business while largely ignoring the
interests of the working class. Jeffrey M. Berry, a professor of political science,
contends that public interest pressure groups have effectively challenged the
political power of big business.

ISSUE 13. Should Government Intervene in a Capitalist Economy?   **230**

YES: **Ernest Erber,** from "Virtues and Vices of the Market: Balanced
Correctives to a Current Craze," *Dissent*   **232**

NO: Milton and Rose Friedman, from *Free to Choose: A Personal Statement*   **239**

Author Ernest Erber argues that capitalism creates serious social problems that require government intervention to correct. Economists Milton and Rose Friedman maintain that the market operates effectively and protects citizens better when permitted to work without the interference of government regulations.

ISSUE 14.   Does Welfare Do More Harm Than Good?   **248**

YES: Charles Murray, from "What to Do About Welfare," *Commentary* **250**

NO: Mark Robert Rank, from *Living on the Edge: The Realities of Welfare in America*   **257**

Researcher and social critic Charles Murray argues that welfare contributes to dependency, illegitimacy, and absent fathers, and that the abolition of welfare will greatly reduce these problems. Sociologist Mark Robert Rank asserts that welfare is not financially lucrative enough to entice people to its way of life.

ISSUE 15.   Is Choice a Panacea for the Ills of Public Education?   **266**

YES: John E. Chubb and Terry M. Moe, from "America's Public Schools: Choice *Is* a Panacea," *The Brookings Review*   **268**

NO: Bill Honig, from "Why Privatizing Public Education Is a Bad Idea," *The Brookings Review*   **274**

Political scientists John E. Chubb and Terry M. Moe contend that school choice will liberate school personnel from bureaucratic controls and enhance school performance through competition. Public school superintendent Bill Honig maintains that the reforms of the 1980s have largely overcome the problems of stifling bureaucracy and that the school choice program would greatly increase educational inequality.

PART 5   CRIME AND SOCIAL CONTROL   **281**

ISSUE 16.   Is Street Crime More Harmful Than White-Collar Crime?   **282**

YES: John J. DiIulio, Jr., from "The Impact of Inner-City Crime," *The Public Interest*   **284**

NO: Jeffrey Reiman, from *The Rich Get Richer and the Poor Get Prison: Ideology, Class, and Criminal Justice,* 3rd ed.   **290**

John J. DiIulio, Jr., an associate professor of politics and public affairs, analyzes the enormous harm done to all of society by street criminals and their activities. Professor of philosophy Jeffrey Reiman argues that the dangers posed by negligent corporations and white-collar criminals pose a greater threat to society than do typical street criminals.

ISSUE 17. Should Drugs Be Legalized?   **300**

YES: Ethan A. Nadelmann, from "Should We Legalize Drugs? Yes,"
American Heritage   **302**

NO: David T. Courtwright, from "Should We Legalize Drugs? No,"
American Heritage   **310**

Ethan A. Nadelmann, an assistant professor of politics and public affairs, argues that drug prohibition exacerbates the drug problem and that controlled legalization would reduce the drug problem in the United States. Professor of history David T. Courtwright argues that the government should continue the war against drugs because legalizing drugs would not eliminate drug-related criminal activity and would increase drug use.

ISSUE 18. Is Incapacitation the Answer to the Crime Problem?   **320**

YES: Morgan O. Reynolds, from "Crime Pays, But So Does Imprisonment," *Journal of Social, Political, and Economic Studies*   **322**

NO: D. Stanley Eitzen, from "Violent Crime: Myths, Facts, and Solutions," *Vital Speeches of the Day*   **331**

Professor of economics Morgan O. Reynolds argues that "crime pays" for most criminals but that catching, convicting, and imprisoning more criminals would greatly reduce the crime rate. Professor emeritus of sociology D. Stanley Eitzen argues that the "get tough with criminals" approach to reducing crime costs too much and does not deal with the fundamental causes of crime.

PART 6   THE FUTURE: POPULATION/
          ENVIRONMENT/SOCIETY   341

ISSUE 19. Does Population and Economic Growth Threaten
           Humanity?   342
YES: Lester R. Brown, from "Nature's Limits," in Lester R. Brown et
al., *State of the World 1995*   344
NO: Julian L. Simon, from "The State of Humanity: Steadily
Improving," *Cato Policy Report*   354

Lester R. Brown, president of the Worldwatch Institute, argues that the environment is deteriorating because of economic and population growth. Julian L. Simon, a professor of economics and business administration, asserts that population and economic growth are benefiting, not threatening, humanity.

ISSUE 20. Are Standards of Living in the United States Improving? 362
YES: W. Michael Cox and Richard Alm, from "The Good Old Days
Are Now," *Reason*   364
NO: Beth A. Rubin, from *Shifts in the Social Contract: Understanding
Change in American Society*   373

Economist and banker W. Michael Cox and business journalist Richard Alm contend that Americans consume more, live better, live longer and healthier, achieve a higher net worth, enjoy more leisure time, and have more income per capita today than in 1970. Sociology professor Beth A. Rubin claims that Americans have lost income on average over the past 25 years and have experienced instability in their family relationships.

Contributors   384

Index   388

INTRODUCTION

Debating Social Issues

Kurt Finsterbusch
George McKenna

WHAT IS SOCIOLOGY?

"I have become a problem to myself," St. Augustine said. Put into a social and secular framework, St. Augustine's concern marks the starting point of sociology. We have become a problem to ourselves, and it is sociology that seeks to understand the problem and, perhaps, to find some solutions. The subject matter of sociology, then, is ourselves—people interacting with one another in groups.

Although the subject matter of sociology is very familiar, it is often useful to look at it in an unfamiliar light, one that involves a variety of theories and perceptual frameworks. In fact, to properly understand social phenomena, it *should* be looked at from several different points of view. In practice, however, this may lead to more friction than light, especially when each view proponent says, "I am right and you are wrong," rather than, "My view adds considerably to what your view has shown."

Sociology, as a science of society, was developed in the nineteenth century. Auguste Comte (1798–1857), the French mathematician and philosopher who is considered to be the father of sociology, had a vision of a well-run society based on social science knowledge. Sociologists (Comte coined the term) would discover the laws of social life and then determine how society should be structured and run. Society would not become perfect, because some problems are intractable, but he believed that a society guided by scientists and other experts was the best possible society.

Unfortunately, Comte's vision was extremely naive. For most matters of state there is no one best way of structuring or doing things that sociologists can discover and recommend. Instead, sociologists debate more social issues than they resolve.

The purpose of sociology is to throw light on social issues and their relationship to the complex, confusing, and dynamic social world around us. It seeks to describe how society is organized and how individuals fit into it. But neither the organization of society nor the fit of individuals is perfect. Social disorganization is a fact of life—at least in modern, complex societies such as the one we live in. Here, perfect harmony continues to elude us, and "social problems" are endemic. The very institutions, laws, and policies that produce benefits also produce what sociologists call "unintended effects"— unintended and undesirable. The changes that please one sector of the society may displease another, or the changes that seem so indisputably healthy at first turn out to have a dark underside to them. The examples are endless. Modern urban life gives people privacy and freedom from snooping neighbors that the small town never afforded; yet, that very privacy seems to breed an uneasy sense of anonymity and loneliness. Take another example: Hierarchy is necessary for organizations to function efficiently, but hierarchy leads to the creation of a ruling elite. Flatten out the hierarchy and you may achieve social equality—but at the price of confusion, incompetence, and low productivity.

This is not to say that all efforts to effect social change are ultimately futile and that the only sound view is the tragic one that concludes "nothing works." We can be realistic without falling into despair. In many respects, the human condition has improved over the centuries and has improved as a result of conscious social policies. But improvements are purchased at a price—not only a monetary price but one involving human discomfort and discontent. The job of policymakers is to balance the anticipated benefits against the probable costs.

It can never hurt policymakers to know more about the society in which they work or the social issues they confront. That, broadly speaking, is the purpose of sociology. It is what this book is about. This volume examines issues that are central to the study of sociology.

CULTURE AND VALUES

A common value system is the major mechanism for integrating a society, but modern societies contain so many different groups with differing ideas and values that integration must be built as much on tolerance of differences as on common values. Furthermore, technology and social conditions change, so values must adjust to new situations, often weakening old values. Some people (often called conservatives) will defend the old values. Others (often called liberals) will make concessions to allow for change. For example, the protection of human life is a sacred value to most people, but some would compromise that value when the life involved is a 90-year-old comatose man on life-support machines who had signed a document indicating that he did not want to be kept alive under those conditions. The conservative would counter that once we make the value of human life relative, we become dangerously open to greater evils—that perhaps society will come to think it acceptable to terminate all sick, elderly people undergoing expensive treatments. This is only one example of how values are hotly debated today. Three debates on values are presented in Part 1. In Issue 1, Everett C. Ladd challenges the common perception that morals have declined in America, while James Patterson and Peter Kim provide empirical support for the declining morality thesis. In Issue 2, the news media, which is a major influence on people's values, is analyzed for its bias. H. Joachim Maitre objects to the news media for being too liberal, while Martin A. Lee and Norman Solomon maintain that it is actually too conservative. In Issue 3, Peter Brimelow argues that the current levels of immigration are too high and that the immigrant cultures are too different from American culture to be assimilated. Thus, immigration is threatening America's cultural unity. Francis Fukuyama, in opposition, maintains that many of the new immigrants have very strong family values and work ethics, which will strengthen—not weaken—American culture.

SEX ROLES, GENDER, AND THE FAMILY

An area that has experienced tremendous value change in the last several decades is sex roles and the family. Women in large numbers have rejected major aspects of their traditional gender roles and family roles while remaining strongly committed to much of the mother role and to many feminine characteristics. In fact, on these issues women are deeply divided. The ones who seek the most change identify themselves as feminists, and they have been at the forefront of the modern women's movement. Now a debate is raging as to whether or not the feminist cause really helps women. In Issue 4, Robert Sheaffer attacks feminism as intellectually unsound and doomed to failure because its goals conflict with biological realities. William H. Chafe identifies many positive changes that feminists have brought about and many changes that are still needed. Issue 5 focuses on date rape, which is an issue that has only recently begun to be taken seriously. One crusader who has made the topic more visible is Robin Warshaw. In Issue 5, she reports research showing that date rape is quite common and is usually suffered in silence. As a result, little has been done to change the situation. Katie Roiphe questions statistics that indicate that there is date rape crisis and argues that women should take more responsibility for what takes place sexually on dates. Issue 6 deals with the gay rights movement and discrimination against homosexuals. Richard D. Mohr argues that homosexuals are unjustly treated. He further contends that homosexuality is neither immoral nor unnatural and that it should be tolerated and respected. Carl F. Horowitz argues that the more blatant behaviors of many homosexuals are deeply offensive to heterosexuals and that communities have the right to control the undesirable behavior of gay men and lesbians. Issue 7, which has been much debated by feminists and their critics, asks, Should traditional families be preserved? David Popenoe is deeply concerned about the decline of the traditional family, while Judith Stacey thinks that such concern amounts to little more than nostalgia for a bygone era.

STRATIFICATION AND INEQUALITY

Issue 8 centers around a perennial sociological debate about whether or not economic inequality is beneficial (functional) to society. George Gilder claims that it is, while William Ryan argues that inequalities should be greatly reduced. Closely related to this debate is the issue of why the poor are poor.

The "culture of poverty" thesis maintains that most long-term poverty in America is the result of a common culture among the poor. The implication is that those who always seek immediate material gratification will not climb out of poverty, even if they are helped by welfare and other social programs. Others see most of the poor as victims of adverse conditions; they consider the culture of poverty thesis a way of "blaming the victim." Issue 9 offers two very different views on this issue, with Edward Banfield arguing that "lower-class culture" does perpetuate poverty, and Jonathan Kozol arguing that very adverse conditions of life or personal pathologies and health problems are the primary causes of poverty.

Today one of the most controversial issues regarding inequalities is affirmative action. Is equality promoted or undermined by such policies? Arch Puddington and Roger Wilkins take opposing sides on this question in Issue 10. The final issue under the topic of stratification deals with those who are closest to the bottom of American society: the homeless. Who are the homeless, and why do they live in the streets? This is a divisive issue because people have very different feelings toward and notions about the homeless. In Issue 11, Myron Magnet minimizes their numbers and portrays them as largely socially and mentally pathological. Jonathan Kozol maximizes their numbers and depicts the majority of them as regular people who have been very unfortunate.

POLITICAL ECONOMY

Sociologists study not only the poor, the workers, and the victims of discrimination but also those at the top of society—those who occupy what the late sociologist C. Wright Mills used to call "the command posts." The question is whether the "pluralist" model or the "power elite" model is the one that best fits the facts in America. Does a single power elite rule the United States, or do many groups contend for power and influence so that the political process is accessible to all? In Issue 12, John C. Berg argues that the business elite have a dominating influence in government decisions and that no other group has nearly as much power. Jeffrey M. Berry counters that liberal citizen groups have successfully opened the policy-making process and made it more participatory. Currently, grassroots groups of all kinds have some power and influence. The question is, how much?

The United States is a capitalist welfare state, and the role of the state in capitalism (more precisely, the market) and in welfare is examined in the next two issues. Issue 13 considers whether or not the government should step in and attempt to correct for the failures of the market through regulations, policies, and programs. Ernest Erber argues that an active government is needed to protect consumers, workers, and the environment; to bring about greater equality; and to guide economic and social change. Milton and Rose Friedman argue that even well-intended state interventions in the market usually only make matters worse and that governments cannot serve the public good as effectively as competitive markets can. One way in which the government intervenes in the economy is by providing welfare to people who cannot provide for their own needs in the labor market. Issue 14 debates the wisdom of current welfare policies. In it, Charles Murray contends that many welfare programs of the Great Society have mired people in dependency, spawned illegitimacy, and should be abandoned. Mark Robert Rank interviews many welfare recipients and finds that most of them are driven to welfare by economic crises. Welfare, he asserts, is too stingy to entice people to its way of life.

Education is one of the biggest jobs of government as well as the key to individual prosperity and the success of the economy. For decades the American system of education has been severely criticized. Recently the criticism has brought education into an ideological debate over the proper role of the government, private enterprise, and markets in public education. In Issue 15, John E. Chubb and Terry M. Moe argue that under the current system, governments cannot run schools well, because they must rely too much on bureaucratic controls, which prevent teachers from doing their jobs well. They conclude that school choice and the competition it induces will remove most of the counterproductive, top-down controls and will reward performance. Bill Honig argues that radical educational reforms are not necessary because the reforms of the 1980s have largely overcome the problems of stifling bureaucracy. He fears that the school choice program would greatly increase educational inequality.

CRIME AND SOCIAL CONTROL

Crime is interesting to sociologists because crimes are those activities that society makes illegal and will use force to stop. Why are some acts made illegal and others (even those that may be more harmful) not made illegal? Surveys indicate that concern about crime is extremely high in America. Is the fear of crime, however, rightly placed? Americans fear mainly street crime, but Jeffrey Reiman argues in Issue 16 that corporate crime—also known as "white-collar crime"—causes far more death, harm, and financial loss to Americans than street crime. In contrast, John DiIulio points out the great harm done by street criminals, even to the point of social disintegration in some poor neighborhoods. Much of the harm that DiIulio describes is related to the illegal drug trade, which brings about such bad consequences that some people are seriously talking about legalizing drugs in order to kill the illegal drug business. Ethan A. Nadelmann argues this view in Issue 17, while David T. Courtwright argues that legalization would greatly expand the use of dangerous drugs and increase the personal tragedies and social costs resulting therefrom. Finally, Issue 18 examines the extent to which deterrence or tough sentencing of criminals reduces crime. The debate is whether American society should focus on deterrence by meting out sentencing on a tougher and more uniform basis or whether the emphasis should be on rehabilitating criminals and eliminating the social conditions that breed crime. These alternatives are explored in the debate by Morgan O. Reynolds and D. Stanley Eitzen.

THE FUTURE: POPULATION/ENVIRONMENT/SOCIETY

Many social commentators speculate on "the fate of the earth." The environmentalists have their own vision of apocalypse. They see the possibility that the human race could overshoot the carrying capacity of the globe. The resulting collapse could lead to the extinction of much of the human race and the end of free societies. Population growth and increasing per capita levels of consumption, say some experts, are leading us to this catastrophe. Others believe that these fears are groundless. In Issue 19, Lester R. Brown and Julian L. Simon argue over whether or not the world is threatened by population and economic growth.

The last issue in this book tries to assess the status in America of people's standards of living. In Issue 20, Beth A. Rubin presents trends showing that Americans are losing out economically, socially, and psychologically. W. Michael Cox and Richard Alm, in contrast, argue that Americans have never had it so good. Although they may not make as much money in real terms, they buy more with their money and live longer and healthier lives.

THE SOCIAL CONSTRUCTION OF REALITY

An important idea in sociology is that people construct social reality in the course of interaction by attaching social meanings to the reality they are experiencing and then responding to those meanings. Two people can walk down a city street and derive very different meanings from what they see around them. Both, for example, may see homeless people—but they may see them in different contexts. One fits them into a picture of once-vibrant cities dragged into decay and ruin because of permissive policies that have encouraged pathological types to harass citizens; the other observer fits them into a picture of an America that can no longer hide the wretchedness of its poor. Both feel that they are seeing something deplorable, but their views of what makes it deplorable are radically opposed. Their differing views of what they have seen will lead to very different prescriptions for what should be done about the problem. And their policy arguments will be based upon the pictures in their heads, or the constructions they have made of reality.

The social construction of reality is an important idea for this book because each author is socially constructing reality and working hard to persuade you to see his or her point of view; that is, to see the definition of the situation and the set of meanings he or she has assigned to the situation. In doing this, each author presents a carefully selected set of facts, arguments, and values. The arguments contain assumptions or theories, some of which are spelled out and some of which are unspoken. The critical reader has to judge the evidence for the facts, the logic and soundness of the arguments, the importance of the values, and whether or not omitted facts, theories, and values invalidate the thesis. This book facilitates this critical thinking process by placing authors in opposition. This puts the reader in the position of critically evaluating two constructions of reality for each issue instead of one.

CONCLUSION

Writing in the 1950s, a period that was in some ways like our own, the sociologist C. Wright Mills said that Americans know a lot about their "troubles" but that they cannot make the connections between seemingly personal concerns and the concerns of others in the world. If they could only learn to make those connections, they could turn their concerns into *issues*. An issue transcends the realm of the personal. According to Mills, "An issue is a public matter: some value cherished by publics is felt to be threatened. Often there is a debate about what the value really is and what it is that really threatens it."

It is not primarily personal troubles but social issues that we have tried to present in this book. The variety of topics in it can be taken as an invitation to discover what Mills called "the sociological imagination." This imagination, said Mills, "is the capacity to shift from one perspective to another—from the political to the psychological; from examination of a single family to comparative assessment of the national budgets of the world.... It is the capacity to range from the most impersonal and remote transformations to the most intimate features of the human self—and to see the relations between the two." This book, with a range of issues well suited to the sociological imagination, is intended to enlarge that capacity.

PART 1

Culture and Values

Sociologists recognize that a fairly strong consensus on the basic values of a society contributes greatly to the smooth functioning of that society. The functioning of modern, complex urban societies, however, often depends on the tolerance of cultural differences and equal rights and protections for all cultural groups. In fact, such societies can be enriched by the contributions of different cultures. But at some point the cultural differences may result in a pulling apart that exceeds the pulling together. Three areas where the issue of cultural consensus or cultural clashes is prominent today are moral decline, the news media, and the immigration of peoples from different cultures. Analysis of these issues involves strongly held value differences.

- Is the Moral Decline of America a Myth?

- Does the News Media Have a Liberal Bias?

- Does Third World Immigration Threaten America's Cultural Unity?

ISSUE 1

Is the Moral Decline of America a Myth?

YES: Everett C. Ladd, from "The Myth of Moral Decline," *The Responsive Community* (vol. 4, no. 1, 1993/1994)

NO: James Patterson and Peter Kim, from "The Decline and Fall: An Alarmed Perspective," *The Responsive Community* (vol. 4, no. 1, 1993/1994)

ISSUE SUMMARY

YES: Everett C. Ladd, president of the Roper Center for Public Opinion, empirically tests the moral decline thesis and finds that, according to the indicators that he employs, it is a myth.

NO: Businessmen and community volunteers James Patterson and Peter Kim survey a wide variety of indicators suggesting that America is in moral decline and that its central institutions are suffering.

Morality is the glue that holds society together. It enables people to deal with each other in relative tranquility and generally to their mutual benefit. Morality influences us both from the outside and from the inside. The morality of others affects us from outside as social pressure. Our conscience is morality affecting us from inside, even though others, especially parents, influence the formation of our conscience. Because parents, churches, schools, and peers teach us their beliefs and values (their morals) and the rules of society, most of us grow up wanting to do what is right. We also want to do things that are pleasurable. In a well-functioning society the right and the pleasurable are not too far apart, and most people lead morally respectable lives. On the other hand, no one lives up to moral standards perfectly. In fact, deviance from some moral standards is common, and when it becomes very common the standard changes. Some people interpret this as moral decline, while others interpret it as simply a change in moral standards or even as progress.

The degree of commitment to various moral precepts varies from person to person. Some people even act as moral guardians and take responsibility for encouraging others to live up to the moral standards. One of their major tactics is to cry out against the decline of morals. There are a number of such voices speaking out in public today. In fact, many politicians seem to try to outdo each other in speaking out against crime, teenage pregnancy, divorce, violence in the media, latchkey children, irresponsible parenting, etc.

Cries of moral decline have been ringing out for centuries. In earlier times the cries were against sin, debauchery, and godlessness. Today the cries are often against various aspects of individualism. Parents are condemned for sacrificing their children for their own needs, including their careers. Divorced people are condemned for discarding spouses instead of working hard to save their marriages. Children of elderly parents are condemned for putting their parents into nursing homes to avoid the inconvenience of caring for them. The general public is condemned for investing so little time in others and their communities while pursuing their own interests. These criticisms against individualism may have some validity. On the other hand, individualism has some more positive aspects, including enterprise and inventiveness, which contribute to economic growth; individual responsibility; advocacy of human rights; reduced clannishness and prejudice toward other groups; and an emphasis on self-development, which includes successful relations with others.

The morality debate is important because moral decline not only increases human suffering but also weakens society and hinders the performance of its institutions. The following selections require some deep reflection on the moral underpinnings of American society as well as other societies, and they invite the reader to strengthen those underpinnings.

Everett C. Ladd denies the common viewpoint that a serious moral decline is in progress. He argues that numerous morality indicators do not show the decline that the decline thesis expects. Therefore, even in the face of the statistics on crime and divorce, Ladd concludes that there has not been "a deterioration of moral conduct." James Patterson and Peter Kim examine numerous indicators and find that the conventional view of moral decline is not a myth. They argue that Americans do not recognize moral authorities but set themselves "as the sole arbiter of moral life." In other words, morality is becoming privatized, which could be dangerous in the long run.

YES

Everett C. Ladd

THE MYTH OF MORAL DECLINE

The moral state of the United States is the subject of enormous attention and concern. Although this has been a recurring theme throughout American history, there is some indication that concern has grown in our own time. Rushworth M. Kidder, President of the Institute for Global Ethics, recently noted in *The Public Perspective* that dozens of ethics organizations are springing up across the nation, hundreds of executive ethics seminars are conducted every year, and thousands of students are participating in character education at school. The press is now full of discussions of ethics issues. Kidder cites data showing, for example, that between 1969 and 1989 the number of stories found under "ethics" in the *New York Times* index increased four-fold.

Survey data also indicate that the proportion of the public troubled by what they perceive to be serious deficiencies in the moral state of the nation is not only large but expanding. True, throughout the span of our history for which we have survey data, large majorities have expressed dissatisfaction with such matters as the honesty and standards of behavior of their fellow citizens. Nonetheless, the proportions today are at the highest levels we have seen. For instance, in 1938, when asked if the "general morals" of young unmarried people were better or worse than they had been 10 years earlier, 42 percent of those interviewed by the Roper Organization said they were worse, compared to just 13 percent who said they were better. In 1987, 60 percent of those interviewed in a Yankelovich Clancy Shulman poll said teenagers were "less moral in their behavior at present than when [the respondents] were growing up," while only 11 percent described young people as more moral. Every time we have located a pair of queries like this from the 1930s–50s span on the one hand, and from the 1980–90s on the other, we have found the same pattern: Majorities always profess to see decline in moral standards, but the majority is larger in the contemporary period than earlier.

Again and again, polls show Americans expressing this kind of values nostalgia. But has there in fact been a deterioration in moral conduct in the United States, as compared to, say, the 1950s? Ethical norms and moral

From Everett C. Ladd, "The Myth of Moral Decline," *The Responsive Community*, vol. 4, no. 1 (1993/1994). Copyright © 1993/1994 by *The Responsive Community*. Reprinted by permission.

conduct are of great importance to the health of the American society and polity, and it certainly matters which way the great engines of contemporary society are pulling us with regard to them. Yet for all the importance of this question and the attention it has received, the data are not as clear as the polls might suggest.

THERE'S ALWAYS SO MUCH WRONG

One obstacle standing in the way of productive analysis involves the fact that at every point in time, in the view of many thoughtful people, ethical standards and moral conduct leave much to be desired. Michael Josephson and his colleagues have attempted empirical work on Americans' moral judgments and behavior which, they say, reveals that a "disturbingly high proportion of young people regularly engage in dishonest and irresponsible behavior." What an extraordinary way to put it! It is, after all, a little late in human history to present as a finding that a disturbingly high proportion of people variously err and sin. The Josephson study documents that many young people are struggling and stumbling ethically, but it tells us nothing about whether things are actually getting better or worse.

Is the contemporary U.S. beset with moral decline? If we had a "Morality Index," on which 100 was utopia and zero the modern equivalent of Sodom and Gomorrah, and found the U.S. standing at 50, that should be cause for national concern. But it would be one thing if we also found that the country's position on this mythic measure had been 80 in 1867, 70 in 1917, and 60 in 1957, quite another if we found that it had been hovering around 50 in each of those earlier years.

We don't have such an index, nor do we have the kind of imaginative and thorough data-gathering such a measure would require. We only know that moral conduct today is "deficient." I have no intention of making light of this when I note that part of the reason we think today's problems are so pressing is that they are the ones we face. Since we can do absolutely nothing about previous sins, present problems are the "worst" in the sense that they are the ones that occupy us and require our efforts at remedy....

CHANGING STANDARDS AND PERCEPTIONS

Assessing the moral state of the union is made more difficult by the fact that our standards keep changing. Moreover, the institutions through which the public gains a sense of the moral state of the nation now tend to portray social and political institutions in a negative light.

As to changing standards, consider the area of race relations. Surely we have made enormous strides along this dimension of national moral conduct since the 1850s. We have ended slavery and, all too belatedly, we must acknowledge, eradicated the system of gross exclusion of African-Americans from various facilities and entitlements, known as "Jim Crow." Survey data on racial attitudes and various behavioral data alike attest to the spread and strengthening of public support for extending to African-Americans the Declaration's lofty insistence that all people are created equal and possess inalienable rights.

But in assessing moral conduct, we seem largely to ignore this historical perspective. Is America now living in satisfactory accord with the norm set forth in the Declaration of Independence and in other statements of national ideals? Of course not. But today's shortcomings are the ones that now occupy us—even when we recognize marked gains from times past. *We expect more of ourselves in this area than we did 50 or 150 years ago—and we come up short.*

Media studies have for some time examined the issue of political negativism or cynicism, suggesting that press bias results not so much from political preferences as from professional outlook The press often portrays various national institutions as seamy and even unworthy of support. Austin Ranney argues that there is not so much "a political bias in favor of liberalism or conservatism, as a structural bias . . ." which encourages a cynical and excessively manipulative view of politics. Michael Robinson's research has supported the view that the press fosters a pervasive cynicism:

> Events are frequently conveyed by television news through an inferential structure that often injects a negativistic, contentious, or anti-institutional bias. These biases, frequently dramatized by film portrayals of violence and aggression, evoke images of American politics and social life which are inordinately sinister and despairing.

In addition to America's historic sense of creedal anxiety, then, recent factors, such as changing standards of justice and press negativism, may be encouraging an even more pessimistic view. At the very least, all these factors suggest there is reason to doubt that the apparently widespread sense of moral decline is simply a reflection of the actual progression.

WHAT THE DATA ACTUALLY SHOW

The various factors sketched above present terrible difficulties for the literature which purports to provide thoughtful guidance on the matter of which way we are headed. As a result, analysts often seem to be led to the conclusion that deterioration is occurring, even when available information is inconclusive or flat-out says otherwise.

When we look at the status of religion in America and a number of moral norms, it is not at all clear America is in moral decline. The country's religious life, for instance, is often considered a moral barometer. A decade ago, I was asked to prepare a conference paper reviewing what surveys had to say about the religious beliefs and practices of the American people. As the Reverend Richard John Neuhaus observed at the New York Conference, the conventional wisdom had it that "America is or is rapidly becoming a secular society."

I began my paper by acknowledging that on this subject, as on so many, there are severe limits as to what polls can tell us. They are blunt instruments, unable to help us much with the searching, the ambiguity, the depth and subtlety that necessarily surround any basic set of human needs and values. Nevertheless, the story told by survey research was remarkably clear and unambiguous with regard to the general character and directions of Americans' religious life: namely, the U.S. is distinguished from most other advanced industrial democracies by the persisting strength of religious beliefs and of organized religious practice. As Seymour Martin Lipset argued in *The First New Nation*, published in 1963, "the one empirical generalization which does seem justified about American religion is that from the early nineteenth century down to the present, the United States has been among the most religious countries in the Christian world." Similarly, James Reichley concluded his examination of *Religion in American Life* with the assessment that "Americans remain, despite recent incursions of civil humanism among cultural elites and relentless promotion of egoism by advertising and entertainment media, overwhelmingly, in Justice [William O.] Douglas's words, 'a religious people'."

My own assessments of available survey information have supported these observations. Americans continue, for example, in virtually unchanging proportions to describe religion as important in their own lives. The proportion describing themselves as members of a church or synagogue, while down just a bit from the levels of the 1930–50s, has, on the whole, remained both high and constant. Surveys conducted by the National Opinion Research Center have continued to find overwhelming majorities of the public describing the Bible as either "the actual word of God . . . to be taken literally, word for word," (the response of 33 percent in 1993); or as "the inspired word of God, but not everything in it should be taken literally, word for word" (49 percent stating this). Only 15 percent categorized the Bible as "an ancient book of fables, legends, history, and moral precepts recorded by men." Also, prayer remains integral to Americans, even among young adults and high-income citizens (65 percent and 69 percent of whom, respectively, agreed with the statement that "prayer is an important part of my daily life").

Perhaps most striking is the extent to which the U.S. differs religiously from other advanced industrial democracies.

In 1981, Gallup conducted a series of surveys cross-nationally which found 79 percent of Americans saying they gained strength from religion, compared to 46 percent in Britain, 44 percent of West Germans, and 37 percent of the French. Similarly, 84 percent of those interviewed in the U.S. said they believed in heaven, as against 57 percent in Britain, 31 percent in West Germany, 27 percent in France, and 26 percent in Sweden.

This isn't to say that there have been no changes in the structure of American religious life. We know, for example, that over the last 30 to 40 years, while the proportion of the population which is "churched" has remained basically constant, the denominational mix has changed quite strikingly. Sociologist Benton Johnson notes that American religious groups have differed greatly in terms of membership gains and losses. He points out that evangelical churches have prospered even as main-line Protestant denominations have suffered serious membership losses during this period.

Taking a longer view of American religious experience from the eighteenth century to the present, we see many substantial shifts. Interesting enough, though, these shifts are more often than not in the opposite direction from those assumed in most commentary. That is, *the long movement over time in the U.S. seems clearly to be toward religion,* not away from it. Pointing to the decline of organized atheism and church membership gains in the nineteenth century, sociologist Theodore Caplow suggested:

One concedes too much when one says we're just about as religious as we used to be. We may be a good deal more religious than we used to be.

Yet, while virtually all the scholars who have reviewed the systematic data which are available to us have reached the same conclusions on American religious experience, most of the group assembled at the New York conference strongly rejected the idea that American religious commitments are notably strong and enduring. For example, George Marsden, a leading student of evangelicalism and fundamentalism, dismissed most of the findings on religious belief as essentially meaningless because, as he saw it, they picked up only an insubstantial, superficial, essentially trivial commitment. "As you know," Marsden argued, "the common comment on fundamentalism is that it is just secularism in disguise. It is a way of endorsing a materialistic, self-centered lifestyle. And that's something that could be said about a lot of American Christianity."

Marsden brought up the often-cited remark which is attributed (perhaps entirely incorrectly, according to some historians) to Dwight Eisenhower. Ike is reputed to have said: "Our government makes no sense unless it is founded on a deeply religious faith—and I don't care what it [that faith] is." This hollow, instrumental approach to faith encapsulates, Marsden argued, what's wrong with religion in the U.S.

Political scientist Stanley Rothman had a perspective similar to Marsden's:

In a public opinion survey people are asked, "Do you believe in hard work?" Sure, everyone may mouth that. But there's a difference between saying that and actually doing it.... And I would say the same thing about religious attitudes among the population as a whole. Modernization of the west has led to the erosion of the traditional structures and beliefs...

now there is evidence that people no longer take religion so seriously, unless they redefine it in some ways. I think there has been a general redefinition, not among the whole population, but among substantial segments of the population, so as to fit religion into their own wishes and desires.... Unfortunately this cannot be proven with data.

And so it went. Most of the participants were convinced that in a deeper sense, whatever the numbers seem to show, religious belief is in precipitous decline in modern America.

Nor is religion the only area in which our perceptions of deterioration conflict with other measures of experience. While there are important areas where Americans are in deep disagreement about what constitutes the proper moral or ethical standards—the case of abortion is certainly a prime example—far more often than not the data point to broad agreement on the norm. As Table 1 shows, norms condemning various forms of cheating, lying, and stealing seem firmly entrenched across most of the population. If we are going to hell in a handbasket, it's not because the preponderance of Americans have abandoned their attachment to many of the older verities.

But does this simply suggest that hypocrisy is on the rise—that we have become more inclined to act contrary to our professed standards? Not necessarily. Take the case of cheating. A lot of people, including many educators, seem to believe that cheating is on the rise—even though young Americans continue to condemn cheating. But many of the best survey data available to us say otherwise. The Gallup Youth Surveys, for example, show that many more young people describe cheating at their own schools as *more infrequent* now than three

Table 1
Professed Norms Are Strong and Conventional

Tax Fraud	Extramarital Affairs
Question: Do you feel it is wrong if . . . a taxpayer does not report all of his income in order to pay less income taxes?	**Question:** Do you think it is always wrong or sometimes okay for . . . a married person to have sex with someone other than his/her spouse?
Wrong: 94% Not Wrong: 4%	**Always Wrong: 87% Sometimes OK: 11%**
Source: Survey by NORC for the International Social Survey Program (ISSP), Feb.–April 1991.	*Source:* Survey by Yankelovich Clancy Shulman for Time/CNN, June 4–5, 1991.
Question: Have you ever cheated on your federal income taxes, or not?	**Question:** (If ever married) Have you ever had sex with someone other than your husband or wife while you were married?
No: 95% Yes: 4%	**No: 83% Yes: 17%**
Source: Survey by the Gallup Organization, March 28–30, 1991.	*Source:* Survey by NORC-GSS, February–April 1993.
Lying	**Stealing**
	Question: The . . . eighth commandment is . . . Do not steal . . . Does the way you live these days completely satisfy . . . or not at all satisfy that commandment?
Question: Do you think it is sometimes justified to lie to friends or to family members or do you think lying is never justified?	
Never: 73% Depends: 10% Justified: 18%	**Completely: 86% Not at All: 2%**
Source: Survey by CBS News/New York Times, December 7–9, 1992.	*Source:* Survey by Barna Research Group, January 1992.

decades ago. The proportion saying that they themselves have cheated at some time or another, while high, seems to be decreasing.

We know that people often fail to live up to standards to which they express adherence. But we also know that norms matter—that is, they actually regulate conduct, if imperfectly—and that large changes in conduct rarely, if ever, take place without correspondingly large changes in professed norms. Consider, for example, premarital sexual relations. Behavior has clearly shifted mightily in the "sexual revolution" of the last several decades, but so too has the professed norm. When there is a problem, as in the latter area, the survey findings readily pick it up.

One of the things that seem to be bothering Americans most is the sense that the old-time standards-setting, which was centered around the institutions of family and church, is being replaced by new ones, centered in remote and morally vacuous institutions, such as popular music, TV, and movies. Data presented in Table 2 demonstrate this concern clearly. But as we see in the figure, other data show that most of us say that, for us personally, the old order of standards-setting still holds. Furthermore, a Roper Organization survey for *Good Housekeeping* in 1991 found that 86 percent of women shared

Table 2
Where Do Today's Values Come From?

Question: What do you think (has/should have) the most influence on the values of young people today?

	Has	Should Have
TV & Movies	34%	1%
Parents	20	74
Young People	19	1
Musicians & Music Videos	10	0
Celebrities, Athletes	6	1
Teachers	5	9
Political Leaders	2	1
Religious Leaders	1	11
Military Leaders	1	0

Source: Survey by Mellman & Lazarus for Massachusetts Mutual Life Insurance Co., September 1991.

Question: What do you feel has been the single most important factor in influencing your beliefs about what is right or wrong?

Parents	47%
Religion	28%
Personal Experience	8%
Other	8%
Not sure	9%

Source: Survey by Yankelovich Clancy Shulman for Time, January 19–21, 1987.

the values of their parents, 10 percent had somewhat different values, and only 4 percent had very different values. In the same survey, 85 percent of the women who were mothers thought their children would have the same values.

Once again, there is a striking tension between the perceived deterioration in moral norms and conduct nationally on the one hand, and the sense of strength and continuity drawn from personal experience on the other. We see this again and again across many areas. Thus 63 percent of respondents in a Gallup survey of November 1992 said that "religion as a whole" is losing its influence on American life, while only 27 percent described religion's influence as increasing. As we have seen, though, a great deal of the data indicates that religion in America continues to flourish.

INDIVIDUALISM: STRENGTH OR WEAKNESS?

The moral shortcomings of this society often grow out of the same elements that enhance national life. The positives and negatives are frequently but flip sides of a single structure of national values. As many analysts from Alexis de Tocqueville on down to the present have observed, the core of the sociopolitical ideology on which the U.S. was founded is a uniquely insistent and far-reaching individualism —a view of the individual person which gives unprecedented weight to his or her choices, interests, and claims. This distinctive individualism has always enriched the moral life of the country in important regards and posed serious challenges to it in yet others....

An abundance of data from our own time show that this dynamic sense of individual responsibility and capabilities has continued. Philanthropy has also increased dramatically: in 1955, individuals gave more than $5 billion to charity; this amount rose to $102 billion in 1990 (a rate of increase that outpaced inflation significantly). Surveys suggest that, in recent years, the proportion of the populace giving of its time for charitable and social service activities has actually been increasing. The moral life of the nation is thus strengthened.

Individualism has contributed much historically to the vitality of American family life and created a distinctively American type of family. Children, nineteenth century visitors often remarked, didn't occupy a subordinate place—"to be seen and not heard"—like their European counterparts, but were exuberant, vociferous, spoiled participants. Similarly, visiting commentators often remarked on the effects of America's pervasive individualism on the status of women. Bryce, for example, saw women's rights more widely recognized in the U.S. than in Europe. This had resulted, he argued, because "the root idea of democracy cannot stop at defining men as male human beings, anymore than it could ultimately stop at defining them as white human beings.... Democracy is in America more respectful of the individual... than it has shown itself in Continental Europe, and this regard for the individual enured to the benefit of women."

But just as the country's demanding individualism has liberated individuals to achieve productive lives for themselves and contribute to a dynamic public life, so it has also been a source of distinctive problems. Many analysts have argued that these problems with the American ideology are evident not so much in the fact that these ideals are sometimes unachieved, as that their achievement may create terrible difficulties....

Present-day critics of the "dark side" of individualist America charge that individualism has come to emphasize the gratification of the self over the needs of various important social institutions including, above all, the family. In *Habits of the Heart: Individualism and Commitment in American Life*, Robert Bellah and colleagues grant that "our highest and noblest aspirations, not only for ourselves, but for those we care about, for our society in the world, are closely linked to our individualism." Moreover, America cannot abandon its individualism, for "that would mean for us to abandon our deepest identity."

Still, Bellah *et al.* insist, "some of our deepest problems both as individuals and as a society are also closely linked to our individualism." It has become far too unrestrained. Historically in the U.S., the natural tendencies within individualism toward narrow self-service were mitigated by the strength of religion and the ties of the local community. No longer. In their view, individualism has been transmogrified by a radical insistence upon individual autonomy, so profoundly corrosive of the family and other collective institutions that depend upon substantial subordination of individual claims for social goods.

The recent historical record suggests that neither the boosters nor the knockers of individualism quite have it right. On the positive side, factors like the continued strength of voluntarism in America signal the degree to which individualism strengthens moral conduct by stressing individual responsibility and encouraging the view that "what I do" can really matter. Also, the individualistic ethic in America has fueled important advances for women and African-Americans under the banner of the "inalienable rights" to "Life, Liberty and the pursuit of Happiness." On the other hand, that ethic constantly runs the risk of leaving the individual far too radically autonomous. It suggests that whatever serves a person's sense of his/her rights and entitlements is, miraculously, good for the society or, at the least, something which the society may not lightly challenge.

But the down-side of contemporary individualism does not quite play itself out in the way that recent arguments suggest. Individualism does not necessarily equal "selfishness." Rather, it seems to be that Americans are construing their own self-interest too narrowly. Hence, many of the men and women implicated in the rise in divorce and single-parent households—which has posed difficulties for many children and communities—would seem to have a "narrow" sense of self-interest, which is not serving them or their children very well. They need to be reminded, as Tocqueville argued, that self-interest is only justified when it is "properly understood" in a communal context, which is to say that individuals can only flourish in robust communities....

Has there been a deterioration of moral conduct? Probably not. But we have been given ample proof that extending commitment to our national idea, which centers around a profound individualism, is by no means an unmixed blessing. As the U.S. has progressed in recognizing the worth and the claims of people previously excluded from the Declaration's promise, it has also encouraged tendencies which have destructive possibilities, liable to see the individual as too radically autonomous and leave him too narrowly self-serving. In seeking to improve the moral conduct of the nation, earlier generations of Americans have had to build on the positive elements of the country's individualist ethic, so as to curb its dark side. Ours is surely no exception.

NO James Patterson and Peter Kim

THE DECLINE AND FALL:
AN ALARMED PERSPECTIVE

Americans have become increasingly alienated from family, church, calling, community, and nation. By the late 1980s, we were living our lives as isolated individuals, islands unto ourselves, detached and self-interested.

Social institutions to which individuals have traditionally looked for moral support and guidance—community, family, religion, work-place, public and political institutions, and our leadership—are less central to everyday American life than they once were.

COMMUNITY

The prospects for community—in both the moral and sociological sense—are in serious jeopardy. Seventy-two percent of Americans don't know their neighbors well; 66 percent have never worked with others trying to solve community problems; 65 percent refuse to donate any time to community activities; Americans rate their level of community activity a "3" on a scale of "1" to "10"; two-in-three cannot name their local member of Congress.

When asked what traits contemporary Americans are more likely to embody than Americans of the past, our respondents selected such negative adjectives as materialistic, greedy, selfish, criminal, phony, mean, devious, and skeptical. On the other hand, when asked to select traits that Americans of 30 years ago were more likely to embody, they selected neighborliness, civic-mindedness, patriotism, volunteerism, religiousness, honesty, morality, hard work, compassion, and charity. In short, all of the traits we generally associate with community were associated with the past, while the traits we associate with selfishness, narcissism, calculation, and anti-social behavior are associated with the present.

FAMILY

The American family is crumbling. Over 50 percent of Americans assert that there is no need for people living together ever to marry; 60 percent of Americans who were married have considered divorce or been divorced; 39 percent of Americans believe that "till death do us part," is an outdated concept; 31 percent of currently married Americans have cheated on their spouses; 43 percent of married respondents aren't sure they would marry the same person if they had it to do over; 25 percent would abandon their families for $10 million.

RELIGION

Religion has little impact on the moral life of the majority of Americans. Most Americans aren't sure of their church's position on the great moral issues of the day—from school busing, capital punishment, book-banning, affirmative action, birth control, homosexuality, teaching creationism in the schools, pornography, and premarital sex to civil rights. Eighty-four percent of Americans report being willing to violate the teachings of their own faith if those teachings conflict with their own personal sense of right and wrong. And although we are a predominantly Christian nation, only 11 percent report believing in all 10 of the Ten Commandments (42 percent of African-Americans report believing in five or fewer).

WORK

The work ethic has given way to hedonism, and the spirit of capitalism has gone awry. Sixty-four percent of Americans confess to malingering, procrastinating, or abusing alcohol or drugs in the workplace; 33 percent conduct personal chores on company time; fewer than one in four Americans report giving their maximum effort at work. Americans report goofing-off about 20 percent of the time while at work; only 24 percent of Americans report that they work in order to realize their full potential (the rest do it for the money); 13 percent regularly leave work early and 10 percent regularly arrive late.

PUBLIC INSTITUTIONS

Our public institutions have lost much of their legitimacy. From 1973/74 to 1989, the proportion of Americans expressing a great deal of confidence in each of the institutions below declined by the amount shown:

- organized religion (-55 percent);
- organized labor (-50 percent);
- educational institutions (-39 percent);
- television (-39 percent);
- the press (-35 percent);
- the executive branch (-31 percent);
- the Congress (-26 percent);
- major companies (-23 percent).

LEADERSHIP

We face a serious crisis in leadership. Seventy-two percent of Americans do not think that any public figure provides moral leadership; 68 percent cannot name a single American leader they admire; 70 percent do not think America has any more heroes; 68 percent do not think there are any adequate role models in public life for their children to follow.

THE AGE OF MORAL AMBIGUITY

More and more, the isolated individual, disconnected from external moral reference points, has come to view himself/herself as the sole arbiter of moral life. In fact, 93 percent of all Americans report that they alone determine what is moral in their lives.

As a consequence of this lack of external structures of moral support, Americans are increasingly coming to view the great moral issues of the day as "gray" issues without a clear right and wrong. More than a third of Americans believes there is no clear right or wrong position when it comes to the following issues: affirmative action (54 percent); creationism in schools (52 percent); premarital sex (52 percent); the right to die (44 percent); school busing (44 percent); homosexuality (43 percent); flag burning (38 percent); pornography (38 percent); capital punishment (37 percent).

CRIME AND PUNISHMENT IN A POST-MORAL SOCIETY

One need no longer read Dostoevsky, Camus, or Genet to probe the significance of crime and punishment in everyday life. One is tempted to speculate that a decline of moral support-structures and the rise of the self have led to a society in which it is increasingly difficult to maintain social order. If individuals no longer believe in the moral legitimacy of the community, what is there to keep them from flouting its rules? We found that systematic rule-breaking was one such consequence.

Crime has become so rampant, as to be a part of everyday life: fully 60 percent of Americans have been the victim of at least one crime in their lifetimes, and fully 35 percent have been victimized more than once; 39 percent of Americans readily confess to having committed some kind of crime themselves.

Violence has become so commonplace as to have become "normalized" to an extent. Sixty-four percent of Americans believe the use of physical force is sometimes justified; 59 percent admit to having used physical force on another

person; fewer than half (45 percent) of those who have used physical force regret it; 12 percent of Americans report having injured someone enough to send them to the hospital; 9 percent have threatened someone with a knife (6 percent used it); 9 percent have threatened someone with a gun (4 percent used it).

THE END OF CHILDHOOD

In our society, childhood has traditionally been a time of innocence. No one aspect stood for childhood innocence more than sexual innocence and naivete. Even Freud, who placed sexuality at the very heart of his world view, attributed a period of "dormancy" to childhood sexuality. However, today, we are facing a radically new phenomenon: we are living in an age of sexually precocious children.

Discussions of the "sexual revolution" go back to the coming of age of baby boomers in the 1960s. Indeed, our data found that baby boomers were significantly less likely to have been virgins when they married (29 percent), than either their parents' generation (42 percent) or their grandparents (41 percent). Clearly, baby boomers had disconnected sex from marriage.

However, baby boomers do not report having started sexual activity at an earlier age than either their parents or grandparents. The baby boomers and their parents both became sexually active at about the same age; the only difference is that baby boomer's parents married younger. For both baby boomers and their parents, only a relative few had become sexually active by age 13 (less than 5 percent). What is so striking about those between the ages of 18 and 24 is that more than one in five has lost their virginity by age 13 and almost two-thirds by age 16.

A THOUSAND POINTS OF DARKNESS: THE PRIVATIZATION OF SOCIAL RESPONSIBILITY

With the end of the 1980s, we found Americans retreating into an ever-more private and isolated existence, and are becoming less willing to confront the social issues and social problems of the day. Poverty and race are being redefined as private problems, more the fault of those "afflicted" than social problems that need to be addressed by society as a whole. Forty-two percent of Americans believe that the poor are poor because they are lazy or because of other faults of their own. And when it comes to race, Americans clearly believe that the problem lies with African-Americans and not with white America: two in three believe that African-Americans have the same opportunities as whites; 68 percent believe that some races are harder working than others.

POSTSCRIPT

Is the Moral Decline of America a Myth?

The selections by Ladd and by Patterson and Kim serve well as the opening round of the debate on the moral decline thesis, but they provide the basis for only tentative conclusions. The data presented by Patterson and Kim show that the current situation is quite unsatisfactory from a moral point of view, but almost all of these data are not trend data. We do not know whether situations were worse or better in the past. The authors do present trend data showing a marked decline in the public's confidence in eight public institutions. This supports their thesis that Americans have become less attached to the "social institutions to which individuals have traditionally looked for moral support and guidance," but it does not clearly show moral decline. They do show a shift in moral life, but the reader must decide whether or not this shift is really a decline. The shift involves a growing disconnection from external moral reference points to sole reliance on one's own moral judgment. Ladd accepts that Americans have become more individualistic, but he does not believe that this represents moral decline. In addition, he argues that religion and morality have not declined.

Most of the relevant literature is on aspects of the moral decline. Few works challenge the decline thesis. Richard Stivers attributes the moral decline to a culture of cynicism in *The Culture of Cynicism: American Morality in Decline* (Basil Blackwell, 1994). The most sophisticated exposition of the moral decline thesis is Gertrude Himmelfarb's *The De-Moralization of Society: From Victorian Virtues to Modern Values* (Alfred A. Knopf, 1995). The strongest statement on moral decline is Charles Derber's *The Wilding of America: How Greed and Violence Are Eroding Our Nation's Character* (St. Martin's Press, 1996). His focus is on the increasing selfishness that pervades American culture.

Two highly visible public figures have recently proposed other solutions to the current moral crisis. John W. Gardner, the founder of the citizens' lobby Common Cause, proposes a large-scale mobilization for national renewal, which has signed up more than 100 organizations for the cause. See "National Renewal," *National Civic Review* (Fall–Winter 1994). Retiring senator Bill Bradley proposes many small actions for revitalizing civil society in "America's Challenge: Revitalizing Our National Community," *National Civic Review* (Spring 1995). In addition, a new intellectual movement named communitarianism, which seeks to curb excessive individualism and bring back a greater balance between individual and community interests, has developed. *The Spirit of Community* by Amitai Etzioni (Crown Publishers, 1993) is the fullest statement of the communitarian position.

ISSUE 2

Does the News Media Have a Liberal Bias?

YES: H. Joachim Maitre, from "The Tilt to the News: How American Journalism Has Swerved from the Ideal of Objectivity," *The World and I* (December 1993)

NO: Martin A. Lee and Norman Solomon, from *Unreliable Sources: A Guide to Detecting Bias in News Media* (Carol Publishing Group, 1992)

ISSUE SUMMARY

YES: Journalism professor H. Joachim Maitre argues that news reporters are liberals who allow their political views to seep into their reporting.

NO: Media critics Martin A. Lee and Norman Solomon argue that the media are owned and operated by men and women whose bias in reporting is toward the conservative status quo.

"A small group of men, numbering perhaps no more than a dozen 'anchormen,' commentators and executive producers... decide what forty to fifty million Americans will learn of the day's events in the nation and the world." The speaker was Spiro Agnew, vice president of the United States during the Nixon administration. The thesis of Agnew's speech, delivered to an audience of midwestern Republicans in 1969, was that the television news media are controlled by a small group of liberals who foist their liberal opinions on viewers under the guise of "news." The upshot of this control, said Agnew, "is that a narrow and distorted picture of America often emerges from the televised news." Many Americans, even many of those who were later shocked by revelations that Agnew took bribes while serving in public office, agreed with Agnew's critique of the "liberal media."

Politicians' complaints about unfair news coverage go back much further than Agnew and the Nixon administration. The third president of the United States, Thomas Jefferson, was an eloquent champion of the press, but after six years as president, he could hardly contain his bitterness. "The man who never looks into a newspaper," he wrote, "is better informed than he who reads them, inasmuch as he who knows nothing is nearer to truth than he whose mind is filled with falsehoods and errors."

The press today is much different than it was in Jefferson's day. Newspapers then were pressed in hand-operated frames in many little printing shops around the country; everything was local and decentralized, and each paper averaged a few hundred subscribers. Today, newspaper chains have taken over most of the once-independent local newspapers. The remaining independents rely heavily on national and international wire services. Almost all major magazines have national circulations; some newspapers, like *USA Today* and the *Wall Street Journal*, do too. Other newspapers, like the *New York Times* and the *Washington Post*, enjoy nationwide prestige and help set the nation's news agenda. Geographical centralization is even more obvious in the case of television. About 70 percent of the national news on television comes from three networks whose programming originates in New York City.

A second important difference between the media of the eighteenth century and the media today has to do with the ideal of "objectivity." In past eras, newspapers were frankly partisan sheets, full of nasty barbs at the politicians and parties the editors did not like; they made no distinction between "news" and "editorials." The ideal of objective journalism is a relatively recent development. It traces back to the early years of the twentieth century. Disgusted with the sensationalist "yellow journalism" of the time, intellectual leaders urged that newspapers cultivate a core of professionals who would concentrate on accurate reporting and who would leave their opinions to the editorial page. Journalism schools cropped up around the country, helping to promote the ideal of objectivity. Although some journalists now openly scoff at it, the ideal still commands the respect—in theory, if not always in practice —of working reporters.

These two historical developments, news centralization and news professionalism, play off against one another in the current debate over news "bias." The question of bias was irrelevant when the press was a scatter of little independent newspapers. If you did not like the bias of one paper, you picked another one—or you started your own, which could be done with modest capital outlay. Bias started to become an important question when newspapers became dominated by chains and airwaves by networks, and when a few national press leaders like the *New York Times* and the *Washington Post* began to emerge. Although these "mainstream" news outlets have been challenged in recent years by opinions expressed in a variety of alternative media—such as cable television, talk radio, newsletters, and computer mail —they still remain powerful conveyers of news.

Is media news reporting biased? The media constitutes a major socializing institution, so this is an important question. Defenders of the media usually hold that although journalists, like all human beings, have biases, their professionalism compels them to report news with considerable objectivity. Media critics insist that journalists constantly interject their biases into their news reports. The critics, however, often disagree about whether such bias is liberal or conservative, as is the case with this issue. In the following selections, H. Joachim Maitre argues that the news media tilt to the left, while Martin A. Lee and Norman Solomon contend that the slant of the news media supports a conservative status quo.

YES

H. Joachim Maitre

THE TILT TO THE NEWS: HOW AMERICAN JOURNALISM HAS SWERVED FROM THE IDEAL OF OBJECTIVITY

"Mr. President," said the nation's second-ranked television news anchorman on May 27 [1993] and via satellite, "if we could be one-hundredth as great as you and Hillary Rodham Clinton have been in the White House, we would take it right now and walk away winners.... Thank you very much, and tell Mrs. Clinton we respect her and we are pulling for her."

Dan Rather's declaration of adoration and active support for the presidential couple was not meant for public viewing but—recorded through a technical glitch—caused yet another puncture in the perforated armor of American journalism. In professionally purer times, Rather's indiscretion would have destroyed what was left of his credibility as an honest news broker. He had shown his tilt.

Finally, after years of heated public debates and often tedious scholarly discourse over alleged institutional liberal bias in the American news media, there is no argument on the basics any longer. "Everyone knows," said political scientist James Q. Wilson in the June 21, 1993, edition of the *New Republic*, "that the members of the national media are well to the left of the average voter."

For those skeptics still demanding statistical evidence that journalists tend to hold liberal political views, numbers were provided in a summer 1992 survey of fourteen hundred journalists, reported in *The American Journalist in the 1990s*, published by the New York–based Freedom Forum Media Studies Center. It concluded that 44.1 percent of those polled consider themselves Democrats and only 16.3 percent Republicans. The gap had grown since 1982, when a similar survey was done, and is now far larger than among the general population.

BIAS CREEPS INTO REPORTING

These figures as such would be of limited interest if they did not strengthen the suspicion that the journalist's personal political and philosophical preferences, his system of beliefs, his world-view would—unavoidably—seep into his reporting and that the stated imbalance between liberal and conservative leanings and loyalties already is gravely affecting the ways and worth of news reporting in this country. Slant is becoming ever more visible, nowhere more so than on television "news."

Examples of liberal bias and resulting slant abound. President Clinton had been in office less than a month when megastar Dan Rather offered his helping hand: Clinton's program "will include money to put people back to work repairing this country's infrastructure, roads, bridges, and other public works" (CBS, February 17). Rather's unspoken message: The Clinton administration will rebuild the America run down through years of neglect by Clinton's Republican predecessors in the White House. Bill Clinton will create the employment lost in previous years. News, or partisan propaganda?

Soon, Dan Rather's new coanchor, Connie Chung, another Clinton fan, identified Clinton's adversary: "The Senate Republicans are threatening to block the president's $16 billion job creation program" (CBS, April 1). Or: "Held up in the Senate is President Clinton's $16 billion plan to bring unemployment down" (CBS, April 2). And: "President Clinton says the $16 billion is crucial to boosting the economy" (CBS, April 6).

But what was the opposition's line of argumentation? Neither Rather nor Chung ever addressed the conceptual base for Republican resistance to Clinton's ambitious employment program and to "Clintonomics" in general, to wit: In free societies, the creation of jobs is a central task for private enterprise, not for the government and its various bureau-

cracies. This concept in its implementation resulted in the creation of millions of jobs in the 1980s, but that had been under President Reagan—anathema for the liberal mind-set.

The rule of liberal media bias starts with terminology. The term *liberal* is generally used in a positive sense in America. "Liberal social policies" are good by implication; "restrictive social policies" are bad. To be "liberal" suggests generosity and open-mindedness; to be "conservative" implies selfishness and closed-mindedness. Derived from the Latin word *liber* (free), *liberal* once stood for persons and ideas that favored freedom. In many European countries, that original meaning still prevails. Not so in America, where—in particular when applied to public policy—*liberal* has come to mean favoring government intervention and control to secure economic and social justice.

Thus, the expansion of government activities and the growth of government itself are favored by today's liberals, while liberating commerce (through deregulation) and the economy from government intervention and control has become a conservative ideal. Classic liberal spokesmen for a free economy such as Friedrich von Hayek and Milton Friedman (both recipients of the Nobel Prize in economics) have been relegated to conservative status by the liberal class dominant in the media and in politics. At the same time, contemporary America's most successful advocate of government intervention in commerce and the economy, Sen. Edward Kennedy, is also America's best-known "liberal"—or socialist, in reality.

Television news coverage of American economic affairs has been the subject of an in-depth report by Ted Smith of Virginia Commonwealth University.

The study, titled *The Vanishing Economy: Television Coverage of Economic Affairs, 1982–87*, involved systematic analysis of three full years of coverage during the Reagan presidency and found a highly consistent pattern of emphasis and omission. Smith demonstrates that network news journalists have chosen not only to stress problems and failures but to limit or eliminate coverage of gains and success. In some instances, Smith says, "those restrictions have been so extreme that it would be difficult or impossible for a person who relied exclusively on television evening news for his knowledge of the world to form an accurate understanding of the world." He concludes: "To be blunt, systematic suppression of positive information, economic or otherwise, is nothing less than systematic censorship. As such, it strikes at the foundations of the democratic process."

THE MEDIA AND THE DEMOCRATS: SUPPRESSING NEGATIVE INFORMATION

With Clinton's election and the return of the Democrats to majority rule in Congress, television's coverage of economic affairs faces the challenge of liberal economic policies and their implementation. Chances are that the "systematic suppression of positive information," as found by Smith, will be replaced by systematic suppression of negative information. Liberal policies and plans will be granted the benefit of the doubt. During the budget debates of the past summer, criticism of Reagan policies far outweighed serious analysis of Clinton's campaign platform and his economic package, advertised as seeking a "deficit reduction."

The purpose of the phrase *deficit reduction* was to avoid the more candid term *tax increase* and, at the same time, to mislead Americans into thinking "that the change has something to do with reducing the federal budget," says Tom Bethell, one of the country's few nonconforming journalists, in an article in the September 1993 issue of the *American Spectator*. Bethell reveals numbers and trends that easily could have been published in prestigious newspapers (but were not) or made public on television news programs (but were not thought newsworthy) and concludes:

The Clinton economic plan has all along been an exercise in deception, with the news media acting as collaborators or dupes.... On April 8, the Office of Management and Budget [OMB] published the 1994 federal budget. The next day, major newspapers published full-page stories on the budget, but all failed to give the outlay and revenue totals. It has become a convention among journalists that only the deficit, or "difference," should be published. The difference between what and what? We are rarely told. The failure to publish the totals, of course, disguises the extent to which they continue to rise. An uncritical Washington press corps has permitted Clinton to talk of "spending cuts" without publishing the numbers on which his claim is based.

Many ordinary citizens agree with this assessment of today's media. One man, Douglas Losordo, chastised the *Boston Globe* in a letter printed on September 7, 1993, for repeatedly referring to "spending reductions" in the Clinton budget "when in fact the only proposed real decreases in spending are in the defense budget."

Losordo cited OMB figures to the effect that outlays (spending) will increase from $1.468 trillion [in 1993] to $1.781 trillion in 1998, while defense spending will drop from $277 billion to $239 billion over the same period. "How is this a spending cut?" Losordo asks, charging that the *Globe* is "simply repeating the distortions of fact presented by our politicians."

[In 1986] social scientists Robert Lichter, Stanley Rothman, and Linda Lichter published *The Media Elite*, a ground-breaking study of political leanings and perspectives among the nation's leading journalists and how those preferences affected their work. They concluded:

> The media elite are a homogeneous and cosmopolitan group, who were raised at some distance from the social and cultural traditions of small-town middle America. Drawn mainly from big cities in the Northeast and North Central states, their parents tended to be well-off, highly educated members of the middle class. Most have moved away from any religious heritage, and very few are regular churchgoers. In short, the typical leading journalist is the very model of the modern Eastern urbanite. The dominant perspective of this group is equally apparent. Today's leading journalists are politically liberal and alienated from traditional norms and institutions. Most place themselves to the left of center and regularly vote the Democratic ticket. Yet theirs is not the New Deal liberalism of the underprivileged, but the contemporary social liberalism of the urban sophisticate. They favor a strong welfare state within a capitalist framework. They differ most from the general public, however, on the divisive social issues that have emerged since the 1960s—abortion, gay rights, affirmative action, et cetera. Many are alienated from the "system" and quite critical of America's world role. They would like

to strip traditional powerbrokers of their influence and empower black leaders, consumer groups, intellectuals, and... the media.

These findings were complemented by an article in the summer 1986 edition of *Policy Review* magazine by Dinesh D'Souza, who analyzed television network conformism:

> No matter where he comes from... the aspiring TV journalist typically adopts a left-liberal worldview as he picks up the tools of his trade. There is nothing conspiratorial in this. To get their stories on the air, TV journalists have to embrace the culture of network news, either consciously or unconsciously.... And since the culture of television journalism is liberal, it is hardly surprising that reporters get their idea of what is news— ultimately the most ideological question in journalism—from a whole range of left-liberal assumptions, inclinations, and expectations.

THE EDITOR AS IDEOLOGICAL GATEKEEPER

In television as well as newspaper journalism, the reporter's role in the running of the newsroom and production of the final copy is subservient to that of the desk editor; it is certainly secondary or insignificant when measured against the power of managing editors and executive editors and of their television news counterparts. The reporter and the editor are both "journalists." It is the editor, however, in his function as gatekeeper, who determines which story will be covered, what news is "fit to print," and who gets hired and fired.

Take the *New York Times*, the nation's ranking and undisputedly liberal newspaper. Max Frankel, its executive editor, is not known for having hired any openly conservative reporter or editor during his seven-year tenure. Moreover, "one of the first things I did was stop the hiring of nonblacks and set up an unofficial little quota system," Frankel boasted in an interview with Ken Auletta.

Auletta, writing in the June 18, 1992, issue of the *New Yorker*, added: "The new publisher [Arthur Ochs Sulzberger, Jr.] applauded Frankel's hiring policies and also the newsroom's more extensive coverage of women and gays, despite grumbling by some members of the staff that the *Times* was becoming politically correct."

Grumbling over hiring practices and program content seems to be no longer an issue at the partly tax-supported National Public Radio (NPR), which is liberal to the core. (Think of Nina Totenberg, NPR's correspondent at the Supreme Court, and her stubborn effort to prevent Clarence Thomas from being confirmed as a justice of the Court.) A rare insight into the inner workings of NPR was offered in the Washington, D.C., weekly *City Paper* by Glenn Garvin, who conducted intensive research on the radio station:

It's not that the network's editorial brain trust meets each morning to plot the day's campaign to rid America of Republican taint. It's that the newsroom is composed almost entirely of like-minded people who share one another's major philosophical precepts.... Their thinking is apparent both in what they report and their approach to it. They believe that government is the fundamental agent of change, that government can and should solve most problems. They believe most of those solutions involve spending large sums of money. They believe that taxes are not only an appropriate way of raising money, but an impor-

tant social responsibility. They believe that, although individuals cannot always be trusted to make correct choices, bureaucrats usually can. In short, NPR reporters are the kind of people who voted for Michael Dukakis and Bill Clinton, not as the lesser evils, but enthusiastically, in the firm belief that what the world needs is better social engineering.

Like-minded people who share one another's major philosophical precepts and operate under unofficial but nonetheless binding rules of political correctness are not journalists. They are today's Media, less a profession than a culture and secular religion, attempting to reform society according to their left-radical agenda. The guiding motto of the *New York Times* —"All the news that's fit to print"—has been turned into a tool of self-censorship. Especially on feminism, the homosexual rights campaign, and pop culture, the *Times* "has in recent years become crassly partisan in an essentially frivolous way," writes critic Richard Neuhaus in the June/July edition of *First Things* magazine. "There is an absence of *gravitas* ... it has become a generally vulgar and strident paper that is hostile to nuance and, it seems, editorially incapable of self-doubt or a modicum of intellectual curiosity."

The *Times* is still held to be the flagship of American journalism, but its traditional in-depth coverage of national and international events has been weakened by trendy treatment, obviously caused by imitating television coverage. Peter Steinfels, who writes the *Times'* Beliefs section, claims that journalists themselves know the problem: "The news media are sometimes less adept in telling truly new stories than in retelling old stories in new ways."

Steinfels, writing in the August 21, 1993, edition of the *Times*, offers a telling example of a tilt threatening to turn institutional: the coverage of Pope John Paul II's voyage to Colorado [summer 1993]. Steinfels observes:

> For the better part of a mid-August week some of the nation's most prized air time, from morning shows to evening newscasts, was devoted to Pope John Paul II's visit.... So were front-page stories in most newspapers.... No one can dispute that this reporting and commentary conveyed some powerful images of a charismatic religious leader and exuberant teenagers.... Nonetheless, fair questions can be raised about how much this impressive effort advanced the public's knowledge and understanding about the Pope, about the current state of Catholicism, about young people and about the moral issues that Pope John Paul II highlighted.

What was reported instead, in print and on the screen? "Journalists recounted," Steinfels wrote, "in some cases a bit breathlessly, the fact that many American Catholics disagree with their church's official teachings on birth control, ordaining women to the priesthood, and other questions about sex and roles for women." While the pope "repeatedly lamented the loss of belief in objective truth and in universally valid principles of morality," reporters wallowed in stereotypes: "Their estimates should have reflected the fact that the Pope's language might escape the ideological grid of American politics and the American news media."

The belief in objective truth and in universally valid principles, so central to Western culture, runs counter to the "anything goes" relativism of the counterculture, where truth is subject to debate and negotiation.

"Why do journalists tend to be liberals?" asks Michael Kinsley in a short, instructive essay tellingly titled "Bias and Baloney" in the December 14, 1992, edition of the *New Republic.* Conceding that the general liberal inclination of many journalists would be hard to deny, the much-in-demand liberal talk show host and columnist for the *Washington Post* and the *New Republic* states, only partly tongue-in-cheek:

> My own political views are more or less liberal. They were not genetically implanted, and I hold them under no form of compulsion except that of reason. It seems to me they are the sort of views a reasonable, intelligent person would hold. Since most journalists I meet are reasonable, intelligent people, the mystery to me is not why journalists tend to be liberals but why so many other reasonable, intelligent people are not.

Kinsley's smugness typifies the conviction of intellectual and moral superiority apparently shared by many contemporary liberal journalists. He rejects all conspiracy theories: "People freely choose their politics and freely choose their careers. No one is forcing journalists to hold liberal political views, and no one is preventing or even discouraging conservatives from becoming journalists. If it just happens to work out that way, so what?"

Kinsley also rejects the suspicion that a journalist's personal political worldview might taint his professional product through bias, claiming that "a political preference is not itself a 'bias.' "

THE DEATH OF PROFESSIONAL DETACHMENT AND OBJECTIVITY

Why, then, do political liberal preferences show so frequently, often blatantly, on network news programs, the average American's favored information watering holes? Why are the leading anchormen—Peter Jennings, Dan Rather, Tom Brokaw—known everywhere as liberal in their views and liberal in their presence on the screen? And why is there no conservative news anchor on network television? Is it because the medium of television, by its very nature, is hostile to balanced news presentation? That still would leave open the question of domination by liberals, a fact that had been documented and analyzed in John Corry's ground-breaking 1986 study *TV News and the Dominant Culture.*

Kinsley's flippant observation that "no one is preventing or even discouraging conservatives from becoming journalists" begs the larger question, which has nothing to do with personal political views or convictions: What happened to professional detachment, to objectivity?

Television news has long ceased to strive for objectivity, that forlorn ideal of yesteryear. Television news delivers "infotainment" instead, where whirl is king, tilt is trendy, and slant rules supreme. Likewise, objectivity has been driven from the pages of the nation's weekly newsmagazines. They also have surrendered to the lure of entertainment, allegedly expected or demanded by the viewing public, bored by print.

And commentary, the legitimate exercise of subjective opinion, once restricted to editorial and op-ed pages, is advancing glacierlike into the news pages of the *New York Times* and *Washington Post,* the nation's "prestige papers."

Driven by commercial television's soft assault, journalism attempts to adjust through imitation, thus betraying its mission and professional standards.

A new force is born: The Media. Or is it only show business with a mask?

NO

Martin A. Lee and
Norman Solomon

POLITICIANS AND THE PRESS

More than 20 years after Vice President Spiro Agnew's famous attack on the American press, the myth of the "liberal media" endures.

Agnew decried "the trend toward the monopolization of the great public information vehicles and the concentration of more and more power over public opinion in fewer and fewer hands." True enough, but his oratory targeted only the *Washington Post* and other major media outlets lacking enthusiasm for the Nixon administration. "Agnew was hypocritical in his attack on press monopolies," a critic later remarked. "Giant chains like Newhouse and Hearst—among the good guys in Agnew's press lord pantheon—escaped his ire."

Likewise, conservative owners of magazines with huge circulations, like *Reader's Digest* and *Parade*, received no brickbats from the White House. An outspoken Federal Communications Commissioner, Nicholas Johnson, observed at the time that Agnew was simply going public with "what corporate and government officials have been doing for years in the privacy of their luncheon clubs and paneled offices. They cajoled and threatened publishers and broadcasters in an effort to manage news and mold images."

Agnew's rhetorical barrage in November 1969 was to reverberate into the century's last decade. However deceptive, it struck a populist chord of resentment against media conglomerates. Rather than challenge the "liberal media" myth, right-leaning owners have encouraged it—and media under their control have popularized it.

The Vice President conveniently neglected to mention that a year earlier the majority of endorsing newspaper editorials backed the Nixon-Agnew ticket. And three years later, running for reelection, the same Republican duo received a whopping 93 percent of the country's newspaper endorsements. (Since 1932 every Republican presidential nominee except Barry Goldwater has received the majority of endorsements from U.S. daily newspapers. Ronald Reagan got 77 percent in 1980, and 86 percent in 1984; George Bush got 70 percent in 1988.) Before resigning in disgrace from the vice presidency, Agnew never explained why the "liberal" media so consistently favored conservative presidential candidates.

From Martin A. Lee and Norman Solomon, *Unreliable Sources: A Guide to Detecting Bias in News Media* (Carol Publishing Group, 1992). Copyright © 1992 by Carol Publishing Group. Reprinted by permission.

Reporters' "liberalism" has been exaggerated quite a bit, as Duke University scholar Robert Entman found when he examined the study most commonly cited by purveyors of the cliché. Entman discovered that the study relied on "a non-random sample that vastly overrepresented perhaps the most liberal segment of journalism"—employees of public TV stations in Boston, New York and Washington. These journalists were much more heavily surveyed about their political attitudes than the personnel putting together the far more weighty *New York Times* and national CBS television news.

The much-ballyhooed conclusion that journalists are of a predominantly leftish bent failed to square with data compiled by researchers without a strongly conservative agenda. A Brookings Institution study, for instance, found that 58 percent of Washington journalists identified themselves as either "conservative or middle of the road."

A 1985 *Los Angeles Times* survey, comparing 3,000 journalists to 3,000 members of the general public, found that journalists were more conservative when asked if the government should act to reduce the gap between rich and poor. Fifty-five percent of the general public supported such measures, compared to only 50 percent of the "news staff" and 37 percent of the editors.

But all the heated number-crunching may be much ado about little. The private opinions of media workers are much less important than the end products. Mark Hertsgaard has astutely pinpointed "the deeper flaw in the liberal-press thesis" —"it completely ignored those whom journalists worked for. Reporters could be as liberal as they wished and it would not change what news they were allowed to report or how they could report it. America's major news organizations were owned and controlled by some of the largest and richest corporations in the United States. These firms were in turn owned and managed by individuals whose politics were, in general, anything but liberal. Why would they employ journalists who consistently covered the news in ways they did not like?"

If there's a political tilt to news coverage, it derives principally from mass media owners and managers, not beat reporters. "Admittedly," said sociologist Herbert Gans, "some journalists have strong personal beliefs and also the position or power to express them in news stories, but they are most often editors; and editors, like producers in television, have been shown to be more conservative than their news staffs." To the extent that personal opinions influence news content, Gans added, "they are most often the beliefs of the President of the United States and other high federal, state and local officials, since they dominate the news."

However baseless, accusations by conservatives that the media lean left have made many journalists compensate by tilting in the other direction. In this sense, the liberal media canard has been effective as a pre-emptive club, brandished to encourage self-censorship on the part of reporters who "bend over backwards not to seem at all critical of Republicans," commented Mark Crispin Miller. "Eager to evince his 'objectivity,' the edgy liberal reporter ends up just as useful to the right as any ultra-rightist hack."

And there are plenty of those, dominating America's highest-profile forums for political commentary on television and newspaper editorial pages. "In terms of the syndicated columnists, if there is an ideological bias, it's more and more to the right," President Reagan's media point man David Gergen declared in a 1981 interview. As the decade wore on, the imbalance grew more extreme.

The syndicated likes of George Will, Patrick Buchanan, Robert Novak, William F. Buckley and John McLaughlin achieved monotonous visibility on national TV, thanks to producers casting nets wide for right-wing pundits. As a tedious ritual they were paired with bland centrists, so that supposed "debates" often amounted to center-right discussions —on PBS's *MacNeil/Lehrer NewsHour*, Gergen with the *Washington Post's* charmingly mild Mark Shields; on ABC's *This Week With David Brinkley*, Will with the network's stylized but politically tepid Sam Donaldson; on CNN's *Crossfire*, Buchanan or Novak with somnolent ex-CIA-exec Tom Braden. (In late 1989, Braden yielded his seat "on the left" to Michael Kinsley of the *New Republic* magazine, but this didn't make the show any less unbalanced. "Buchanan is much further to the right than I am to the left," Kinsley acknowledged. As Howard Rosenberg wrote in the *Los Angeles Times*, "*Crossfire* should at least get the labeling right: Pat Buchanan from the far right and Michael Kinsley from slightly left of center.")

In early 1989, columnist Jack Newfield counted eight popular political opinion talk shows on national television. "These shows all have certifiably right-wing hosts and moderators," wrote Newfield. "This is not balance. This is ideological imbalance that approaches a conservative monopoly... Buchanan, who calls AIDS a punishment from God for sin, and campaigns against the prosecution of Nazi war criminals hiding in America, is about as far right as you can get."

A fixture on CNN, and often made welcome on the biggest TV networks, Buchanan has flaunted his admiration for prominent fascists past and present, like the Spanish dictator Francisco Franco (who came to power allied with Hitler) and Chile's bloody ruler Augusto Pinochet. "A soldier-patriot like Franco, General Pinochet saved his country from an elected Marxist who was steering Chile into Castroism," Buchanan effused in a September 1989 column, going on to defend the apartheid regime in South Africa: "The Boer Republic is the only viable economy in Africa. Why are Americans collaborating in a U.N. conspiracy with sanctions?"

Sharing much of the remaining op-ed space are others from the hard right, including former U.N. ambassador Jeane Kirkpatrick; William Safire (like Buchanan, an ex-speechwriter for the Nixon-Agnew team); erstwhile segregationist James J. Kilpatrick; Charles Krauthammer; former NBC News correspondent and Moral Majority vice president Cal Thomas; neo-conservative prophet Norman Podhoretz, and Ray Price (yet another Nixon speechwriter). Aside from a handful of left-leaning liberals, most of the other op-ed mainstays are establishment-tied middle-roaders such as Flora Lewis, David Broder, Jeff Greenfield, Georgie Anne Geyer, and Meg Greenfield.

The more honest conservatives readily admit to an asymmetry in their favor. Blunt acknowledgement has come from Adam Meyerson, editor of *Policy Review* magazine at the Heritage Foundation, the Washington think tank that drew up much of the Reaganite agenda. "Journalism today is very different from what it was 10 to 20 years ago," he said in 1988. "Today, op-ed pages are dominated by conservatives." The media market's oversupply of right-wingers was not without a drawback: "If Bill Buckley were to come out of Yale today, nobody would pay much attention to him ... [His] ideas would not be exceptional at all, because there are probably hundreds of people with those ideas already there, and they have already got syndicated columns ..." As for becoming an editorial writer, Meyerson could not be encouraging. "There are still a few good jobs here and there, but there's a glut of opinions, especially conservative opinions."

Factor in the proliferation of televangelists and far-right religious broadcasters, and the complaints about the "liberal media" ring even more hollow. By 1987, religious broadcasting had become a $2 billion a year industry, with more than 200 full-time Christian TV stations and 1,000 full-time Christian radio stations. This means that evangelical Christians control about 14 percent of the television stations operating in the U.S. and 10 percent of the radio stations, which bombard the American public with a conservative theo-political message. TV ministries continue to thrive, despite the widely-publicized preacher sex and money scandals of the late 1980s.

Some journalists may reject the mythology about liberal prejudice, but when addressing what *is* going on they're prone to denial. Instead of identifying the thumbs on news-media scales, the preference is to call the whole contraption neutral. "Everybody talks about media biases to the right or the left," syndicated columnist Ellen Goodman pooh-poohed in 1989. "The real media bias is against complexity, which is usually terminated with the words: 'I'm sorry, we're out of time.'" Of course, electronic news media are surface-skimming operations. Views that

seriously challenge the status quo, however, have few occasions to be interrupted, since they're so rarely heard at all.

As he celebrated Thanksgiving in 1989, Spiro Agnew had reason to be pleased on the twentieth anniversary of his bombast. Agnew's polemical legacy hadn't stopped refracting the light under which journalists in Washington furrowed their brows. Tagged as "liberal" despite the evidence, mass media continued to shy away from tough, independent reporting.

OFFICIAL SCANDALS: FROM WATERGATE TO CONTRAGATE

Although big media are an integral part of the American power structure, it doesn't mean that reporters never challenge a President or other members of the governing class. A number of Presidents have gotten into nasty spats with the press, which has been credited with exposing the Watergate scandal that drove Richard Nixon from the vestibules of authority.

While the orthodox view of Watergate depicts it as the ultimate triumph of a free and independent press, there is a contrary view held by award-winning investigative journalist Seymour Hersh. "Far from rooting Nixon out in Watergate, I would say the press made Watergate inevitable," Hersh told us.

Hersh's thesis is simple. During his first term, Nixon conducted several illegal and unconstitutional policies with hardly a whimper from the mainstream media: the secret bombing of Cambodia, subversive operations that toppled Chile's democratically-elected government, CIA domestic spying against antiwar dissenters, wholesale wiretapping of

American officials and other citizens. "If the press had been able to break any one of these stories in 1971," Hersh reflected, "we might have been able to save the President from himself. He might have been afraid to do some of the things he did in 1972, and this would have changed the course of history. But the press failed utterly to do anything during Nixon's first term, thereby making it easy for Nixon to walk into his own trap in Watergate."

Having gotten away with so much for so long, Nixon didn't think twice about launching a covert assault against leaders of the other established political party. When Nixon's private spies—the plumbers—were caught red-handed in the headquarters of the Democratic National Committee in June 1972, most media accepted White House claims that it was just a two-bit burglary. The pundits said there was no story there; *Washington Post* reporters Bob Woodward and Carl Bernstein were dismissed as a couple of precocious upstarts out to make trouble for the President.

Nearly all media were slow to delve into what proved to be a monumental political scandal. As Bernstein told an audience at Harvard University in 1989, "At the time of Watergate, there were some 2,000 full-time reporters in Washington, working for major news organizations. In the first six months after the break-in... 14 of those reporters were assigned by their news organizations to cover the Watergate story on a full-time basis, and of these 14, half-a-dozen on what you might call an investigative basis." Bernstein added: "The press has been engaged in a kind of orgy of self-congratulations about our performance in Watergate and about our performance in covering the

news since. And it seems to me no attitude could be more unjustified."

"We realize that we did a lousy job on Watergate," said United Press International's Helen Thomas of the White House press corps. "We just sat there and took what they said at face value." Television was even slower than print media. As author Donna Woolfolk Cross wrote, "TV news did not pursue the story until it was already a well-established matter of discussion in the press and among politicians. During the times when Americans might have profited most from a full exploration of the scandal—before a national election—TV news was still presenting the story as the administration billed it: a 'second-rate burglary.'"

When the Iran-contra scandal broke in November 1986, comparisons with Watergate quickly came into vogue. Once again there were tales of a crusading press corps—journalistic Davids slaying White House Goliaths. But the wrong analogy was being drawn. A more accurate appraisal of the two scandals would not have been very flattering to the U.S. media. For if members of the press corps snoozed through Nixon's first term, they also winked and nodded off during almost six years of the Reagan presidency. Small wonder there were those in the Reagan administration who felt they could get away with escapades even more outlandish than Watergate.

Nixon, of course, was eventually forced to resign from office. Reagan managed to elude such a fate, in part because his aides pursued a more sophisticated media strategy. Whereas Nixon's people were often overtly hostile to the press, waging both a public and private war against journalists, the Reagan White House eschewed brass-knuckle tactics in favor of a more amicable relationship. When the *Washington Post* persisted in publishing detrimental Watergate revelations, Nixon threatened to revoke the broadcasting license of the *Post's* parent company. The Reagan administration tried a more enticing approach, expanding the number of lucrative broadcast affiliates that media corporations could own.

Reagan also benefited from the fact that the media's ideological pendulum had swung rightward since Nixon's final days—largely in reaction to Watergate. Media executives felt that perhaps they had gone too far when Nixon resigned. Roger Wilkins, who wrote *Washington Post* editorials about Watergate, later remarked that the press sought to prove "in the wake of Watergate that they were not irresponsible, that they did have a real sense of the national interest, that they had wandered out of this corporate club... But that essentially they were members in good standing of the club and they wanted to demonstrate that."

Nixon's fall from grace in 1974 came during a period of intense conflict within America's governing circles about the Vietnam War, economic policy and other matters. Nixon loyalists believe, probably correctly, that Woodward and Bernstein were used by unnamed U.S. intelligence sources—including their main source, nicknamed "Deep Throat"—to derail the Nixon presidency. This is not to detract from their accomplishments, but Woodward and Bernstein clearly had help from powerful, well-placed sources.

Shadowboxing in Washington

When Reagan became President in 1981, there was a high degree of consensus within America's corporate and political elites about domestic and foreign policy.

Abdicating the role of a real opposition party, Democratic leaders in Congress were more eager to put on a show than put up a fight. Sometimes the media used the passivity of the Democrats to justify their own. Either way, as Walter Karp put it, "the private story behind every major non-story during the Reagan administration was the Democrats' tacit alliance with Reagan."

It was a convenient arrangement for each of the three principals. The Reagan administration got credit for superb political smarts, and—after its nadir, the unraveling of the Iran-contra scandal —admirable resiliency. ("Howard Baker restored order to the White House," etc.) The Democrats scored points for slugging it out with the Reaganites. And the media reported the shadowboxing as a brawl instead of a contest that kept being thrown before it ever got bloody.

"For eight years the Democratic opposition had shielded from the public a feckless, lawless President with an appalling appetite for private power," Karp wrote. "That was *the* story of the Reagan years, and Washington journalists evidently knew it. Yet they never turned the collusive politics of the Democratic party into news. Slavishly in thrall to the powerful, incapable of enlightening the ruled without the consent of the rulers, the working press, the 'star' reporters, the pundits, the sages, the columnists passed on to us, instead, the Democrats' mendacious drivel about the President's 'Teflon shield.' For eight years, we saw the effects of a bipartisan political class in action, but the press did not show us that political class acting, exercising its collective power, making things happen, contriving the appearances that were reported as news.

One of the chronically contrived appearances was President Reagan's great popularity—phenomenal only in that it was a distortion. In April 1989, the *New York Times* reminded readers that Reagan was "one of the most popular Presidents in American history." Authoritative, but false—as University of Massachusetts political science professor Thomas Ferguson promptly documented for the umpteenth time. "It is tiresome," he wrote in *The Nation* magazine, "always to be pointing out that this ever-popular and seemingly indestructible refrain monumentally distorts the truth. But it does." The past half-century of polling data from Gallup Report showed Reagan's average public approval rating while in office (52 percent) to be lower than Presidents Johnson (54 percent), Kennedy (70 percent), Eisenhower (66 percent), and Roosevelt (68 percent). What's more, Reagan barely bested his three immediate predecessors —Carter (47 percent), Ford (46 percent) and Nixon (48 percent). Of the last nine Presidents, Reagan's approval ranking was a mediocre fifth.

POSTSCRIPT

Does the News Media Have a Liberal Bias?

As the opposing arguments in this issue indicate, we can find critics on both the Left and the Right who agree that the media are biased. What divides such critics is the question of whether the bias is left-wing or right-wing. Defenders of the news media may seize upon this disagreement to bolster their own claim that "bias is in the eye of the beholder." But the case may be that the news media are unfair to both sides. If that were true, however, it would seem to take some of the force out of the argument that the news media have a distinct ideological tilt at all.

Edward Jay Epstein's *News from Nowhere* (Random House, 1973) remains one of the great studies of the factors that influence television news shows. In *Media Events: The Live Broadcasting of History* (Harvard University Press, 1992), Daniel Dayan and Elihu Katz argue that live television coverage of major events helps to create the events and serves an important integrative role for society by deepening most citizens' experience of a common history. A study by S. Robert Lichter et al., *The Media Elite* (Adler & Adler, 1986), tends to support Maitre's contention that the media slant leftward, as does William Rusher's *The Coming Battle for the Media* (William Morrow, 1988), whereas Ben Bagdikian's *The Media Monopoly* (Beacon Press, 1983) and Mark Hertsgaard's *On Bended Knee: The Press and the Reagan Presidency* (Schocken, 1989) lend support to Lee and Solomon's view. A more recent S. Robert Lichter book, coauthored with Linda Lichter and Stanley Rothman, is *Watching America* (Prentice Hall, 1991), which surveys the political and social messages contained in television "entertainment" programs. Lichter has also written a media textbook with Thomas Dye and Harmon Ziegler entitled *American Politics in the Media Age*, 4th ed. (Brooks-Cole, 1992). David Halberstam's *The Powers That Be* (Alfred A. Knopf, 1979), a historical study of CBS, the *Washington Post*, *Time* magazine, and the *Los Angeles Times*, describes some of the political and ideological struggles that have taken place within major media organizations.

Edward Jay Epstein's book, previously cited, uses as an epigraph the following statement by Richard Salant, president of CBS News in the 1970s: "Our reporters do not cover stories from *their* point of view. They are presenting them from *nobody's* point of view." Most probably, Salant had not intended to be facetious or ironic, but the statement so amused Epstein that he parodied it in the title of his book: *News from Nowhere*.

ISSUE 3

Does Third World Immigration Threaten America's Cultural Unity?

YES: Peter Brimelow, from *Alien Nation: Common Sense About America's Immigration Disaster* (Random House, 1995)

NO: Francis Fukuyama, from "Immigrants and Family Values," *Commentary* (May 1993)

ISSUE SUMMARY

YES: Peter Brimelow, a writer and senior editor of *Forbes* and *National Review*, asserts that the large influx of immigrants from non-European countries threatens to undermine the cultural foundations of American unity.

NO: Francis Fukuyama, a former deputy director of the U.S. State Department's policy planning staff, argues that today's immigrants share many of America's traditional values and may actually strengthen America's cultural foundations.

In his 1996 State of the Union speech, President Bill Clinton promised a 50 percent increase in border patrols to try to dramatically reduce illegal immigration. Polls show that this stand is a popular one. There is also much support for cutting back on legal immigration.

Today the number of legal immigrants to America is close to 1 million per year, and illegal ("undocumented") immigrants probably number well over that figure. In terms of numbers, immigration is now comparable to the level it reached during the early years of the twentieth century, when millions of immigrants arrived from southern and eastern Europe. A majority of the new immigrants, however, do not come from Europe but from what has been called the "Third World"—the underdeveloped nations. The largest percentages come from Mexico, the Philippines, Korea, and the islands of the Caribbean, while European immigration has shrunk to about 10 percent. Much of the reason for this shift has to do with changes made in U.S. immigration laws during the 1960s. Decades earlier, in the 1920s, America had narrowed its gate to people from certain regions of the world by imposing quotas designed to preserve the balance of races in America. But in 1965 a series of amendments to the Immigration Act put all the world's people on an equal footing in terms of immigration. The result, wrote journalist Theodore H. White, was "a stampede, almost an invasion" of Third World immigrants. Indeed, the 1965 amendments made it even easier for Third World immigrants to enter the country because the new law gave preference to those with a family member already living in the United States. Since most of the European immigrants who settled in the early part of the century had died off, and since few Europeans had immigrated in more recent years, a greater percentage of family-reuniting immigration came from the Third World.

Immigrants move to the United States for various reasons: to flee tyranny and terrorism, to escape war, or to join relatives who have already settled. Above all, they immigrate because in their eyes America is an island of affluence in a global sea of poverty; here they will earn many times what they could only hope to earn in their native countries. One hotly debated question is, What will these new immigrants do to the United States—or for it?

Part of the debate has to do with bread-and-butter issues: Will new immigrants take jobs away from American workers? Or will they fill jobs that American workers do not want anyway, which will help stimulate the economy? Behind these economic issues is a more profound cultural question: Will these new immigrants add healthy new strains to America's cultural inheritance, broadening and revitalizing it? Or will they cause the country to break up into separate cultural units, destroying America's unity? Of all the questions relating to immigration, this one seems to be the most sensitive.

In 1992 conservative columnist Patrick Buchanan set off a firestorm of controversy when he raised this question: "If we had to take a million immigrants next year, say Zulus or Englishmen, and put them in Virginia, which group would be easier to assimilate and cause less problems for the people of Virginia?" Although Buchanan later explained that his intention was not to denigrate Zulus or any other racial group but to simply talk about assimilation into Anglo-American culture, his remarks were widely characterized as racist and xenophobic (related to a fear of foreigners). Whether or not that characterization is justified, Buchanan's question goes to the heart of the cultural debate over immigration, which is the tension between unity and diversity.

In the selections that follow, Peter Brimelow contends that immigrants are harming America both economically and culturally. He argues that the sheer number of immigrants from other cultures threatens to overwhelm traditional safeguards against cultural disintegration. This foreign influx is changing America from a nation into a collection of separate nationalities. Francis Fukuyama insists that, in some respects, the values and customs of new immigrants to the United States are more traditionally "American" than those of many native-born Americans. Whereas American families are falling apart, he asserts, immigrant families tend to be more tightly knit. And although illegitimacy, drug addiction, and other social problems are on the rise in America, many immigrants lead exemplary lives.

YES

Peter Brimelow

ALIEN NATION: COMMON SENSE ABOUT AMERICA'S IMMIGRATION DISASTER

THE IMMIGRATION INUNDATION

In 1991, the year of Alexander's birth, the Immigration and Naturalization Service reported a total of over 1.8 million legal immigrants. That was easily a record. It exceeded by almost a third the previous peak of almost 1.3 million, reached eighty-four years earlier at the height of the First Great Wave of Immigration, which peaked just after the turn of the century.

The United States has been engulfed by what seems likely to be the greatest wave of immigration it has ever faced. The INS estimates that 12 to 13 million legal and illegal immigrants will enter the United States during the decade of the 1990s. The Washington, D.C.–based Federation for American Immigration Reform (FAIR), among the most prominent of the groups critical of immigration policy, thinks the total will range between 10 and 15 million. An independent expert, Daniel James, author of *Illegal Immigration—An Unfolding Crisis*, has argued that it could be as high as 18 million.

And the chaotic working of current U.S. immigration law has created a peculiar, but little-understood, reality. *The extraordinary truth is that, in almost all cases, Americans will have little more say over the arrival of these new claimants on their national community—and voters on their national future—than over the arrival of Alexander.*

This is because it's not just illegal immigration that is out of control. So is legal immigration. *U.S. law in effect treats immigration as a sort of imitation civil right, extended to an indefinite group of foreigners who have been selected arbitrarily and with no regard to American interests.*

Whether these foreigners deign to come and make their claim on America —and on the American taxpayer—is pretty much up to them.

AMERICA'S ONE-WAY IMMIGRATION DEBATE

Everyone knows that there are two sides to every question, except the typical American editor ordering up a story about immigration, for whom there is only one side: immigration good, concern about immigration bad.

This results in the anecdotal happy-talk good-news coverage of immigration that we all know and love:

XYZ was just Harvard's valedictorian —XYZ arrived in the U.S. speaking no English three months ago—XYZ PROVES THE AMERICAN DREAM IS STILL ALIVE!—despite those nasty nativists who want to keep all the XYZs out.

Now, the achievement of immigrants to the United States (more accurately, of some immigrants to the United States) is indeed one of the most inspiring, and instructive, tales in human history. Nevertheless, there are still two sides to the question. Thus we might, equally reasonably, expect to see balancing anecdotal coverage like this:

In January 1993, a Pakistani applicant for political asylum (and, simultaneously, for amnesty as an illegal immigrant) opens fire on employees entering CIA headquarters, killing two and wounding three! In February 1993, a gang of Middle Easterners (most illegally overstaying after entering on non-immigrant visas— one banned as a terrorist but admitted on a tourist visa in error) blow up New York's World Trade Center, killing six and injuring more than 1,000!! In December 1993, a Jamaican immigrant (admitted as a student but stayed, illegal status automatically regularized after marriage to a U.S. citizen) opens fire on commuters on New York's Long Island Rail Road, killing six and wounding 19!!! WHAT'S GOING ON??!!?

The case of Colin Ferguson, arrested in the Long Island Rail Road shootings, is particularly instructive....

Ferguson's own writings showed him to be motivated by hatred of whites. And this racial antagonism is a much deeper problem. In any rational mind, it must raise the question: *Is is really wise to allow the immigration of people who find it so difficult and painful to assimilate into the American majority?*

Because the fact cannot be denied: if Ferguson and the others had not immigrated, those fourteen Americans would not have been killed.

Although we might reasonably expect to see such balancing media coverage of immigration, don't hold your breath. There are powerful taboos preventing it.... The result, however, is that the American immigration debate has been a one-way street. Criticism of immigration, and news that might support it, just tends not to get through.

This is no mere journalism-school game of balancing anecdotes. It involves the broadest social trends. For example, the United States is in the midst of a serious crime epidemic. Yet almost no Americans are aware that *aliens make up one quarter of the prisoners in federal penitentiaries*—almost three times their proportion in the population at large.

Indeed, many problems that currently preoccupy Americans have an unspoken *immigration dimension....*

The education crisis. Americans are used to hearing that their schools don't seem to be providing the quality of education that foreigners get. Fewer of them know that the U.S. education system is also very expensive by international standards. Virtually none of them know anything about the impact of immigration on that education system.

Yet the impact of immigration is clearly serious. For example, in 1990 almost one child in every twenty enrolled in American public schools either could not speak English or spoke it so poorly as to need language-assistance programs.

This number is increasing with striking speed: only six years earlier, it had been one child in thirty-one. Current law is generally interpreted as requiring schools to educate such children in their native language. To do so, according to one California estimate, requires spending some 65 percent more per child than on an English-speaking child....

[T]he immigration resulting from current public policy

1. is dramatically larger, less skilled and more divergent from the American majority than anything that was anticipated or desired
2. is probably not beneficial economically—and is certainly not necessary
3. is attended by a wide and increasing range of negative consequences, from the physical environment to the political
4. is bringing about an ethnic and racial transformation in America without precedent in the history of the world —an astonishing social experiment launched with no particular reason to expect success...

WHAT ABOUT MY GRANDFATHER?

Many Americans have difficulty thinking about immigration restriction because of a lurking fear: *This would have kept my grandfather out....*

But it must also be stressed: *that was then; this is now.* There are important differences between the last Great Wave of Immigration and today's.

1. Then, there was an "Open Door" (essentially—and with the major exception of the restriction on Asians). Now, the 1965 reform has reopened the border in a perversely unequal way. Essentially, it has allowed immigrants from some countries to crowd out immigrants from others....
2. Then, immigrants came overwhelmingly from Europe, no matter how different they seemed at the time; now, immigrants are overwhelmingly visible minorities from the Third World. Not withstanding which—
3. Then, there was an aggressive public and private "Americanization" campaign...; now, there's "multiculturalism"—i.e., immigrants are officially not expected to assimilate.
4. Then, there was no welfare state and immigrants who failed often went home; now, there is a welfare state —and fewer immigrants leave.
5. Then, *immigration was stopped.* There was a pause for digestion—the Second Great Lull—that lasted some forty years. Now, there's no end in sight.

... [A]n implicit accusation of racism is the common reaction of a vocal minority of Americans to news of their country's shifting ethnic balance....

I say a vocal minority because I think the vast majority of Americans regard as just a matter of common sense that the composition of a country's population cannot, in fact, be changed without risking dramatic consequences....

[T]here are some extraordinary aspects of the impending ethnic revolution that, by any standard, deserve discussion in a democracy:

- *It is unprecedented in history.* No sovereign state has ever undergone such a radical and rapid transformation.
- *It is wholly and entirely the result of government policy.* Immigration is causing both the shifting American ethnic balance and also the projected massive increase in overall population.

Left to themselves, pre-1965 Americans would be stabilizing both their ethnic proportions and their overall numbers.

... [T]here's a plain fact to be considered: the evidence that multiracial societies work is—what shall we say?—*not very encouraging.*

There have, of course, been multiracial societies (strictly speaking, usually multiethnic) in the past. Famous examples are the Roman Empire, or the Arab Caliphate, which briefly ruled from Spain to Samarkand in the name of Muhammad. But these were old-fashioned despotisms, not modern democracies. And, even so, ethnic divisions still kept surfacing. The ancestors of the modern Iranians repeatedly rebelled against Arab rule, although they tended to justify their revolts in terms of a convenient Islamic heresy.

Heterogeneous empires that lasted, such as the Eastern Roman Empire of Byzantium, which survived until 1453, were generally based on a core ethnic group—distinctly like our old friend, the "racial hegemony of white Americans." In the case of Byzantium, for instance, this core group was Greek.

In modern times, there has been a lot of seductive murmuring about internationalism, united nations, new world orders, and so on. But, meanwhile, the role of ethnicity and race has proved to be elemental—absolute—fundamental. Look at the record, working back from the present:

- *Eritrea,* a former Italian colony ruled by Ethiopia since 1952, revolt begins in 1960s, finally splits off 1993.
- *Czechoslovakia,* founded 1918, splits into Czech and Slovak ethnic components, 1993.
- *Soviet Union,* founded 1922, splits into multiple underlying ethnic components, 1991. (Some of the underlying components are themselves promptly threatened with further ethnic fragmentation—Georgia, Moldova.)
- *Yugoslavia,* founded 1918, splits into multiple underlying ethnic components, 1991. (An earlier breakup averted by imposition of royal dictatorship, 1929.)
- *Lebanon,* founded 1920, progressive destabilization caused by its Muslim component's faster growth results in civil war, effective partition under Syrian domination, after 1975.
- *Cyprus,* independent 1960, repeated violence between Greeks and Turks results in military intervention by Turkey, effective partition with substantial ethnic cleansing, 1974.
- *Pakistan,* independent 1947, ethnically distinct eastern component rebels, splits off after Indian military intervention, 1971.
- *Malaysia,* independent 1963, political conflict between ethnic Malays and Chinese, Chinese-dominated Singapore expelled, 1965.

And these are just the cases where ethnic and racial differences have actually succeeded in breaking a country up. Many other cases are not yet resolved, because of often-bloody repression.

Here's a partial list: *India*—protracted separatist revolts by Sikhs, Kashmiris, northeastern hill tribes. *Sri Lanka*—protracted separatist revolt by Tamils. *Turkey, Iraq, Iran*—separatist revolts by Kurds. *Sudan, Chad*—endemic warfare between Arab north, black south. *Nigeria*—secession of Ibo-majority "Biafra" crushed in 1967–70 civil war. *Liberia*—English-speaking descendants of freed American slaves overthrown by tribal forces 1981, civil war renders more than half the population refugees. *Ulster*—protracted campaign by members of province's Catholic Irish minority to force the Ulster Protestant ("Scotch-Irish") majority to accept its transfer to the Irish Republic. Some of these conflicts have been very violent—over 1 million deaths each in Nigeria and Sudan.

And there's a whole further category of disputes that are being conducted, mostly, through political means. For example: *Belgium*—Flemish and Walloon; *Canada*—French and English; even *Brazil* —a movement in the predominantly white southern states Rio Grande do Sul, Santa Catarina and Paraná to separate from the mixed-race north.

What a record! You would think it would inspire at least some caution about the prospects for multiethnic, multiracial, multicultural harmony within the same political framework.

But you would be wrong. The recent record seems to have made very little impression on the American political elite....

HOW MUCH ECONOMIC GROWTH ARE WE TALKING ABOUT ANYWAY?

Oddly, American economists have made very little effort to measure the overall economic benefits of immigration. But the answer seems to be clear: *immigration doesn't contribute that much to economic growth....*

In 1992, the economic surplus generated by immigrants and accruing to native-born Americans was very small: about one to three tenths of 1 percent of total U.S. economic output, or between $6 billion and $18 billion.

That's 0.2 or 0.3 percent! In an economy whose long-run average annual growth is about 2 percent anyway!! Within the normal margin of error for economic projections—*so it may be, for practical purposes, infinitesimal!!!...*

Another point:

If immigration is indeed causing a net loss to taxpayers of $16 billion— as George Borjas estimates—that means its economic effects are neutral. It's a wash!!!

America is being transformed for— *nothing?*

Yep. That's what it looks like.

However, note that this Borjas back-of-the-envelope calculation has a subtle but ugly implication:

The overall economic surplus generated by immigrants and accruing to native-born Americans might be very small —but immigration might still be causing a significant redistribution of income within the native-born American community.

This happens because the small amount by which immigrants drive down the wages for all American workers, nationwide, adds up to a sizeable sum—which goes to American owners of capital. Borjas estimates it could be 2 percent of GNP, or as much as $120 billion....

However, this is the ugly implication: the American elite's support for immigration may not be idealistic at all, but self-interested—as a way to prey on their fellow Americans....

IS THE UNITED STATES STILL CAPABLE OF ABSORBING IMMIGRANTS?

Let's be clear about this: the American experience with immigration has been triumphant success. It has so far transcended anything seen in Europe as to make the application of European lessons an exercise to be performed with care.

But there are very clear reasons why the American nation has been able to absorb and assimilate immigrants. In considering further immigration, its enthusiasts must ask themselves honestly: *do these reasons still apply?*

One reason America could assimilate immigrants, as we have seen, is that there were regular pauses for digestion. Another reason is that the American political elite *wanted the immigrants to assimilate.* And it did not hesitate to ensure that they did.

Over two hundred years of U.S. history, a number of tried-and-true, but undeniably tough, assimilation techniques had been perfected. But today, they have been substantially abandoned.

The economic culture of the United States has changed significantly—from classical liberalism to government-regulated welfare statism. Earlier immigrants were basically free to succeed or fail. And many failed: as we have seen, as many as 40 percent of the 1880–1920 immigrants went back home. But now, public policy interposes itself, with the usual debatable results. . . .

And it's not just the American economic culture that has changed. So has the political culture. Almost a century ago, the last Great Wave of immigrants were met with the unflinching demand that they "Americanize." Now they are told that they should retain and reinforce their diversity. . . .

Is the United States still capable of absorbing immigrants? Is it still trying? Consider these policies:

1. *Massive, heterogeneous immigration.*
2. *"Bilingualism"*—i.e., foreign languageism—and
3. *"Multiculturalism"*—i.e., non-Americanism—in the education system.
4. *"Affirmative Action"*—i.e., government-mandated discrimination against white Americans.
5. *Systematic attack on the value of citizenship,* by making it easier for aliens to vote, receive government subsidies, etc.

Sounds much more like deconstructionism—the deconstruction of the American nation as it existed in 1965.

NO

Francis Fukuyama

IMMIGRANTS AND FAMILY VALUES

At the Republican convention in Houston last August, Patrick J. Buchanan announced the coming of a block-by-block war to "take back our culture." Buchanan is right that a cultural war is upon us, and that this fight will be a central American preoccupation now that the cold war is over. What he understands less well, however, is that the vast majority of the non-European immigrants who have come into this country in the past couple of decades are not the enemy. Indeed, many of them are potentially on his side....

II

The most articulate and reasoned recent conservative attack on immigration came last summer in an article in *National Review* by Peter Brimelow. Brimelow, a senior editor at *Forbes* and himself a naturalized American of British and Canadian background, argues that immigration worked in the past in America only because earlier waves of nativist backlash succeeded in limiting it to a level that could be successfully assimilated into the dominant Anglo-Saxon American culture. Brimelow criticizes pro-immigration free-marketeers like Julian Simon for ignoring the issue of the skill levels of the immigrant labor force, and their likely impact on blacks and others at the bottom end of the economic ladder. But his basic complaint is a cultural one. Attacking the *Wall Street Journal*'s Paul Gigot for remarking that a million Zulus would probably work harder than a million Englishmen today, Brimelow notes:

> This comment reveals an utter innocence about the reality of ethnic and cultural differences, let alone little things like tradition and history—in short, the greater part of the conservative vision. Even in its own purblind terms, it is totally false. All the empirical evidence is that immigrants from developed countries assimilate better than those from underdeveloped countries. It is developed countries that teach the skills required for success in the United States... it should not be necessary to explain that the legacy of [the Zulu kings] Shaka and Cetewayo—overthrown just over a century ago—is not that of Alfred the Great, let alone Elizabeth II or any civilized society.

Elsewhere, Brimelow suggests that culture is a key determinant of economic performance, and that people from certain cultures are therefore likely to do less well economically than others. He implies, furthermore, that some immigrants are more prone to random street crime because of their "impulsiveness and present-orientation," while others are responsible for organized crime which is, by his account, ethnically based. Finally, Brimelow argues that the arrival of diverse non-European cultures fosters the present atmosphere of multiculturalism, and is, to boot, bad for the electoral prospects of the Republican party.

A similar line of thought runs through Buchanan's writings and speeches, and leads to a similar anti-immigrant posture. Buchanan has explicitly attacked the notion that democracy represents a particularly positive form of government, and hence would deny that belief in universal democratic principles ought to be at the core of the American national identity.[1] But if one subtracts democracy from American nationality, what is left? Apparently, though Buchanan is somewhat less explicit on this point, a concept of America as a Christian, ethnically European nation with certain core cultural values that are threatened by those coming from other cultures and civilizations.

* * *

There is an easy, Civics 101-type answer to the Brimelow-Buchanan argument. In contrast to other West European democracies, or Japan, the American national identity has never been directly linked to ethnicity or religion. Nationality has been based instead on universal concepts like freedom and equality that are in theory open to all people. Our Constitution forbids the establishment of religion, and the legal system has traditionally held ethnicity at arm's length. To be an American has meant to be committed to a certain set of ideas, and not to be descended from an original tribe of *ur*-Americans. Those elements of a common American culture visible today—belief in the Constitution and the individualist-egalitarian principles underlying it, plus modern American pop and consumer culture—are universally accessible and appealing, making the United States, in Ben Wattenberg's phrase, the first "universal nation."

This argument is correct as far as it goes, but there is a serious counterargument that reaches to the core of last year's debate over "family values." It runs as follows:

America began living up to its universalist principles only in the last half of this century. For most of the period from its revolutionary founding to its rise as a great, modern, industrial power, the nation's elites conceived of the country not just as a democracy based on universal principles, but also as a Christian, Anglo-Saxon nation.

American democracy—the counterargument continues—is, of course, embodied in the laws and institutions of the country, and will be imbibed by anyone who learns to play by its rules. But virtually every serious theorist of American democracy has noted that its success depended heavily on the presence of certain pre-democratic values or cultural characteristics that were neither officially sanctioned nor embodied in law. If the Declaration of Independence and the Constitution were the basis of America's *Gesellschaft* (society), Christian Anglo-Saxon culture constituted its *Gemeinschaft* (community).

Indeed—the counterargument goes on—the civic institutions that Tocqueville observed in the 1830's, whose strength and vitality he saw as a critical manifestation of the Americans' "art of associating," were more often than not of a religious (i.e., Christian) nature, devoted to temperance, moral education of the young, or the abolition of slavery. There is nothing in the Constitution which states that parents should make large sacrifices for their children, that workers should rise early in the morning and labor long hours in order to get ahead, that people should emulate rather than undermine their neighbors' success, that they should be innovative, entrepreneurial, or open to technological change. Yet Americans, formed by a Christian culture, possessed these traits in abundance for much of their history, and the country's economic prosperity and social cohesion arguably rested on them.

It is this sort of consideration that underlay the family-values controversy during last year's election. Basic to this line of thought is that, all other things being equal, children are better off when raised in stable, two-parent, heterosexual families. Such family structures and the web of moral obligations they entail are the foundation of educational achievement, economic success, good citizenship, personal character, and a host of other social virtues.

... [W]hile many Americans did not sign on to last year's family-values theme, few would deny that the family and community are in deep crisis today. The breakdown of the black family in inner-city neighborhoods around America in the past couple of generations shows in particularly stark form the societal consequences of a loss of certain cultural values. And what has happened among blacks is only an extreme exten-sion of a process that has been proceeding apace among whites as well.

The issue, then, is not whether the questions of culture and cultural values are important, or whether it is legitimate to raise them, but whether immigration really threatens those values. For while the values one might deem central either to economic success or to social cohesion may have arisen out of a Christian, Anglo-Saxon culture, it is clear that they are not bound to that particular social group: some groups, like Jews and Asians, might come to possess those values in abundance, while Wasps themselves might lose them and decay. The question thus becomes: which ethnic groups in today's America are threatening, and which groups are promoting, these core cultural values?

III

The notion that non-European immigrants are a threat to family values and other core American cultural characteristics is, in a way, quite puzzling. After all, the breakdown of traditional family structures, from extended to nuclear, has long been understood to be a disease of advanced industrial countries and not of nations just emerging from their agricultural pasts.

Some conservatives tend to see the third world as a vast, global underclass, teeming with the same social pathologies as Compton in Los Angeles or Bedford-Stuyvesant in Brooklyn. But the sad fact is that the decay of basic social relationships evident in American inner cities, stretching to the most intimate moral bonds linking parents and children, may well be something with few precedents in human history. Economic conditions in most third-world countries simply would not permit a social group suffering so total a collapse of family structure to survive: with absent fathers and no source of income, or mothers addicted to drugs, children would not live to adulthood.

But it would also seem *a priori* likely that third-world immigrants should have stronger family values than white, middle-class, suburban Americans, while their work ethic and willingness to defer to traditional sources of authority should be greater as well. Few of the factors that have led to family breakdown in the American middle class over the past couple of generations—rapidly changing economic conditions, with their attendant social disruptions; the rise of feminism and the refusal of women to play traditional social roles; or the legitimization of alternative life-styles and consequent proliferation of rights and entitlements on a retail level—apply in third-world situations. Immigrants coming from traditional developing societies are likely to be poorer, less educated, and in possession of fewer skills than those from Europe, but they are also likely to have stronger family structures and moral inhibitions. Moreover, despite the greater ease of moving to America today than in the last century, immigrants are likely to be a self-selecting group with a much greater than average degree of energy, ambition, toughness, and adaptability.

These intuitions are largely borne out by the available empirical data, particularly if one disaggregates the different parts of the immigrant community.

The strength of traditional family values is most evident among immigrants from East and South Asia, where mutually supportive family structures have long been credited as the basis for their economic success. According to Census Bureau statistics, 78 percent of Asian and Pacific Islander households in the United States were family households, as opposed to 70 percent for white Americans. The size of these family households is likely to be larger: 74 percent consist of three or more persons, compared to 57 percent for white families. While Asians are equally likely to be married as whites, they are only half as likely to be divorced.[2] Though dropping off substantially in the second and third generations, concern for elderly parents is high in Chinese, Japanese, and Vietnamese households; for many, the thought of sticking a mother or father out of sight and out of mind in a nursing home continues to be anathema. More importantly, most of the major Asian immigrant groups are intent on rapid assimilation into the American mainstream, and have not been particularly vocal in pressing for particularistic cultural entitlements.

* * *

While most white Americans are ready to recognize and celebrate the social strengths of Asians, the real fears of cultural invasion surround Latinos. Despite their fast growth, Asians still constitute less than 3 percent of the U.S. population, while the number of Hispanics increased from 14.6 to over 22 million between 1980 and 1990, or 9 percent of the population. But here as well, the evidence suggests that most Latin American immigrants may be a source of strength with regard to family values, and not a liability.

Latinos today constitute an extremely diverse group. It is certainly the case that a segment of the Latino community has experienced many of the same social problems as blacks. This is particularly true of the first large Latino community in the U.S.: Puerto Ricans who came to the mainland in the early postwar period and settled predominantly in New York and other cities of the Northeast. Forty percent of Puerto Rican families are headed by women, compared to 16 percent for the non-Hispanic population; only 57 percent of Puerto Rican households consist of families, while their rate of out-of-wedlock births is almost double the rate for non-Hispanics. In New York, Puerto Ricans have re-exported social pathologies like crack-cocaine use to Puerto Rico over the past generation.

Other Latino groups have also brought social problems with them: the Mariel boat lift from Cuba, during which Castro emptied his country's jails and insane asylums, had a measurable impact on crime in the U.S. Many war-hardened immigrants from El Salvador and other unstable Central American countries have contributed to crime in the U.S., and Chicano gangs in Los Angeles and other Southwestern cities have achieved their own notoriety beside the black Bloods and Crips. Half of those arrested in the Los Angeles riot last year were Latinos.

Such facts are highly visible and contribute to the impression among white Americans that Latinos as a whole have joined inner-city blacks to form one vast, threatening underclass. But there are very significant differences among Latino groups. Latinos of Cuban and Mexican origin, for example, who together constitute 65 percent of the Hispanic community, have a 50-percent lower rate of female-headed households than do Puerto Ricans—18.9 and 19.6 percent versus 38.9 percent. While the rate of Puerto Rican out-of-wedlock births approaches that of blacks (53.0 vs. 63.1 percent of live births), the rates for Cuban and Mexican-origin Latinos

are much lower, 16.1 and 28.9 percent, respectively, though they are still above the white rate of 13.9 percent.[3]

When looked at in the aggregate, Latino family structure stands somewhere between that of whites and blacks. For example, the rates of female-headed families with no husband present as a proportion of total families is 13.5 percent for whites, 46.4 percent for blacks, and 24.4 percent for Hispanics. If we adjust these figures for income level, however, Hispanics turn out to be much closer to the white norm.

Poverty is hard on families regardless of race; part of the reason for the higher percentage of Latino female-headed households is simply that there are more poor Latino families. If we compare families below the poverty level, the Hispanic rate of female-headed families is very close to that of whites (45.7 vs. 43.6 percent), while the comparable rate for blacks is much higher than either (78.3 percent). Considering the substantially higher rate of family breakdown within the sizable Puerto Rican community, this suggests that the rate of single-parent families for Cuban- and Mexican-origin Latinos is actually lower than that for whites at a comparable income level.

Moreover, Latinos as a group are somewhat more likely to be members of families than either whites or blacks.[4] Another study indicates that Mexican-Americans have better family demographics than do whites, with higher birth-weight babies even among low-income mothers due to taboos on smoking, drinking, and drug use during pregnancy. Many Latinos remain devout Catholics, and the rate of church attendance is higher in the Mexican community than for the U.S. as a whole as well. But even if one does not believe that the United States is a "Christian country," the fact that so many immigrants are from Catholic Latin America should make them far easier to assimilate than, say, Muslims in Europe.

These statistics are broadly in accord with the observations of anyone who has lived in Los Angeles, San Diego, or any other community in the American Southwest. Virtually every early-morning commuter in Los Angeles knows the streetcorners on which Chicano day-laborers gather at 7:00 A.M., looking for work as gardeners, busboys, or on construction sites. Many of them are illegal immigrants with families back in Mexico to whom they send their earnings. While they are poor and unskilled, they have a work ethic and devotion to family comparable to those of the South and East European immigrants who came to the U.S. at the turn of the century. It is much less common to see African-Americans doing this sort of thing.

* * *

Those who fear third-world immigration as a threat to Anglo-American cultural values do not seem to have noticed what the real sources of cultural breakdown have been. To some extent, they can be traced to broad socioeconomic factors over which none of us has control: the fluid, socially disruptive nature of capitalism; technological change; economic pressures of the contemporary workplace and urban life; and so on. But the ideological assault on traditional family values—the sexual revolution; feminism and the delegitimization of the male-dominated household; the celebration of alternative life-styles; attempts ruthlessly to secularize all aspects of American public life; the acceptance of no-fault divorce and the consequent rise of single-parent households—was not the creation of recently-arrived Chicano agricultural workers or Haitian boat people, much less of Chinese or Korean immigrants. They originated right in the heart of America's well-established white, Anglo-Saxon community. The "Hollywood elite" that created the now celebrated Murphy Brown, much like the establishment "media elite" that Republicans enjoy attacking, does not represent either the values or the interests of most recent third-world immigrants.

In short, though the old, traditional culture continues to exist in the United States, it is overlaid today with an elite culture that espouses very different values. The real danger is not that these elites will become corrupted by the habits and practices of third-world immigrants, but rather that the immigrants will become corrupted by them. And that is in fact what tends to happen.

While the first generation of immigrants to the United States tends to be deferential to established authority and preoccupied with the economic problems of "making it," their children and grandchildren become aware of their own entitlements and rights, more politicized, and able to exploit the political system to defend and expand those entitlements. While the first generation is willing to work quietly at minimum- or subminimum-wage jobs, the second and third generations have higher expectations as to what their labor is worth. The extension of welfare and other social benefits to noncitizens through a series of court decisions has had the perverse effect of hastening the spread of welfare dependency. Part of the reason that Puerto Ricans do less well than other Latino groups may be that they were never really immigrants at all, but U.S. citizens, and therefore eligible for social benefits at a very early stage.

As Julian Simon has shown, neither the absolute nor the relative levels of immigration over the past decade have been inordinately high by historical standards. What *is* different and very troubling about immigration in the present period is that the ideology that existed at the turn of the century and promoted assimilation into the dominant Anglo-Saxon culture has been replaced by a multicultural one that legitimates and even promotes continuing cultural differentness.

* * *

The intellectual and social origins of multiculturalism are complex, but one thing is clear: it is both a Western and an American invention. The American Founding was based on certain Enlightenment notions of the universality of human equality and freedom, but such ideas have been under attack within the Western tradition itself for much of the past two centuries. The second half of the late Allan Bloom's *The Closing of the American Mind* (the part that most buyers of the book skipped over) chronicles the way in which the relativist ideas of Nietzsche and Heidegger were transported to American shores at mid-century. Combined with an easygoing American egalitarianism, they led not just to a belief in the need for cultural tolerance, but to a positive assertion of the equal moral validity of all cultures. Today the writings of Michel Foucault, a French epigone of Nietzsche, have become the highbrow source of academic multiculturalism.

France may have produced Foucault, but France has not implemented a multicultural educational curriculum to anything like the degree the U.S. has. The origins of multiculturalism here must therefore be traced to the specific circumstances of American social life. Contrary to the arguments of multiculturalism's promoters, it was not a necessary adjustment to the reality of our pluralistic society. The New York City public-school system in the year 1910 was as diverse as it is today, and yet it never occurred to anyone to celebrate and preserve the native cultures of the city's Italians, Greeks, Poles, Jews, or Chinese.

The shift in attitudes toward cultural diversity can be traced to the aftermath of the civil-rights movement, when it became clear that integration was not working for blacks. The failure to assimilate was interpreted as an indictment of the old, traditional mainstream Anglo-Saxon culture: "Wasp" took on a pejorative connotation, and African-Americans began to take pride in the separateness of their own traditions. Ironically, the experience of African-Americans became the model for subsequent immigrant groups like Latinos who could have integrated themselves into mainstream society as easily as the Italians or Poles before them.

It is true that Hispanic organizations now constitute part of the multiculturalist coalition and have been very vocal in pushing for bilingual/bicultural education. There is increasing evidence, however, that rank-and-file immigrants are much more traditionally assimilationist than some of their more vocal leaders. For example, most Chinese and Russian immigrant parents in New York City deliberately avoid sending their children to the bilingual-education classes offered to them by the public-school system, believing that a cold plunge into English will be a much more effective means of learning to function in American society.

Hispanics generally show more support for bilingual education, but even here a revealing recent study indicates that an overwhelming number of Hispanic parents see bilingualism primarily as a means of learning English, and not of preserving Hispanic culture.[5] This same study indicates that most Hispanics identify strongly with the United States, and show a relatively low level of Spanish maintenance in the home. By contrast, multiculturalism is more strongly supported by many other groups—blacks, feminists, gays, Native Americans, etc.—whose ancestors have been in the country from the start.

* * *

Brimelow's *National Review* piece suggests that even if immigrants are not responsible for our anti-assimilationist multiculturalism, we need not pour oil on burning waters by letting in more immigrants from non-Western cultures. But this argument can be reversed: even if the rate of new immigration fell to zero tomorrow, and the most recent five million immigrants were sent home, we would still have an enormous problem in this country with the breakdown of a core culture and the infatuation of the school system with trendy multiculturalist educational policies.

The real fight, the central fight, then, should not be over keeping newcomers out: this will be a waste of time and energy. The real fight ought to be over the question of assimilation itself: whether we believe that there is enough to our Western, rational, egalitarian, democratic civilization to force those coming to the country to absorb its language and rules, or whether we carry respect for other cultures to the point that Americans no

longer have a common voice with which to speak to one another.

Apart from the humble habits of work and family values, opponents of immigration ought to consider culture at the high end of the scale. As anyone who has walked around an elite American university recently would know, immigration from Asia is transforming the nature of American education. For a country that has long prided itself on technological superiority, and whose economic future rests in large part on a continuing technical edge, a depressingly small number of white Americans from long-established families choose to go into engineering and science programs in preference to business and, above all, law school. (This is particularly true of the most dynamic and vocal part of the white population, upwardly mobile middle-class women.) The one bright spot in an otherwise uniform horizon of decline in educational test scores has been in math, where large numbers of new Asian test-takers have bumped up the numbers.[6] In Silicon Valley alone, there are some 12,000 engineers of Chinese descent, while Chinese account for two out of every five engineering and science graduates in the University of California system.

Indeed, if one were to opt for "designer immigration" that would open the gates to peoples with the best cultural values, it is not at all clear that certain European countries would end up on top.

In the past decade, England's percapita GNP [Gross National Product] has fallen behind Italy's, and threatens to displace Portugal and Greece at the bottom of the European Community heap by the end of the decade. Only a fifth of English young people receive any form of higher education, and despite Margaret Thatcher's best efforts, little progress has been made over the past generation in breaking down the stifling social rigidities of the British class system. The English working class is among the least well-educated, most state- and welfare-dependent and immobile of any in the developed world. While the British intelligentsia and upper classes continue to intimidate middle-class Americans, they can do so only on the basis of snobbery and inherited but rapidly dwindling intellectual capital. Paul Gigot may or may not be right that a million Zulus would work harder than a million English, but a million Taiwanese certainly would, and would bring with them much stronger family structures and entrepreneurship to boot.

IV

This is not to say that immigration will not be the source of major economic and social problems for the United States in the future. There are at least three areas of particular concern.

The first has to do with the effects of immigration on income distribution, particularly at the low end of the scale. The growing inequality of American income distribution over the past decade is not, as the Democrats asserted during the election campaign, the result of Reagan-Bush tax policies or the failure of "trickle-down" economics. Rather, it proceeds from the globalization of the American economy: low-skill labor increasingly has to compete with low-skill labor in Malaysia, Brazil, Mexico, and elsewhere. But it has also had to compete with low-skill immigrant labor coming into the country from the third world, which explains why Hispanics themselves tend to oppose further Hispanic immigration. The country as a whole

may be better off economically as a result of this immigration, but those against whom immigrants directly compete have been hurt, just as they will be hurt by the North American Free Trade Agreement (NAFTA), the General Agreement on Tariffs and Trade (GATT), and other trade-liberalizing measures that are good for the country as a whole. In a city like Los Angeles, Hispanics with their stronger social ties have displaced blacks out of a variety of menial jobs, adding to the woes of an already troubled black community.

The second problem area has to do with the regional concentration of recent Hispanic immigration. As everyone knows, the 25 million Hispanics in the United States are not evenly distributed throughout the country, but are concentrated in the Southwest portion of it, where the problems normally accompanying the assimilation of immigrant communities tend to be magnified. The L.A. public-school system is currently in a state of breakdown, as it tries to educate burgeoning numbers of recent immigrants on a recession-starved budget.

The third problem concerns bilingualism and the elite Hispanic groups which promote and exist off of it. As noted earlier, the rank-and-file of the Hispanic community seems reasonably committed to assimilation; the same cannot be said for its leadership. Bilingualism, which initially began as a well-intentioned if misguided bridge toward learning English, has become in the eyes of many of its proponents a means of keeping alive a separate Spanish language and culture. Numerous studies have indicated that students in bilingual programs learn English less well than those without access to them, and that their enrollments are swelled by a large number of Hispanics who can already speak English perfectly well.[7] In cities with large Hispanic populations like New York and Los Angeles, the bilingual bureaucracy has become something of a monster, rigidly tracking students despite the wishes of parents and students. The *New York Times* recently reported the case of a Hispanic-surnamed child, born in the United States and speaking only English, who was forced by New York City officials to enroll in an English as a Second Language Class. Bilingualism is but one symptom of a much broader crisis in American public education, and admittedly makes the problems of assimilation much greater.

These problems can be tackled with specific changes in public policy. But the central issue raised by the immigration question is indeed a cultural one, and as such less susceptible of policy manipulation. The problem here is not the foreign culture that immigrants bring with them from the third world, but the contemporary elite culture of Americans —Americans like Kevin Costner, who believes that America began going downhill when the white man set foot here, or another American, Ice-T, whose family has probably been in the country longer than Costner's and who believes that women are bitches and that the chief enemy of his generation is the police. In the upcoming block-by-block cultural war, the enemy will not speak Spanish or have a brown skin. In Pogo's words, "He is us."

NOTES

1. See, for example, his article, "America First— and Second, and Third," the *National Interest*, Spring 1990.

2. Census Bureau Press Release CB92–89, "Profile of Asians and Pacific Islanders."

3. Data taken from Linda Chavez, *Out of the Barrio* (Basic Books, 1991), p. 103.

4. Figures taken from *Poverty in the United States: 1991*, Bureau of the Census, Series P-60, no. 181, pp. 7–9; the percentage of people in families for whites, blacks, and Hispanics is 84.5, 84.8, and 89.0, respectively (pp. 2–3).

5. See Rodolfo O. de la Garza, Louis DeSipio, *et al.*, *Latino Voices: Mexican, Puerto Rican, and Cuban Perspectives on American Politics* (Westview Press, 1992).

6. This same group of Asians appears also to have lowered verbal scores, though this is something that will presumably be corrected over time.

7. On this point, see Linda Chavez's *Out of the Barrio*, pp. 9–38.

POSTSCRIPT

Does Third World Immigration Threaten America's Cultural Unity?

Both Brimelow and Fukuyama oppose "multicultural" education, which they think neglects and even denigrates America's unifying traditions. Where the two clearly differ is in the way they frame the issue and their attitudes toward today's immigrant peoples.

In Fukuyama's view, many of the cultural traits that Asian and Latino immigrants commonly have resemble those that Americans once had but are now losing. In some respects, Fukuyama seems to say, the new immigrants are more American than the Americans.

Brimelow asserts that the value congruence of most immigrants is a myth. He also worries that, although the new immigrants may want to assimilate, they have now reached such a critical mass that the United States has lost the ability to absorb everyone into its own, slowly dissipating culture. The result is that immigrants are encouraged to maintain and promote the cultures that they arrive with, which further dilutes the original culture of America.

For a fascinating study of the roots of American traditional culture, see David Hackett Fischer, *Albion's Seed: Four British Folkways in America* (Oxford University Press, 1989). Stanley Lieberson and Mary C. Waters, in *From Many Strands* (Russell Sage Foundation, 1988), argue that ethnic groups with European origins are assimilating, marrying outside their groups, and losing their ethnic identities. Richard D. Alba's recent study "Assimilation's Quiet Tide," *Public Interest* (Spring 1995) confirms these findings.

Several major works debate whether or not immigrants, on average, economically benefit America and can assimilate. Those who argue that immigrants largely benefit America include Julian L. Simon, *The Economic Consequences of Immigration* (Basil Blackwell, 1989); John C. Harles, *Politics in the Lifeboat: Immigrants and the American Democratic Order* (Westview, 1993); and Thomas Muller, *Immigrants and the American City* (New York University Press, 1993). See also Ben Wattenberg and Karl Zinmeister, "The Case for More Immigration," *Commentary* (April 1990); Glenn Garvin, "No Fruits, No Shirts, No Service," *Reason* (April 1995) and "Bringing the Border War Home," *Reason* (October 1995); and Nathan Glazer, "Immigration and the American Future," *The Public Interest* (Winter 1995). Those who argue that immigrants have more negative than positive impacts include George Borjas, *Friends or Strangers* (Basic Books, 1990) and "Know the Flow," *National Review* (April 17, 1995); Lawrence Auster, *The Path to National Suicide: An Essay on Immigration and Multiculturalism* (AICF, 1990); and Richard D. Lamm, "Enough," *Across the Board* (March 1995). Vernon M. Biggs, Jr., and Stephen Moore debate each other on the economic impacts of immigration in *Still an Open Door? U.S. Immigration Policy and the American Economy* (American University Press, 1994). Lawrence E. Harrison, in "America and Its Immigrants," *National Interest* (Summer 1992), argues in favor of selective immigration, which would allow only those people with the "correct" skills and values to immigrate to the United States. Given the great need for a haven for those who must flee persecution and desperation, there are many humanitarian aspects to the immigration issue that must be brought into the discussion. See Gil Loescher, *Beyond Charity: International Cooperation and the Global Refugee Crisis* (Oxford University Press, 1993).

PART 2

Sex Roles, Gender, and the Family

*The modern feminist movement has advanced the causes of
women to the point where there are now more women in the
workforce in the United States than ever before. Professions
and trades that were traditionally regarded as the provinces of
men have opened up to women, and women now have easier
access to the education and training necessary to excel in these
new areas. But what is happening to sex roles, and what are
the effects of changing sex roles? How have related problems
such as date rape and the deterioration of the traditional family
structure affected men and women and children? Is feminism
as a universal philosophy harmful in any way? The issues in
this part address these sorts of questions.*

- Is Feminism a Harmful Ideology?
- Is There a Date Rape Crisis in Society?
- Should Society Be More Accepting of
  Homosexuality?
- Should Traditional Families Be Preserved?

ISSUE 4

Is Feminism a Harmful Ideology?

YES: Robert Sheaffer, from "Feminism, the Noble Lie," *Free Inquiry* (Spring 1995)

NO: William H. Chafe, from *The Paradox of Change: American Women in the Twentieth Century* (Oxford University Press, 1991)

ISSUE SUMMARY

YES: Robert Sheaffer, a consulting editor for *Skeptical Inquirer,* faults feminism for supporting its political agenda with fraudulent research and for trying to impose an inappropriate equality on men and women that conflicts with basic biological differences between the genders.

NO: William H. Chafe, a professor at Duke University, presents the history of feminism since the early 1960s and portrays the injustices that needed to be corrected. He maintains that the vast improvements that women have made and the obvious need to end continuing discrimination demonstrate the value of feminism.

The publication of Betty Friedan's *The Feminine Mystique* (W. W. Norton, 1963) is generally thought of as the beginning of the modern women's movement, and since that time significant changes have occurred in American society. Occupations and professions, schools, clubs, associations, and governmental positions that were by tradition or law previously reserved for men only are now open to women. Women are found in increasing numbers among lawyers, judges, physicians, and elected officials. In 1981 President Ronald Reagan appointed the first woman, Sandra Day O'Connor, to the Supreme Court. In 1983 the first American woman astronaut, Sally Ride, was included in the crew of a space shuttle, and women have been on more recent space shuttle missions as well. The service academies have accepted women since 1976, and women in the military participated in the U.S. invasion of Panama in December 1989 and the Persian Gulf War in 1990–1991. There are ongoing debates in Congress and among the armed services about whether or not to lift restrictions on women serving in combat. And Elizabeth Watson became the first woman to head a big-city police department when the mayor of Houston appointed her chief of police in January 1990.

These sorts of changes—quantifiable and highly publicized—may signal a change in women's roles, at least to this extent: women now engage in occupations that were previously exclusive to men, and women can pursue the necessary training and education required to do so. But three decades after Friedan's book, to what extent do females and males have equal standing? Are femininity and femaleness prized or valued the same as maleness and masculinity? What is happening to society's concepts of both? Even as changes are occurring in the public world, what is happening on a personal level to the roles of men and women? How do we value the domestic sphere? What is happening to child care? to our concept of the family?

Feminism—an ideology that, in its most basic form, directly opposes sexism by supporting gender equality and portraying women and men as essentially equals—has been a driving force in shaping the modern women's movement. The final legal victory of the women's movement was supposed to be the passage of the Equal Rights Amendment to the Constitution (ERA), which would have made a person's sex an irrelevant distinction under the law. The ERA passed both houses of Congress by overwhelming margins in 1972, but it failed to win ratification from the required three-fourths of the state legislatures. The amendment was not ratified in part due to the efforts of a coalition of groups, composed overwhelmingly of women, who went to battle against it. Thus, the women's movement did not represent the views of all women; many continued to believe in traditional gender roles.

In the readings that follow, Robert Sheaffer argues that feminists falsely reconstruct gender realities to deny that biological differences contribute significantly to gender inequalities. Sheaffer asserts that feminists assume that current inequalities are due to socialization and are thus malleable, or are due to discrimination and are thus best redressed by regulations. But he concludes that their program of action will have largely adverse impacts. A favorable view of feminism is presented by William H. Chafe, who defines feminism by what feminists have tried to change. He discusses three variants of feminism, all of which he says have brought about important reforms in society.

YES   Robert Sheaffer

FEMINISM, THE NOBLE LIE

In the *Republic*, Plato argues that, in order to build a proper Utopia, it would be necessary to depict the gods as virtuous. Hence censorship and deception were seen as requisite for instilling virtue: "The lie in words is in certain cases useful and not hateful."[1] This has come to be known as Plato's "Noble Lie." In the present age, another would-be builder of utopias has, almost unnoticed, adopted the Noble Lie in pursuit of its goals, while somehow yet retaining an aura of moral rectitude: the politically correct feminist movement, which reigns virtually unchallenged in academe and in government.

The world as depicted by contemporary feminism is a peculiar one. It teaches a history that is at variance with that taught in history departments, a view of science incorporating only selectively that taught in science departments, and a paradoxical, illiberal approach to morality in which the correctness of an action depends to a large extent on who is performing it. The world-view created by contemporary feminism has much in common with that of the illusionist, who can conjure an impressive scenario, but only when viewed from a certain angle, and only when all attempts at critical scrutiny are muted. Indeed, it is difficult to quell the suspicion that the reason feminists have always insisted on a separate department for Women's Studies is because they require exemption from the peer review and critical scrutiny that their material would otherwise receive were it taught as history, philosophy, or science.

Feminists have largely gotten away with these deceptions because the widespread and highly successful inculcation of male guilt allows them to claim that any critical scrutiny of their claims amounts to "blaming the victim." Additionally, chivalrous feelings make most men feel it is somehow unfair to attack women, even if those same women are spouting bizarre nonsense in the process of vigorously attacking men. The result has been that a great deal of selective truth, half-truth, and even untruth has been unquestioningly accepted by a large portion of the educated public. In Plato's Utopian state, the rulers would have a monopoly on the right to tell lies; through the enforcement of "hostile speech" codes on campus (and in some instances questioning feminist doctrine has been construed as hostile speech), modern-day academic feminists seek the same privilege.

* * *

... The harsh reality is that the entire history of the human race, from the present to the earliest written texts, is an unbroken record of so-called patriarchy, presumably extending back at least as far as our early primate ancestors (since chimp society displays extreme male dominance). In every human society, without exception, leadership is associated with the male and the nurturing of children with the female.

Those who argue that socialization must somehow explain sex roles find themselves unable to explain *why* socialization always proceeds in a uniform direction, when according to their assumptions it ought to proceed randomly, resulting in a patchwork of matriarchies, interspersed with patriarchies. Why does every society, without exception, socialize men for leadership and women for domestic tasks? Why not the reverse?

Thus, the strict environmentalist explanation falls into an infinite regress, and finds itself postulating an uncaused cause: the male dominance we observe in every society is said to be caused by socialization, yet the socialization has no cause, and somehow always was.

Steven Goldberg argues persuasively that the popular claim of socialization to explain sex roles gets the causality backward. He writes that feminist theorists "make the mistake of treating the social environment as an independent variable, thereby failing to explain *why* the social environment always conforms to limits set by, and takes a direction concordant with, the physiological (i.e., never

does environment act as sufficient counterpoise to enable a society to avoid male dominance of hierarchies)."[2] Societies observe the patterns of behavior that biology seems to render inevitable, then attempt to socialize women and men into roles that it expects they will be able to fulfill. Hence, according to Goldberg, socialization is the *dependent* variable, not the independent one, as is commonly supposed.

If sex roles really are arbitrary constructs of society, created to keep women "in their place," why is it necessary to give transsexuals—individuals who already display many characteristics of the opposite sex—hormones of that opposite sex, prior to and separate from any surgery, to enable them to genuinely fit into their new role? Invariably these male or female hormones are reported as having profound mood-altering characteristics. For example, in the documentary film *Max* by the lesbian director Monika Treut, a pre-surgical female-to-male transsexual comments on the profound effects experienced upon being administered male hormones in the course of treatment. She reported that her energy level suddenly increased dramatically, as did her sex drive. Her moods were greatly affected, and she found herself unable to cry as much and as easily as she did before. Feminists, however, attribute such behavior in men to "socialization."

Now if the feminist "society-is-responsible" hypothesis were true, sex hormones would have no effect on behavior, and transsexuals could presumably be trained into their new roles just by reading a book. The reason that the feminist theorist attempts to force us to ignore the powerful role of male and female hormones as determinants of behavior is that we would then have to acknowledge that sex roles are not only arbitrary, but are in fact permanent and ineradicable (short of radical medical intervention).

Contemporary politically correct feminists, like Marxists, feel obligated to postulate a purely environmental explanation for all sex-related differences in behavior, because, as soon as biological differences are admitted as relevant factors, the presumption that women's career choices are forced by discrimination cannot be supported. Should any male/female differences in behavior and career choices be admitted as innate and real, then the null hypothesis—the assumption that in the absence of discrimination, no differences in the two groups would be observed—is no longer tenable. The feminist would then be placed in the position of needing to separate the effects of so-called discrimination from those of biology, a clearly impossible task. Hence, male/female differences in biology must be declared *ipso facto* to have no possible observable consequences. Biologist Garrett Hardin notes that the epithet "biological determinism," carrying "implications of absolute rigidity," is "a straw man set up for the convenience of polemicists; we would do well to ignore it." He adds,

to suppose that human behavior is uninfluenced by heredity is to say that man is not a part of nature. The Darwinian assumption is that he is; Darwinians insist that the burden of proof falls on those who assert the contrary.

Philosopher Michael Levin wryly describes feminist theory as a form of Creationism, which he defines as

any refusal to apply evolutionary theory to man. It is irrelevant whether this refusal is sustained by a literal reading of scripture or commitment to a secular ideology.

He chides scientists like Richard Lewontin and Stephen Jay Gould, who take a wholly naturalistic stance toward all living creatures apart from man.[3]

The fact that men have much greater physical strength than women cannot possibly be admitted as a factor causing men to predominate in strenuous jobs; the dearth of women in such jobs is instead attributed to a hostile working environment created by sexist men. If it is admitted that few women actually *want* to do such work, this must be explained away as a consequence of them having been brainwashed into accepting negative patriarchal stereotypes. That men predominate in higher-paying positions is itself seen as evidence of a vast conspiracy to keep women out of better jobs, in spite of the fact that, when we correct for factors such as the number of hours worked, the number of years of education and in the position, etc., the differences all but vanish. If it were really true that women were being paid fifty-nine cents (or whatever number you choose to believe) for every dollar that men make, for doing the same work at the same level of skill, then no business could possibly be competitive if it employed any men.

That differences in career choices might arise from mutual preferences and independent choices made by two groups having significant innate psychological differences is not a permissible hypothesis, even though it has seemed obvious to every other society except our own. No explanation will be satisfactory to contemporary feminists unless it depicts men as exploiters and women as victims (a depiction that itself belies the feminists' claim to believe in strict equality).

In order to defend the employment conspiracy hypothesis, feminists must argue either that there are no genuine, innate differences in the skills, attitudes, and abilities of women and men, or else that such differences may exist but have absolutely no observable effect. As soon as such differences are admitted as a meaningful factor influencing career choices and performance, the case for the supposed omnipresent discrimination vanishes.

Most feminists will reluctantly admit that, at least in sports, the difference in performance between women and men is a result of innate factors and not social conditioning. No amount of political indoctrination will transform a female athlete into a respectable linebacker for the National Football League. This then places the feminist in the curious position of arguing that innate factors account for the profound difference in male/female performance in sports, but in absolutely nothing else. This violates parsimony. Michael Levin argues that it is absurd to claim that there is *no* paid job outside athletics where the kind of skill, stamina, and speed manifested in athletics conveys advantage.[5] Truly, it is ideology, not logic, that prompts the hypothesis of absolute male/female interchangeability (most feminists will disavow the claim of interchangeability, yet vigorously defend everything that follows from it!).

Contemporary politically correct feminism with its emphasis on group rights and group offenses is fundamentally illiberal, a dramatic break from the long humanistic tradition that emphasizes individual rights, rewards, and punishments. It attacks free speech wherever freedom is used in ways it does not approve; many feminists have recently joined forces with the religious right to attack so-called pornography. (Another coalition of feminists with the religious right, crusading against alleged satanic cults, threatens to become a witch-hunt in a literal sense! And the zealous use of highly dubious "repressed memories" to uncover supposed "forgotten incest" is largely a feminist-led campaign.)

This ideology seeks to replace the liberal ideal of "equality under the law" with the sinister "some are more equal than others," awarding women special rights and special protections unavailable to men. One of the most glaring examples concerns the status of single-sex schools. The small number of remaining all-male colleges, mostly of military orientation, such as Virginia Military Institute and The Citadel, are under unrelenting political and legal pressure from feminists to end their single-sex policy, which is held to be discriminatory. Yet, when a few years back the directors of all-female Mills College decided to begin admitting men students, this same relentless feminist juggernaut came down upon them to *preserve* same-sex education, forcing them to reverse their decision.

The justification offered was that men tend to dominate classroom environments owing to their greater aggressiveness. Feminists who argue this way, however, are in the delicate position of maintaining that, while male dominance of classrooms is caused by the male's greater aggressiveness, male dominance of the business world is entirely the result of a conspiracy against women.

* * *

It is invariably objected that the kinds of positions and doctrines described above are those of extremists and that reasonable feminists and feminist organizations do not hold them. The question I next ask is: just *where are* all these reasonable feminists? The answer invariably is that they are sitting next to me, or in the office down the hall; yet somehow these supposed voices of moderation manage to play absolutely no role whatsoever in the formulation of public policy. We are asked to believe that the largest feminist organization in America, and the largest-circulation feminist magazine, each of which endlessly promotes the image of women as victims while vigorously lobbying for special preferences and quotas (and each is or recently was headed up by a lesbian), are somehow unrepresentative of what the supposedly typical feminist does and believes. Again, this is just a cheap rhetorical trick: by definition, the largest organizations and publications in any movement are representative of that movement. Were they unrepresentative, some other spokeswomen would step forth, and gather a following larger still.

No reasonable person could deny that women and men ought to have the same legal rights in matters of a career, property ownership, etc. Likewise, no reasonable person could expect that equality of opportunity would automatically turn into equality of result when two groups are as different as women and men. It also seems to me that no reasonable person could deny the moral equality of women and men: that neither sex has any credible claim to greater goodness or cooperative behavior than the other. Yet, this is precisely what contemporary feminism attempts to deny, with its incessant depiction of men as cruel exploiters and women as their innocent victims.

The rhetoric of the feminist movement portrays history as a dismal scenario of the unending oppression and subjugation of women for the selfish benefit of men. (That men might themselves be a "victim" class, given that men have made up almost 100 percent of the cannon fodder of every battle in history, is not worthy of consideration.) But the depiction of woman as perpetual victim does not survive critical scrutiny. Whatever rights women may not have had at various points in history, such as the right to vote, had typically only been won by men a short time earlier. Throughout most of history, *nobody* had any rights, outside the ruling elite! And the very real *informal* power women hold in families and other situations is simply ignored when painting the weepy scenario.

As for contemporary American society: women live an average of seven years longer than men; female-headed households have a net worth that averages 41 percent higher than those of male-headed ones (and this in spite of the fact that the average woman works far fewer hours per year than the average man). Women, supposedly discriminated against in education, make up 55 percent of current college graduates. They claim to be discriminated against in politics, yet cast seven million more votes than men in electing presidents. They win almost automatically in child custody disputes. Victims of violent crime are overwhelmingly male, and wives assault husbands *more frequently* than the reverse. Women can murder a sleeping husband or lover in cold blood, then claim the "battered woman" defense and very likely receive only the lightest sentence or perhaps even no sentence at all, even in the absence of any proof that they were actually battered. (There is no "battered man" defense.)

If convicted of a felony, a man serves out a sentence averaging more than 50 percent longer than a woman convicted of the same crime, and a man in prison is more than ten times as likely to die there than is a woman. Men's suicide rate is four times that of women. Twenty-four out of the twenty-five jobs ranked worst in terms of pay and working conditions by the Jobs Related Almanac have one thing in common: they are all 95 percent to 100 percent male. Of those killed in work-related accidents, 94 percent are men, as were 96 percent of those killed in the Gulf War. If men have supposedly arranged everything to be so wonderful for themselves, then why are they dying, being mutilated, murdered, or killing themselves at rates vastly higher than those of women, who end up having more money in spite of having worked less?[6] It makes much more sense to call contemporary American women "privileged" than "oppressed!"

The world-view erected by contemporary politically correct feminism, the only kind that plays any role in shaping public policy, is a house of cards. It requires its adherents to jump from one unsteady limb to another, never quite sure whether sex differences in behavior are illusory or very real but insignificant; uncertain whether women behave exactly the same as men, or are emotionally and morally superior, oriented toward life (unlike men, who love death); switching from "absolute *égalité*" to "special provisions," depending on which confers greater advantage. Women are simultaneously strong and independent, fully prepared to prevail in the hell of combat, yet at the same time so weak as to need special rules under which they receive compensatory advantages to assist them in competition with men; they also

need special protection against unwanted sexual advances and dirty jokes. This is much like a magician's silk that appears to have a different color each time it is revealed. It is predictable that this article will be answered far more with *ad hominem* insults and expressions of moral outrage than with reasoned argument; such are the defenses employed by illusionists who are infuriated when their deceptions are revealed.

But there can be great harm in falsehood unopposed, especially when it results in suspicion, hostility, and envy between the sexes, where love frequently used to exist as recently as a generation before. In no other countries has politically correct feminism gained such power as in the United States and Canada (which is itself interesting: why have European women largely declined to fight in the war against men?). As a consequence, we have here what is almost certainly the highest divorce rate in the world, a crumbling educational system, and a seemingly unstoppable spiral of rising crime and related social pathology. Recent studies demonstrated a powerful correlation between this social pathology and the children of fatherless families.[7] It remains to be seen whether any society can remain intact largely without viable families in which to raise psychologically healthy children. One can argue that the U.S. family died of natural causes at precisely the same time feminists began shooting at it; after examining the depth and ferocity of the feminist attack against women's roles as wives and mothers, one can be convinced.

Nietzsche warned against systems of morality grounded in what he called *ressentiment*, pretending to represent compassion while actually embodying the covert destructiveness of those who impotently desire revenge against those they envy. He cited Christian morality as the primary example of such a system.[8] While feigning an attitude of passivity and love, the early Christian actually worked to bring down any person or institution esteemed for worldly success. We must not fail to note that contemporary politically correct feminism and Marxism are both manifestations of *ressentiment*.[9]

In spite of its success in masquerading as a harmless, even noble, movement dedicated to simple fairness, the contemporary feminist movement is in fact a Noble Lie. No matter how many people may have been sincerely persuaded to believe its pronouncements, the empress has no clothes. And a Noble Lie is nonetheless a lie.

NOTES

1. *The Republic*, Book II (382c).

2. Steven Goldberg, *When Wish Replaces Thought* (Buffalo, N.Y.: Prometheus Books, 1991) p. 173.

3. Garrett Hardin, *Naked Emperors: Essays of a Taboo Stalker* (Los Altos, Calif.: William Kaufmann, Inc., 1982), Chapter 8. Michael Levin, *Feminism and Freedom* (New Brunswick, N.J.: Transaction Books, 1987), Chapter 3.

4. See, for example, George Gilder's *Wealth and Poverty* (New York: Bantam Books, 1982) Chapter 12.

5. Michael Levin, *Feminism and Freedom* (New Brunswick, N.J.: Transaction Books, 1987) Chapter 10.

6. These statistics come from Warrent Farrell *The Myth of Male Power* (New York: Simon & Schuster, 1993).

7. See "Dan Quayle Was Right," *Atlantic Monthly*, April 1993.

8. Nietzsche, *The Genealogy of Morals*, Book 1. See also Robert Sheaffer, *The Making of the Messiah* (Prometheus Books, 1991) Chapter 2.

9. Simone de Beauvoir is generally acknowledged as the Founding Mother of contemporary feminism. In her tome *The Second Sex*, she plainly grounds her theory of the "exploitation" of women in "historical materialism" (i.e., Marxism), and in particular in the now-discredited historical speculations of Engels. Today, the feminist establishment and socialists, are on the same side of every significant political issue.

NO

William H. Chafe

THE POSTWAR REVIVAL OF FEMINISM

THE REVIVAL OF FEMINISM

HELMAN: Before all else, you are a wife and mother.
NORA: That I no longer believe. I believe that before all else, I am a human being, just as much as you are—or at least that I should try to become one.

—Henrik Ibsen, *A Doll's House* (1879)

In the fall of 1962, the editors of *Harper's* observed a curious phenomenon. An extraordinary number of women seemed "ardently determined to extend their vocation beyond the bedroom, kitchen and nursery," but very few showed any interest in feminism. Both observations were essentially correct. In the years during and after World War II, millions of women had joined the labor force, many of them leaving the home to take jobs; but the expansion of their "sphere" occurred without fanfare and was not accompanied either by progress toward equality or an organized effort to protest traditional definitions of "woman's place." If many women were dissatisfied with what one housewife called the endless routine of "dishwashing, picking up, ironing and folding diapers," they had no collective forum to express their grievances. Women examined their futures privately and with an unmilitant air. There seemed to be no sanctioned alternative.

Eight years later, feminism competed with the war in Vietnam, student revolts, and inflation for headlines in the daily press. Women activists picketed the Miss America pageant, demonstrated at meetings of professional associations to demand equal employment opportunities, and insisted on equal access to previously all-male bars and restaurants in New York. They called a national strike to commemorate the 50th anniversary of woman suffrage, wrote about the oppression of "sexual politics," and sat in at the editorial offices of *Newsweek* and the *Ladies' Home Journal*. In an era punctuated by protest, feminism had once again come into its own. If not all women enlisted in the new struggle for equality, few could claim to be unaffected by it.

From William H. Chafe, *The Paradox of Change: American Women in the Twentieth Century* (Oxford University Press, 1991). Copyright © 1991 by Oxford University Press. Reprinted by permission.

The evolution of any protest movement, of course, is a complicated process. In general, however, a series of preconditions are necessary: political currency and sanction for the ideas around which a movement grows; a catalyst to initiate protest; support from an energetic minority, at least, of the aggrieved group; and a social atmosphere that is conducive to reform. To an extent unmatched since the last days of the suffrage fight, all these elements were present during the 1960s. The accumulated grievances of individual women found expression in a growing number of feminist voices whose writings gave focus to the movement; the civil-rights struggle helped to trigger a renewal of women's rights activism; a substantial number of women, young and old, were ready to respond; and the society at large was more sensitive than at any time in the twentieth century to the quest for social justice. No one development could have fostered the resurgence of feminism, but the several acting together created a context in which, for the first time in five decades, feminism became again a force to be reckoned with.

* * *

The most widely noted indictment of America's system of sex inequality came from the pen of Betty Friedan. Although other books and articles exerted just as much influence on key groups of women activists, Friedan's acerbic look at *The Feminine Mystique* (1963) generated the kind of attention that made feminism a popular topic of conversation once again. According to Friedan, American women had been held captive by a set of ideas that defined female happiness as total involvement in the roles of wife and mother. Advertisers manipulated women into believing that they could achieve fulfillment by using the latest model vacuum cleaner or bleaching their clothes a purer white. Women's magazines romanticized domesticity and presented an image of women as "gaily content in a world of bedroom, kitchen, sex, babies and home." And psychiatrists popularized the notion that any woman unhappy with a full-time occupation as housewife must be neurotic. As a result, Friedan charged, a woman's horizons were circumscribed from childhood on by the assumption that her highest calling in life was to be a servant to her husband and children. In effect, the home had become a "comfortable concentration camp" that infantilized its female inhabitants and forced them to "give up their adult frame of reference." Just as Victorian culture had repressed women's sexual instincts, modern American culture had destroyed their minds and emotions.

Other observes came to the same conclusions. Adopting a more academic perspective, Ellen and Kenneth Keniston pointed out that young women had no positive models of independent women to emulate and that with no culturally approved alternative to homemaking, many women accepted a "voluntary servitude" in the home rather than risk losing their femininity. The sociologist Alice Rossi made the same point. "There are few Noras in contemporary society," she observed, "because women have deluded themselves that a doll's house is large enough to find complete fulfillment within it." As a result, however, children were treated like "hothouse plants," women overidentified with their offspring, and a vicious cycle of repression and frustration ensured. The family became a breeding ground for discontent and unhappiness, with suburban bliss exploding into skyrocketing divorce rates, addiction to pills and alcohol, and an epidemic of mental illness.

At the heart of this diagnosis was the assertion that women had been deprived of the chance to develop an identity of their own. Assigned to a "place" solely on the basis of their sex, women were kept from seeing themselves as unique human beings. All women participated equally in the undifferentiated roles of housewife and mother, but many lacked a more precise image of themselves as individuals. As one young mother wrote to Friedan:

> I've tried everything women are supposed to do—hobbies, gardening, pickling, canning, and being very social with my neighbors.... I can do it all, and I like it, but it doesn't leave you anything to think about—any feeling of who you are.... I love the kids and Bob and my home.... But I'm desperate. I begin to feel that I have no personality. I'm a server of food and putter-on of pants and a bedmaker, somebody who can be called on when you want something. But who am I?

To Friedan and others like her, the question struck at the core of the alienation of modern women and could be answered only if wives and mothers rejected cultural stereotypes and developed lives of their own. If women pursued their own careers, Alice Rossi noted, they would demand less of their husbands, provide a "living model" of independence and responsibility to their children, and regain a sense of their own worth as persons. With an independent existence outside the home, they would cease to be parasites living off the activities of those around them and, instead, became full and equal partners in the family community.

There were a number of problems with this analysis. First, it reflected an extraordinary middle- and upper-class bias, ignoring both the circumstances and aspirations of those women who were not white and not affluent. Second, it failed to do justice to those women who were content with their lives—three out of five according to a 1962 Gallup poll. And third, it presumed that the ideas of "the feminine mystique" were a post–world War II phenomenon, when in fact they went even further back than the "cult of true womanhood" in the nineteenth century. Nor could it fairly be said that women in the 1950s were more "victimized" than they had been at other times in history.

Nevertheless, the fact that a feminist analysis had gained political currency proved to be enormously important. For years, talk about women's discontent had been rife, but now there was an assessment of that discontent that compelled attention. With eloquence and passion, Friedan had dramatized through case studies the boredom and alienation of those afflicted by "the problem that has no name." In addition, she was able to take her readers behind the scenes to editorial offices and advertising firms where they could see firsthand the way in which the image of the feminine mystique was formed. It was hard not to be outraged after reading how advertising men—who themselves viewed housework as menial —tried to sell cleaning products as an answer to drudgery and as a means of expressing creativity. If, as Friedan claimed, the women frustrated by such manipulation were legion, her book helped to crystallize a sense of grievance and to provide an ideological explanation with which the discontented could identify. *The Feminine Mystique* sold more than a million copies, and if not all its readers agreed with the conclusions, they could not help but reexamine their own lives in light of the questions it raised.

... [T]he time was right in the mid-1960s for feminism to make a profound impact, with substantial support from both younger and older women. Fortuitously, the woman's movement of the 1960s and 1970s was operating in tandem with rather than in opposition to long-term social developments. During the 1910s and 1920s, suffragist calls for greater economic and social independence for women ran counter to patterns of behavior that found most married and middle-class women still conforming to traditional norms. Now, feminists calls for the same kind of independence coincided with women leaving the home in ever greater numbers and learning firsthand how pervasive sex discrimination was. Fertility rates, attitudes toward sexuality and the double standard, changes in long-term employment curves-all these seemed to be working *for*, not against, the demands of women activists....

* * *

Although outside observers were impressed by the apparent fervor with which large numbers of activists supported abortion reform, ERA [Equal Rights Amendment], and child care, there existed beneath the surface of the women's movement an ongoing set of conflicts over the tactics, goals, and values of the new feminism. From the nineteenth century onward, women's rights activists had struggled with a series of troubling dilemmas. Were women different from men or similar to them? *Should* women accept or seek differential treatment from society? Was the best method of securing equality to assimilate into the society, adopting integration as a means as well as an end, or did separatism make more sense as a strategy and tactic? Should women join in coalition with others in behalf of shared goals, or should women act only on their own behalf and pursue their own agenda regardless of potential alliances? Was reform or revolution the goal, and if revolution, who was the enemy to be overthrown? Obviously, such questions were not easy to answer, nor did they pose the kind of choices that could readily be solved by compromise....

At least three different kinds of feminism competed during the early 1970s for the allegiance of women activists. Broadly defined, these can be labeled as liberal feminism, radical feminism, and socialist feminism. Each in its own way developed a different analysis and set of answers to the key questions of the sources of women's oppression, the possibilities of coalition to end that oppression, and the goal of reform or revolution. Radical feminism and socialist feminism shared in common a collectivist approach to women's dilemma and an antipathy to the individualist priorities of liberal feminism. Yet both radicals and socialists at different times shared a commitment to some of the programmatic goals of liberal feminism and might join the ranks of such liberal organizations as NOW [National Organization for Women] and WEAL [Women's Equity Action League]. The conflicts were stark, but it was not at all unlikely that the same person could—at different stages of ideological perception—be identified with all three kinds of feminism.

To casual observers, liberal feminism was clearly the dominant force in women's rights activity in the years after

1968. Associated primarily with personalities like Betty Friedan and organizations like NOW, liberal feminism sought to work politically within the existing social and economic framework to secure reforms for women and progress toward full equality of opportunity between the sexes....

[T]he goal of liberal feminism was complete integration of women into American society. Assimilation, not separatism, was the desired end, with victory being defined as the total acceptance of women—as individuals—in all jobs, political organizations, and voluntary associations *without regard to their sex*. Implicitly, then, NOW and other liberal feminist groups embraced a natural-rights philosophy that all individuals should be treated the same, that sex and gender should be discounted, and that eradication of a "separate-sphere" ideology was a *sine qua non* [essential] for progress toward equality.

Within this framework, liberal feminists concentrated on a series of pragmatic reforms. Recognizing that equal access for women into the "opportunity structure" necessitated at least acknowledging past barriers, NOW and other similar groups endorsed affirmative-action programs to promote women in compensation for prior neglect and the creation of social institutions such as federally funded child-care centers to ease conflicts between family and work. Liberal feminists emphasized compliance with equal-opportunity legislation, enactment of the ERA to guarantee that women would be treated exactly like men under the law, and advancement of women into careers that previously had been dominated by men. Typical of NOW's initiatives in the late 1960s were campaigns to eliminate sex identification from employment advertisements in newspapers ("Male Only Jobs," "Female Only Jobs"), a blistering indictment of one airline that offered "Men only" executive flights from Chicago to New York at the end of the business day, and insistence on open admission to clubs and bars previously off-limits to women. Clearly, the message was that women wanted to join, as individuals with equal rights, all the institutions of the society and that separate classification of spheres by sex was no longer acceptable.

Although for many Americans at the time these positions seemed extreme, liberal feminists themselves were —within the overall women's movement —perceived to be pragmatic and even conservative. They were "liberals," after all, who believed in incremental change and the possibility of persuading individuals through reason of the need for reform. They neither wished to topple the power structure nor to create their own. Rather, they wanted to join the existing social and economic system. As a consequence, they were more likely to eschew radical rhetoric and shy away from controversy, lest they alienate some of those *within* the structure of power whom they needed as allies. Thus, in the early years at least, NOW preferred to avoid the issue of sexual preference, lest lesbian-baiting be used to defeat their other goals. When NOW did take a strong stand in favor of abortion reform and reproductive freedom, some of its members were distressed enough to form the Women's Equity Action League (WEAL) in 1969, a group that would concentrate exclusively on economic and political issues in an effort to avoid losing the backing of those who adamantly opposed abortion and gay rights.

Within the overall spectrum of women's activism, then, the position of liberal feminists was fairly clear. They were political, and they were activist—but their activism focused on reform of mainstream institutions, often through the existing electoral system, with the goal of integration by women as individuals within the prevailing social and economic order. Groups like the National Women's Political Caucus might be formed to promote women's issues and women politicians, but any such "separatist" tactics were premised on acceptance of the fundamental health of American institutions and on a belief that reform would eventually eliminate the need for such separate organizations. Although NOW and other liberal feminist groups espoused programs that would benefit poor and minority women as well as the middle class, it was clear that their primary constituency consisted of well-educated, upwardly mobile and independent women who wished to take their place next to men in America's dominant social and economic institutions.

Radical feminists, by contrast, saw men as the enemy, patriarchy as a system that must be overthrown, and separatism as an important strategy and tactic—for achieving the revolution. The adjective "radical" naturally evokes an association with the New Left or the student movements of the late 1960s but in reality it speaks more to the position of activists on a woman-defined scale, not one dictated by male political affiliations —that is, feminists were radical vis à vis their diagnosis of women's oppression as a function of male supremacy rather than vis à vis their position on the war in Vietnam or capitalism.

At the same time, it would be a mistake not to recognize the extent to which New Left machismo played a role in shaping radical feminism. In the early stages of the women's liberation movement, for example, women participants in the civil-rights struggle and the anti-war movement sought repeatedly to bring their concerns before male-dominated New Left organizations. Yet when they did so, they were treated with disdain, contempt, and outrageous sexism. *Ramparts* magazine, one journalistic voice of the New Left, dismissed women petitioners at a Students for a Democratic Society (SDS) conference as a "mini-skirted caucus." When Jo Freeman and Shulamith Firestone brought resolutions on women's rights to the National Conference on New Politics in December 1967, they were told that their concerns were irrelevant. "Calm down, little girl," the man presiding at the convention said. And when a representative of women's groups sought to present two statements on women's issues to the anti-Vietnam War mobilization rally in November 1968, she was greeted with raucous heckling. "Take it off," men around the platform yelled.... Eventually, the speaker was forced to leave the stage, a male anti-war leader saying it was "for her own good." "If radical men can be so easily provoked into acting like red-necks," one woman observer noted, "what can we expect from others? What have we gotten ourselves into?"

Such experiences simply reinforced the inclination of many women to organize separate groups, free of interruption and domination by men. "We need not only separate groups, but a separate movement, free of preconceptions," Ellen Willis wrote. "It is also clear that a genuine alliance with male radicals will not be possible until sexism sickens them as much as racism. This will not be accomplished through persuasion, conciliation or love, but through independence and solidarity." ...

By virtue of their analysis and prescription for change, radical feminists were identified with a series of issues and processes that while shared with other groups as well were perhaps more characteristic of radical feminist groups than others. Consciousness-raising, for example, provided an organizational tactic for most women's liberation groups, but the process was especially associated with radical feminists. When groups of ten to fifteen women gathered to share their common concerns about the second-class treatment women were accorded in American society, one of the bonds that united them was the stories they told each other about growing up female, being pressured into subservient roles, responding to sexual pressures from men, having to "perform" for an audience with a preordained script on how women should act. As the stories became more intimate and the sense of solidarity more profound, consciousness-raising became the symbol for women standing together against men and society. They found within their group identity and process the model for separatist institution-building and the empowerment to pursue change. If becoming woman-identified was the philosophical core of radical feminism, what better way to initiate and perpetuate the process than by reinforcing every week the experiences and bonds that tied women to each other.

Similarly, while gay rights represented an issue with which every feminist group eventually identified, radical feminists were more likely than others to see the question of sexual preference as pivotal. Not only did lesbianism embody the politics of being a "woman-identified woman"; it also clearly celebrated the empowerment of being self-sufficient and free of men in *every* aspect of life, including the sexual. Women who lived together, worked together, and slept together made separatism the pragmatic as well as philosophical *raison d'être* of their lives. In an age of reproductive technology that promised to bypass heterosexuality as a precondition for pregnancy, it was possible to envision an entire life free of men. And if women could thereby establish their freedom from patriarchy, they could create a world where class oppression based on sex no longer existed.

Toward that end, radical feminists also focused their energies on developing women-run institutions. To break the shackles of the male-dominated health professions, especially gynecology, women built their own health clinics, taught self-examination, and with books like *Our Bodies, Our Selves* created a mass-market resource that would liberate countless others from medical views of women that reflected a man's point of view. Feminist publishing houses commissioned, edited, and printed their own literature, from children's books that were nonsexist to literary and political journals. Abortion clinics, child-care centers, separate caucuses in professional associations, and food cooperatives all represented ways in which women could structure their own lives and institutions so that men were not in control. Although usually associated with groups like New York Radical Women (1968) and New York Radical Feminists (1970), the radical feminist perspective was widespread throughout the country and helped substantially to shape the ideological direction of the entire movement. While not political in electoral or legislative terms, radical feminism gave support to causes, institutions, and alliances that reflected the power of separatist thinking and the importance of women's distinctive cultural voice in reshaping gender relations in society at large.

The third major expression of feminist thought was also radical, but more in the mainstream sense than in a "woman-identified" sense. Comprised of people often referred to as "politicos," these women were Marxist, called themselves socialist-feminists, and emphasized the inextricable links between race, class, and gender oppression. Rather than advocating separatism, with men as the enemy, socialist-feminists championed solidarity by oppressed peoples everywhere, male or female, with capitalism as the enemy. Like radical feminists, the socialists were contemptuous of the existing social order and sought revolution, but theirs was a revolution where men were potential allies and where the goal was a complete abolition of race, gender, and class hierarchies, not a separate, woman-defined world....

Socialist-feminists saved their harshest criticism, however, for the reformism of liberal feminist groups like NOW. Marlene Dixon, a Marxist, regretted the extent to which "the political consciousness of women [was frozen] at a very primitive level: the struggle against the attitudinal expression of institutionalized white male supremacy... particularly as it impinged upon sexual relationships. The early actions of the movement—bra burnings, Miss America protests, Playboy Club demonstrations—reflected a political consciousness which had been stunted in the long debate confined within personal relationships."

... [S]ocialist-feminists adopted perhaps the most visionary scheme of all. Not only should women organize to liberate themselves from oppression, but they should constitute a vanguard revolutionary force who—together with blacks, Hispanics, Indians, the poor, and other "victims" of capitalism—could transform the entire social and economic order. Women could be free only if the reign of capitalism ended, but women's captivity was neither separate nor different from the captivity of other groups. Hence, alliance with these groups, whatever the limitations of *their* sexual politics, was a prerequisite for change. Of all the activist visions that inspired women in the late 1960s and early 1970s, the socialist-feminists' was perhaps the most programmatic and political, and certainly the most collectivist, the most severely critical of traditional liberal individualism....

To outside observers,... the unity, vigor, and enthusiasm of feminism seemed far more impressive (or threatening) than any internal divisions. Although comedians might scorn women's liberation and ridicule women who insisted on being admitted to "men's" bars or who protested the Miss America pageant as a "meat market," the measure of derision was, in fact, a testimony to how effectively feminists were entering the public consciousness with their positions. By the early 1970s, countless Americans were debating what could only be described as "feminist" issues, whether the focus was on the Equal Rights Amendment, child care, abortion, "open marriage," greater sharing of household responsibilities, or the sexual revolution. In every kitchen, living room, and bedroom, feminists contended, women—and men—were facing, for the first time in their lifetimes, the centrality of women's liberation to *all aspects* of daily life.

Indeed, what remained most impressive was the growing support that feminist positions seemed to be gathering in the body politic. In 1962, George Gallup asked a cross-section of American women whether they felt themselves to be victims of discrimination. Two-thirds of the women responding said no. Eight years later—three years after the women's movement began—the same question was asked again. This time, 50 percent of the respondents said that they were victims of discrimination. In 1974, the question was asked a third time. Now, with more than seven years of experience with the women's movement, two out of three respondents said that they were victims of discrimination, and even more supported such feminist policies as the Equal Rights Amendment and the right of a woman to have an abortion.

... By the early 1970s, the pollster Daniel Yankelovich commented on the "wide and deep" acceptance of women's liberation positions among the young. In two years, the number of students who viewed women as an oppressed group had doubled, and nearly 70 percent of college women declared agreement with the statement that "the idea that a woman's place is in the home is nonsense." The expression of such feminist viewpoints coincided with the greatest period of success in securing support for public policies promoting sex equality that had occurred in more than half a century....

THE BEST OF TIMES, THE WORST OF TIMES

In many respects, the 1970s and 1980s provided an ideal barometer for measuring the impact on women's status of the changes that had occurred during the postwar era. The 1940s and 1950s had been a time of paradox, with significant behavioral changes in women's economic activities occurring simultaneously with a resurgence of traditional patriarchal attitudes that defined women's "place"—rigidly and anachronistically—as being strictly in the home. With the revitalization of a dynamic feminist movement in the 1960s, however, an opportunity arose for reconciling attitudes and behavior and, potentially at least, for creating an ideological mandate for moving toward substantive equality between the sexes.

As the 1970s and 1980s unfolded, however, it became clear that the relationship between attitudes and practice would remain complicated. The feminist movement careened through its own roller-coaster journey, achieving enormous successes, only to have these followed by disastrous defeats. Extraordinary changes continued to occur in the family and workplace, resulting in giant strides forward for a number of women who, two decades earlier, would have been unable even to conceive of some of the choices they now faced; yet other women, caught in the same vortex of change, saw their opportunities diminish and the degree of their oppression deepen, not diminish. In the end, the story of these two decades was reminiscent of what Charles Dickens wrote in *The Tale of Two Cities*: "it was the best of times, it was the worst of times; it was a spring of hope, a winter of discontent." The fact that both characterizations were true said worlds about the divided mind of American society when it came to women's role in life and about the continuing power of race and class to interact with gender and shape women's possibilities and circumstances.

As a result, it was possible to predict that by the beginning of a new century, some white women of decent education and economic security would have more equality with men than women had ever experienced in America before and that many poor women—especially of minority background—would be caught in a cycle of poverty and hopelessness not exceeded at any time before in the twentieth century....

* * *

One explanation for why the 1970s and 1980s were "the best of times, the worst of times" centers on the extent to which America was becoming much more a two-tiered society. The 1960s had spawned passionate crusades for social justice. With a degree of energy, collective mobilization, and ideological fervor not seen for more than a century, Americans from a variety of backgrounds had come together to struggle against racism, sexism, poverty, and war. Many of these movements had gone through similar stages of evolution. Beginning as moderate reform efforts, premised on the ability of social institutions to respond readily to proof of injustice, they had become rapidly radicalized as the depth of resistance to change became more obvious. By the end of each movement's history, some participants had become revolutionaries, some had dropped out, and some had joined in accepting whatever reforms had been achieved, choosing to work within the established order rather than try to overthrow it....

When looking carefully at the experience of women during these decades, it seems clear that important reforms did take place, resulting in substantial elimination of barriers in law and custom that had denied women the freedom to pursue their own destinies. Just as the civil-rights movements led to the passage of public-accommodations laws, desegregation of many educational institutions, and destruction of Jim Crow, the women's rights movement brought a toppling of ancient barriers to women in the professions and support for a whole series of freedoms in personal behavior that had not been permitted before. Whether the issue was reproductive freedom, access to a career in corporate America, or greater flexibility of choice in one's mating or childbearing patterns, enormous changes had taken place. It would not be going too far to say that within the framework of the legal system at least, barriers to individual freedom based on race and gender had largely been eliminated.

What this meant, in reality, was that individual women and individual members of minority groups now had the opportunity to join the mainstream (a) as long as they had the economic base and educational qualifications for doing so; and (b) as long as they accepted the rules that governed mainstream institutions and agreed to operate within the prevailing norms of the status quo. Thus, large numbers of black Americans, including women, succeeded in getting college degrees in desegregated institutions and in joining the middle class through securing access to well-paid positions in corporate America. Similarly, large numbers of women, including some minorities, were able to enter business and professional schools, move into elite law firms and corporations, and create a life that combined professional achievement and personal fulfillment in a way that had never been available to their mothers and grandmothers.

In all of this, those in positions of power responded, albeit reluctantly, as long as basic structures remained intact. It was all right to admit blacks, Hispanics, or women into the corporate boardroom; it was not all right to abolish the boardroom or place blacks, Hispanics, or women in control. Reform was permissible; structural change was not.

In this context, the demands of liberal feminism were far more tolerable than those of radical feminism or of socialist-feminism. Liberal feminists wanted access for women to decent jobs, prestigious clubs, high-powered meetings; they wanted to abolish "male only" or "female only" job classifications; they sought the kind of self-determination for women as individuals that men had always had as individuals. And frequently, they asked for more radical changes as well. But it was impossible for those with power to respond to the first set of demands because these were familiar requests, with compelling morality and logic behind them, and *they could be accepted without changing the rules of the game*, except in terms of defining who could play.

Radical feminists and socialist-feminists, by contrast, sought to redesign both the ballpark and the rules. Both insisted in placing collective priorities ahead of individual freedom of choice. In one case, it was all women *qua* women seeking to be treated as a class, with their own separatist institutions and values dedicated to ending patriarchy; in the other case, it was all oppressed people as a class seeking to destroy capitalism. But in both cases, the goal was radical transformation, not moderate accommodation.

In contradiction to the reform aspirations of the liberal feminists, the revolutionary demands of radical feminists and socialist-feminists were not absorbable. Basic structures would be challenged and changed. Power would be redistributed. The rules would be altered. And countless Americans—women and men—who were devoted to a different view of gender roles mobilized to resist these demands. Those in the opposition also organized to defeat the more frightening ideas of liberal feminists, or at least their version of these ideas. Hence, the ERA went down to defeat because antifeminists said that it threatened to abolish all distinctions between the sexes, subvert the family, and sanction sexual deviancy. Still, people might resist the ERA and also be pleased that their own daughters could go to law school or become a bank manager. . . .

Ultimately, the paradox of these years being both the best and the worst of times is no paradox at all. It is rather the key to how American society has functioned in this era and a vantage point from which to better understand the persistent power of race and class—together with sex—to determine women's experience.

POSTSCRIPT

Is Feminism a Harmful Ideology?

Sheaffer states that his most convincing arguments are made against extremist positions, which "reasonable feminists" might not hold. But since he cannot find the voice of reasonable feminists in the current public debate, he feels justified in representing all feminists by their extreme positions. But do feminists deny the significance of hormones and other biological differences between women and men? Does their demand for truly equal opportunity and affirmative action only require the premise that the similarities between men and women are greater than the differences? On the other hand, have feminists cultivated an antipathy to men as their oppressors? Has the feminist program adversely affected the family and gender relations? Do feminists deny that nondiscriminatory bases exist for many inequalities between men and women?

Over the past 30 years, there has been a deluge of books, articles, and periodicals devoted to expounding feminist positions. Among the earliest feminist publications was Betty Friedan's book *The Feminine Mystique* (W. W. Norton, 1963).

Friedan later wrote *The Second Stage* (Summit Books, 1981), which was less antagonistic to men and more accepting of motherhood and traditional women's roles. An analysis of the current status of the women's movement is Susan Faludi's *Backlash: The Undeclared War on American Women* (Crown Publishers, 1991). A superb analysis of the full range of gender issues is found in *Paradoxes of Gender* by Judith Lorber (Yale University Press, 1994). Christine Hoff Sommers advocates equity (liberal) feminism while criticizing feminist extremists and sloppy research in *Who Stole Feminism? How Women Have Betrayed Women* (Simon & Schuster, 1994). For radical feminist views, see Catharine A. MacKinnon's *Feminism Unmodified* (Harvard University Press, 1987); Marilyn French's *Beyond Power* (Summit Books, 1985); and Margaret Randall's *Gathering Rage: The Failure of Twentieth-Century Revolutions to Develop a Feminist Agenda* (Monthly Review Press, 1992). For a radical feminist analysis of the oppression of women, see Marilyn French, *The War Against Women* (Summit Books, 1992). An analytical and historical discussion of women's movements over the past century and a half is provided by Steven M. Buechler in *Women's Movements in the United States: Suffrage, Equal Rights, and Beyond* (Rutgers University Press, 1990). For an insightful analysis of how ideology has been used by men to mute the rebellion of women against exploitative and subordinate relations, see Mary R. Jackman, *The Velvet Glove: Paternalism and Conflict in Gender, Class, and Race Relations* (University of California Press, 1994). A rich analysis of gender inequality and its social and psychological roots is provided by Sandra Lipsitz Bem in *The Lenses of Gender: Transforming the Debate on Sexual Inequality* (Yale University Press, 1994). Other important feminist voices are Suzanne Gordon, *Prisoners of Men's Dreams: Striking Out for a New Feminine Future* (Little, Brown, 1991); Paula Kamen, *Feminist Fatale: Voices from the "Twentysomething" Generation Explore the Future of the "Women's Movement"* (Donald I. Fine, 1991); and Naomi Wolf, *Fire With Fire: The New Female Power and How It Will Change the Twenty-First Century* (Random House, 1993).

Antifeminist works are rarer. One antifeminist, Nicholas Davidson, charges that it is "extremely difficult to find a publisher for a work critical of feminism." See Davidson's *The Failure of Feminism* (Prometheus Books, 1988). Other antifeminist arguments may be found in Maggie Gallagher's *Enemies of Eros* (Bonus Books, 1993); Michael Levin's *Feminism and Freedom* (Transaction Books, 1987); Midge Decter's *The New Chastity and Other Arguments Against Women's Liberation* (Putnam, 1974); George Gilder's *Sexual Suicide* (Times Books, 1973); and Phyllis Schlafly's *The Power of Positive Woman* (Arlington House, 1977). For a defense of men against the accusations of feminists see Warren Farrell, *The Myth of Male Power* (Simon & Schuster, 1993) and David Thomas, *Not Guilty: The Case in Defense of Men* (William Morrow, 1993).

ISSUE 5

Is There a Date Rape Crisis in Society?

YES: Robin Warshaw, from *I Never Called It Rape: The* Ms. *Report on Recognizing, Fighting, and Surviving Date and Acquaintance Rape* (Harper & Row, 1988)

NO: Katie Roiphe, from "Date Rape's Other Victim," *The New York Times Magazine* (June 13, 1993)

ISSUE SUMMARY

YES: Journalist Robin Warshaw reports the findings of a major study of college students that shows that about one-fourth of college women are victims of date rape, though few report the crime to authorities. She maintains that although the public tends to blame the date rape victim for enticing the man or failing to send clear signals, when men force sex on unwilling women, that is rape.

NO: Author Katie Roiphe challenges the statistics about date rape, which she feels are based on a very broad definition of rape. She analyzes the political agenda of those who contend that there is a date rape crisis and faults these crusaders for undermining the autonomy of women.

How often does date rape happen? Have most sexually active women experienced unwanted intercourse? Have most sexually active men raped a date in the sense of achieving intercourse despite their partner's reluctance? Clearly the prevalence of date rape depends on the definition of rape. How much resistance on the woman's part and how much force on the man's part are required to cross the line from seduction to rape? When date rape does occur, how much responsibility does each party have for the outcome?

It is important to treat date rape as a moral issue, but it should also be treated as a sociological issue. One of sociology's major theses is that social reality is socially constructed. When social events take place, people label, define, and construct a reality out of them. The process normally involves conflicting viewpoints, and sociologists focus on whose perspective dominates the process. It is informative to look at all of social life using this perspective. For example, marriage is a constructed reality between spouses, much of it mutual but some of it sharply contested. Political reality is manufactured out of the babble of the many competing voices of politicians and media pundits.

The social construction perspective is particularly helpful in looking at social problems. Unfortunate conditions often become social problems when constructed by vocal activists who persuade politicians and the media that certain conditions should be addressed. One of the latest social problems to run this course is date rape. Until recently, male definitions of male-female relations have dominated. The male viewpoint was that a male was to be the active partner in the dating game, including the sexual aspect. Often this meant that a man would go as far as a woman would allow and then would try to encourage in her the desire and willingness to go further. Naturally, misunderstandings occurred as to whether the woman's "no" was a "final no" or just a "not yet, I need more encouragement." Sometimes the woman felt molested, but the man thought that he was just being persistent. Other times the woman felt raped when the man recognized her resistance but felt that she had gotten him so sexually aroused she was obligated to go through with the act. In many other ways men's definitions of their sexual practices minimized their problematic aspects. Times have changed, and women have become much more vocal about their grievances and have achieved greater political influence and media impact. Now, some say, there is a date rape crisis. Has the behavior of men gotten worse? Probably not, but now women's voices have a much bigger role in the construction of the reality of male-female relationships. From a democratic viewpoint, suppressed voices should be heard because only then can greater justice be achieved. Justice requires that both men and women understand and honor each other, and this requires equal voice and equal power. It also requires the legal system to justly handle sexual victimization cases such as date rape. The difficulty for the legal system is the incidence of false accusations, which are frequently a problem when participants in an event operate out of different constructed realities.

The issue for debate is whether or not there is a date rape crisis. The reality constructed by many highly vocal women is that women are frequently violated by men through countless acts of subordination, many of which are minor, with date rape being the extreme. But some women do not have this view of reality. They do not see subordination and injustice in everyday male-female relationships. So they may think that what some people call "date rape" is a bad misunderstanding but not a crime.

If a reality is to be redefined in the public mind, crusaders must convince the public that the problem of date rape is serious and that behavior that had not been heavily sanctioned before should now be condemned. In the following selections, Robin Warshaw argues that men who continue sexual advances past a woman's "no" are not mistaken lovers but rapists. They forcibly violate and emotionally harm their victims. Katie Roiphe does not condone men's forcing themselves sexually upon unwilling women, but she does believe that women should take more responsibility for what happens sexually on dates. She thinks that the date rape crusaders are teaching women that they are powerless, naive, and easily manipulated.

YES

Robin Warshaw

THE REALITY OF ACQUAINTANCE RAPE

Women raped by men they know—acquaintance rape—is not an aberrant quirk of male-female relations. If you are a woman, your risk of being raped by someone you know is *four times greater* than your risk of being raped by a stranger.

A recent scientific study of acquaintance rape on 32 college campuses conducted by *Ms.* magazine and psychologist Mary P. Koss showed that significant numbers of women are raped on dates or by acquaintances, although most victims never report their attacks.

Ms. Survey Stats

- 1 in 4 women surveyed were victims of rape or attempted rape.
- 84 percent of those raped knew their attacker.
- 57 percent of the rapes happened on dates.

Those figures make acquaintance rape and date rape more common than left-handedness or heart attacks or alcoholism. These rapes are no recent campus fad or the fantasy of a few jilted females. They are real. And they are happening all around us.

THE EXTENT OF "HIDDEN" RAPE

Most states define rape as sexual assault in which a man uses his penis to commit vaginal penetration of a victim against her will, by force or threats of force or when she is physically or mentally unable to give her consent. Many states now also include unwanted anal and oral intercourse in that definition and some have removed gender-specific language to broaden the applicability of rape laws.

In acquaintance rape, the rapist and victim may know each other casually—having met through a common activity, mutual friend, at a party, as neighbors, as students in the same class, at work, on a blind date, or while traveling. Or they may have a closer relationship—as steady dates or former sexual partners. Although largely a hidden phenomenon because it's the least reported type of rape (and rape, in general, is the most underreported crime against a person), many organizations, counselors, and social researchers agree that acquaintance rape is the most prevalent rape crime today.

Only 90,434 rapes were reported to U.S. law enforcement agencies in 1986, a number that is conservatively believed to represent a minority of the actual rapes of all types taking place. Government estimates find that anywhere from three to ten rapes are committed for every rape reported. And while rapes by strangers are still underreported, rapes by acquaintances are virtually nonreported. Yet, based on intake observations made by staff at various rape-counseling centers (where victims come for treatment, but do not have to file police reports), 70 to 80 percent of all rape crimes are acquaintance rapes.

Those rapes are happening in a social environment in which sexual aggression occurs regularly. Indeed, less than half the college women questioned in the *Ms.* survey reported that they had experienced *no* sexual victimization in their lives thus far (the average age of respondents was 21). Many had experienced more than one episode of unwanted sexual touching, coercion, attempted rape, or rape. Using the data collected in the study... the following profile can be drawn of what happens in just one year of "social life" on America's college campuses:

Ms. **Survey Stats**

In one year 3,187 women reported suffering:

- 328 rapes (as defined by law)
- 534 attempted rapes (as defined by law)
- 837 episodes of sexual coercion (sexual intercourse obtained through the ag-

gressor's continual arguments or pressure)
- 2,024 experiences of unwanted sexual contact (fondling, kissing, or petting committed against the woman's will)

Over the years, other researchers have documented the phenomenon of acquaintance rape. In 1957, a study conducted by Eugene J. Kanin of Purdue University in West Lafayette, Indiana, showed that 30 percent of women surveyed had suffered attempted or completed forced sexual intercourse while on a high school date. Ten years later, in 1967, while young people donned flowers and beads and talked of love and peace, Kanin found that more than 25 percent of the male college students surveyed had attempted to force sexual intercourse on a woman to the point that she cried or fought back. In 1977, after the blossoming of the women's movement and countless pop-culture attempts to extol the virtues of becoming a "sensitive man," Kanin found that 26 percent of the men he surveyed had tried to force intercourse on a woman and that 25 percent of the women questioned had suffered attempted or completed rape. In other words, two decades had passed since Kanin's first study, yet women were being raped by men they knew as frequently as before.

... A random sample survey of 930 women living in San Francisco, conducted [in 1984] by researcher Diana Russell, showed that 44 percent of the women questioned had been victims of rape or attempted rape—and that 88 percent of the rape victims knew their attackers. A Massachusetts Department of Public Health study, released in 1986, showed that two-thirds of the rapes reported at crisis centers were committed by acquaintances....

RAPE IS RAPE

Rape that occurs on dates or between people who know each other should not be seen as some sort of misguided sexual adventure: Rape is violence, not seduction. In stranger rape *and* acquaintance rape, the aggressor makes a decision to force his victim to submit to what he wants. The rapist believes he is entitled to force sexual intercourse from a woman and he sees interpersonal violence (be it simply holding the woman down with his body or brandishing a gun) as an acceptable way to achieve his goal.

"All rape is an exercise in power," writes Susan Brownmiller in her landmark book *Against Our Will: Men, Women and Rape*. Specifically, Brownmiller and others argue, rape is an exercise in the imbalance of power that exists between most men and women, a relationship that has forged the social order from ancient times on.

Today, that relationship continues. Many men are socialized to be sexually aggressive—to score, as it were, regardless of how. Many women are socialized to submit to men's wills, especially those men deemed desirable by society at large. Maintaining such roles helps set the stage for acquaintance rape.

But despite their socialization, most men are not rapists. That is the good news.

The bad news, of course, is that so many are.

Ms. Survey Stat

1 in 12 of the male students surveyed had committed acts that met the legal definitions of rape or attempted rape.

BLAMING THE ACQUAINTANCE-RAPE VICTIM

Without question, many date rapes and acquaintance rapes could have been prevented by the woman—if she hadn't trusted a seemingly nice guy, if she hadn't gotten drunk, if she had acted earlier on the "bad feeling" that many victims later report they felt but ignored because they didn't want to seem rude, unfriendly, or immature. But acknowledging that in some cases the woman might have prevented the rape by making a different decision does not make her responsible for the crime. Says a counselor for an Oregon rape-crisis agency: "We have a saying here: 'Bad judgment is not a rapeable offense.'"

As a society, we don't blame the victims of most crimes as we do acquaintance-rape survivors. A mugging victim is not believed to "deserve it" for wearing a watch or carrying a pocketbook on the street. Likewise, a company is not "asking for it" when its profits are embezzled; a store owner is not to blame for handing over the cash drawer when threatened. These crimes occur because the perpetrator decides to commit them.

Acquaintance rape is no different. There are ways to reduce the odds, but, like all crimes, there is no way to be certain that it will not happen to you.

Yet acquaintance-rape victims are seen as responsible for the attacks, often more responsible than their assailants. "Date rape threatens the assumption that if you're good, good things happen to you. Most of us believe that bad things don't happen out of the blue," says psychologist Koss, chief investigator of the *Ms.* study, now affiliated with the department of psychiatry at the University of Arizona Medical School in Tucson, Arizona. Society, in general, is so disturbed by the idea that a "regular guy" could do such a thing—and, to be sure, many "regular guys" are made uncomfortable by a concept that views their actions as a crime—that they would rather believe that something is wrong with the woman making such an outlandish claim: She is lying, she has emotional problems, she hates men, she is covering up her own promiscuous behavior. In fact, the research in the *Ms.* survey shows that women who have been raped by men they know are not appreciably different in any personal traits or behaviors than women who are not raped.

Should we ask women not to trust men who seem perfectly nice? Should we tell them not to go to parties or on dates? Should we tell them not to drink? Should we tell them not to feel sexual? Certainly not. *It is not the victim who causes the rape.*

But many persist in believing just that. An April 1987 letter to syndicated columnist Ann Landers from a woman who had been raped by two different men she dated reportedly drew heavy negative reader mail after Landers responded supportively to the woman. "Too bad you didn't file charges against those creeps," Landers wrote. "I urge you to go for counseling immediately to rid yourself of the feeling of guilt and rage. You must get it through your head that you were not to blame."

So far, so good, but not for long. Three months later, Landers published a letter from an irate female reader who noted that the victim said she and the first man had "necked up a storm" before he raped her. Perhaps the raped woman hadn't intended to have intercourse, the reader said, "but she certainly must accept responsibility for encouraging the guy and making him think she was a willing partner. The trouble starts when she changes her mind after his passions are out of control. Then it's too late."

Landers bought this specious argument—a variant on the old "men can't help themselves" nonsense. In her reply to the follow-up letter she wrote, "Now I'm convinced that I must rethink my position and go back to telling women, 'If you don't want a complete sexual experience, keep a lively conversation going and his hands off you.'"

In other words, if you get raped, it's your own fault.

DATE RAPE AND ACQUAINTANCE RAPE ON COLLEGE CAMPUSES

Despite philosophical and political changes brought about by the women's movement, dating relationships between men and women are still often marked by passivity on the woman's part and aggression on the man's. Nowhere are these two seen in stronger contrast than among teenagers and young adults who often, out of their own fears, insecurity, and ignorance, adopt the worst sex-role stereotypes. Such an environment fosters a continuum of sexual victimization—from unwanted sexual touching to psychologically coerced sex to rape—that is tolerated as normal. "Because sexually coercive behavior is so common in our male-female interactions, rape by an acquaintance may not be perceived as rape," says Py Bateman, director of Alternatives to Fear, a Seattle rape-education organization....

Not surprising, then, that the risk of rape is four times higher for women aged 16 to 24, the prime dating age, than for any other population group. Approximately half of all men arrested for rape are also 24 years old or younger. Since 26 percent of all 18- to 24-year-olds in the United States attend college, those institutions have become focal points for studying date rape and acquaintance rape, such as the *Ms.* research.

Ms. Survey Stat

For both men and women, the average age when a rape incident occurred (either as perpetrator or victim) was $18 1/2$ years old.

Going to college often means going away from home, out from under parental control and protection and into a world of seemingly unlimited freedoms. The imperative to party and date, although strong in high school, burgeons in this environment. Alcohol is readily available and often used in stultifying amounts, encouraged by a college world that practically demands heavy drinking as proof of having fun. Marijuana, cocaine, LSD, methamphetamines, and other drugs are also often easy to obtain....

When looking at the statistical results of the *Ms.* survey, it's important to remember that many of these young people still have years of socializing and dating ahead of them, years in which they may encounter still more acquaintance rape. Students, parents of college students, and college administrators should be concerned. But many are not, lulled by the same myths that pervade our society at large: Rape is not committed by people you know, against "good" girls, in "safe" places like university campuses.

THE OTHER VICTIMS OF ACQUAINTANCE RAPE

Date rape and acquaintance rape aren't confined to the college population,

however. Interviews conducted across the country showed that women both younger and older than university students are frequently acquaintance-rape victims as well.

A significant number of teenage girls suffer date rape as their first or nearly first experience of sexual intercourse... and most tell no one about their attacks. Consider Nora, a high school junior, who was raped by a date as they watched TV in his parents' house or Jenny, 16, who was raped after she drank too much at a party. Even before a girl officially begins dating, she may be raped by a schoolmate or friend.

Then there are the older women, the "hidden" population of "hidden" rape victims—women who are over 30 years old when their rapes occur. Most are socially experienced, yet unprepared for their attacks nonetheless. Many are recently divorced and just beginning to try the dating waters again; some are married; others have never married. They include women like Helene, a Colorado woman who was 37 and the mother of a 10-year-old when she was raped by a man on their third date, and Rae, who was 45 when she was raped by a man she knew after inviting him to her Oklahoma home for coffee.

"I NEVER CALLED IT RAPE"

Ms. Survey Stat

Only 27 percent of the women whose sexual assault met the legal definition of rape thought of themselves as rape victims.

Because of her personal relationship with the attacker, however casual, it often takes a woman longer to perceive an action as rape when it involves a man she knows than it does when a stranger assaults her. For her to acknowledge her experience as rape would be to recognize the extent to which her trust was violated and her ability to control her own life destroyed.

Indeed, regardless of their age or background, many women interviewed... told no one about their rapes, never confronted their attackers, and never named their assaults as rape until months or years later.

NO

Katie Roiphe

DATE RAPE'S OTHER VICTIM

One in four college women has been the victim of rape or attempted rape. One in four. I remember standing outside the dining hall in college, looking at a purple poster with this statistic written in bold letters. It didn't seem right. If sexual assault was really so pervasive, it seemed strange that the intricate gossip networks hadn't picked up more than one or two shadowy instances of rape. If I was really standing in the middle of an "epidemic," a "crisis" —if 25 percent of my women friends were really being raped—wouldn't I know it?

These posters were not presenting facts. They were advertising a mood. Preoccupied with issues like date rape and sexual harassment, campus feminists produce endless images of women as victims—women offended by a professor's dirty joke, women pressured into sex by peers, women trying to say no but not managing to get it across.

This portrait of the delicate female bears a striking resemblance to that 50's ideal my mother and other women of her generation fought so hard to leave behind. They didn't like her passivity, her wide-eyed innocence. They didn't like the fact that she was perpetually offended by sexual innuendo. They didn't like her excessive need for protection. She represented personal, social and intellectual possibilities collapsed, and they worked and marched, shouted and wrote to make her irrelevant for their daughters. But here she is again, with her pure intentions and her wide eyes. Only this time it is the feminists themselves who are breathing new life into her.

* * *

Is there a rape crisis on campus? Measuring rape is not as straightforward as it might seem. Neil Gilbert, a professor of social welfare at the University of California at Berkeley, questions the validity of the one-in-four statistic. Gilbert points out that in a 1985 survey undertaken by Ms. magazine and financed by the National Institute of Mental Health, 73 percent of the women categorized as rape victims did not initially define their experience as rape; it was Mary Koss, the psychologist conducting the study, who did.

One of the questions used to define rape was: "Have you had sexual intercourse when you didn't want to because a man gave you alcohol or drugs?"

From Katie Roiphe, "Date Rape's Other Victim," *The New York Times Magazine* (June 13, 1993). Adapted from Katie Roiphe, *The Morning After* (Little, Brown, 1993). Copyright © 1993 by Katherine Ann Roiphe. Reprinted by permission of Little, Brown and Company.

The phrasing raises the issue of agency. Why aren't college women responsible for their own intake of alcohol or drugs? A man may give her drugs, but she herself decides to take them. If we assume that women are not all helpless and naïve, then they should be held responsible for their choice to drink or take drugs. If a woman's "judgment is impaired" and she has sex, it isn't necessarily always the man's fault; it isn't necessarily always rape.

As Gilbert delves further into the numbers, he does not necessarily disprove the one-in-four statistic, but he does clarify what it means—the so-called rape epidemic on campuses is more a way of interpreting, a way of seeing, than a physical phenomenon. It is more about a change in sexual politics than a change in sexual behavior. Whether or not one in four college women has been raped, then, is a matter of opinion, not a matter of mathematical fact.

That rape is a fact in some women's lives is not in question. It's hard to watch the solemn faces of young Bosnian girls, their words haltingly translated, as they tell of brutal rapes; or to read accounts of a suburban teen-ager raped and beaten while walking home from a shopping mall. We all agree that rape is a terrible thing, but we no longer agree on what rape is. Today's definition has stretched beyond bruises and knives, threats of death or violence to include emotional pressure and the influence of alcohol. The lines between rape and sex begin to blur. The one-in-four statistic on those purple posters is measuring something elusive. It is measuring her word against his in a realm where words barely exist. There is a gray area in which one person's rape may be another's bad night. Definitions become entangled in passionate ideological battles. There hasn't been a remarkable change in the number of women being raped; just a change in how receptive the political climate is to those numbers.

The next question, then, is who is identifying this epidemic and why. Somebody is "finding" this rape crisis, and finding it for a reason. Asserting the prevalence of rape lends urgency, authority to a broader critique of culture.

In a dramatic description of the rape crisis, Naomi Wolf writes in "The Beauty Myth" that "Cultural representation of glamorized degradation has created a situation among the young in which boys rape and girls get raped *as a normal course of events.*" The italics are hers. Whether or not Wolf really believes rape is part of the "normal course of events" these days, she is making a larger point. Wolf's rhetorical excess serves her larger polemic about sexual politics. Her dramatic prose is a call to arms. She is trying to rally the feminist troops. Wolf uses rape as a red flag, an undeniable sign that things are falling apart.

From Susan Brownmiller—who brought the politics of rape into the mainstream with her 1975 best seller, "Against Our Will: Men, Women and Rape"—to Naomi Wolf, feminist prophets of the rape crisis are talking about something more than forced penetration. They are talking about what they define as a "rape culture." Rape is a natural trump card for feminism. Arguments about rape can be used to sequester feminism in the teary province of trauma and crisis. By blocking analysis with its claims to unique pandemic suffering, the rape crisis becomes a powerful source of authority.

Dead serious, eyes wide with concern, a college senior tells me that she believes one in four is too conservative an estimate. This is not the first time I've heard this. She tells me the right statistic is closer to one in two. That means one in two women are raped. It's amazing, she says, amazing that so many of us are sexually assaulted every day.

What is amazing is that this student actually believes that 50 percent of women are raped. This is the true crisis. Some substantial number of young women are walking around with this alarming belief: a hyperbole containing within it a state of perpetual fear.

* * *

"Acquaintance Rape: Is Dating Dangerous?" is a pamphlet commonly found at counseling centers. The cover title rises from the shards of a shattered photograph of a boy and girl dancing. Inside, the pamphlet offers a sample date-rape scenario. She thinks:

"He was really good looking and he had a great smile.... We talked and found we had a lot in common. I really liked him. When he asked me over to his place for a drink I thought it would be O.K. He was such a good listener and I wanted him to ask me out again."

She's just looking for a sensitive boy, a good listener with a nice smile, but unfortunately his intentions are not as pure as hers. Beneath that nice smile, he thinks:

"She looked really hot, wearing a sexy dress that showed off her great body. We started talking right away. I knew that she liked me by the way she kept smiling and touching my arm while she was speaking. She seemed pretty relaxed so I asked her back to my place for a drink. ... When she said 'Yes' I knew that I was going to be lucky!"

These cardboard stereotypes don't just educate freshmen about rape. They also educate them about "dates" and about sexual desire. With titles like "Friends Raping Friends: Could It Happen to You?" date-rape pamphlets call into question all relationships between men and women. Beyond warning students about rape, the rape-crisis movement produces its own images of sexual behavior, in which men exert pressure and women resist. By defining the dangerous date in these terms—with this type of male and this type of female, and their different expectations—these pamphlets promote their own perspective on how men and women feel about sex: men are lascivious, women are innocent.

The sleek images of pressure and resistance projected in rape education movies, videotapes, pamphlets and speeches create a model of acceptable sexual behavior. The don'ts imply their own set of do's. The movement against rape, then, not only dictates the way sex *shouldn't be* but also the way it *should be*. Sex should be gentle, it should not be aggressive; it should be absolutely equal, it should not involve domination and submission; it should be tender, not ambivalent; it should communicate respect, it shouldn't communicate consuming desire.

In "Real Rape," Susan Estrich, a professor of law at the University of Southern California Law Center, slips her ideas about the nature of sexual encounters into her legal analysis of the problem of rape. She writes: "Many feminists would argue that so long as women are powerless relative to men, viewing a 'yes' as a sign of true consent is misguided.... Many women who say yes to men they know, whether on dates or on the job, would say no if they could.... Women's silence sometimes is the product not of passion and desire but of pressure and fear."

Like Estrich, most rape-crisis feminists claim they are not talking about sex; they're talking about violence. But, like Estrich, they are also talking about sex. With their advice, their scenarios, their sample aggressive male, the message projects a clear comment on the nature of sexuality: women are often unwilling participants. They say yes because they feel they have to, because they are intimidated by male power.

The idea of "consent" has been redefined beyond the simple assertion that "no means no." Politically correct sex involves a yes, and a specific yes at that. According to the premise of "active consent," we can no longer afford ambiguity. We can no longer afford the dangers of unspoken consent. A former director of Columbia's date-rape education program told New York magazine, "Stone silence throughout an entire physical encounter with someone is not explicit consent."

This apparently practical, apparently clinical proscription cloaks retrograde assumptions about the way men and women experience sex. The idea that only an explicit yes means yes proposes that, like children, women have trouble communicating what they want. Beyond its dubious premise about the limits of female communication, the idea of active consent bolsters stereotypes of men just out to "get some" and women who don't really want any.

Rape-crisis feminists express nostalgia for the days of greater social control, when the university acted in loco parentis and women were protected from the insatiable force of male desire. The rhetoric of feminists and conservatives blurs and overlaps in this desire to keep our youth safe and pure.

By viewing rape as encompassing more than the use or threat of physical violence to coerce someone into sex, rape-crisis feminists reinforce traditional views about the fragility of the female body and will. According to common definitions of date rape, even "verbal coercion" or "manipulation" constitute rape. Verbal coercion is defined as "a woman's consenting to unwanted sexual activity because of a man's verbal arguments not including verbal threats of force." The belief that "verbal coercion" is rape pervades workshops, counseling sessions and student opinion pieces. The suggestion lurking beneath this definition of rape is that men are not just physically but also intellectually and emotionally more powerful than women.

Imagine men sitting around in a circle talking about how she called him impotent and how she manipulated him into sex, how violated and dirty he felt afterward, how coercive she was, how she got him drunk first, how he hated his body and he couldn't eat for three weeks afterward. Imagine him calling this rape. Everyone feels the weight of emotional pressure at one time or another. The question is not whether people pressure each other but how our minds and our culture transform that pressure into full-blown assault. There would never be a rule or a law or even a pamphlet or peer counseling group for men who claimed to have been emotionally raped or verbally pressured into sex. And for the same reasons—assumption of basic competence, free will and strength of character—there should be no such rules or groups or pamphlets about women.

In discussing rape, campus feminists often slip into an outdated sexist vocabulary. But we have to be careful about using rape as metaphor. The sheer physical fact of rape has always been loaded with cultural meaning. Throughout history, women's bodies have been seen as property, as chaste objects, as virtuous vessels to be "dishonored," "ruined," "defiled." Their purity or lack of purity has been a measure of value for the men to whom they belonged.

"Politically, I call it rape whenever a woman has sex and feels violated," writes Catharine MacKinnon, a law professor and feminist legal scholar best known for her crusade against pornography. The language of virtue and violation reinforces retrograde stereotypes. It backs women into old corners. Younger feminists share MacKinnon's vocabulary and the accompanying assumptions about women's bodies. In one student's account of date rape in the Rag, a feminist magazine at Harvard, she talks about the anguish of being "defiled." Another writes, "I long to be innocent again." With such anachronistic constructions of the female body, with all their assumptions about female purity, these young women frame their experience of rape in archaic, sexist terms. Of course, sophisticated modern-day feminists don't use words like honor or virtue anymore. They know better than to say date-rape victims have been "defiled." Instead, they call it "post-traumatic stress syndrome." They tell the victim she should not feel "shame," she should feel "traumatized." Within their overtly political psychology, forced penetration takes on a level of metaphysical significance: date rape resonates through a woman's entire life.

Combating myths about rape is one of the central missions of the rape-crisis movement. They spend money and energy trying to break down myths like "She asked for it." But with all their noise about rape myths, rape-crisis feminists are generating their own. The plays, the poems, the pamphlets, the Take Back the Night speakouts, are propelled by the myth of innocence lost....

As long as we're taking back the night, we might as well take back our own purity. Sure, we were all kind of innocent, playing in the sandbox with bright red shovels—boys, too. We can all look back through the tumultuous tunnel of adolescence on a honey-glazed childhood, with simple rules and early bedtimes. We don't have to look at parents fighting, at sibling struggles, at casting out one best friend for another in the Darwinian playground. This is not the innocence lost; this is the innocence we never had.

The idea of a fall from childhood grace, pinned on one particular moment, a moment over which we had no control, much lamented, gives our lives a compelling narrative structure. It's easy to see why the 17-year-old likes it; it's easy to see why the rape-crisis feminist likes it. It's a natural human impulse put to political purpose. But in generating and perpetuating such myths, we should keep in mind that myths about innocence have been used to keep women inside and behind veils. They have been used to keep them out of work and in labor....

* * *

People have asked me if I have ever been date-raped. And thinking back on complicated nights, on too many glasses of wine, on strange and familiar beds, I would have to say yes. With such a sweeping definition of rape, I wonder how many people there are, male or female, who haven't been date-raped at one point or another. People pressure and manipulate and cajole each other into all sorts of things all of the time. As Susan

Sontag wrote, "Since Christianity upped the ante and concentrated on sexual behavior as the root of virtue, everything pertaining to sex has been a 'special case' in our culture, evoking peculiarly inconsistent attitudes." No human interactions are free from pressure, and the idea that sex is, or can be, makes it what Sontag calls a "special case," vulnerable to the inconsistent expectations of double standard.

With their expansive version of rape, rape-crisis feminists are inventing a kinder, gentler sexuality. Beneath the broad definition of rape, these feminists are endorsing their own utopian vision of sexual relations: sex without struggle, sex without power, sex without persuasion, sex without pursuit. If verbal coercion constitutes rape, then the word rape itself expands to include any kind of sex a woman experiences as negative.

When Martin Amis spoke at Princeton, he included a controversial joke: "As far as I'm concerned, you can change your mind before, even during, but just not after sex." The reason this joke is funny, and the reason it's also too serious to be funny, is that in the current atmosphere you can change your mind afterward. Regret can signify rape. A night that was a blur, a night you wish hadn't happened, can be rape. Since "verbal coercion" and "manipulation" are ambiguous, it's easy to decide afterwards that he manipulated you. You can realize it weeks or even years later. This is a movement that deals in retrospective trauma.

Rape has become a catchall expression, a word used to define everything that is unpleasant and disturbing about relations between the sexes. Students say things like "I realize that sexual harassment is a kind of rape." If we refer to a whole range of behavior from emotional pressure to sexual harassment as "rape," then the idea itself gets diluted. It ceases to be powerful as either description or accusation.

Some feminists actually collapse the distinction between rape and sex. Catharine MacKinnon writes: "Compare victims' reports of rape with women's reports of sex. They look a lot alike.... In this light, the major distinction between intercourse (normal) and rape (abnormal) is that the normal happens so often that one cannot get anyone to see anything wrong with it."

There are a few feminists involved in rape education who object to the current expanding definitions of sexual assault. Gillian Greensite, founder of the rape prevention education program at the University of California at Santa Cruz, writes that the seriousness of the crime "is being undermined by the growing tendency of some feminists to label all heterosexual miscommunication and insensitivity as acquaintance rape." From within the rape-crisis movement, Greensite's dissent makes an important point. If we are going to maintain an *idea* of rape, then we need to reserve it for instances of physical violence, or the threat of physical violence.

But some people want the melodrama. They want the absolute value placed on experience by absolute words. Words like "rape" and "verbal coercion" channel the confusing flow of experience into something easy to understand. The idea of date rape comes at us fast and coherent. It comes at us when we've just left home and haven't yet figured out where to put our new futons or how to organize our new social lives. The rhetoric about date rape defines the terms, gives names to nameless confusions and sorts through mixed feelings with a sort of insistent consistency. In the first rush of sexual experience, the fear of date rape offers a tangible framework to locate fears that are essentially abstract.

When my 55-year-old mother was young, navigating her way through dates, there was a definite social compass. There were places not to let him put his hands. There were invisible lines. The pill wasn't available. Abortion wasn't legal. And sex was just wrong. Her mother gave her "mad money" to take out on dates in case her date got drunk and she needed to escape. She had to go far enough to hold his interest and not far enough to endanger her reputation.

Now the rape-crisis feminists are offering new rules. They are giving a new political weight to the same old no. My mother's mother told her to drink sloe gin fizzes so she wouldn't drink too much and get too drunk and go too far. Now the date rape pamphlets tell us: "Avoid excessive use of alcohol and drugs. Alcohol and drugs interfere with clear thinking and effective communication." My mother's mother told her to stay away from empty rooms and dimly lighted streets. In "I Never Called It Rape," Robin Warshaw writes, "Especially with recent acquaintances, women should insist on going only to public places such as restaurants and movie theaters."

There is a danger in these new rules. We shouldn't need to be reminded that the rigidly conformist 50's were not the heyday of women's power. Barbara Ehrenreich writes of "re-making love," but there is a danger in re-making love in its old image. The terms may have changed, but attitudes about sex and women's bodies have not. Rape-crisis feminists threaten the progress that's been made. They are chasing the same stereotypes our mothers spent so much energy escaping.

One day I was looking through my mother's bookshelves and I found her old battered copy of Germaine Greer's feminist classic, "The Female Eunuch." The pages were dogeared and whole passages marked with penciled notes. It was 1971 when Germaine Greer fanned the fires with "The Female Eunuch" and it was 1971 when my mother read it, brand new, explosive, a tough and sexy terrorism for the early stirrings of the feminist movement.

Today's rape-crisis feminists threaten to create their own version of the desexualized woman Greer complained of 20 years ago. Her comments need to be recycled for present-day feminism. "It is often falsely assumed," Greer writes, "even by feminists, that sexuality is the enemy of the female who really wants to develop these aspects of her personality.... It was not the insistence upon her sex that weakened the American women student's desire to make something of her education, but the insistence upon a *passive* sexual *role* [Greer's italics]. In fact, the chief instrument in the deflection and perversion of female energy is the denial of female sexuality for the substitution of femininity or sexlessness."

It is the passive sexual role that threatens us still, and it is the denial of female sexual agency that threatens to propel us backward.

POSTSCRIPT

Is There a Date Rape Crisis in Society?

Warshaw's thesis is that both stranger and acquaintance rape constitute rape. "In stranger rape *and* acquaintance rape, the aggressor... believes he is entitled to force sexual intercourse from a woman and he sees interpersonal violence (be it simply holding the woman down with his body or brandishing a gun) as an acceptable way to achieve his goal." In both cases women are victims. Warshaw also has a political thesis: "Rape is an exercise in the imbalance of power that exists between most men and women, a relationship that has forged the social order from ancient times on." Her crusade is thus against both forced sex and the imbalance of power between men and women. Roiphe also would join these crusades, but she questions the way feminists like Warshaw construct their reality about date rape. She would deflate the statistics and encourage women to take more responsibility for themselves and not backslide into the victim role.

Since the mid-1980s a sizeable literature on date or acquaintance rape has emerged. Easy access to this literature is provided by Sally K. Ward et al. in their annotated bibliography of over 400 items of research literature entitled *Acquaintance and Date Rape: An Annotated Bibliography* (Greenwood Press, 1994). On the prevalence of date or acquaintance rape, see Mary Koss, "Hidden Rape: Sexual Aggression and Victimization in a National Sample of Students in Higher Education," in Ann Wolbert Burgess, ed., *Rape and Sexual Assault II* (Garland Publishing, 1988). The classic statement of the feminist political view of rape is Susan Brownmiller's *Against Our Will: Men, Women, and Rape* (Simon & Schuster, 1975). For an extensive treatment of the issue of acquaintance rape, see Vernon R. Wiehe and Ann L. Richards, *Intimate Betrayal: Understanding and Responding to the Trauma of Acquaintance Rape* (Sage Publications, 1995). For discussions of rape and other forms of sexual violence, see Linda A. Fairstein, *Sexual Violence: Our War Against Rape* (William Morrow, 1993) and Alice S. Vachss, *Sex Crimes* (Random House, 1993).

The legal aspects of date rape are covered in Cassia Spohn and Julie Horney, *Rape Law Reform: A Grassroots Revolution and Its Impact* (Plenum Press, 1992). Works that discuss how to deal with the rape problem include Mary P. Koss and Mary R. Harvey, *The Rape Victim: Clinical and Community Interventions* (Sage Publications, 1991) and Carol Bohmer and Andrea Parrot, *Sexual Assault on Campus: The Problem and the Solution* (Lexington Books, 1993). For the best analysis of overall sexual practices of Americans, see Edward O. Laumann et al., *The Social Organization of Sexuality: Sexual Practices in the United States* (University of Chicago Press, 1994).

ISSUE 6

Should Society Be More Accepting of Homosexuality?

YES: Richard D. Mohr, from *A More Perfect Union: Why Straight America Must Stand Up for Gay Rights* (Beacon Press, 1994)

NO: Carl F. Horowitz, from "Homosexuality's Legal Revolution," *The Freeman* (May 1991)

ISSUE SUMMARY

YES: Philosophy professor Richard D. Mohr argues that homosexuals suffer from unjust discrimination and that homosexuality is neither immoral nor unnatural.

NO: Carl F. Horowitz, a policy analyst at the Heritage Foundation, argues that legal acceptance of homosexuality has gone too far. He maintains that open displays of homosexual affection, the creation of gay neighborhoods, and gay mannerisms are deeply offensive to heterosexuals.

In 1979 in Sioux Falls, South Dakota, Randy Rohl and Grady Quinn became the first acknowledged homosexual couple in America to receive permission from their high school principal to attend the senior prom together. The National Gay Task Force hailed the event as a milestone in the progress of human rights. It is unclear what the voters of Sioux Falls thought about it, since it was not put up to a vote, but if their views were similar to those of voters in Dade County, Florida; Houston, Texas; Wichita, Kansas; and various localities in the state of Oregon, they probably were not as enthusiastic as the National Gay Task Force. In referenda held in these and other areas, voters have reversed decisions by legislators and local boards to ban discrimination by sexual preference. Even in New York City, which is well known for its liberal attitudes, parents in some school districts have fought battles against school administrators over curricula that promote tolerance of gay lifestyles.

Yet the attitude of Americans toward gay rights is not easy to pin down. On one hand, voting majorities in many localities have defeated or overturned resolutions designating sexual orientation as a protected right. In 1993 alone, 19 localities passed measures that are considered antihomosexual by gay rights leaders. However, voters have also defeated resolutions like the one in California in 1978 that would have banned the hiring of gay schoolteachers, or the one on the Oregon ballot in 1992 identifying homosexuality as "abnormal, wrong, unnatural and perverse." In some states, notably Colorado, voters have approved initiatives widely perceived as antigay, but, almost invariably, these resolutions have been carefully worded so as to appear to oppose "special" rights for gays. In general, polls show that a large majority of Americans believe that homosexuals should have equal rights with heterosexuals with regard to job opportunities. On the other hand, many persist in viewing homosexuality as morally wrong.

President Bill Clinton experienced both of these views in 1992 and 1993. When he ran for president, Clinton caused no particular stir when he openly supported gay rights and promised that if elected he would issue an executive order lifting the ban on homosexuals in the military services. Once in office, however, and faced with demands from gay rights groups to deliver on his pledge, Clinton encountered bitter opposition. The locus of the opposition was the armed services and their supporters in Congress, but these vocal opponents also enjoyed considerable support from the public at large. Clinton ended up accepting a modified version of what he had promised—a "don't ask, don't tell, don't pursue" policy that fell far short of fully accepting homosexuality in the armed services.

Homosexuality was once commonly viewed as "deviant." The adjective may still be acceptable by both sides of the controversy if it simply means behavior considered different by the majority. But in popular usage, "deviant" means considerably more than this. It carries the connotation of "sick" and "immoral," which is why homosexuals are working hard to redefine homosexuality as normal, natural, and an acceptable lifestyle in a pluralist society. A more accepting attitude seems to be growing, especially among younger, college-educated Americans, but the recent referendum results suggest that widespread opposition to gay rights measures still exists.

In the selections that follow, Richard D. Mohr argues that the refusal to accept homosexuality is simply another form of bigotry, in the same category as racial or sexual discrimination, and that the time is long past due for granting full civil rights to homosexuals. Carl F. Horowitz argues that society's legal acceptance of homosexuality is already excessive because the rights of homosexuals are impinging on those of heterosexuals.

YES   Richard D. Mohr

PREJUDICE AND HOMOSEXUALITY

Who are gays anyway? Though the number of gays in America is hotly
disputed, studies agree that gays are distributed through every stripe and
stratum of Americans. Who are homosexuals? They are your friends, your
minister, your teacher, your bankteller, your doctor, your mailcarrier, your
officemate, your roommate, your congressional representative, your sibling,
parent, and spouse. They are we. We are everywhere, virtually all ordinary,
virtually all unknown.

Ignorance about gays, however, has not stopped people's minds from being
filled with stereotypes about gays. Society holds two oddly contradictory
groups of anti-gay stereotypes. One revolves around an individual's allegedly
confused gender identity: lesbians are females who want to be, or at least
look and act like, men—bulldykes, diesel dykes; while gay men are males
who want to be, or at least look and act like, women—queens, fairies, nances,
limp-wrists, nellies, sissies, aunties. These stereotypes of mismatches between
biological sex and socially defined gender provide the materials through
which lesbians and gay men become the butts of ethniclike jokes. These
stereotypes and jokes, though derisive, basically view lesbians and gay men as
ridiculous. For example: "How many fags does it take to change a light bulb?"
Answer: "Eight—one to replace it and seven to scream 'Faaaaaabulous!' "

The other set of stereotypes revolves around gays as a pervasive sinister
conspiratorial threat. The core stereotype here is that of the gay person—
especially gay man—as child molester, and more generally as sex-crazed
maniac. Homosexuality here is viewed as a vampirelike corruptive contagion.
These stereotypes carry with them fears of the very destruction of family and
civilization itself. Now, that which is essentially ridiculous can hardly have
such a staggering effect. Something must be afoot.

Clarifying the nature of stereotypes can help make sense of this incoherent
amalgam. Stereotypes are not simply false generalizations from a skewed
sample of cases examined. Admittedly, false generalizing plays some part in
the stereotypes society holds about gays and other groups. If, for instance,
one takes as one's sample gay men who are in psychiatric hospitals or prisons, as was done in nearly all early investigations, not surprisingly one will

probably find them to be of a crazed or criminal cast. Such false generalizations, though, simply confirm beliefs already held on independent grounds, ones that likely led the investigator to the prison and psychiatric ward to begin with. Evelyn Hooker, who in the late 1950s carried out the first rigorous studies of nonclinical gay men, found that psychiatrists, when presented with case files including all the standard diagnostic psychological profiles—but omitting indications of sexual orientation—were unable to distinguish gay files from non-gay ones, even though they believed gay men to be crazy. These studies proved a profound embarrassment to the psychiatric establishment, which has profited throughout the century by attempting to "cure" allegedly insane gays. The studies led eventually to the decision by the American Psychiatric Association in 1973 to drop homosexuality from its registry of mental illnesses. Nevertheless, the stereotype of gays as "sick" continues to thrive in the mind of America....

* * *

Partly because lots of people suppose they don't know any gay people and partly through the maintaining of stereotypes, society at large is unaware of the many ways in which gays are subject to discrimination in consequence of widespread fear and hatred. Contributing to this social ignorance of discrimination is the difficulty for gay people, as an invisible minority, even to complain of discrimination. If one is gay, the act of registering a complaint suddenly targets oneself as a stigmatized person, and so, especially in the absence of any protection against discrimination, simply invites additional discrimination. So, discrimination against gays, like rape, goes

seriously underreported. Even so, known discrimination is massive.

Annual studies by the National Gay and Lesbian Task Force have consistently found that over 90 percent of gay men and lesbians have been victims of violence or harassment in some form on the basis of their sexual orientation. Greater than one in five gay men and nearly one in ten lesbians have been punched, hit, or kicked; a quarter of all gays have had objects thrown at them; a third have been chased; a third have been sexually harassed, and 14 percent have been spit on, all just for being perceived to be gay.

The most extreme form of anti-gay violence is queerbashing—where groups of young men target a person who they suppose is a gay man and beat and kick him unconscious and sometimes to death amid a torrent of taunts and slurs. Few such cases with gay victims reach the courts. Those that do are marked by inequitable procedures and results. Frequently judges will describe queerbashers as "just all-American boys." A District of Columbia judge handed suspended sentences to queerbashers whose victim had been stalked, beaten, stripped at knife point, slashed, kicked, threatened with castration, and pissed on, because the judge thought the bashers were good boys at heart—they went to a religious prep school. In 1989, a judge in Dallas handed a sentence he acknowledged as light to the eighteen-year-old murderer of two gay men because the murderer had killed them in a gay cruising zone, where the judge said they might have been molesting children. The judge thereby justified a form of vigilantism that bears a striking resemblance to the lynching of black men on the grounds that they might molest white women. Indeed, queerbashing has the same function that past lynchings of blacks had—to keep a whole stigmatized group in line. As with lynchings, society has routinely averted its eyes, giving its permission or even tacit approval to violence and harassment.

Police and juries often will simply discount testimony from gays; they frequently construe assaults on and murders of gays as "justified" self-defense. The killer simply claims his act was an understandably panicked response to a sexual overture. Alternatively, when guilt seems patent, juries will accept highly implausible "diminished capacity" defenses, as in the case of Dan White's 1978 assassination of openly gay San Francisco city councilman Harvey Milk. Hostess Twinkies made him do it, or so the successful defense went. These inequitable procedures collectively show that the life and liberty of gays, like those of blacks, simply count for less than the life and liberty of members of the dominant culture.

Gays are also subject to widespread discrimination in employment. Governments are leading offenders here. They do a lot of discriminating themselves, require that others do it, and set precedents favoring discrimination in the private sector. First and foremost, the armed forces discriminate against lesbians and gay men. The federal government has also denied gay men and lesbians employment in the CIA, FBI, and the National Security Agency—and continues to defend such discrimination in the courts. The government refuses to give security clearances to gays and so forces the country's considerable private sector military and aerospace contractors to fire employees known to be gay and to avoid hiring those perceived to be gay. State and local governments regularly fire gay teachers, policemen, firemen, social workers, and

anyone who has contact with the public. Further, state licensing laws (though frequently honored only in the breach) officially bar gays from a vast array of occupations and professions—everything from doctors, lawyers, accountants, and nurses to hairdressers, morticians, even used-car dealers.

Gays are subject to discrimination in a wide variety of other ways, including private-sector employment, public accommodations, housing, insurance of all types, custody, adoption, and zoning regulations that bar "singles" or "nonrelated" couples from living together. A 1988 study by the Congressional Office of Technology Assessment found that a third of America's insurance companies openly admit that they discriminate against lesbians and gay men. In nearly half the states, same-sex sexual behavior is illegal.

Legal sanctions, discrimination, and the absorption by gays of society's hatred all interact to impede and, for some, block altogether the ability of gay men and lesbians to create and maintain significant personal relations with loved ones. Every facet of life is affected by discrimination. Only the most compelling reasons could possibly justify it.

* * *

Many people suppose society's treatment of gays is justified because they think gays are extremely immoral. To evaluate this claim, different senses of "moral" must be distinguished. Sometimes "morality" means the values generally held by members of a society—its mores, norms, and customs. On this understanding, gays certainly are not moral: lots of people hate them, and social customs are designed to register widespread disapproval of gays. The problem here is that this sense of morality is merely a descriptive one. Every society has this kind of morality—even Nazi society, which had racism and mob rule as central features of its "morality" understood in this sense. Before one can use the notion of morality to praise or condemn behavior, what is needed is a sense of morality that is prescriptive or normative.

As the Nazi example makes clear, the fact that a belief or claim is descriptively moral does not entail that it is normatively moral. A lot of people in a society saying that something is good, even over aeons, does not make it so. The rejection of the long history of the socially approved and state-enforced institution of slavery is another good example of this principle at work. Slavery would be wrong even if nearly everyone liked it. So consistency and fairness require that one abandon the belief that gays are immoral simply because most people dislike or disapprove of gays.

Furthermore, recent historical and anthropological research has shown that opinion about gays has been by no means universally negative. It has varied widely even within the larger part of the Christian era and even within the Church itself. There are even current societies—most notably in Papua New Guinea—where compulsory homosexual behavior is integral to the rites of male maturity. Within the last thirty years, American society has undergone a grand turnabout from deeply ingrained, nearly total condemnation to nearly total acceptance on two emotionally charged "moral" or "family" issues—contraception and divorce. Society holds its current descriptive morality of gays not because it has to, but because it chooses to.

Clearly popular opinion and custom are not enough to ground moral condemnation of homosexuality. Religious arguments are also frequently used to condemn homosexuality. Such arguments usually proceed along two lines. One claims that the condemnation is a direct revelation of God, usually through the Bible. The other sees condemnation in God's plan as manifested in nature; homosexuality (it is claimed) is "contrary to nature."

One of the more remarkable discoveries of recent gay research is that the Bible may not be as univocal in its condemnation of homosexuality as many have believed. Christ never mentions homosexuality. Recent interpreters of the Old Testament have pointed out that the story of Lot at Sodom is probably intended to condemn inhospitality rather than homosexuality. Further, some of the Old Testament condemnations of homosexuality seem simply to be ways of tarring those of the Israelites' opponents who happen to accept homosexual practices when the Israelites themselves did not. If so, the condemnation is merely a quirk of history and rhetoric rather than a moral precept.

What does seem clear is that those who regularly cite the Bible to condemn an activity like homosexual sex do so by reading it selectively. Do clergy who cite what they take to be condemnations of homosexuality in Leviticus maintain in their lives all the hygienic, dietary, and marital laws of Leviticus? If they cite the story of Lot at Sodom to condemn homosexuality, do they also cite the story of Lot in the Cave to condone incestuous rape? It seems then not that the Bible is being used to ground condemnations of homosexuality as much as society's dislike of homosexuality is being used to interpret the Bible.

Even if a consistent portrait of condemnation could be gleaned from the

Bible, what social significance should it be given? One of the guiding principles of society, enshrined in the Constitution as a check against the government, is that decisions affecting social policy are not made on religious grounds. The Religious Right has been successful in thwarting sodomy law reform, in defunding gay safe-sex literature and gay art, and in blocking the introduction of gay materials into school curriculums. If the real ground of the alleged immorality invoked by governments to discriminate against gays is religious (as it seems to be in these cases), then one of the major commitments of our nation is violated. Religious belief is a fine guide around which a person might organize his own life, but an awful instrument around which to organize someone else's life.

In the second kind of religious argument, people try to justify society's treatment of gays by saying they are unnatural. Though the accusation of unnaturalness looks whimsical, it is usually hurled against homosexuality with venom of forethought. It carries a high emotional charge, usually expressing disgust and evincing queasiness. Probably it is nothing but an emotional charge. For people get equally disgusted and queasy at all sorts of things which are perfectly natural and which could hardly be fit subjects for moral condemnation. Two typical examples in current American culture are some people's responses to mothers breastfeeding in public and to women who do not shave body hair. Similarly people fling the term "unnatural" at gays in the same breath and with the same force as when they call gays "sick" and "gross." When people have strong emotional reactions, as they do in these cases, without being able to give good reasons for them, they can hardly be thought of

as operating morally, but more likely as obsessed and manic.

When "nature" is taken in technical rather than ordinary usages, it also cannot ground a charge of homosexual immorality. When unnatural means "by artifice" or "made by humans," it can be pointed out that virtually everything that is good about life is unnatural in this sense. The chief feature that distinguishes people from other animals is people's very ability to make over the world to meet their needs and desires. Indeed people's well-being depends upon these departures from nature. On this understanding of human nature and the natural, homosexuality is perfectly unobjectionable; it is simply a means by which some people adapt nature to fulfill their desires and needs....

But (it might also be asked) aren't gays willfully the way they are? It is widely conceded that if sexual orientation is something over which an individual— for whatever reason—has virtually no control, then discrimination against gays is presumptively wrong, as it is against racial and ethnic classes.

Attempts to answer the question whether or not sexual orientation is something that is reasonably thought to be within one's own control usually appeal simply to various claims of the biological or "mental" sciences. But the ensuing debate over genes, hormones, hypothalamuses, twins, early childhood development, and the like is as unnecessary as it is currently inconclusive. All that is needed to answer the question is to look at the actual experience of lesbians and gay men in current society, and it becomes fairly clear that sexual orientation is not likely a matter of choice.

... [I]f people were persecuted, threatened with jail terms, shattered careers, loss of family and housing, and the like for eating, say, Rocky Road ice cream, no one would ever eat it. Everyone would pick another easily available flavor. That gay people abide in being gay even in the face of persecution suggests that being gay is not a matter of easy choice.

... Typically, gays-to-be simply find themselves having homosexual encounters and yet, at least initially, resisting quite strongly the identification of being homosexual. Such a person even very likely resists having such encounters, but ends up having them anyway. Only with time, luck, and great personal effort, but sometimes never, does the person gradually come to accept her or his orientation, to view it as a given material condition of life, coming as all materials do with certain capacities and limitations. The person begins to act in accordance with his or her orientation and its capacities, seeing its actualization as a requisite for an integrated personality and as a central component of personal well-being. As a result, the experience of coming out to oneself has for gays the basic structure of a discovery, not the structure of a choice. And far from signaling immorality, coming out to others affords one of the few remaining opportunities in ever more bureaucratic, technological, and socialistic societies to manifest courage.

How would society at large be changed if gays were socially accepted? Suggestions to change social policy with regard to gays are invariably met with claims that to do so would invite the destruction of civilization itself: after all isn't that what did Rome in? Actually, Rome's decay paralleled not the flourishing of homosexuality but its repression under the later Christianized emperors. Predictions of American civilization's imminent demise have been as premature as they have been frequent. Civilization has shown itself to be rather resilient here, in large part because of the country's traditional commitments to respect for privacy, to individual liberties, and especially to people minding their own business. These all give society an open texture and the flexibility to try out things to see what works. And because of this, one now need not speculate about what changes reforms in gay social policy might bring to society at large. For many reforms have already been tried.

Half the states have decriminalized lesbian and gay male sex acts. Can you guess which of the following states still have sodomy laws: Wisconsin, Minnesota; New Mexico, Arizona; Vermont, New Hampshire; Nebraska, Kansas? One from each pair does and one does not have sodomy laws. And yet one would be hard pressed to point out any substantial social differences between the members of each pair. (If you're interested: the second of each pair still has them.) Empirical studies have shown that there is no increase in other crimes in states that have decriminalized homosexual sex acts.

Neither has the passage of legislation barring discrimination against gays ushered in the end of civilization. Nearly a hundred counties and municipalities, including some of the country's largest cities (like Chicago and New York City), have passed such statutes, as have eight states: Wisconsin, Connecticut, Massachusetts, Hawaii, New Jersey, Vermont, California, and Minnesota. Again, no more brimstone has fallen on these places than elsewhere. Staunchly anti-gay cities, like Miami and Houston, have not been spared the AIDS crisis.

Berkeley, California, followed by a couple dozen other cities including New York, has even passed "domestic partner" legislation giving gay couples at least some of the same rights to city benefits as are held by heterosexually married couples, and yet Berkeley has not become more weird than it already was. A number of major universities (including Harvard, Stanford, and the University of Chicago) and respected corporations (including Levi Strauss and Company, the Montefiore Medical Center of New York, and Apple Computer, Inc.) have also been following Berkeley's lead. Lesbian and gay marriages are legal in Denmark (as of 1989) and in Norway (1993). In May of 1993, Hawaii's Supreme Court ruled that the state's law requiring spouses to be of different genders is a violation of the state's Equal Rights Amendment and can be upheld in further litigation only if the law's discrimination against same-sex couples (implausibly) can be shown to be necessary to a compelling state interest.

Seemingly hysterical predictions that the American family would collapse if such reforms passed have proven false, just as the same dire predictions that the availability of divorce would lessen the ideal and desirability of marriage proved unfounded. Indeed if current discrimination, which drives gays into hiding and into anonymous relations, ended, far from seeing gays destroying American families, one would see gays forming them.

If discrimination ceased, gay men and lesbians would enter the mainstream of the human community openly and with self-respect. The energies that the typical gay person wastes in the anxiety of leading a day-to-day existence of systematic disguise would be released

for use in personal flourishing. From this release would be generated the many benefits that accrue to a society when its individual members thrive.

Society would be richer for acknowledging another aspect of human diversity. Families with gay members would develop relations based on truth and trust rather than lies and fear. And the heterosexual majority would be better off for knowing that they are no longer trampling their gay friends and neighbors.

Finally and perhaps paradoxically, in extending to gays the rights and benefits it has reserved for its dominant culture, America would confirm its deeply held vision of itself as a morally progressing nation, a nation itself advancing and serving as a beacon for others—especially with regard to human rights. The words with which our national pledge ends—"with liberty and justice for all"—are not a description of the present, but a call for the future. America is a nation given to a prophetic political rhetoric which acknowledges that morality is not arbitrary and that justice is not merely the expression of the current collective will. It is this vision that led the black civil rights movement to its successes. Those senators and representatives who opposed that movement and its centerpiece, the 1964 Civil Rights Act, on obscurantist grounds, but who lived long enough and were noble enough, came in time to express their heartfelt regret and shame at what they had done. It is to be hoped and someday to be expected that those who now grasp at anything to oppose the extension of that which is best about America to gays will one day feel the same.

NO   Carl F. Horowitz

HOMOSEXUALITY'S LEGAL REVOLUTION

Last April, a brief series of events occurred in a Madison, Wisconsin, restaurant that spoke volumes about the current character of the homosexual rights movement. An employee of the Espresso Royal Cafe asked two women—presumably lesbians—to refrain from passionately kissing as they sat at a window table. Madison's gay community was not amused. The very next day, about 125 homosexual demonstrators showed up on the premises, and conducted a "kiss-in" for several minutes. A spokeswoman for the protesters, Malvene Collins, demanded, "You say gays and lesbians cannot show affection here? Why not here but in every other restaurant in Madison?" The establishment's chastised owner, Donald Hanigan, assured the crowd, "I regret that this incident ever happened. I want all of you to come in here every day."

In October, several dozen homosexual males, many of them dressed in women's clothing, openly hugged and kissed in a terminal of Seattle-Tacoma Airport, and handed out condoms and leaflets to travelers. Matt Nagel, spokesman for the Seattle chapter of . . . [the] homosexual organization, Queer Nation, seemed to sum up the feeling among militants in the local homosexual community. "We're going to homophobic bars, we're going to pack them, we're going to be openly affectionate, we're going to dance together and make it uncomfortable for all the straight people there."

At the same time in Chicago, six homosexual couples staged a "kiss-in" at the cosmetics counter of a Bloomingdale's department store until they were escorted out by security guards. Far from being deterred, the couples shortly went down to the cafeteria of a nearby office building, where they resumed their public display of affection.

A BID FOR LEGITIMACY

After some two decades of confrontation, the homosexual rights movement is consolidating its bid for legitimacy. The phrase, "Out of the closet, and into the streets," sounds quaint. That battle has already been won. Openly homosexual adults are certainly in the streets—and in stores, airports, and "homophobic" bars. Openly gay television characters, each with handsome, well-scrubbed looks, populate daytime and evening drama. Gay-oriented news programming is available on radio and television. Homosexual activists have all but completed their campaign to persuade the nation's educational establishment that homosexuality is normal "alternative" behavior, and thus any adverse reaction to it is akin to a phobia, such as fear of heights, or an ethnic prejudice, such as anti-Semitism.

The movement now stands on the verge of fully realizing its use of law to create a separate homosexual society paralleling that of the larger society in every way, and to intimidate heterosexuals uncomfortable about coming into contact with it. Through aggressive lobbying by such gay organizations as the Human Rights Campaign Fund, the Lambda Legal Defense and Education Fund, and the National Gay and Lesbian Task Force, the first part of that mission has enjoyed enormous success. About 90 counties and municipalities now have ordinances banning discrimination on the basis of gender orientation. There are roughly 50 openly gay public officials, up from less than a half-dozen in 1980.

Gay couples are increasingly receiving the full benefits of marriage, if not through state recognition of homosexual marriage ceremonies, then through enactment of domestic partnership laws. The State of California recently took a big step toward legalization of such marriages: this December [1990] it announced that "non-traditional" families, including homosexual couples, could formally register their unions as "unincorporated non-profit associations." Divorced gay parents are receiving with increasing frequency the right to custody of natural children. Gay adults without children are increasingly receiving the right to adopt them. Aspiring homosexual clergy are demanding—and receiving—the right to be ordained. Openly gay teachers are teaching in public schools. Homosexual soldiers, aware that their sexual orientation is grounds for expulsion from the military, openly declare their proclivities.

A Federal gay rights bill is the ultimate prize, and homosexual activists are blunt and resolute in pursuing such legislation. For example, Jeff Levi, spokesman for the National Gay and Lesbian Task Force, remarked at a press conference coinciding with the national gay march on Washington in October 1987:

> ...we are no longer seeking just a right to privacy and a protection from wrong. We also have a right—as heterosexual Americans already have—to see government and society affirm our lives.... until our relationships are recognized in the law —through domestic partner legislation or the definition of beneficiaries, for example—until we are provided with the same financial incentives in tax law and government programs to affirm our family relationships, then we will not have achieved equality in American society.

Yet, homosexual activists know that this legal revolution will never succeed without the unpleasant task of coercing heterosexuals into masking their displeasure with homosexuality. It is thus not enough merely to break down all existing barriers to homosexual affection being expressed through marriage, child-rearing, or employment. The law must additionally be rewritten to make it as difficult as possible for heterosexuals to avoid contact with such displays, or to show discomfort toward them.

This two-edged approach would create a world in which stringent laws at all levels, aggressively enforced and strictly interpreted, force business owners to refuse to discriminate against the openly homosexual in patronage, leasing, and hiring. Removing overtly homosexual patrons from a bar, an airport, or any other public space would result in heavy fines and even jail sentences against property owners or their employees (or in lieu of these sanctions, mandatory purgation). Derogatory remarks directed at homosexuals, even with sexuality only incidental, would likewise result in criminal penalties.

1990: A PIVOTAL YEAR

The year 1990 was pivotal for the homosexual legal revolution. The states of Massachusetts and Wisconsin in the late 1980s had enacted laws forbidding discrimination against homosexuals. The victories would come quickly now, especially at the local level. In March, the City of Pittsburgh voted to include sexual orientation as a right protected under the City Code. In October, Stanford University allowed homosexual couples to qualify for university student housing. In November, voters in San Francisco, buoyed by a heavy turnout of that city's large gay population, produced a "lavender sweep," not only passing Proposition K, a city initiative to allow homosexuals to register as domestic partners at City Hall (a similar measure was defeated in 1989), but electing two openly lesbian candidates to the City Board of Supervisors, and an openly homosexual male candidate to the Board of Education.

Voters in Seattle refused to repeal an existing gender orientation ordinance. Congress did its part early in the year by overwhelmingly passing the Hate Crimes Statistics Act (or Hate Crimes Act), which requires the Justice Department to publish hate crime statistics according to classifications that include sexual orientation....

"GAY CIVIL RIGHTS"

The homosexual lobby speaks of itself as struggling for "civil rights." "The gay community's goal is integration—just as it was with Martin Luther King," argues homosexual activist and San Francisco Board of Supervisors President Harry Britt.[10] Yet, underneath the surface, gay civil rights seems analogous to black "civil rights" *after* Reverend King's death. Far from seeking integration with the heterosexual world, it vehemently avoids it. More important, the movement seeks to win sinecures through the state, and over any objections by "homophobic" opposition. With a cloud of a heavy fine or even a jail sentence hanging over a mortgage lender, a rental agent, or a job interviewer who might be discomforted by them, homosexuals under these laws can win employment, credit, housing, and other economic entitlements. Heterosexuals would have no right to discriminate against homosexuals, but apparently, not vice versa. Libertarians as well as traditionalists ought to be troubled by this.

Consider a recent controversy in Madison, Wisconsin, as noted earlier a national bastion of "enlightened" attitudes. Three single women had recently moved into the same apartment, and one announced that she was a lesbian. The other two, not unreasonably, asked her to move. The lesbian filed a grievance with the local Human Rights Board, and, predictably, won. The shock came in the punishment. The two heterosexual women had to pay

$1,500 in "damages" to the lesbian, send her a public letter of apology, attend a two-hour "briefing" on homosexuality (conducted, needless to say, by homosexuals), and submit to having their living arrangements monitored for two years.

With such laws in effect, this outcome would not be so much played out as simply avoided. Let one hypothetical example suffice, one that no doubt *has* been played out regularly, and that goes a long way in explaining why in any metropolitan area gays tend to cluster in a few neighborhoods.

A man enters an apartment rental office, inquiring about a vacancy. He openly indicates he is a homosexual, or at least implies as much through certain mannerisms. For good measure, he brings along his lover. The rental manager fudges, clears his throat, and says, "Well, er, several people are looking at the apartment. Call me later." An hour later, a second man, alone, walks in. He does not announce his sexuality. Who gets the apartment?

In the absence of gay protectionism, and assuming equal incomes, the manager (sighing with relief) would probably award the apartment to the second applicant. Gay militants would cry, "Discrimination!"—and miss the point. Discrimination based on sexual orientation is fundamentally different from that based on race. Homosexuality constitutes a behavioral, not a genetic trait. It is within the moral right of a landlord, job interviewer, banker, or anyone else performing a "gatekeeper" function to discourage economically risky behavior, sexual or otherwise. Libertarian columnist Doug Bandow articulates this:

The point is, homosexuals have no right to force others to accept or support their lifestyle. Certainly government has no business discriminating against them: Anti-sodomy laws, for instance, are a vicious intrusion in the most intimate form of human conduct. And gays who pay taxes have as much right to government services and employment as anyone else.

But someone who decides to live openly as a homosexual should accept the disapproval of those around him. For many Americans still believe that there is a fundamental, unchangeable moral code by which men are to live....

Using government to bludgeon homophobics into submission is even more intolerant than the original discrimination.

Under normal circumstances, the rental manager would not want to lease to gays who, once moved in, might tell their friends that the neighborhood could have possibilities as a "gay" one. Word-of-mouth travels fast within their world. Beyond a certain "tipping-point," many heterosexual residents near and within the complex, rather than risk feeling stigmatized, would choose to move. Their places largely would be taken by overt homosexuals.

In fact this is exactly how neighborhoods such as Castro (San Francisco), West Hollywood (formerly part of Los Angeles, now separately incorporated largely due to gay pressure), the West Village (New York City), and Dupont Circle (Washington, D.C.) all rapidly developed reputations as "gay neighborhoods," and how large sections of Martha's Vineyard, Fire Island, and Rehoboth Beach became "gay resorts." The tipping-point principle also applies to public facilities such as restaurants. At the Grapevine Cafe in Columbus, Ohio, for example, heterosexual customers stopped coming when the clientele became heavily gay.

What would happen with a sexual orientation law in place? The rental manager knows that if he turns down an openly homosexual applicant, he risks prosecution. Any rejection can serve as proof of discriminatory intent, even with factors such as length of employment, income, and previous tenant record taken into account. In response to such a fear, the manager, though reluctantly, is likely to award the apartment to the homosexual.

For gay activists, therein lies the pay-off. By codifying into law "protection" of homosexual mannerisms, they can intimidate gatekeepers into providing job security and housing for the openly homosexual. Thus, without necessarily mentioning anything about quotas or, for that matter, homosexuality, law in the U.S. is increasingly mandating *homosexual affirmative action*. ...

THE GROWING THREAT OF VIOLENCE

There is something about encountering homosexuality in its militant and pugnacious form that touches a deep, almost reflexive anger, even among most heterosexual liberals. That is why attempts at "mainstreaming" gay culture, even when holding an olive branch, are bound to fail. One of the saddest books to appear in recent years is *After the Ball: How America Will Conquer Its Fear and Hatred of Gays in the 90s.*[29] The authors, Marshall Kirk and Hunter Madsen, both homosexual, advocate a national campaign to cheerfully "sell" gay culture. They suggest, for example, that gay organizations buy up advertising space in "straight" newspapers with pictures of historical figures such as

Alexander the Great, asking: "Did you know he was gay?"

Kirk and Madsen, like their surlier compatriots, fail to grasp that public homosexuality strikes at both a heterosexual's fear of loss of sexual identity and sense of belonging to a family. For even in this age of artificial insemination, families are not sustainable without heterosexuality. No matter how much the homosexual activist naively protests, "Gays are people, too," such a plea will receive in return grudging respect, and little else.

In a summary piece for *Newsweek's* March 12, 1990, cover story, "The Future of Gay America," Jonathan Alter revealed a rare understanding of this dynamic. He notes, " 'Acting gay' often involves more than sexual behavior itself. Much of the dislike for homosexuals centers not on who they are or what they do in private, but on so-called affectations —'swishiness' in men, the 'butch' look for women—not directly related to the more private sex act." Quite rightly so—one doubts if more than a tiny fraction of heterosexuals have even *inadvertently* witnessed a homosexual act. Alter then gets to the core of the issue. "Heterosexuals," he writes, "tend to argue that gays can downplay these characteristics and 'pass' more easily in the straight world than blacks can in a white world. ... This may be true, but it's also irrelevant. For most gays those traits aren't affectations but part of their identities; attacking their swishiness is the same as attacking *them*."

Yet if gays, through their carefully practiced "gay" mannerisms, know fully well they are antagonizing many heterosexuals, then why do they display them? Is it not in part to make heterosexuals sweat? By aggressively politicizing these traits, and demanding that those objecting must grin and bear it, they are in a sense restricting heterosexual freedom of speech. Male and even female opposition to persons with these traits is slowly taking a nasty turn, moving from violence of language to violence of fists. And yet, given the emerging legal climate, one discovers within oneself a disquieting empathy with the inchoate rage behind such acts.

Most heterosexuals are reasonably libertarian; an October 1989 Gallup Poll indicted that by a 47-to-36 margin (with the remainder undecided), Americans prefer legalization of homosexual relations between consenting adults. This is all to the good. Anti-sodomy laws serve no purpose but to intimidate people out of private, consensual acts. On the other hand, the brazen, *open* display of homosexuality—as if to taunt, to tease, to maliciously sow confusion into sexual identities—is something most heterosexuals do not handle gracefully. With an unofficial government mandate for preferential treatment, it is not difficult to imagine a backlash....

The principal motive of the gay movement is coming into focus with each passing month: to bait heterosexuals' less morally sturdy side, goading them into verbal or (better) physical assaults against the openly homosexual. That way, cries of homosexual victimhood would carry even more self-fulfilling prophecy, so much the better to vilify heterosexuals.

Gay militants aren't hesitant about admitting to such motives. Some want nothing less than war in the streets. Homosexual playwright and ACT-UP founder, Larry Kramer, recently called upon a gay audience to take gun practice for use in eventual combat against police and gay-bashers. "They hate us anyway," he rationalized. A cover of a recent issue of *Outweek* displayed a lesbian pointing a gun at the reader, with the headline, "Taking Aim at Bashers," while another cover announced, "We Hate Straights." ...

The crowning legacy of the new gay legalism may yet be widespread violence, a violence brought on by state inhibition of rational dialogue at the behest of gay radicals, and in the name of "sensitivity." That alone is enough reason to oppose it.

POSTSCRIPT

Should Society Be More Accepting of Homosexuality?

The issue of gay rights raises many issues of social control. Most people would agree that all members of a just society should have equal rights and should not have to endure the harassment and discrimination that Mohr reports gays and lesbians often experience. But how many Americans will fully defend with actions the rights of people with dramatically different lifestyles? This is where people's commitment to democracy and justice meets a real test. Tolerance for alternative lifestyles is increasing in America, but will tolerant citizens take actions against the harassment of homosexuals? On the other hand, the few gays and lesbians who practice a flagrant gay lifestyle can be criticized for offending the values of the community. Shouldn't gays respect community norms? But does full subordination to community norms deny gays the right to maintain a lifestyle that does not harm others? (Harmful lifestyles, whether homosexual or heterosexual, are rightfully condemned.) Finally, the normalization of gay lifestyles requires that it be openly practiced. So the issue is partly a matter of rights and partly a matter of courteous respect for others, whether homosexuals or heterosexuals.

There is a considerable literature on homosexuality. A basic source is Wayne Dynes, ed., *The Encyclopedia of Homosexuality* (Garland Publishing, 1990). Other general works include Michelangelo Signorile, *Queer in America: Sex, the Media, and the Closets of Power* (Random House, 1993); Didi Herman, *Rights of Passage: Struggles for Lesbian and Gay Equality* (University of Toronto Press, 1994); and Larry Gross, *Contested Closets: The Politics and Ethics of Outing* (University of Minnesota Press, 1993). Randy Shilts, in *Conduct Unbecoming: Gays and Lesbians in the U.S. Military* (St. Martin's Press, 1993), investigates the situation of lesbians and gays in the military over the last three decades. See also Lois Shawver, *And the Flag Was Still There: Straight People, Gay People, and Sexuality in the U.S. Military* (Haworth Press, 1995). Eugene T. Gomulka, in "Why No Gays?" *Proceedings* (December 1992), makes the case for maintaining the ban on gays in the military. Joseph Nicolosi argues that homosexuality can be cured and sexual orientation changed in "Let's Be Straight: A Cure Is Possible," while Carlton Cornett answers him in "Gay Ain't Broke; No Need to Fix It," *Insight on the News* (December 6, 1993). The best work on human sexual practices is Edward O. Laumann, John H. Gagnon, Robert T. Michael, and Stuart Michaels, *The Social Organization of Sexuality: Sexual Practices in the United States* (University of Chicago Press, 1994).

ISSUE 7

Should Traditional Families Be Preserved?

YES: David Popenoe, from "The American Family Crisis," *National Forum: The Phi Kappa Phi Journal* (Summer 1995)

NO: Judith Stacey, from "Dan Quayle's Revenge: The New Family Values Crusaders," *The Nation* (July/August 1994)

ISSUE SUMMARY

YES: Sociologist David Popenoe contends that families play important roles in society but how the traditional family functions in these roles has declined dramatically in the last several decades, with very adverse effects on children.

NO: Sociologist Judith Stacey argues that the claims of the current traditional family values crusade are false. She finds that high-conflict marriages are more harmful to children than low-conflict divorces and that single-parent families are roughly as good for children as two-parent families when income and self-esteem are the same.

The crisis of the American family deeply concerns many Americans. About 50 percent of marriages end in divorce, and only 27 percent of children born in 1990 are expected to be living with both parents by the time they reach age 17. Most Americans, therefore, are affected personally or are close to people who are affected by structural changes in the family. Few people can avoid being exposed to the issue: violence in the family and celebrity divorces are standard fare for news programs, and magazine articles decrying the breakdown of the family appear frequently. Politicians today try to address the problems of the family. Academics have affirmed that the family crisis has numerous significant negative effects on children, spouses, and the rest of society.

Sociologists pay attention to the role that the family plays in the functioning of society. For a society to survive, its population must reproduce (or take in many immigrants), and its young must be trained to perform adult roles and to have the values and attitudes that will motivate them to contribute to society. Procreation and socialization are two vital roles that families traditionally have performed. In addition, the family provides economic and emotional support for its members, which is vital to their effective functioning in society.

Today the performance of the family is disappointing in all of these areas. Procreation outside of marriage has become rather common, and it has been found to lead to less than ideal conditions for raising children. The scorecard on American family socialization is hard to assess, but there is concern about such issues as parents' declining time with and influence on their children and latchkey children whose parents work and who must therefore spend part of the day unsupervised. There is a prevalence of poverty among single-parent families as well as a potential for financial difficulties within families that have only one income earner. These indicators suggest that the modern family will fail economically unless each family contains two spouses that both work.

Although most experts agree that the American family is in crisis, there is little agreement about what, if anything, should be done about it. After all, most of these problems result from the choices that people make to try to increase their happiness. People end unhappy marriages. Married women work for fulfillment or financial gain. Unwed mothers decide to keep their children. The number of couples who choose to remain childless is growing rapidly. The high divorce rate and the frequency of child and spouse abuse indicate that the modern family fails to provide adequate social and emotional support.

Individual choices are not the only factors that have contributed to the weakening of the family (economic and legal changes have also played an important role). This trend cannot be changed unless people start choosing differently. As yet there is no sign of this happening. Does this mean that the weakening of the family is desirable? Few would advocate such an idea, but is it a reasonable position if free choice is a leading value? Sociologists recognize that the free choices of individuals do not always produce good results at the aggregate or societal level. For example, people choose to smoke, drink, and take drugs for their pleasure, but the costs in lost production, medical services, and socially harmful behaviors are immense. Is the traditional family undergoing this type of problem?

In the selections that follow, David Popenoe argues that the family is the key institution in society. Since it plays many important roles, its functional decline, which is largely due to cultural trends, has many adverse social impacts, including greatly harming children. He concludes by suggesting what needs to be done to strengthen families and family life. Judith Stacey tries to stop the bandwagon that is promoting the traditional family and castigating divorce and alternative family arrangements. Stacey argues that traditionalists misinterpret data to show that divorce and single parenting harms children.

YES

David Popenoe

THE AMERICAN FAMILY CRISIS

Throughout our nation's history, we have depended heavily on the family to provide both social order and economic success. Families have provided for the survival and development of children, for the emotional and physical health of adults, for the special care of the sick, injured, handicapped, and elderly, and for the reinforcement of society's values. Today, America's families face growing problems in each of these areas, and by many measures are functioning less well than ever before—less well, in fact, than in other advanced, industrialized nations.

The most serious negative effects of the functional decline of families have been on children. Evidence suggests that today's generation of children is the first in our nation's history to be less well-off psychologically and socially than their parents were at the same age. Alarming increases have occurred in such pathologies as juvenile delinquency, violence, suicide, substance abuse, eating disorders, nonmarital births, psychological stress, anxiety, and unipolar depression.

Such increases are especially troubling because many conditions for child well-being have improved. Fewer children are in each family today; therefore, more adults are theoretically available to care for them. Children are in some respects healthier and materially better off; they have completed more years in school, as have their parents. Greater national concern for children's rights, for child abuse, and for psychologically sound childrearing practices is also evident.

FAMILY ORIGINS AND HISTORY

As the first social institution in human history, the family probably arose because of the need for adults to devote a great amount of time to childrearing. Coming into the world totally dependent, human infants must, for a larger portion of their lives than for any other species, be cared for and taught by adults. To a unique degree, humans nurture, protect, and educate their offspring. It is hard to conceive of a successful society, therefore, that does not have families that are able to raise children to become adults who have the capacity to love and to work, who are committed to such positive social values as honesty, respect, and responsibility, and who pass these values on to the next generation.

Infants and children need, at minimum, one adult to care for them. Yet, given the complexities of the task, childrearing in all societies until recent years has been shared by many adults. The institutional bond of marriage between biological parents, with the essential function of tying the father to the mother and child, is found in virtually every society. Marriage is the most universal social institution known; in no society has nonmarital childbirth, or the single parent, been the cultural norm. In all societies the biological father is identified where possible, and in almost all societies he plays an important role in his children's upbringing, even though his primary task is often that of protector and breadwinner.

In the preindustrial era, however, adult family members did not necessarily consider childrearing to be their primary task. As a unit of rural economic production, the family's main focus typically was economic survival. According to some scholars, rather than the family being for the sake of the children, the children, as needed workers, were for the sake of the family. One of the most important family transitions in history was the rise in industrial societies of what we now refer to as the "traditional nuclear family": husband away at work during the day and wife taking care of the home and children full time. This transition took place in the United States beginning in the early 1800s. The primary focus of this historically new family form was indeed the care and nurturing of children,

and parents dedicated themselves to this effort.

Over the past thirty years, the United States (along with other modern societies) has witnessed another major family transformation—the beginning of the end of the traditional nuclear family. Three important changes have occurred:

- The divorce rate increased sharply (to a level currently exceeding 50 percent), and parents increasingly decided to forgo marriage, with the consequence that a sizable number of children are being raised in single-parent households, apart from other relatives.
- Married women in large numbers left the role of full-time mother and housewife to go into the labor market, and the activities of their former role have not been fully replaced.
- The focus of many families shifted away from childrearing to the psychological well-being and self-development of their adult members. One indication of this latter focus is that, even when they have young children to raise, parents increasingly break up if their psychological and self-fulfillment needs are unmet in the marriage relationship.

We can never return to the era of the traditional nuclear family, even if we wanted to, and many women and men emphatically do not. The conditions of life that generated that family form have changed. Yet the one thing that has not changed through all the years and all the family transformations is the need for children to be raised by mothers and fathers. Indeed, in modern, complex societies in which children need an enormous amount of education and psychological security to succeed, active and nurturing relationships with adults may be more critical for children than ever.

Unfortunately, the amount of time children spend with adults, especially their parents, has been dropping dramatically. Absent fathers, working mothers, distant grandparents, anonymous schools, and transient communities have become hallmarks of our era. Associated with this trend in many families, and in society as a whole, is a weakening of the fundamental assumption that children are to be loved and valued at the highest level of priority.

THE INDIVIDUALISM TREND

To understand fully what has happened to the family, we must look at the broader cultural changes that have taken place, especially changes in the values and norms that condition everyday choices. Over recent centuries in industrialized and industrializing societies, a gradual shift has occurred from a "collectivist" culture (I am using this term with a cultural and not a political meaning) toward an individualistic culture. In the former, group goals take precedence over individual ones. "Doing one's duty," for example, is more important than "self-fulfillment," and "social bonds" are more important than "personal choice." In individualistic cultures, the welfare of the group is secondary to the importance of such personal goals as self-expression, independence, and competitiveness.

Not surprisingly, individualistic societies rank higher than collectivist societies in political democracy and individual development. But the shift from collectivism to individualism involves social costs as well as personal gains —especially when it proceeds too far. Along with political democracy and individual development, individualistic societies tend to have high rates of individual deviance, juvenile delinquency, crime, loneliness, depression, suicide, and social alienation. In short, these societies have more free and independent citizens but less social order and probably a lower level of psychological well-being.

"Communitarian" Individualism

The United States has long been known as the world's most individualistic society. Certainly, we place a high value on this aspect of our society, and it is a major reason why so many people from other countries want to come here. Yet for most of our history, this individualism has been balanced, or tempered, by a strong belief in the sanctity of accepted social organizations and institutions, such as the family, religion, voluntary associations, local communities, and even the nation as a whole. While individualistic in spirit, people's identities were rooted in these social units, and their lives were directed toward the social goals that they represented. Thus, the United States has been marked for much of its history, not by a pure form of individualism, but by what could be termed a "communitarian" or balanced individualism.

"Expressive" Individualism

As the individualism trend has advanced, however, a more radical or "expressive" individualism has emerged, one that is largely devoted to "self-indulgence" or "self-fulfillment" at the expense of the group. Today, we see a large number of people who are narcissistic or self-oriented, and who show concern for social institutions only when these directly affect their own well-being. Unfortunately, these people have a tendency to distance themselves from the social and community groupings that have long been the basis for personal security and social order. Since the 1950s, the number of people being married, visiting informally with others, and belonging to voluntary associations has decreased, and the number of people living alone has increased.

In turn, the traditional community groupings have been weakened. More people are viewing our once accepted social institutions with considerable skepticism. As measured by public opinion polls, confidence in such public institutions as medicine, higher education, the law, the press, and organized religion has declined dramatically. As measured by people voting with their feet, trust in the institution of marriage also had declined dramatically. And, as we see almost every night on the news, our sense of cultural solidarity seems to be diminishing.

The highly disturbing actions of inner-city residents that we have witnessed in the urban riots of recent years could be considered less a departure from everyday American cultural reality than a gross intensification of it. Few social and cultural trends found in the inner city are not also present in the rest of the nation. Indeed, with respect to the family, the characteristics of the African American family pronounced by President Lyndon Johnson in 1965 to be in a state of "breakdown" are very similar to the family characteristics of America as a whole in 1994!

In summary, for the good of both the individual and society, the individualism trend in the United States has advanced too far. The family holds the key. People need strong families to provide them with the identity, belonging, discipline, and values that are essential for full individual development. The social institutions of the surrounding community depend on strong families to teach those "civic" values—honesty, trust, self-sacrifice, personal responsibility, respect for others—that enable them to thrive. But let us not forget that strong families depend heavily on cultural and social supports. Family life in an unsupportive community is always precarious and the social stresses can be overwhelming.

NOT TO FORGET THE GAINS

While I have presented a fairly grim picture in describing these cultural changes, it is important to add that not every aspect of our society has deteriorated. In several key areas, this nation has seen significant social progress. For instance, we are a much more inclusive society today—segregation and racism have diminished, and we now accept more African Americans, Hispanics, and other minority groups into the mainstream. The legal, sexual, and financial emancipation of women has become a reality as never before in history. With advances in medicine, we have greater longevity and, on the whole, better physical health. And our average material standard of living, especially in the possession of consumer durables, has increased significantly.

THE NUCLEAR FAMILY AND MARRIAGE

Given our nation's past ability to accept positive social change, we can have some confidence in our capacity to solve the problem of family decline. In seeking solutions, we should first consider what family structure is best able to raise children who are autonomous and socially responsible, and also able to meet adult needs for intimacy and personal attachment. Considering the available evidence, as well as the lessons of recent human experience, unquestionably the family structure that works best is the nuclear family. I am not referring to the traditional nuclear family, but rather to the nuclear family that consists of a male and a female who marry and live together and share responsibility for their children and for each other.

Let us look, for a moment, at other family forms. No advanced, Western society exists where the three-generation extended family is very important and where it is not also on the wane. Some scholars suggest that a new extended family has emerged with the trend toward "step" and "blended" families. "Isn't it nice," they say, "that we now have so many new relatives!" The final verdict is not yet in on stepfamilies, but preliminary evidence from the few empirical studies that have been done sends quite the opposite message, and it is a chilling one. For example, a recent British study of 17,000 children born in 1958 concluded that "the chances of stepchildren suffering social deprivation before reaching twenty-one are even greater than those left living after divorce with a lone parent." Similar findings are turning up in the United States.

How are the single-parent families doing? Accumulating evidence on the personal and social consequences of this family type paints an equally grim picture. A 1988 survey by the National Center for Health Statistics found, for example, that children from single-parent families are two to three times more likely to have emotional and behavioral problems than children from intact families, and reduced family income is by no means the only factor involved. In their new book *Growing Up With a Single Parent*, Sara McLanahan and Gary Sandefur, after examining six nationally representative data sets containing over 25,000 children from a variety of racial and social class backgrounds, conclude that "children who grow up with only one of their biological parents are disadvantaged across a broad array of outcomes... they are twice as likely to drop out of high school, 2.5 times as likely to become teen mothers, and 1.4 times as likely to be idle—out of school and out of work—as children who grow up with both parents." The loss of economic resources, they report, accounts for only about 50 percent of the disadvantages associated with single parenthood.

TOWARD SOLUTIONS

Of course, many people have no other choice than to live in step-and single-parent families. These families can be successful, and their members deserve our continuing support. Nevertheless, the benefits that strong nuclear families bring to a high-achieving, individualistic, and democratic society are absolutely clear. For example, a committed marriage, which is the basis of the strong nuclear family, brings enormous benefits to adults. It is ironic in this age of self-fulfillment, when people are being pulled away from marriage, that a happy marriage seems to provide the best source of self-fulfillment. By virtually every measure, married individuals are better off than single individuals.

Another reason for supporting strong nuclear families is that society gains enormously when a high percentage of men are married. While unmarried women take relatively good care of themselves, unmarried men often have difficulty in this regard. In general, every society must be wary of the unattached male, for he is universally the cause of numerous social ills. Healthy societies are heavily dependent on men being attached to a strong moral order, which is centered in families, both to discipline sexual behavior and to reduce competitive aggression. Men need the moral and emotional instruction of women more than vice versa. Family life, especially having children, is for men a civilizing force of no mean proportions.

We should be seriously concerned, therefore, that men currently spend more time living apart from families than at probably any other time in American history. About a quarter of all men aged twenty-five to thirty-four live in nonfamily households, either alone or with an unrelated individual. In 1960, average Americans spent 62 percent of their adult lives with spouse and children, which was the highest in our history; by 1980, they spent 43 percent, the lowest in our history. This trend alone may help to account for the high and rising crime rates over the past three decades. During this period, the number of reported violent crimes per capita, largely committed by unattached males, increased by 355 percent.

Today, a growing portion of American men are highly involved in child care, providing more help with the children than their own fathers did. Yet, because they did not stay with or marry the mothers of their children, or because of divorce, a large number of men have abandoned their children entirely.

Between 1960 and 1990 the percentage of children living apart from their biological fathers more than doubled, from 17 percent to 36 percent. In general, childrearing women have become increasingly isolated from men. This is one of the main reasons why nothing would benefit the nation more than a national drive to promote strong marriages.

THE NEW FAMILISM: A HOPEFUL TREND

One bright spot in this picture is what some of us have called "the new familism," a growing realization in America that, "yes, the family really is in trouble and needs help." Public opinion polls indicate that nearly two-thirds of Americans believe "family values have gotten weaker in the United States." Both major political parties and our President now seem to be in agreement.

Two primary groups are involved in this cultural mini-shift: the maturing baby boomers, now at the family stage of their life cycle, and the "babyboom echo" children of the divorce revolution. The middle-aged baby boomers, spurred by growing evidence that children have been hurt by recent family changes, have been instrumental in shifting the media in a profamily direction. And many of the echo children of the 1970s, with their troubled childhoods, are coming into adulthood with a resolve not to repeat their parents' mistakes. They tend to put a high premium on marital permanence, perhaps because they have been unable to take the family for granted as many of their parents—the children of the familistic 1950s—did. But one concern is this: will they have the psychological stability to sustain an intimate relationship, or will their insecure childhoods make it impossible for them to fulfill their commitment to a lasting marriage?

Unfortunately, studies of the long-term effects of divorce on children and adolescents provide no optimism in this regard.

A couple of other factors seem to be working in a profamily direction. One is AIDS, which has now noticeably slowed the sexual revolution. As one entertainment figure recently said (with obvious dismay), "dating in Hollywood just isn't what it used to be." Neither, I must add, is dating what it used to be on the college campus, but the changes so far have not been very remarkable. Another factor is that cultural change is often reflected in cycles, and some cycles of change are patterned in generational terms. We know that not all cultural values can be maximized simultaneously. What one generation comes to value because they have less of it, their parents' generation rejected. This factor leads us to believe that the nation as a whole may be primed in the 1990s to run away from the values of radical individualism and more fully embrace the ideals of family and other social bonds.

CONCLUSION

In thinking about how to solve America's family crisis, we should keep the following considerations uppermost in mind:

- As a society, we cannot return to the era of the traditional nuclear family. But, we must do everything possible to strengthen the husband-wife nuclear family that stays together and takes responsibility for its children. Every child both wants—and needs—a mother and a father.
- Fundamental to strengthening the nuclear family is a renewed emphasis on the importance of marriage, which is the social institution designed primarily to hold men to the mother-child unit. It is extremely important for our children, and for our society, that men are attached to childrearing families.
- With even the strongest of marriages, parents have great difficulty raising children in an unsupportive and hostile environment. We must seek to renew the sinews of community life that can support families, maintain social order, and promote the common good. We should give as much attention to recreating a "family culture" as we are now giving to strengthening a "work culture."
- As an overall approach to promoting family life, nothing is more important than trying to diminish and even turn back the trend toward radical individualism. Social bonds, rather than personal choice, and community needs, rather than individual autonomy, must be accorded a higher priority in our culture—and in our lives.

NO   Judith Stacey

DAN QUAYLE'S REVENGE: THE NEW FAMILY VALUES CRUSADERS

On election eve in 1992, I optimistically anticipated a respite from the family wars. After all, Murphy Brown had triumphed over Dan Quayle, and the ultramoralistic Republican convention had self-destructed on national television. The family values brigades seemed routed. Who could have predicted that even the liberal media would scramble to rehabilitate the former Vice President's image and warmly embrace family values before Clinton had survived his blistering first 10 days?

"Dan Quayle Was Right," decreed the April 1993 *Atlantic Monthly*, a magazine popular with the very cultural elite Quayle had blamed for the decline of Western civilized family life. Just as Clinton's job stimulus package suffered a silent demise, Jeremiahs from The *New York Times* to the *Chronicle of Higher Education*, from *This Week With David Brinkley* to The *MacNeil/Lehrer News Hour*, chanted kaddish for those fifties families, whose romanticized virtues grow ever more mythic with their passing. Because the rhetoric is numbingly familiar, few seem aware that the media's current family fervor signals the considerable success of a well-orchestrated new campaign. Old-style family values warriors like Quayle, Pat Buchanan and Jerry Falwell are reactionary Republicans and fundamentalist Christians—overtly antifeminist, antigay and, at least at the moment, on the defensive. In contrast, the revisionist family values campaign is explicitly centrist and coming on strong.

A creation of academicians rather than clerics, the campaign grounds its claims not in religious authority but in social science. During the late 1980s, a network of research and policy institutes, think tanks and commissions began mobilizing to forge a national consensus on family values and to shape the family politics of the "new" Democratic Party. Central players are the Institute for American Values, led by David Blankenhorn and Barbara Dafoe Whitehead (author of the *Atlantic* article), and its offshoot, the Council on Families in America, co-chaired by social scientists David Popenoe and Jean Bethke Elshtain. President Clinton's domestic policy adviser, William Galston, is one of the council's seventeen academic members, and Louis

Sullivan, George Bush's Secretary of Health and Human Services, gave the keynote address at its inaugural meeting.

"This is an attempt to bring people together who could convince the liberal intelligentsia that the family was in trouble and that this was a big problem," Popenoe told me when I interviewed him recently. "Most of us are neoliberal—you know, New Democrats, affiliated with the Progressive Policy Institute. We try to keep to the middle of the road." The political networks of these center-laners entwine tightly with those of the communitarians—a movement characterized by its founder, sociologist Amitai Etzioni, as "struggling for the soul of the Clinton Administration." Galston, Blankenhorn, Popenoe and Elshtain are all communitarians. So is Clinton's housing secretary, Henry Cisneros; and Al Gore spoke at a 1991 communitarian teach-in. The groups led by Blankenhorn, Popenoe and Etzioni draw on the same funding sources, according to Popenoe, who concedes that more of their benefactors are conservative than liberal. These include the Randall, Smith Richardson, Mott and Scaife foundations; the Brookings Institution; and the American Enterprise Institute.

Declaring that "the principal source of family decline over the past three decades has been cultural," Whitehead and her colleagues have mounted a crusade to restore the privileged status of lifelong, heterosexual marriage. The effects on intimate behaviors remain to be seen, but these new family values warriors have already achieved astonishing influence over the Clinton Administration. It took scarcely a year to convert Clinton from a proud icon of a single mom's glory into a repentant Quayle acolyte. *Newsweek* published the President's revised family credo last December: "Remember the Dan Quayle speech? There were a lot of very good things in that.... Would we be a better-off society if babies were born to married couples? You bet we would."

The belief that married-couple families are superior is probably the most pervasive prejudice about family life in the Western world, and the centrists are busy transmuting it into a social scientific "truth." They claim that research demonstrates that having two married, biological parents is the passport to a child's welfare, and thereby to society's welfare. Joining Daniel Patrick Moynihan on the "family breakdown" trail he has trekked since the sixties, they identify fatherless families as the root of everything from poverty, violence, drug addiction, crime and declining standards in education and civility to teen pregnancy, sexually transmitted disease, narcissism and the Los Angeles uprising. Claiming that research proves that divorce and unwed motherhood inflict devastating harm on children, centrists seek to revive the social stigma that once marked these "selfish" practices. They want to restore fault criteria to divorce proceedings and impose new restrictions, like mandatory waiting periods and counseling. They also favor welfare caps on unwed mothers.

By endlessly repeating and cross-citing one another's views, the centrists seem to have convinced most of the media, the public and Clinton that the superiority of the family values they espouse is, as Popenoe puts it, "a confirmed empirical generalization." Their efforts paved the yellow brick road to the shockingly respectful response that Charles Murray, an American Enterprise fellow, has received to his punitive quest to restigmatize "illegitimacy" and to terminate "all economic support for single mothers." The revisionist cultural onslaught has been so potent that even Donna Shalala, Clinton's Secretary of Health and Human Services and the Administration's token progressive feminist, seems to feel compelled to recite its mantra. "I don't like to put this in moral terms, but I do believe that having children out of wedlock is just wrong," Shalala told *Newsweek*, while a "dyed in the wool, but curious White House liberal" confided, off the record, that he'd "like to see the Murray solution tried somewhere—just to see, y'know, what might happen."

Although the revisionists sound like card-carrying conservatives who traded in leisure suits for academic tweed, they take wiser note of present demographic and cultural terrain than do their right-wing counterparts. They eschew antifeminism for a postfeminist family ethic and attempt to address some of the dilemmas currently plaguing working parents. They promote greater public commitment to lifting families out of poverty than conservatives can stomach, as well as more reforms like flextime, family allowances, flexible career paths and paid family leave. Disdainful of the Republicans' crude antifeminism, centrists gesture toward gender equality. Blankenhorn, for example, insists that "strengthening family life in the 1990s cannot and should not mean the repeal of the past thirty years of new opportunities for women in the workplace and in public life." Centrists also call for greater familial responsibility from men. Blankenhorn has joined forces with Don Eberly, a former aide to Jack Kemp, to form a national organization of fathers to "restore to fatherhood a sense of pride, duty and reward."

No other "advanced" industrial nation subjects working mothers to as anguishing a work/family conflict as does the United States. Burned-out supermoms, devalued housewives and women suffering the effects of divorce, deadbeat dads, feckless sexual partners or asymmetrical job and courtship markets may be excused if they indulge, like unapologetic male chauvinists, in some backlash nostalgia for simpler family times. While centrists effectively exploit this yearning, progressive social scientists have been backed into ideological corners and marginalized. So before the feeble ranks of remnant, "dyed in the wool" liberals succumb to "curiosity" over what the Murray solution might accomplish, I want to expose the most egregious flaws in the centrists' social science and to confront the kernels of truth embedded in their family sermons.

*   *   *

Contrary to centrist claims, most social scientists do not agree that a family's structure is more important than the quality of the relationships. Revisionists employ academic sleights of hand to evade this consensus. For example, they rest claims on misleading comparison groups and on studies, like Judith Wallerstein's widely cited research on divorcing parents, that do not use any comparison groups at all. It is true that, on average, children of divorce fare somewhat worse than those in intact families, but this tells us nothing about how divorce affects children. To address that question, we must compare children of divorce not with all children of married parents but with those whose unhappily married parents do not divorce. Research indicates that high-conflict marriages harm children more than do low-conflict divorces.

Centrists use another statistical trick to exaggerate advantages that some children from two-parent families enjoy over their single-parented peers—treating small and relative differences as though they were gross and absolute. In fact, most children from both kinds of families turn out reasonably well, and when other parental resources—like income, education, self-esteem and a supportive social environment—are roughly similar, signs of two-parent privilege largely disappear. Most research, like that summarized in Frank Furstenberg and Andrew Cherlin's *Divided Families*, indicates that a stable, intimate relationship with one responsible, nurturant adult is a child's surest path to becoming one too. In short, the research scale tips toward those who stress the quality of family relationships over their form. Moreover, it is untenable to appeal to a child-centered doctrine to impugn the "selfishness" of single women who choose to become mothers. Because no child asks to be born, almost all intentional parenting is selfish.

The centrists have it backward when they argue that the collapse of traditional family values is at the heart of our social decay. The losses in real earnings and in breadwinner jobs, the persistence of low-wage work for women and the corporate greed that has accompanied global economic restructuring have wreaked far more havoc on Ozzie and Harriet Land than have the combined effects of feminism, sexual revolution, gay liberation, the counterculture, narcissism and every other value flip of the past half-century.

In all cultures and eras, stable marriage systems have rested upon coercion—overt or veiled—and on inequality. Proposals to restrict access to divorce and parenting implicitly recognize this. Without coercion, divorce and single motherhood will remain commonplace. Marriage became increasingly fragile as it became less obligatory, particularly for women. It seems a poignant commentary on the benefits to women of modern marriage that even when women retain chief responsibility for children, when they earn much less than men with similar "cultural capital" and when they and their children suffer major economic loss after divorce, so many regard divorce as the lesser evil.

Yet most centrists avert their eyes from this injustice. Whitehead, for example, celebrates signs of a "New Familism" in which, "both parents give up something in their work lives in order to foster their family lives. The woman makes the larger concession, but it is one she actively elects." Postfeminist family ideology appropriates feminist critiques of traditional masculine priorities while appealing to those maternal values that feminists like Carol Gilligan have made popular. They also build upon a body of thought I once termed "new conservative feminism," whose defining feature is distaste for sexual politics. Revisionists offer tepid support, at best, for abortion rights, often supporting restrictions like spousal and parental notification, partly in the service of making men more accountable. Moreover, as Etzioni puts it, "there are some issues, such as abortion and gay rights, that we know communitarians cannot agree on, so we have completely avoided them."

Homophobia also plays a closeted role in the centrists' campaign, one that could prove more insidious than Buchanan-style gay bashing. Moynihan's conviction that children need to grow up in families that provide a "stable relationship to male authority" is echoed by Whitehead's undocumented claim that research demonstrates "the importance of both a mother and a father in fostering the emotional well-being of children." Elshtain unapologetically concedes that "we are privileging relations of a particular kind in which certain social goods are at stake" by affirming a heterosexual family model. Ignoring consistent research findings that lesbian and gay parents are at least as successful as heterosexual ones, the council she co-chairs refuses to advocate equal marriage, adoption or childbearing rights for gays.

Nor do the centrists seem much concerned with the class and race prejudices their crusade exhibits. Having studied families struggling to sustain body, soul and kin ties in Silicon Valley during the mid-1980s recession, I wonder what sort of bourgeois, bubble world folks like Whitehead, Popenoe and the other communitarians inhabit. I do not know whether their moralistic images of hedonistic adults who place selfish emotional, erotic and "career" ambitions above the needs of neglected children derive from close observation of occupants of some professional/corporate cocoon. I do know that such caricatures bear scant resemblance to the family realities of the working people—married or single, lesbian or straight, employed, laid off or retired—that I studied, nor, I would venture, to those of most of the rest of us. Few can enjoy the luxury of a "new familism" that places children's needs above the demands of a job. Wherever class bias flourishes, race is seldom far behind. Dan Quayle's attack on Murphy Brown was an attempt to play the Willie Horton card in whiteface. Without resorting to overt racism, he conjured up frightening hordes of black welfare "queens" rearing infant fodder for sex, drugs and videotaped rebellions, such as had just erupted in L.A. The greatest contrast

in family patterns and resources in the country today is between steady-earner and single-mother households, and these divide visibly along racial lines. Voting patterns in the 1992 election registered a wider "family gap" than gender gap. Unmarried voters' heavy preference for Clinton shored up his precarious margin of victory. Clearly, a campaign that sets two- and single-parent families at odds has political consequences. Centrist Democrats hope their family values campaign will erode the advantage Republicans now enjoy among the largely white, middle-class, heterosexual, two-parent family set. Such a strategy is unlikely to succeed. As Quayle and Christian right leaders recognize, family values ardor more readily promotes their reactionary agenda.

But to halt the stampede to a conservative cultural consensus, progressives must do more than expose the errors of the centrists. We must also dodge the ideological corners into which they deftly paint us, resisting knee-jerk responses to their reductionist logic, like one feminist bumper sticker—"Unspoken Traditional Family Values: Abuse, Alcoholism, Incest"—that Whitehead cites to mock feminists. Nor should we tolerate an image as an overzealous cheering squad for unwed single motherhood. Certainly, aiding women's struggles to resist unequal, hostile, dangerous marriages remains a crucial project, but one we cannot advance by denying that many women, many of them feminists, want committed, intimate relationships with men. The best interests of women, men and children do *not* always coincide. Some divorces *are* better for the adults, who choose them, than for the children, who do not. Just as there are his and hers marriages, divorce is often better for one spouse than the other.

We should also recognize that in most industrial societies teenage motherhood (married or not) often does not augur well for the offspring. Without rejecting the view that most teens now lack the maturity and resources to parent effectively, we might note that this is as true of those whom Charles Murray would shame and starve into shotgun marriages as of those whose dads lack shotguns. The rising age of marriage since the 1950s is a positive trend, but one of its consequences is more nonmarital sexuality and pregnancy. The drive to restigmatize "illegitimacy" demands a renewed struggle to destigmatize abortion and make it accessible, along with contraception and sex education. It seems time to revive Margaret Sanger's slogan, "every child a wanted child."

To show solidarity with single mothers, we need not deny that two responsible, loving parents generally *can* offer children more than one parent can. Of course, three or four might prove even better. Programs encouraging child-free adults to form supportive ties with the children of overburdened parents (a category from which few parents are exempt) might give many kinds of families common cause. Once we grasp the distinctions between right-wing and centrist family values, we can support the latter's "family friendly" reforms while struggling for a more democratic definition of the term. We can employ family values logic to extend full family rights to gays, but to succeed we should help heal the rift between them and blacks that right-wing family values folks are effectively exploiting.

Unless a full-spectrum rainbow coalition comes to recognize shared stakes in democratizing family rights and resources, the future of no kind of family is secure. Communitarian doctrine urges greater collective responsibility for the common good, but its enthusiasm for privatistic, narrowly defined family values is self-canceling. What we need above all is an inclusive movement for *social* values. We won't find this in the middle of the road.

POSTSCRIPT

Should Traditional Families Be Preserved?

Popenoe admits that there are many positive aspects to the recent changes that have affected families, but he sees the negative consequences, especially for children, as necessitating actions to counter them. He recommends a return to family values and speaks out against the individualistic ethos. Stacey believes that the focus should shift from family structure to the quality of family relationships, and from selfishness as the root of the problems of the family to declining real earnings and other societal conditions. In the end she shows a lot of sympathy for "family friendly reforms" as long as they can be free of the subordination and abuse of women that she so strongly associates with the traditional family.

Support for Stacey's point of view can be found in Stephanie Coontz, *The Way We Never Were* (Basic Books, 1992) and "The American Family and the Nostalgia Trap," *Kappan Special Report* (March 1995); E. L. Kain, *The Myth of Family Decline* (D.C. Heath, 1990); and J. F. Gubrium and J. A. Holstein, *What Is a Family?* (Mayfield, 1990). Arlene Skolnick argues that the family is not only changing but it is also in a crisis in *Embattled Paradise: The American Family in an Age of Uncertainty* (Basic Books, 1991). In contrast to the family crisis view, Andrew M. Greeley presents a positive portrait of the family in *Faithful Attraction* (Tor Books, 1991). Change is emphasized in Andrew Cherlin's two books *Marriage, Divorce, Remarriage*, rev. ed. (Harvard University Press, 1992) and *The Changing American Family and Public Policy* (Urban Institute Press, 1988). For major works on aspects of familial changes see David Blankenhorn, *Fatherless America: Confronting Our Most Urgent Social Problem* (Basic Books, 1995); Martha Albertson Fineman, *The Neutered Mother, the Sexual Family and Other Twentieth Century Tragedies* (Routledge, 1995); Ailsa Burns and Cath Scott, *Mother-Headed Families and Why They Have Increased* (Lawrence Erlbaum, 1994); Sara McLanahan and Gary Sandefur, *Growing Up With a Single Parent: What Hurts and What Helps* (Harvard University Press, 1994); Kathleen Gerson, *No Man's Land: Men's Changing Commitments to Family and Work* (Basic Books, 1993); John Snarey, *How Fathers Care for the Next Generation: A Four-Decade Study* (Harvard University Press, 1993); Ronald J. Angel and Jacqueline L. Angel, *Painful Inheritance: Health and the New Generation of Fatherless Families* (University of Wisconsin Press, 1993); and Valerie Polakow, *Lives on the Edge: Single Mothers and Their Children in the Other America* (University of Chicago Press, 1993). For a discussion of equality in the family and society, see Mary Frances Berry, *The Politics of Parenthood* (Viking Penguin, 1993).

PART 3

Stratification and Inequality

Although the ideal of equal opportunity for all is strong in the United States, many charge that the American political and economic system is unfair. Various affirmative action programs have been implemented to remedy unequal opportunities, but some argue that this is discrimination in reverse. Others argue that minorities should depend on themselves, not the government, to overcome differences in equality. Does poverty continue to exist in the United States despite public assistance programs because it has become a deeply ingrained way of life for individuals? Or is poverty as well as homelessness a result of the failure of policymakers to live up to U.S. egalitarian principles? Social scientists debate these questions in this part.

- Is Economic Inequality Beneficial to Society?

- Are the Poor Responsible for Their Poverty?

- Should Affirmative Action Policies Be Discontinued?

- Do Social and Mental Pathologies Largely Account for Homelessness?

ISSUE 8

Is Economic Inequality Beneficial to Society?

YES: George Gilder, from *Wealth and Poverty* (Basic Books, 1981; reissue, ICS Press, 1993)

NO: William Ryan, from *Equality* (Pantheon Books, 1981)

ISSUE SUMMARY

YES: Social critic George Gilder praises the American political economy because it provides many incentives for people to get ahead and make money. He maintains that the economy is dynamic and that all classes of people benefit.

NO: Professor of psychology William Ryan contends that income inequalities in America are excessive and immoral because they vastly exceed differences of merit and result in tremendous hardship for the poor.

The cover of the January 29, 1996, issue of *Time* magazine bears a picture of 1996 Republican presidential candidate Steve Forbes and large letters reading: "DOES A FLAT TAX MAKE SENSE?" During his campaign Forbes expressed his willingness to spend $25 million of his own wealth in pursuit of the presidency, with the major focus of his presidential campaign being a flat tax, which would reduce taxes substantially for the rich. It seems reasonable to say that if the rich pay less in taxes, others would have to pay more. Is it acceptable for the tax burden to be shifted away from the rich in America? Forbes believed that the flat tax would benefit the poor as well as the rich. He theorized that the economy would surge ahead because investors would shift their money from relatively nonproductive, but tax-exempt, investments to productive investments. This is an example of the trickle-down theory, which claims that helping the rich stimulates the economy, which helps the poor. In fact, the trickle-down theory is the major rationalization for the view that economic inequality benefits society.

Inequality is not a simple subject. For example, America is commonly viewed as having more social equality than the more hierarchical societies of Europe and Japan, but America has more income inequality than almost all other industrial societies. This apparent contradiction is explained when one recognizes that American equality is not in income but in the opportunity to obtain higher incomes. The issue of economic inequality is further complicated by other categories of equality/inequality, which include political power, social status, and legal rights.

Americans believe that everyone should have an equal opportunity to compete for jobs and awards. This belief is backed up by free public school education, which provides poor children with a ladder to success, and by laws that forbid discrimination. Americans, however, do not agree on many specific issues regarding opportunities or rights. For example, should society compensate for handicaps such as disadvantaged family backgrounds or the legacy of past discrimination? This issue has divided the country. Americans do not agree on programs such as income-based scholarships, quotas, affirmative action, or the Head Start compensatory education program for poor preschoolers. In the abstract, everyone supports equality of legal rights, but it is often violated in practice.

America's commitment to political equality is strong in principle, though less strong in practice. Everyone over 18 years old gets one vote, and all votes are counted equally. However, the political system tilts in the direction of special interest groups; those who do not belong to such groups are seldom heard. Furthermore, as in the case of Forbes, money plays an increasingly important role in political campaigns.

The final dimension of equality/inequality is status. Inequality of status involves differences in prestige, and it cannot be eliminated by legislation. Ideally, the people who contribute the most to society are the most highly esteemed. To what extent does this principle hold true in the United States?

The Declaration of Independence proclaims that "all men are created equal," and the Founding Fathers who wrote the Declaration of Independence went on to base the laws of the land on the principle of equality. The equality they were referring to was equality of opportunity and legal and political rights for white, property-owning males. They did not mean equality of income or status, though they recognized that too much inequality of income would jeopardize democratic institutions. In the two centuries following the signing of the Declaration, nonwhites and women struggled for and won considerable equality of opportunity and rights. Meanwhile, income gaps in the United States have been widening (except from 1929 to 1945, when the stock market crash harmed the wealthy and wartime full employment favored the poor).

Should America now move toward greater income equality? Must this dimension of inequality be rectified in order for society to be just? George Gilder strongly believes that people must work hard, innovate, compete, aspire, and accept risks, and that inequality of income is needed to motivate them accordingly. He maintains that welfare, highly progressive taxes, and many other egalitarian measures are sapping American initiative, crippling American enterprise, slowing the American economy, and perpetuating the poverty of the poor. William Ryan makes the case that the existing income inequalities are obscene and offensive to moral sensibilities. He believes that reduction of inequalities is essential to social justice.

YES

George Gilder

THE DIRGE OF TRIUMPH

The most important event in the recent history of ideas is the demise of the socialist dream. Dreams always die when they come true, and fifty years of socialist reality, in every partial and plenary form, leave little room for idealistic reverie. In the United States socialism chiefly rules in auditoria and parish parlors, among encounter groups of leftist intellectuals retreating from the real world outside, where socialist ideals have withered in the shadows of Stalin and Mao, Sweden and Tanzania, gulag and bureaucracy.

The second most important event of the recent era is the failure of capitalism to win a corresponding triumph. For within the colleges and councils, governments and churches where issue the nebulous but nonetheless identifiable airs and movements of new opinion, the manifest achievements of free enterprise still seem less comely than the promise of socialism betrayed. . . .

A prominent source of trouble is the profession of economics. Smith entitled Book One of *The Wealth of Nations*, "Of the Causes of Improvement in the productive Powers of Labour and the Order according to which its Produce is naturally distributed among the different Ranks of the people." He himself stressed the productive powers, but his followers, beginning with David Ricardo, quickly became bogged down in a static and mechanical concern with distribution. They all were forever counting the ranks of rich and poor and assaying the defects of capitalism that keep the poor always with us in such great numbers. The focus on distribution continues in economics today, as economists pore balefully over the perennial inequalities and speculate on brisk "redistributions" to rectify them.

This mode of thinking, prominent in foundation-funded reports, best-selling economics texts, newspaper columns, and political platforms, is harmless enough on the surface. But its deeper effect is to challenge the golden rule of capitalism, to pervert the relation between rich and poor, and to depict the system as "a zero-sum game" in which every gain for someone implies a loss for someone else, and wealth is seen once again to create poverty. As Kristol has said, a free society in which the distributions are widely seen as unfair cannot long survive. The distributionist mentality thus strikes at the living heart of democratic capitalism.

From George Gilder, *Wealth and Poverty* (Basic Books, 1981; reissue, ICS Press, 1993). Copyright © 1981 by George Gilder. Reprinted by permission of Georges Borchardt, Inc., for the author.

Whether of wealth, income, property, or government benefits, distributions always, unfortunately, turn out bad: highly skewed, hugely unequal, presumptively unfair, and changing little, or getting worse. Typical conclusions are that "the top 2 percent of all families own 44 percent of all family wealth, and the bottom 25 percent own none at all"; or that "the top 5 percent get 15.3 percent of the pre-tax income and the bottom 20 percent get 5.4 percent." . . .

Statistical distributions, though, can misrepresent the economy in serious ways. They are implicitly static, like a picture of a corporate headquarters, towering high above a city, that leaves out all the staircases, escalators, and elevators, and the Librium® on the executive's desk as he contemplates the annual report. The distribution appears permanent, and indeed, like the building, it will remain much the same year after year. But new companies will move in and out, executives will come and go, people at the bottom will move up, and some at the top will leave their Librium® and jump. For example, the share of the tobacco industry commanded by the leading four firms has held steady for nearly thirty years, but the leader of the 1950s is now nearly bankrupt. The static distributions also miss the simple matter of age; many of the people at the bottom of the charts are either old, and thus beyond their major earning years, or young, and yet to enter them. Although the young and the old will always be with us, their low earnings signify little about the pattern of opportunity in a capitalist system.

Because blacks have been at the bottom for centuries now, economists often miss the dynamism within the American system. The Japanese, for example, were interned in concentration camps during World War II, but thirty years later they had higher per capita earnings than any other ethnic group in America except the Jews. Three and one-half million Jewish immigrants arrived on our shores around the turn of the century with an average of nine dollars per person in their pockets, less than almost any other immigrant group. Six decades later the mean family income of Jews was almost double the national average. Meanwhile the once supreme British Protestants (WASPs) were passed in per capita earnings after World War II not only by Jews and Orientals but also by Irish, Italians, Germans, and Poles (which must have been the final Polish joke), and the latest generation of black West Indians.

It is a real miracle that learned social scientists can live in the midst of these continuing eruptions and convulsions, these cascades and cataracts of change, and declare in a tone of grim indignation that "Over the last fifty years there has been no shift in the distribution of wealth and income in this country." . . .

The income distribution tables also propagate a statistical illusion with regard to the American rich. While the patterns of annual income changed rather little in the 1970s, there was a radical shift in the distribution of wealth. In order to understand this development, it is crucial to have a clear-eyed view of the facts and effects of inflation, free of the pieties of the Left and the Right: the familiar rhetoric of the "cruelest tax," in which all the victims seem to be widows and orphans. In fact, widows and orphans—at least the ones who qualified for full social security and welfare benefits—did rather well under inflation. Between 1972 and 1977, for example, the median household income of the elderly rose from 80 to 85 percent of the entire population's. As Christopher Jencks of Harvard University and Joseph Minarek of the Brookings Institution, both men of the Left, discovered in the late 1970s, inflation hit hardest at savers and investors, largely the rich....

Wealth consists of assets that promise a future stream of income. The flows of oil money do not become an enduring asset of the nation until they can be converted into a stock of remunerative capital—industries, ports, roads, schools, and working skills—that offer a future flow of support when the oil runs out. Four hundred years ago, Spain was rich like Saudi Arabia, swamped by a similar flood of money in the form of silver from the mines of Potosi in its Latin American colonies. But Spain failed to achieve wealth and soon fell back into its previous doldrums, while industry triumphed in apparently poorer parts of Europe.

A wealthy country must be able to save as well as to consume. Saving is often defined as deferred consumption. But it depends on investment: the ability to produce consumable goods at that future date to which consumption has been deferred. Saving depends on having something to buy when the deposit is withdrawn. For an individual it sounds easy; there must always be *something* to buy after all. But for a nation, with many savers, real wealth is hard work, requiring prolonged and profitable production of goods....

Work, indeed, is the root of wealth, even of the genius that mostly resides in sweat. But without a conception of goals and purposes, well-paid workers consume or waste all that they earn. Pop singers rocking and rolling in money, rich basketball stars who symbolize wealth to millions, often end up deep in debt with nothing solid to show for their efforts, while the poorest families can often succeed in saving enough to launch profitable businesses. The old adages on the importance of thrift are true not only because they signify a quantitative rise in investible funds, but because they betoken imagination and purpose, which make wealth. Few businesses begin with bank loans, and small businesses almost never do. Instead they capitalize labor.

For example, ten years ago a Lebanese family arrived in Lee, Massachusetts, with a few dollars and fewer words of English. The family invested the dollars in buying a woebegone and abandoned shop beside the road at the edge of town, and they started marketing vegetables. The man rose at five every morning to drive slowly a ramshackle truck a hundred miles to farms in the Connecticut Valley, where he purchased the best goods he could find as cheaply as possible to sell that morning in Lee. It was a classic entrepreneurial performance, arbitrage, identifying price differentials in different markets, and exploiting them by labor. But because both the labor and the insight was little compensated, it was in a sense invisibly saved and invested in the store. All six children were sources of accumulating capital as they busily bustled about the place. The store remained open long hours, cashed checks of locals, and began to build a clientele. A few years later one had to fight through the crowds around it in summer, when the choice asparagus or new potted plants went on sale. Through the year it sold flowers and Christmas trees, gas and dry goods, maple syrup and blackberry jam, cider and candies, and wines and liquors, in the teeth of several supermarkets, innumerable gas stations, and other shops of every description, all better situated, all struggling in an overtaxed and declining Massachusetts economy.

The secret was partly in the six children (who placed the family deep in the statistics of per capita poverty for long after its arrival) and in the entrepreneurial vision of the owner, which eluded all the charts. Mr. Michael Zabian is the man's name, and he recently bought the biggest office building in the town, a three-story structure made of the same Lee marble as the national capitol building. He owns a large men's clothing store at street level and what amounts to a small shopping center at his original site; and he preens in three-piece suits in the publicity photos at the Chamber of Commerce.

As extraordinary as may seem his decade of achievement, though, two other Lebanese have performed similar marvels in the Berkshires and have opened competing shops in the area. Other immigrants in every American city—Cubans in Miami, Portuguese in Providence and Newark, Filipinos in Seattle, Koreans in Washington, D.C., and New York, Vietnamese in Los Angeles, to mention the more recent crop—have performed comparable feats of commerce, with little help from banks or government or the profession of economics.

Small firms, begun by enterprising men, can rise quickly to play important roles in the national economy. Berkshire Paper Company, for example, was started by Whitmore (Nick) Kelley of Glendale, Massachusetts, as a maker of scratch pads in the rural town of Great Barrington. One of the array of paper manufacturers along the Housatonic River, the firm endured repeated setbacks, which turned into benefits, and, by 1980, it was providing important capital and consumer goods to some of the nation's largest and fastest growing corporations, though Kelley himself had no inherited wealth or outside support.

From the onset, the company's capital consisted mostly of refuse. Like the copper and steel companies thriving on the contents of slag heaps, Berkshire Paper Company employed paper, machinery, and factory space rejected as useless by other companies. Berkshire Paper, in fact, was launched and grew with almost no recourse to resources or capital that was accorded by any value at all in any national economic accounts. Yet the company has now entered the semiconductor industry and holds virtual monopolies in three sophisticated products. The story of its rise from scratch pads to semiconductor products shows the irrelevance of nearly all the indices of economic value and national wealth employed by the statisticians of our economy.

As a sophomore in college, Nick Kelley used to visit his stepfather at Clark-Aiken, a manufacturer of papermaking machine tools in Lee, Massachusetts. Within and around the factory, he noticed random piles of paper and asked his stepfather what was done with them. He was told they were leftovers from machinery tests and would be loaded into a truck and taken to the Lee dump. Kelley asked whether he could have them instead.

He took a handful of paper to an office-supply store, Gowdy's in Pittsfield, and asked the proprietor what such paper was good for. Scratch pads, he was told. After long trial and error, and several visits to a scratch pad factory in the guise of a student, he figured out how to make the pads. With the help of his stepfather he purchased and repaired a broken paper-cutting machine, and he even found a new method of applying glue, replacing the usual paintbrush with a paint roller. He then scoured much of the Northeast for markets and created a thriving scratch pad business that, again with his stepfather's help, even survived Kelley's stint in Southeast Asia during the Vietnam War.

In every case, setbacks led to innovation and renewed achievement. Deprived of paper from Clark-Aiken, he learned how to purchase it from jobbers in New York. Discovering that it cost two cents a pound more in sheets than in rolls (nine cents rather than seven cents), he computed that the two pennies represented a nearly 30 percent hike in cost and determined to contrive a sheeter out of old equipment. Finally, his worst setback drove him out of the scratch pad business altogether and allowed him to greatly expand his company.

Attempting to extend his marketing effort to Boston, Kelley approached the buyer for a large office-supply firm. The buyer said he doubted that Kelley could meet the competition. Kelley demanded to know how anyone could sell them for less, when the raw materials alone cost some fourteen cents a pound, and he sold the pads for eighteen cents. He went off to investigate his rival, a family firm run by Italians in Somerville. Kelley found a factory in an old warehouse, also filled with old equipment, but organized even more ingeniously than Kelley's own. He had to acknowledge that the owner was "the best." "He had me beat." Kelley said, "I decided then and there to go out of scratch pad manufacturing." Instead he resolved to buy pads from the Somerville factory and use his own marketing skills to sell them. He also purchased printing equipment and began adding value to the pads by printing specified lines and emblems on them.

This effort led to a request from Schweitzer, a large paper firm in the Berkshires, that Kelley print up legal pads, and then later, in a major breakthrough, that he cut up some tea bag paper that the Schweitzer machines could not handle. Although Kelley had only the most crude cutting machinery, he said sure, he could process tea bags. He took a pile of thin paper and spent several days and nights at work on it, destroying a fourth of the sheets before his machine completely jammed and pressed several of the layers together so tightly that he found he could easily cut them. This accident gave Kelley a reputation as a worker of small miracles with difficult and specialized papermaking tasks, and the large companies in the area began channeling their most difficult production problems to him.

These new assignments eventually led to three significant monopolies for the small Berkshire firm. One was in making women's fingernail mending tissue (paper with long fibers that adhere to the nail when it is polished) for cosmetic firms from Avon to Revlon. Another was in manufacturing facial blotting tissue (paper that cleans up dirt and makeup without rubbing) for such companies as Mary Kaye and Bonne Belle. His third and perhaps most important project, though —a task that impelled Kelley to pore endlessly through the literature of semiconductor electronics, trafficking in such concepts as microns (one-thousandth of a centimeter) and angstroms (one thousandth of a micron)—was production of papers for use in the manufacture of microprocessors and other semiconductor devices. This required not only the creation of papers sufficiently lint free to wrap a silicon wafer in (without dislodging an electron), but also a research effort to define for the companies precisely what impurities and "glitches" might remain. Kelley now provides this paper, along with the needed information, to all leading semiconductor companies, from National Semiconductor to Intel and Motorola, and he continues research to perfect his product.

Throughout his career, Kelley had demonstrated that faith and imagination are the most important capital goods in the American economy, that wealth is a product less of money than of mind.

The official measures miss all such sources of wealth. When Heilbroner and Thurow claim that 25 percent of American households owned zero net wealth in 1969, they are speaking of families that held above 5 billion dollars' worth of automobiles, 16 billion dollars of other consumer durables, such as washers and television sets, 11 billion dollars' worth of housing (about one-third had cars and 90 percent TVs), as well as rights in Medicaid, social security, housing, education, and other governmental benefits. They commanded many billions of dollars' worth of human capital, some of it rather depreciated by age and some by youthful irresponsibilities (most of these poor households consisted either of single people or abandoned mothers and their offspring). Their net worth was zero, because their debts exceeded their calculable worth. Yet some 80 percent of these people who were poor in 1969 escaped poverty within two years, only to be replaced in the distributions by others too young, too old, too improvident, or too beset with children to manage a positive balance in their asset accounts.

Now it may be appropriate to exclude from the accounting such items as rights in government welfare and transfer programs, which often destroy as much human worth as they create. But the distribution tables also miss the assets of the greatest ultimate value. For example, they treated as an increment of poverty, bereft of net worth, the explosive infusion of human capital that arrived on our shores from Lebanon in the guise of an unlettered family.

Families of zero wealth built America. Many of the unincorporated businesses that have gained some 500 billion dollars in net value since World War II (six times more than all the biggest corporations combined) were started in households of zero assets according to the usual accounts. The conception of a huge and unnegotiable gap between poverty and wealth is a myth. In the Berkshires, Zabian moving up passed many scions of wealth on their way down....

In the second tier of wealth-holders, in which each member would average nearly 2 million dollars net worth in 1970 dollars, 71 percent reported no inherited assets at all, and only 14 percent reported substantial inheritance. Even in the top group of multimillionaires, 31 percent received no inherited assets, and 9 percent only small legacies. Other studies indicate that among the far larger and collectively more important group of wealth-holders of more than $60,000 in 1969, 85 percent of the families had emerged since 1953. With a few notable exceptions, which are always in the news, fast movement up or down in two generations has been the fate of the American rich....

In attacking the rich, tax authorities make great use of the concept of "unearned income," which means the returns from money earned earlier, heavily taxed, then saved or invested. Inheritances receive special attention, since they represent undemocratic transfers and concentrations of power. But they also extend the time horizons of the economy (that is, business), and retard the destruction of capital. That inheritance taxes are too high is obvious from the low level of revenue they collect and the huge industry of tax avoidance they sustain. But politically these levies have long been regarded as too attractive to forgo at a time of hostility toward the rich.

Nonetheless, some of the most catalytic wealth in America is "unearned." A few years before Michael Zabian arrived on our shores, Peter Sprague, now his Berkshire neighbor, inherited 400,000 dollars, largely from the sale of Sprague Electric Company stock. Many heirs of similar legacies have managed to lose most of it in a decade or so. But Sprague set out on a course that could lose it much faster. He decided on a career in venture capital. To raise the odds against him still further, he eventually chose to specialize in companies that faced bankruptcy and lacked other sources of funds.

His first venture was a chicken hatchery in Iran, which taught him the key principles of entrepreneurship—chiefly that nothing happens as one envisions it in theory. The project had been based on the use of advanced Ralston-Purina technology, widely tested in Latin America, to tap the rapidly growing poultry markets of the Middle East. The first unexpected discovery was two or three feet of snow; no one had told him that it *snowed* in Iran. Snow ruined most of the Ralston-Purina equipment. A second surprise was chicanery (and sand) in the chicken feed business. "You end up buying two hundred pounds of stone for every hundred pounds of grain." But after some seven years of similar setbacks, and a growing capital of knowledge, Sprague began to make money in Iran; growing a million trees fertilized with chicken manure, cultivating mushrooms in abandoned ice houses, and winding up with the largest cold storage facilities in the country. The company has made a profit through most of the seventies.

In 1964, three years after starting his Iranian operations, Sprague moved in on a failing electronics company called National Semiconductor. Sprague considered the situation for a week, bought a substantial stake, and became its chairman. The firm is now in the vanguard of the world-wide revolution in semiconductor technology and has been one of America's fastest growing firms, rising from 300 employees when Sprague joined it to 34,000 in 1980.

Also in the mid-sixties Sprague bought several other companies, including the now fashionable Energy Resources, and rescued Design Research from near bankruptcy (the firm finally folded in 1976). In 1969, he helped found Auton Computing Company, a firm still thriving in the business of detecting and analyzing stress in piping systems in nuclear and other power plants, and in 1970 he conducted a memorably resourceful and inventive but finally unsuccessful Republican campaign for the New York City congressional seat then held by Edward Koch....

He then entered the latest phase of his career rescuing collapsing companies. A sports car buff, he indicated to some friends an interest in reviving Aston-Martin, which had gone out of business six months earlier, in mid-1974. Arriving in England early in 1975 with a tentative plan to investigate the possibilities, he was besieged by reporters and TV cameras. Headlines blared: MYSTERY

YANK FINANCIER TO SAVE ASTON MARTIN. Eventually he did, and the company is now securely profitable....

A government counterpart of Sprague's investment activity was Wedgewood Benn's National Enterprise Board in England, which spent some 8 billion dollars attempting to save various British companies by drowning them in money. Before Sprague arrived in England Benn had adamantly refused to invest in Aston-Martin—dismissing the venerable firm as a hopeless case—and instead subsidized a large number of other companies, most of which, unlike Aston, still lose money, and some of which ended up bankrupt. The British, however, did find 104 million dollars—fifty times more than Sprague had to invest in Aston-Martin—to use in luring John DeLorean's American luxury car project to Northern Ireland and poured 47.8 million dollars into the effort to create Ininos, a British nationalized semiconductor firm that has yet to earn any money and technologically remains well in the wake of Sprague's concern. With 400,000 dollars inheritance and his charismatic skills, Sprague has revived many times more companies than Wedgewood Benn with the British Treasury. One entrepreneur with energy, resolution, and charisma could turn 400,000 dollars into a small fortune for himself and a bonanza for the economy, accomplishing more than any number of committee-bound foundations, while a government agency usually requires at least 400,000 dollars to so much as open an office.

Nonetheless, considering the sometimes unedifying spectacle of the humpty-dumpty heirs of wealth—and often focusing on the most flamboyant and newsworthy consumers of cocaine and spouses—it is all too easy to forget that the crucial role of the rich in a capitalist economy is not to entertain and titillate the classes below, but to invest: to provide unencumbered and unbureaucratized cash. The broad class of rich does, in fact, perform this role. Only a small portion of their money is consumed. Most of it goes to productive facilities that employ labor and supply goods to consumers. The rich remain the chief source of discretionary capital in the economy.

These are the funds available for investment outside the largely sterile channels of institutional spending. This is the money that escapes the Keynesian trap of compounded risk, created by the fact that a bank, like an entrepreneur, may lose most of its investment if an enterprise fails, but only the entrepreneur can win the large possible payoff that renders the risk worthwhile. Individuals with cash comprise the wild card—the mutagenic germ—in capitalism, and it is relatively risky investments that ultimately both reseed the economy and unseat the rich....

The risk-bearing role of the rich cannot be performed so well by anyone else. The benefits of capitalism still depend on capitalists. The other groups on the pyramid of wealth should occasionally turn from the spectacles of consumption long enough to see the adventure on the frontiers of the economy above them —an adventure not without its note of nobility, since its protagonist families will almost all eventually fail and fall in the redeeming struggle of the free economy.

In America the rich should not be compared to the Saudi Arabians or be seen in the image of Midas in his barred cage of gold.... Under capitalism, when it is working, the rich have the anti-Midas touch, transforming timorous liquidity and unused savings into factories and office towers, farms and laboratories, orchestras and museums—turning gold into goods and jobs and art. That is the function of the rich: fostering opportunities for the classes below them in the continuing drama of the creation of wealth and progress....

THE NATURE OF POVERTY

To get a grip in the problems of poverty, one should also forget the idea of overcoming inequality by redistribution. Inequality may even grow at first as poverty declines. To lift the incomes of the poor, it will be necessary to increase the rates of investment, which in turn will tend to enlarge the wealth, if not the consumption, of the rich. The poor, as they move into the work force and acquire promotions, will raise their incomes by a greater percentage than the rich; but the upper classes will gain by greater absolute amounts, and the gap between the rich and the poor may grow. All such analyses are deceptive in the long run, however, because they imply a static economy in which the *numbers* of the rich and the middle class are not growing.

In addition, inequality may be favored by the structure of a modern economy as it interacts with demographic changes. When the division of labor becomes more complex and refined, jobs grow more specialized; and the increasingly specialized workers may win greater rents for their rare expertise, causing their incomes to rise relative to common labor. This tendency could be heightened by a decline in new educated entrants to the work force, predictable through the 1990s, and by an enlarged flow of immigration, legal and illegal. Whatever the outcome of these developments, an effort to take income from the rich, thus diminishing their investment, and to give it to the poor, thus reducing their work incentives, is sure to cut American productivity, limit job opportunities, and perpetuate poverty.

Among the beneficiaries of inequality will be the formerly poor. Most students of the problems of poverty consider the statistics of success of previous immigrant groups and see a steady incremental rise over the years, accompanied by the progressive acquisition of educational credentials and skills. Therefore, programs are proposed that foster a similar slow and incremental ascent by the currently poor. But the incremental vision of the escape from poverty is mostly false, based on a simple illusion of statistical aggregates that conceals everything important about upward mobility. Previous immigrants earned money first by working hard; their children got the education.

The rising average incomes of previous groups signify not the smooth progress of hundreds of thousands of civil-service or bureaucratic careers, but the rapid business and professional successes of a relative few, who brought their families along and inspired others to follow. Poor people tend to rise up rapidly and will be damaged by a policy of redistribution that will always hit new and unsheltered income and wealth much harder than the elaborately concealed and fortified winnings of the established rich. The poor benefit from a dynamic economy full of unpredictable capital gains (they have few capital losses!) more than from a stratified system governed by educational and other credentials that the rich can buy.

The only dependable route from poverty is always work, family, and faith. The first principle is that in order to move up, the poor must not only work, they must work harder than the classes above them. Every previous generation of the lower class has made such efforts. But the current poor, white even more than black, are refusing to work hard. Irwin Garfinkel and Robert Haveman, authors of an ingenious and sophisticated study of what they call *Earning Capacity Utilization Rates,* have calculated the degree to which various income groups use their opportunities —how hard they work outside the home. This study shows that, for several understandable reasons, the current poor work substantially less, for fewer hours and weeks a year, and earn less in proportion to their age, education, and other credentials (even *after* correcting the figures for unemployment, disability, and presumed discrimination) than either their predecessors in American cities or those now above them on the income scale (the study was made at the federally funded Institute for Research on Poverty at the University of Wisconsin and used data from the census and the Michigan longitudinal survey). The findings lend important confirmation to the growing body of evidence that work effort is the crucial unmeasured variable in American productivity and income distribution, and that current welfare and other subsidy programs substantially reduce work. The poor choose leisure not because of moral weakness, but because they are paid to do so.

A program to lift by transfers and preferences the incomes of less diligent groups is politically divisive—and very unlikely—because it incurs the bitter resistance of the real working class. In addition, such an effort breaks the psychological link between effort and reward, which is crucial to long-run upward mobility. Because effective work consists not in merely fulfilling the requirements of labor contracts but "in putting out" with alertness and emotional commitment, workers have to understand and feel deeply that what they are given depends on what they give—that they must supply work in order to demand goods. Parents and schools must inculcate this idea in their children both by instruction and example. Nothing is more deadly to achievement than the belief that effort will not be rewarded, that the world is a bleak and discriminatory place in which only the predatory and the specially preferred can get ahead. Such a view in the home discourages the work effort in school that shapes earnings capacity afterward. As with so many aspects of human performance, work effort begins in family experiences, and its sources can be best explored through an examination of family structure.

Indeed, after work the second principle of upward mobility is the maintenance of monogamous marriage and family. Adjusting for discrimination against women and for child-care responsibilities, the Wisconsin study indicates that married men work between two and one-third and four times harder than married women, and more than twice as hard as female family heads. The work effort of married men increases with their age, credentials, education, job experience, and birth of children, while the work effort of married women steadily declines. Most important in judging the impact of marriage, husbands work 50 percent harder than bachelors of comparable age, education, and skills.

The effect of marriage, thus, is to increase the work effort of men by about half. Since men have higher earnings capacity to begin with, and since the female capacity-utilization figures would be even lower without an adjustment for discrimination, it is manifest that the maintenance of families is the key factor in reducing poverty.

Once a family is headed by a woman, it is almost impossible for it to greatly raise its income even if the woman is highly educated and trained and she hires day-care or domestic help. Her family responsibilities and distractions tend to prevent her from the kind of all-out commitment that is necessary for the full use of earning power. Fewer women with children make earning money the top priority in their lives.

A married man, on the other hand, is spurred by the claims of family to channel his otherwise disruptive male aggressions into his performance as a provider for a wife and children. These sexual differences alone, which manifest themselves in all societies known to anthropology, dictate that the first priority of any serious program against poverty is to strengthen the male role in poor families.

These narrow measures of work effort touch on just part of the manifold interplay between family and poverty. Edward Banfield's *The Unheavenly City* defines the lower class largely by its lack of an orientation to the future. Living from day to day and from hand to mouth, lower class individuals are unable to plan or save or keep a job. Banfield gives the impression that short-time horizons are a deep-seated psychological defect afflicting hundreds of thousands of the poor.

There is no question that Banfield puts his finger on a crucial problem of the poor and that he develops and documents his theme in an unrivaled classic of disci-

plined social science. But he fails to show how millions of men, equally present oriented, equally buffeted by impulse and blind to the future, have managed to become farseeing members of the middle classes. He also fails to explain how millions of apparently future-oriented men can become dissolute followers of the sensuous moment, neglecting their jobs, dissipating their income and wealth, pursuing a horizon no longer than the most time-bound of the poor.

What Banfield is in fact describing in his lower-class category is largely the temperament of single, divorced, and separated men. The key to lower-class life in contemporary America is that unrelated individuals, as the census calls them, are so numerous and conspicuous that they set the tone for the entire community. Their congregation in ghettos, moreover, magnifies greatly their impact on the black poor, male and female (though, as Banfield rightly observes, this style of instant gratification is chiefly a male trait).

The short-sighted outlook of poverty stems largely from the breakdown of family responsibilities among fathers. The lives of the poor, all too often, are governed by the rhythms of tension and release that characterize the sexual experience of young single men. Because female sexuality, as it evolved over the millennia, is psychologically rooted in the bearing and nurturing of children, women have long horizons within their very bodies, glimpses of eternity within their wombs. Civilized society is dependent upon the submission of the short-term sexuality of young men to the extended maternal horizons of women. This is what happens in monogamous marriage; the man disciplines his sexuality and extends it into the future through the womb of a woman.

The woman gives him access to his children, otherwise forever denied him; and he gives her the product of his labor, otherwise dissipated on temporary pleasures. The woman gives him a unique link to the future and a vision of it; he gives her faithfulness and a commitment to a lifetime of hard work. If work effort is the first principle of overcoming poverty, marriage is the prime source of upwardly mobile work.

It is love that changes the short horizons of youth and poverty into the long horizons of marriage and career. When marriages fail, the man often returns to the more primitive rhythms of singleness. On the average, his income drops by one-third and he shows a far higher propensity for drink, drugs, and crime. But when marriages in general hold firm and men in general love and support their children, Banfield's lower-class style changes into middle-class futurity....

Adolph A. Berle, contemplating the contrast between prosperous and dominantly Mormon Utah and indigent, chiefly secular Nevada next door, concluded his study of the American economy with the rather uneconomic notion of a "transcendental margin," possibly kin to Leibenstein's less glamorous X-efficiency and Christopher Jencks's timid "luck." Lionel Tiger identifies this source of unexplained motion as "evolution-ary optimism—the biology of hope," and finds it in the human genes. Ivan Light, in his fascinating exploration of the sources of difference between entrepreneurial Orientals and less venturesome blacks, resolved on "the spirit of moral community." Irving Kristol, ruminating on the problems of capitalism, sees the need for a "transcendental justification." They are all addressing, in one way or another, the third principle of upward mobility, and that is faith.

Faith in man, faith in the future, faith in the rising returns of giving, faith in the mutual benefits of trade, faith in the providence of God are all essential to successful capitalism. All are necessary to sustain the spirit of work and enterprise against the setbacks and frustrations it inevitably meets in a fallen world; to inspire trust and cooperation in an economy where they will often be betrayed; to encourage the forgoing of present pleasures in the name of a future that may well go up in smoke; to promote risk and initiative in a world where the rewards all vanish unless others join the game. In order to give without the assurance of return, in order to save without the certainty of future value, in order to work beyond the requirements of the job, one has to have confidence in a higher morality: a law of compensations beyond the immediate and distracting struggles of existence.

NO

William Ryan

EQUALITY

It should not surprise us ... that the clause "all men are created equal" can be interpreted in quite different ways. Today, I would like to suggest, there are two major lines of interpretation: one, which I will call the "Fair Play" perspective, stresses the individual's right to pursue happiness and obtain resources; the other, which I will call the "Fair Shares" viewpoint, emphasizes the right of access to resources as a necessary condition for equal rights to life, liberty and happiness.

Almost from the beginning, and most apparently during the past century or so, the Fair Play viewpoint has been dominant in America. This way of looking at the problem of equality stresses that each person should be equally free from all but the most minimal necessary interferences with his right to "pursue happiness." ... Given significant differences of interest, of talents, and of personalities, it is assumed that individuals will be variably success- ful in their pursuits and that society will consequently propel to its surface what Jefferson called a "natural aristocracy of talent," men who because of their skills, intellect, judgment, character, will assume the leading positions in society that had formerly been occupied by the hereditary aristocracy— that is, by men who had simply been born into positions of wealth and power. In contemporary discussions, the emphasis on the individual's unen- cumbered pursuit of his own goals is summed up in the phrase "equality of opportunity." Given at least an approximation of this particular version of equality, Jefferson's principle of a natural aristocracy—spoken of most com- monly today as the idea of "meritocracy"—will insure that the ablest, most meritorious, ambitious, hardworking, and talented individuals will acquire the most, achieve the most, and become the leaders of society. The relative inequality that this implies is seen not only as tolerable, but as fair and just. Any effort to achieve what proponents of Fair Play refer to as "equality of results" is seen as unjust, artificial, and incompatible with the more basic principle of equal opportunity.

The Fair Shares perspective, as compared with the Fair Play idea, concerns itself much more with equality of rights and of access, particularly the implicit rights to a reasonable share of society's resources, sufficient to sustain life at a decent standard of humanity and to preserve liberty and freedom from compulsion. Rather than focusing on the individual's pursuit of his own happiness, the advocate of Fair Shares is more committed to the principle that all members of the society obtain a reasonable portion of the goods that society produces. From his vantage point, the overzealous pursuits of private goals on the part of some individuals might even have to be bridled. From this it follows, too, that the proponent of Fair Shares has a different view of what constitutes fairness and justice, namely, an appropriate distribution throughout society of sufficient means for sustaining life and preserving liberty.

So the equality dilemma is built into everyday life and thought in America; it comes with the territory. Rights, equality of rights—or at least interpretations of them—clash. The conflict between Fair Play and Fair Shares is real, deep, and serious, and it cannot be easily resolved. Some calculus of priorities must be established. Rules must be agreed upon. It is possible to imagine an almost endless number of such rules:

- Fair Shares until everyone has enough; Fair Play for the surplus
- Fair Play until the end of a specified "round," then "divvy up" Fair Shares, and start Fair Play all over again (like a series of Monopoly games)
- Fair Play all the way, except that no one may actually be allowed to starve to death.

The last rule is, I would argue, a perhaps bitter parody of the prevailing one in the United States. Equality of opportunity and the principle of meritocracy are the clearly dominant interpretation of "all men are created equal," mitigated by the principle (usually defined as charity rather than equality) that the weak, the helpless, the deficient will be more or less guaranteed a sufficient share to meet their minimal requirements for sustaining life.

FAIR PLAY AND UNEQUAL SHARES

The Fair Play concept is dominant in America partly because it puts forth two most compelling ideas: the time-honored principle of distributive justice and the cherished image of America as the land of opportunity. At least since Aristotle, the principle that rewards should accrue to each person in proportion of his worth or merit has seemed to many persons one that warrants intuitive acceptance. The more meritorious person —merit being some combination of ability and constructive effort—*deserves* a greater reward. From this perspective it is perfectly consistent to suppose that *unequal* shares could well be *fair* shares; moreover, within such a framework, it is very unlikely indeed that equal shares could be fair shares, since individuals are not equally meritorious.

The picture of America as the land of opportunity is also very appealing. The idea of a completely open society, where each person is entirely free to advance in his or her particular fashion, to become whatever he or she is inherently capable of becoming, with the sky the limit, is a universally inspiring one. This is a picture that makes most Americans proud.

But is it an accurate picture? Are these two connected ideas—unlimited opportunity and differential rewards fairly distributed according to differences in individual merit—congruent with the facts of life? The answer, of course, is yes and no. Yes, we see some vague congruence here and there—some evidence of upward mobility, some kinds of inequalities that can appear to be justifiable. But looking at the larger picture, we must answer with an unequivocal "No!" The fairness of unequal shares and the reality of equal opportunity are wishes and dreams, resting on a mushy, floating, purely imaginary foundation. Let us look first at the question of unequal shares.

Fair Players and Fair Sharers disagree about the meaning, but not about the fact, of unequal shares and of the significant degree of inequality of wealth and income and of everything that goes along with wealth and income—general life conditions, health, education, power, access to services and to cultural and recreational amenities, and so forth. Fair Sharers say that this fact is the very *essence* of inequality, while Fair Players define the inequalities of condition that Fair Sharers decry as obvious and necessary *consequences* of equality of opportunity. Fair Players argue, furthermore, that such inequalities are for the most part roughly proportional to inequalities of merit....

There [are] some patterns of ownership that are reasonably consistent with the Fair Play paradigm. In the distribution of such items as automobiles, televisions, appliances, even homes, there are significant inequalities, but they are not extreme. And if the Fair Player is willing to concede that many inequities remain to be rectified—and most Fair Players are quite willing, even eager, to do so—these inequalities can, perhaps, be swallowed.

It is only when we begin to look at larger aspects of wealth and income—aspects that lie beyond our personal vision—that the extreme and, I believe, gross inequalities of condition that prevail in America become evident. Let us begin with income. How do we divide up the shares of what we produce annually? In 1977 about one American family in ten

had an income of less than $5,000 and about one in ten had an income of $35,000 a year and up ("up" going all the way to some unknown number of millions). It is difficult to see how anyone could view such a dramatic disparity as fair and justified. One struggles to imagine any measure of merit, any sign of membership in a "natural aristocracy," that would manifest itself in nature in such a way that one sizable group of persons would "have" eight or ten or twenty times more of it —whatever "it" might be—than another sizeable group has.

Income in the United States is concentrated in the hands of a few: one-fifth of the population gets close to half of all the income, and the top 5 percent of this segment get almost one-fifth of it. The bottom three-fifths of the population—that is, the majority of us—receive not much more than one-third of all income....

As we move [to] the reality of living standards, the pertinent questions are: How much do people spend and on what? How do the groups at the different tables, that is, different income groups in America, live? Each year the Bureau of Labor Statistics [BLS] publishes detailed information on the costs of maintaining three different living standards, which it labels "lower," "intermediate," and "higher"; in less discreet days it used to call the budgets "minimum," "adequate," and "comfortable." The adequate, intermediate budget is generally considered to be an index of a reasonably decent standard of living. It is on this budget, for example, that newspapers focus when they write their annual stories on the BLS budgets.

To give some sense of what is considered an "intermediate" standard of living, let me provide some details about this budget as it is calculated for a family of four—mother, father, eight-year-old boy, and thirteen-year-old girl. As of the autumn of 1978, for such a family the budget allows $335 a month for housing, which includes rent or mortgage, heat and utilities, household furnishings, and all household operations. It allows $79 a week for groceries, which extends to cleaning supplies, toothpaste, and the like. It allows $123 a month for transportation, including car payments. It allows $130 a month for clothing, clothing care or cleaning, and all personal-care items.

In his book *The Working Class Majority*, Andrew Levinson cites further details about this budget from a study made by the UAW:

A United Auto Workers study shows just how "modest" that budget is: The budget assumes, for example, that a family will own a toaster that will last for thirty-three years, a refrigerator and a range that will each last for seventeen years, a vacuum cleaner that will last for fourteen years, and a television set that will last for ten years. The budget assumes that a family will buy a two-year-old car and keep it for four years, and will pay for a tune-up once a year, a brake realignment every three years, and front-end alignment every four years.... The budget assumes that the husband will buy one year-round suit every four years... and one topcoat every eight and a half years.... It assumes that the husband will take his wife to the movies once every three months and that one of them will go to the movies alone once a year. The average family's two children are each allowed one movie every four weeks. A total of two dollars and fifty-four cents per person per year is allowed for admission to all other events, from football and baseball games to plays or

concerts.... The budget allows nothing whatever for savings.

This budget, whether labeled intermediate, modest, or adequate, is perhaps more accurately described by those who call it "shabby but respectable."...

In 1978 the income needs by an urban family of four in order to meet even this modest standard of living was $18,622. This is a national average; for some cities the figure was much higher: in Boston, it was $22,117, in metropolitan New York, $21,587, in San Francisco, $19,427. More than *half* of all Americans lived *below* this standard. As for the "minimum" budget (which, by contrast with the "intermediate" budget, allows only $62 rather than $79 for groceries, $174 rather than $335 for housing, $67 rather than $123 for transportation, and $93 rather than $130 for clothing and personal care), the national average cost for an urban family in 1978 was $11,546. Three families out of ten could not afford even *that* standard, and one family in ten had an income below $5,000 which is *less than half enough* to meet minimum standards.

These dramatically *unequal* shares are —it seems to me—clearly *unfair* shares. Twenty million people are desperately poor, an additional forty million don't get enough income to meet the minimal requirements for a decent life, the great majority are just scraping by, a small minority are at least temporarily comfortable, and a tiny handful of persons live at levels of affluence and luxury that most persons cannot even imagine.

The myth that America's income is symmetrically distributed—an outstanding few at the top getting a lot, an inadequate few at the bottom living in poverty, and the rest clustered around the middle—could hardly be more false. The grotesquely lopsided distribution of our yearly production of goods and services is well illustrated by Paul Samuelson's famous image:

A glance at the income distribution in the United States shows how pointed is the income pyramid and how broad its base. "There's always room at the top" is certainly true; this is so because it is hard to get there, not easy. If we make an income pyramid out of a child's blocks, with each layer portraying $1000 of income, the peak would be far higher than the Eiffel Tower, but almost all of us would be within a yard of the ground.

When we move from income to wealth —from what you *get* to what you *own* —the *degree* of concentration makes the income distribution look almost fair by comparison. About one out of every four Americans owns *nothing*. Nothing! In fact, many of them *owe* more than they have. Their "wealth" is actually negative. The persons in the next quarter own about 5 percent of all personal assets. In other words, half of us own 5 percent, the other half own 95 percent. But it gets worse as you go up the scale. Those in the top 6 percent own half of all the wealth. Those in the top 1 percent own one-fourth of all the wealth. Those in the top $1/2$ percent own one-fifth of all the wealth. That's one-half of 1 percent —about one million persons, or roughly 300,000 families.

And even this fantastic picture doesn't tell the whole story, because "assets" include homes, cars, savings accounts, cash value of life insurance policies—the kinds of assets that the very rich don't bother with very much. The very rich put their wealth into the ownership of things that produce more wealth—corporate stocks and bonds, mortgages, notes, and the like. Two-thirds of their wealth is in this form and the top 1 percent owns 60 percent of all that valuable paper. The rest of it is owned by only an additional 10 percent, which means that nine people out of ten own none of it—and, if they're like me, they probably have never seen a real stock certificate in their lives.

America, we are sometimes told, is a nation of capitalists, and it is true that an appreciable minority of its citizens have a bank account here, a piece of land there, along with a few shares of stock. But quantitative differences become indisputably qualitative as one moves from the ownership of ten shares of General Motors to the ownership of ten thousand. There are capitalists, and then there are capitalists. . . .

Another way of grasping the extreme concentration of wealth in our society is to try to imagine what the ordinary person would have if that wealth were evenly distributed rather than clumped and clotted together in huge piles. Assuming that all the personal wealth was divided equally among all the people in the nation, we would find that every one of us, man, woman, and child, would *own* free and clear almost $22,000 worth of goods: $7,500 worth of real estate, $3,500 in cash, and about $5,000 worth of stocks and bonds. For a family of four that would add up to almost $90,000 in assets, including $30,000 equity in a house, about $14,000 in the bank, and about $20,000 worth of stocks and bonds. That much wealth would also bring in an extra $3,000 or $4,000 a year in income.

If you have any doubts about the reality of grossly unequal shares, compare the utopian situation of that imaginary "average" family with your own actual situation. For most of us, the former goes beyond our most optimistic fantasies of competing and achieving and getting ahead. Actually only about ten million persons in the country own as much as that, and, as I suggested before, the majority of us have an *average* of less than $5,000 per family including whatever equity we have in a home, our car and other tangible assets, and perhaps $500 in the bank.

Still another way of thinking about this is to remark that the fortunate few at the top, and their children, are more or less guaranteed an opulent standard of living because of what they own, while the majority of American families are no more than four months' pay away from complete destitution.

All of this, of course, takes place in the wealthiest society the world has ever known. If we extended our horizons further and began to compare the handful of developed, industrial nations with the scores of underdeveloped, not to say "over-exploited," nations, we would find inequalities that are even more glaring and appalling....

THE VULNERABLE MAJORITY

Stripped down to its essentials, the rule of equal opportunity and Fair Play requires only that the best man win. It doesn't necessarily specify the margin of victory, merely the absence of unfair barriers. The practical test of equal opportunity is *social mobility*—do talented and hardworking persons, whatever their backgrounds, actually succeed in rising to higher social and economic positions?

The answer to that of course, is that they do. Remaining barriers of discrimination notwithstanding, it is plain that many persons climb up the social and economic ladder and reach much higher rungs than those their parents attained and than those from which they started. Fair Players prize these fortunate levitations as the ultimate justification of their own perspective and as phenomena that must be protected against any erosion caused by excessive emphasis upon Fair Shares.

It is necessary, then, to look seriously at the question of mobility. Among the questions to be asked are the following:

- How much mobility can we observe? No matter how rigidly hierarchical it might be, every society permits some mobility. How much movement up and down the scale is there in ours?
- How far do the mobile persons move?
- Is mobility evident across the whole social and economic range? Do the very poor stay poor, or do they, too, have an equal chance to rise? Are the very rich likely to slide *down* the ladder very often?

Given our great trove of rags-to-riches mythology, our creed that any child (well, any man-child) can grow up to be president—if not of General Motors, at least of the United States —we clearly assume that our society is an extraordinarily open one. And everyone knows, or has a friend who knows, a millionaire or someone on the way to that envied position: the patient, plodding peddler who transformed his enterprise into a great department store; the eccentric tinkerer in his garage whose sudden insight produced the great invention that everyone had been saving his pennies to buy.

At lesser levels of grandeur, we all know about the son of the illiterate cobbler who is now a wealthy neurosurgeon, the daughter of impoverished immigrants who sits in a professional chair at Vassar or Smith—or even Princeton.

In America social mobility is an unquestioned fact.

But how many sons of illiterate cobblers become physicians, on the other hand, and how many become, at best, literate cobblers? And how many settle for a job on the assembly line or in the sanitation department? And all of those daughters of impoverished immigrants —how many went on to get Ph.D.'s and become professors? Very few. A somewhat larger number may have gone to college and gotten a job teaching sixth grade. But many just finished high school and went to work for an insurance company for a while, until they married the sons of other impoverished immigrants, most of them also tugging at their bootstraps without much result.

About all of these facts there can be little dispute. For most people, there is essentially no social mobility—for them, life consists of rags to rags and riches to riches. Moreover, for the relatively small minority who do rise significantly in the social hierarchy, the *distance* of ascent is relatively short. Such a person may start life operating a drill press and eventually become a foreman or even move into the white-collar world by becoming a payroll clerk or perhaps an accountant. Or he may learn from his father to be a cobbler, save his money, and open a little cobbler shop of his own. He hardly ever starts up a shoe factory. It is the son of the owner of the shoe factory who gets to do that. So there is mobility—it is rather common, but also rather modest, with only an occasional dramatic rise from rags to riches.

To provide some specific numbers, it has been calculated that for a young man born into a family in which the father does unskilled, low-wage manual work, the odds against his rising merely to the point of his becoming a nonmanual white-collar worker are at least three or four to one; the odds against his rising to the highest level and joining the wealthy upper class are almost incalculable. For the son of a middle-level white-collar worker, the odds against his rising to a higher-level professional or managerial occupation are two or three to one. On the other hand, the odds are better than fifty to one that the son of a father with such a high-level occupation will not descend the ladder to a position as an unskilled or semiskilled manual worker. Upward mobility is very limited and usually involves moving only one or two levels up the hierachy....

Finally, we have to look carefully to see that, for all our social mobility, the very rich almost all stay at the top and welcome only a select handful to their ranks. The rich of one generation are almost all children of the rich of the previous generation, partly because more than half of significant wealth is inherited, partly because all the other prerogatives of the wealthy are sufficient to assure a comfortable future for Rockefeller and Du Pont toddlers. It may well take more energy, ingenuity, persistence, and single-mindedness for a rich youngster to achieve poverty than for a poor one to gain wealth.

The dark side of the social-mobility machine is that it is, so to speak, a reciprocating engine—when some parts go up, others must come *down*. Downward mobility is an experience set aside almost exclusively for the nonrich, and it is grossly destructive of the quality of life.

The majority of American families are constantly vulnerable to economic disaster—to downward mobility to the point where they lack sufficient income to meet their most basic needs—food, shelter, clothing, heat, and medical care. Included in this vulnerable majority, who have at least an even chance of spending some portion of their lives in economic distress, are perhaps three out of four Americans.

This does not accord with the common view of poverty. We have been given to understand that "the poor" form a fairly permanent group in our society and that those who are above the poverty line are safe and perhaps even on their way up. This thought is comforting but false. A number of small studies have raised serious questions about this static picture; recently we have received massive evidence from one of the most comprehensive social and economic investigations ever mounted. This study, under the direction of James Morgan, has traced the life trajectories of five thousand American families over a period, to date, of eight years, concentrating on the nature of and possible explanations for economic progress or the lack of it.

Five Thousand American Families indicates that over a period of eight years, although only one in ten families is poor during *every one* of the eight years, over one-third of American families are poor for *at least one* of those eight years.

From the Michigan study, the census data, and other sources, we can readily estimate that a few are permanently protected against poverty because they *own things*—property, stocks, bonds—that provide them with income sufficient to meet their needs whether or not they work or have any other source of income. Another small minority of Americans own only *rights*—virtual job tenure, a guaranteed pension—but these rights also give effective protection against poverty. At the bottom of the pyramid, there are a few who might be called per-

manently poor. Between these extremes come persons whose income is primarily or wholly dependent on salaries or wages. This is the core of the vulnerable majority—not poor now, but in jeopardy. In any given year one family out of six in that vulnerable majority will suffer income deficit, will go through a year of poverty. Over a five-year period nearly half of them will be poor for at least one year. If we project this over ten or fifteen years, we find that well over half will be poor for at least one year. On adding this group to the permanently poor, we arrive at the startling fact that a *substantial majority* of American families will experience poverty at some point during a relatively short span of time.

Several elements in our socioeconomic structure help account for income deficiency. Let us consider, for example, those who are more or less permanently poor. Why do they stay mired in poverty? The answer in most cases is simple: they remain poor because it has been deliberately *decided* that they should remain poor. They are, for the most part, dependent on what we impersonally call transfer payments—mostly Social Security, some private pensions, some welfare. To put it as simply as possible, these transfer payments are not enough to live on, not enough to meet basic needs. Countrywide, public assistance payments provide income that is only 75 percent of what is required to pay for sufficient food, adequate shelter, clothing, and fuel; the percentage decreases as the size of the family increases. For very large families, welfare provides only half of what is needed to live on. The poverty of the permanently poor is thus easily explained by the fact that the income assistance that we provide them is simply too small.

For the vulnerables, however, economic hills and valleys are created by the job situation. Economic status, progress, and deficit are determined by what social scientists call "family composition and participation in the labor force." In plain English that means they depend on the number of mouths to be fed and on the number of people working—that is, on how many children there are, on whether both wife and husband are working, and so forth. But this, of course, is only synonymous with the natural ebb and flow in the life of almost any family. It should not be an economic catastrophe, after all, when people get married and have children.... So, children are born and they grow up, sometimes work awhile, and then leave home. One parent, usually the mother, is tied to the home during some periods, free to work during others. A family member finds a job, loses a job, gets sick or injured, sometimes dies tragically young. All of these events are the landmarks in the life of a family, most of them are common enough, and some are inevitable sources of joy or sorrow. Yet these ordinary occurrences have a drastic impact on families, because they lead to greater changes in one or both sides of the ratio of income and needs. In most cases they are direct causes of most of the economic progress or distress that a family experiences....

WHY NOT FAIR SHARES?

I have been trying to show, in a preliminary way, that the beliefs and assumptions associated with the Fair Play rendering of equality are quite inconsistent with the facts of life as we know them, although its principles are paraded as a version—in fact, the correct version—of equality and are widely accepted as quite plausible, indeed obvious. To the extent that there is any competition between Fair Players and Fair Sharers for the mind of the public, the former usually win hands down. Yet, as we have seen, the Fair Play idea appears to condone and often to endorse conditions of inequality that are blatant and, I would say, quite indefensible. Such equal opportunities for advancing in life as do exist are darkly overshadowed by the many head starts and advantages provided to the families of wealth and privilege. As for the workings out of the solemnly revered principles of meritocracy, they are—like many objects of reverence—invisible to most persons and rarely discernible in the lives of the vulnerable majority of us. Barely two centuries after its most persuasive formulation, the Fair Play concept of equality has shriveled to little more than the assertion that a few thousand individuals are fully licensed to gather and retain wealth at the cost of the wasteful, shameful, and fraudulent impoverishment of many millions....

A Fair Shares egalitarian would hold that all persons have a *right* to a reasonable share of material necessities, a right to do constructive work, and a right of unhindered access to education, to gratifying social memberships, to participation in the life and decisions of the community, and to all the major amenities of society. This principle doesn't lend itself to the calculation of "equal results," and it certainly doesn't imply a demand for uniformity of resources. No one in his right mind would entertain some cockeyed scheme in which everyone went to school for precisely thirteen years; consumed each year 19,800 grams of protein and 820,000 calories; read four works of fiction and six of non-fiction; attended two concerts, one opera, and four basketball games, and voted in 54 percent of the elections.... Unfortunately, many persons who are upset about the present state of inequality tend to talk vaguely about the need "to redistribute income" or even "to redistribute wealth." When such ideas are tossed out without consideration of the fact that they will then be discussed within the framework of Fair Play, we have a surefire prescription for disaster. From that viewpoint, which is, after all, the dominant one in America, such ideas appear both extremely inpracticable and not particularly desirable. For example, are we to take redistribution of income to mean that every individual will somehow receive the same compensation, no matter what work he or she does or whether he works at all? And would we try to redistribute wealth by giving every person, say, a share of stock in GM, Exxon, IBM, and the local paper-bag factory? Hardly. Fair Players can make mincemeat of such silly ideas, and they love to pretend that that's what Fair Share egalitarians are proposing. I don't think many of us have strong objections to inequality of monetary income as such. A modest range, even as much as three or four to one, could, I suspect, be tolerable to almost everybody. (And one would suppose that, given some time for adjustment and perhaps some counseling and training in homemaking and budgeting skills, those who now get a lot more could learn to scrape by on something like eight or nine hundred dollars a week.) The current range in annual incomes—from perhaps $3,000 to some unknown number of *millions*—is, however, excessive and intolerable, impossible to justify rationally, and plain inhuman. The problem of wealth is more fundamental. Most of the evils of inequality derive

from the reality that a few thousand families control almost all the necessities and amenities of life, indeed the very conditions of life. The rest of us, some 200 million, have to pay tribute to them if we want even a slight illusion of life, liberty, and the pursuit of happiness. But the solution to this problem is certainly not simply the fragmentation of ownership into tiny units of individual property. This naive solution has been well criticized by serious proponents of equality, perhaps most gracefully by R. H. Tawney:

> It is not the division of the nation's income into eleven million fragments, to be distributed, without further ado, like cake as a school treat, among its eleven million families. It is, on the contrary, the pooling of its surplus resources by means of taxation, and use of the funds thus obtained to make accessible to all, irrespective of their income, occupation, or social position, the conditions of civilization which, in the absence of such measures, can only be enjoyed by the rich....
>
> It can generalize, by collective action, advantages associated in the past with ownership of property.... It can secure that, in addition to the payments made to them for their labour, its citizens enjoy a social income, which is provided from the surplus remaining after the necessary cost of production and expansion have been met, and is available on equal terms for all its members....

The central problem of inequality in America—the concentration of wealth and power in the hands of a tiny minority —cannot, then, be solved, as Tawney makes clear, by any schemes that rest on the process of long division. We need, rather, to accustom ourselves to a different method of holding resources, namely, holding them in common, to be *shared* amongst us all—not divided up and parceled out, but shared. That is the basic principle of Fair Shares, and it is not at all foreign to our daily experience. To cite a banal example, we share the air we breathe, although some breathe in penthouses or sparsely settled suburbs and others in crowded slums. In a similar fashion, we share such resources as public parks and beaches, although, again, we cannot overlook the gross contrast between the size of vast private waterfront holdings and the tiny outlets to the oceans that are available to the public. No one in command of his senses would go to a public beach, count the number of people there, and suggest subdividing the beach into thirty-two-by-twenty-six-foot lots, one for each person. Such division would not only be unnecessary, it would ruin our enjoyment. If I were assigned to Lot No. 123, instead of enjoying the sun and going for a swim, I might sit and watch that sneaky little kid with the tin shovel to make sure he did not extend the sand castle onto my beach. We own it in common; it's *public*; and we just plain *share* it.

We use this mode of owning and sharing all the time and never give it a second thought. We share public schools, streets, libraries, sewers, and other public property and services, and we even think of them as being "free" (many libraries even have the word in their names). Nor do we need the "There's no such thing as a free lunch" folks reminding us that they're not really free; everyone is quite aware that taxes support them. We don't feel any need to divide up all the books in the library among all the citizens. And there's no sensible way of looking at the use of libraries in terms of "equal opportunity" as opposed to "equal results." Looking at the public library as a tiny example of what Fair Shares equality is all about, we note that it satisfies the principle of equal access if no one is *excluded* from the library on the irrelevant grounds of not owning enough or of having spent twelve years in school learning how not to read. And "equal results" is clearly quite meaningless. Some will withdraw many books; some, only a few; some will be so unwise as to never even use the facility.

The *idea* of sharing, then, which is the basic idea of equality, and the *practice* of sharing, which is the basic methodology of Fair Shares equality, are obviously quite familiar and acceptable to the American people in many areas of life. There are many institutions, activities, and services that the great majority believe should be located in the public sector, collectively owned and paid for, and equally accessible to everyone. We run into trouble when we start proposing the same system of ownership for the resources that the wealthy have corralled for themselves....

Most of the good things of life have either been provided free by God (nature, if you prefer) or have been produced by the combined efforts of many persons, sometimes many generations. As all share in the making, so all should share in the use and the enjoyment. This may help convey a bit of what the Fair Shares idea of equality is all about.

POSTSCRIPT

Is Economic Inequality Beneficial to Society?

The spirit of personal initiative seems to be alive in the hearts of Michael Zabian, the vegetable stand owner, Nick Kelley, the scratch pad dealer, and Peter Sprague, the venture capitalist, whose success stories are related by Gilder. But how typical are their experiences? How much do they teach us about American capitalism today, which is dominated by multinational corporations? There are also stories about the government's bailouts of Lockheed and Chrysler, enterprising corporate raiders weakening or destroying sound corporations, and how the spirit of personal initiative created the recent savings and loan scandal. And what about the issues of fairness raised by Ryan? Perhaps the basic question is, Can the system be made more just, fair, and humane without squelching enterprise and drive?

Stratification and social mobility are two central concerns of sociology, and they are addressed by a large literature. Two classic publications on stratification theory based on research on census statistics are Peter M. Blau and Otis Dudley Duncan's *The American Occupational Structure* (John Wiley & Sons, 1967) and Robert M. Hauser and David L. Featherman's *The Process of Social Stratification* (Academic Press, 1972). Blau's other major works on stratification include *Structural Contexts of Opportunities* (University of Chicago Press, 1994). Richard J. Herrnstein and Charles Murray's *The Bell Curve: Intelligence and Class Structure in American Life* (Free Press, 1994) is a controversial work that concludes that the major cause of income inequality is differences in intelligence. For a structural explanation of inequality see Sheldon Danziger and Peter Gottschalk, *America Unequal* (Harvard University Press, 1995). For an examination of the full range of explanations of poverty, see William A. Kelso, *Poverty and the Underclass: Changing Perceptions of the Poor in America* (New York University Press, 1994). A number of important works look at the poor and their disadvantages, including Elliot Liebow, *Tell Them Who I Am: The Lives of Homeless Women* (Free Press, 1993); Lawrence M. Mead, *The New Politics of Poverty* (Basic Books, 1992); Richard H. Ropers, *Persistent Poverty* (Plenum, 1992); Mickey Kaus, *The End of Inequality* (Basic Books, 1992); Jonathan Kozol, *Savage Inequalities: Children in America's Schools* (Harper Perennial, 1992); Rural Sociological Task Force on Persistent Rural Poverty, *Persistent Poverty in Rural America* (Westview, 1993); and Thomas Lyson and William W. Falk, *Forgotten Places: Uneven Development in Rural America* (University of Kansas Press, 1993).

ISSUE 9

Are the Poor Responsible for Their Poverty?

YES: Edward Banfield, from *The Unheavenly City* (Little, Brown, 1970; reissue, Waveland Press, 1990)

NO: Jonathan Kozol, from "Poverty's Children: Growing Up in the South Bronx," *The Progressive* (October 1995)

ISSUE SUMMARY

YES: Sociologist Edward Banfield asserts that it is the cultural outlook of the poor that tends to keep them in poverty.

NO: Author Jonathan Kozol gives an eyewitness account of life in a very poor neighborhood to demonstrate how structural conditions and personal tragedies create poverty independent of any culture of the poor.

The Declaration of Independence proclaims the right of every human being to "life, liberty, and the pursuit of happiness." It never defines happiness, but Americans tend to agree that it includes doing well financially, getting ahead in life, and maintaining a comfortable standard of living.

The fact is that millions of Americans do not do well and do not get ahead. They are mired in poverty and seem unable to get out of it. On the face of it, this fact poses no contradiction to America's commitment to the pursuit of happiness. To pursue is not necessarily to catch; it certainly does not mean that everyone should feel entitled to a life of material prosperity.

"Equality of opportunity," the prototypical American slogan, is vastly different from the socialist dream of "equality of condition," which perhaps is one reason socialism has so few adherents in America.

The real difficulty in reconciling the American ideal with American reality is not the problem of income differentials but the *persistence* of poverty from generation to generation. Often, parent, child, and grandchild seem to be locked into a hopeless cycle of destitution and dependence. One explanation is that a large segment of the poor does not really try to get out of poverty. In its more extreme form this view portrays the poor as lazy, stupid, or base. Their poverty is not to be blamed on defects of American society but on their own defects. After all, many successful Americans have worked their way up from humble beginnings, and many immigrant groups have made progress in one generation. Therefore, the United States provides opportunities for those who work hard.

Another theory for the persistence of poverty is that the poor have few opportunities and many obstacles to overcome to climb out of poverty. If so, then America is not the land of opportunity for the poor, and the American dream is reserved for the more fortunate.

There is a belief that among some groups there is a *culture* that breeds poverty because it is antithetical to the self-discipline and hard work that enable others to overcome poverty. In other words, the poor have a culture all their own that is at variance with middle-class culture and hinders their success. Although it may keep people locked into what seems to be an intolerable life, this culture nevertheless has its own compensations and pleasures: it is full of "action," and it does not demand that people postpone pleasure, save money, or work hard. And it is, for the most part, tolerable to those who live in it.

Furthermore, according to this argument, not all poor people embrace the culture of poverty, and those who embrace middle-class values should be encouraged to escape poverty. But for those poor who embrace the lower-class culture, very little can be done.

According to an opposing view of poverty, most of the poor will become self-supporting if they are given a chance. Their most important need is for decent jobs that have potential for advancement. But often poor people cannot find jobs, and when they do, the jobs are dead-end or degrading. Some need job training or counseling to enable them to navigate the job market. Others need temporary help such as rent supplements, inexpensive housing, income supplements, protection from crime, medical services, or better education to help them help themselves.

The culture of poverty thesis shields the economic system from blame for poverty and honors Americans who are better off. But most of the poor are as committed to taking care of themselves and their families through hard work as is the middle class, and a sense of dignity is common to all classes. Critics judge the culture of poverty thesis to be a self-righteous justification by spokesmen for the middle and upper classes for an economic system that rewards them while subjecting the poor to an intolerable existence. How different is the culture of the poor from the culture of the middle class? If their material conditions were altered, would the culture of the poor change?

Edward Banfield, a proponent of the culture of poverty thesis, maintains that it is not the material that controls the culture but the other way around; only the abandonment of lower-class culture will get the poor out of poverty. On the other side, Jonathan Kozol, who has spent a lot of time with the poor, paints a sympathetic picture of the poor that denigrates the culture of poverty thesis.

YES

Edward Banfield

THE FUTURE OF THE LOWER CLASS

So long as the city contains a sizable lower class, nothing basic can be done about its most serious problems. Good jobs may be offered to all, but some will remain chronically unemployed. Slums may be demolished, but if the housing that replaces them is occupied by the lower class it will shortly be turned into new slums. Welfare payments may be doubled or tripled and a negative income tax instituted, but some persons will continue to live in squalor and misery. New schools may be built, new curricula devised, and the teacher-pupil ratio cut in half, but if the children who attend these schools come from lower-class homes, they will be turned into blackboard jungles, and those who graduate or drop out from them will, in most cases, be functionally illiterate. The streets may be filled with armies of policemen, but violent crime and civil disorder will decrease very little. If, however, the lower class were to disappear—if, say, its members were overnight to acquire the attitudes, motivations, and habits of the working class—the most serious and intractable problems of the city would all disappear with it.

[The] serious problems of the city all exist in two forms—a normal-class and a lower-class form—which are fundamentally different from each other. In its normal-class form, the employment problem, for example, consists mainly of young people who are just entering the labor market and who must make a certain number of trials and errors before finding suitable jobs; in its lower-class form, it consists of people who prefer the "action" of the street to any steady job. The poverty problem in its normal-class form consists of people (especially the aged, the physically handicapped, and mothers with dependent children) whose only need in order to live decently is money; in its lower-class form it consists of people who live in squalor and misery even if their incomes were doubled or tripled. The same is true with the other problems—slum housing, schools, crime, rioting; each is really two quite different problems.

The lower-class forms of all problems are at bottom a single problem: the existence of an outlook and style of life which is radically present-oriented and which therefore attaches no value to work, sacrifice, self-improvement, or service to family, friends, or community. Social workers, teachers,

From Edward Banfield, *The Unheavenly City* (Little, Brown, 1970; reissue, Waveland Press, 1990). Copyright © 1970 by Edward C. Banfield. Reprinted by permission of Waveland Press, Inc.

and law-enforcement officials—all those whom Gans calls "caretakers"—cannot achieve their goals because they can neither change nor circumvent this cultural obstacle....

Robert Hunter described it in 1904:

They lived in God only knows what misery. They ate when there were things to eat; they starved when there was lack of food. But, on the whole, although they swore and beat each other and got drunk, they were more contented than any other class I have happened to know. It took a long time to understand them. Our Committees were busy from morning until night in giving them opportunities to take up the fight again, and to become independent of relief. They always took what we gave them; they always promised to try; but as soon as we expected them to fulfill any promises, they gave up in despair, and either wept or looked ashamed, and took to misery and drink again,—almost, so it seemed to me at times, with a sense of relief.

In Hunter's day these were the "undeserving," "unworthy," "depraved," "debased," or "disreputable" poor; today, they are the "troubled," "culturally deprived," "hard to reach," or "multiproblem." In the opinion of anthropologist Oscar Lewis, their kind of poverty "is a way of life, remarkably stable and persistent, passed down from generation to generation among family lines." This "culture of poverty," as he calls it, exists in city slums in many parts of the world, and is, he says, an adaptation made by the poor in order to defend themselves against the harsh realities of slum life.

The view that is to be taken here [is that] there is indeed such a culture, but that poverty is its effect rather than its cause. (There are societies even poorer than the ones Lewis has described—primitive ones, for example—in which nothing remotely resembling the pattern of behavior here under discussion exists.) Extreme present-orientedness, not lack of income or wealth, is the principal cause of poverty in the sense of "the culture of poverty." Most of those caught up in this culture are unable or unwilling to plan for the future, to sacrifice immediate gratifications in favor of future ones, or to accept the disciplines that are required in order to get and to spend. Their inabilities are probably culturally given in most cases—"multi-problem" families being normal representatives of a class culture that is itself abnormal. No doubt there are also people whose present-orientedness is rationally adaptive rather than cultural, but these probably comprise only a small part of the "hard core" poor.

Outside the lower class, poverty (in the sense of hardship, want, or destitution) is today almost always the result of external circumstances—involuntary unemployment, prolonged illness, the death of a breadwinner, or some other misfortune. Even when severe, such poverty is not squalid or degrading. Moreover, it ends quickly once the (external) cause of it no longer exists. Public or private assistance can sometimes remove or alleviate the cause—for example, by job retraining or remedial surgery. Even when the cause cannot be removed, simply providing the nonlower-class poor with sufficient income is enough to enable them to live "decently."

Lower-class poverty, by contrast, is "inwardly" caused (by psychological inability to provide for the future, and all that this inability implies). Improvements in external circumstances can affect this poverty only superficially: One problem of a "multiproblem" family is no sooner solved than another arises. In principle, it is possible to eliminate the poverty (material lack) of such a family, but only at great expense, since the capacity of the radically improvident to waste money is almost unlimited. Raising such a family's income would not necessarily improve its way of life, moreover, and could conceivably even make things worse. Consider, for example, the H. family:

Mrs. H. seemed overwhelmed with the simple mechanics of dressing her six children and washing their clothes. The younger ones were running around in their underwear; the older ones were unaccounted for, but presumably were around the neighborhood. Mrs. H. had not been out of the house for several months; evidently her husband did the shopping. The apartment was filthy and it smelled. Mrs. H. was dressed in a bathrobe, although it was mid-afternoon. She seemed to have no plan or expectations with regard to her children; she did not know the names of their teachers and she did not seem to worry about their school work, although one child had been retained one year and another two years. Mrs. H. did seem to be somewhat concerned about her husband's lack of activity over the weekend—his continuous drinking and watching baseball on television. Apparently he and she never went out socially together nor did the family ever go anywhere as a unit.

If this family had a very high income —say, $50,000 a year—it would not be considered a "culture of poverty" case. Mrs. H. would hire maids to look after the small children, send the others to boarding schools, and spend her time at fashion shows while her husband drank and watched TV at his club. But with an income of only moderate size—say 100 percent above the poverty line—they would probably be about as badly off as they are now. They might be even worse off, for Mrs. H. would be able to go to the dog races, leaving the children alone, and Mr. H. could devote more time to his bottle and TV set....

Welfare agencies, recognizing the difference between "internally" and "externally" caused poverty, have long been trying first by one means and then another to improve the characters or, as it is now put, to "bring about personal adjustment" of the poor. In the nineteenth century, the view was widely held that what the lower class individual needed was to be brought into a right relation with God or (the secular version of the same thing) with the respectable (that is, middle- and upper-class) elements of the community. The missionary who distributed tracts door to door in the slums was the first caseworker; his— more often, her—task was to minister to what today would be called "feelings of alienation."

The stranger, coming on a stranger's errand, becomes a friend, discharging the offices and exerting the influence of a friend....

Secularized, this approach became the "friendly visitor" system under which "certain persons, under the direction of a central board, pledge themselves to take one or more families who need counsel, if not material help, on their visiting list, and maintain personal friendly relations with them." The system did not work; middle- and upper-class people might be "friendly," but they could not sympathize, let alone communicate, with the lower class. By the beginning of the twentieth century the friendly visitor had been replaced by the "expert." The idea now was that the authority of "the facts" would bring about desired changes of attitude, motive, and habit. As it happened, however, the lower class did not recognize the authority of the facts. The expert then became a supervisor, using his (or her) power to confer or withhold material benefits in order to force the poor to do the things that were supposed to lead to "rehabilitation" (that is, to a middle-class style of life). This method did not work either; the lower class could always find ways to defeat and exploit the system. They seldom changed their ways very much and they never changed them for long. Besides, there was really no body of expertise to tell caseworkers how to produce the changes desired. As one caseworker remarked recently in a book addressed to fellow social service professionals:

> Despite years of experience in providing public aid to poor families precious little is yet known about how to help truly inadequate parents make long term improvements in child care, personal maturity, social relations, or work stability.

Some people understood that if the individual's style of life was to be changed at all, it would be necessary to change that of the group that produced, motivated, and constrained him. Thus, the settlement house. As Robert A. Woods explained:

> The settlements are able to take neighborhoods in cities, and by patience bring back to them much of the healthy village life, so that the people shall again know and care for one another....

When it became clear that settlement houses would not change the culture of slum neighborhoods, the group approach was broadened into what is called "community action." In one type of commu-

nity action ("community development"), a community organizer tries to persuade a neighborhood's informal leaders to support measures (for instance, measures for delinquency control) that he advances. In another form of it ("community organization"), the organizer tries to promote self-confidence, self-respect, and attachment to the group (and, hopefully, to normal society) among lower-class people. He attempts to do this by encouraging them in efforts at joint action, or by showing them how to conduct meetings, carry on discussions, pass resolutions, present requests to politicians, and the like. In still another form ("community mobilization"), the organizer endeavors to arouse the anger of lower-class persons against the local "power structure," to teach them the techniques of mass action—strikes, sit-ins, picketing, and so on—and to show them how they may capture power. The theory of community organization attributes the malaise of the poor to their lack of self-confidence (which is held to derive largely from their "inexperience"); community mobilization theory, by contrast, attributes it to their feelings of "powerlessness." According to this doctrine, the best cure for poverty is to give the poor power. But since power is not "given," it must be seized.

The success of the group approach has been no greater than that of the case-worker approach. Reviewing five years of effort on the part of various community action programs, Marris and Rein conclude:

> ... the reforms had not evolved any reliable solutions to the intractable problems with which they struggled. They had not discovered how in general to override the intransigent autonomy of public and private agencies, at any level of gov-

ernment; nor how to use the social sciences practically to formulate and evaluate policy; nor how, under the sponsorship of government, to raise the power of the poor. Given the talent and money they had brought to bear, they had not even reopened very many opportunities.

If the war on poverty is judged by its ability "to generate major, meaningful and lasting social and economic reforms in conformity with the expressed wishes of poor people," writes Thomas Gladwin, "... it is extremely difficult to find even scattered evidence of success."...

Although city agencies have sent community organizers by the score into slum neighborhoods, the lower-class poor cannot be organized. In East Harlem in 1948, five social workers were assigned to organize a five-block area and to initiate a program of social action based on housing, recreation, and other neighborhood needs. After three years of effort, the organizers had failed to attract a significant number of participants, and those they did attract were upwardly mobile persons who were unrepresentative of the neighborhood. In Boston a "total community" delinquency control project was found to have had "negligible impact," an outcome strikingly like that of the Cambridge-Somerville experiment—a "total caseworker" project—a decade earlier. Even community mobilization, despite the advantages of a rhetoric of

hate and an emphasis on "action," failed to involve lower-class persons to a significant extent. Gangsters and leaders of youth gangs were co-opted on occasion, but they did not suffer from feelings of powerlessness and were not representative of the class for which mobilization was to provide therapy. No matter how hard they have tried to appeal to people at the very bottom of the scale, community organizers have rarely succeeded. Where they have appeared to succeed, as, for example, in the National Welfare Rights Organization, it has been by recruiting people who had some of the *outward* attributes of the lower class—poverty, for example—but whose outlook and values were not lower class; the lower-class person (as defined here) is incapable of being organized. Although it tried strenuously to avoid it, what the Mobilization for Youth described as the general experience proved to be its own experience as well:

> Most efforts to organize lower-class people attract individuals on their way up the social-class ladder. Persons who are relatively responsible about participation, articulate and successful at managing organizational "forms" are identified as lower-class leaders, rather than individuals who actually reflect the values of the lower-class groups. Ordinarily the slum's network of informal group associations is not reached.

NO

Jonathan Kozol

POVERTY'S CHILDREN: GROWING UP IN THE SOUTH BRONX

The Number Six train from Manhattan to the South Bronx makes nine stops in the eighteen-minute ride between East 59th Street and Brook Avenue. When you enter the train, you are in the seventh richest Congressional district in the nation. When you leave, you are in the poorest. The 600,000 people who live here and the 450,000 people who live in Washington Heights and Harlem, across the river, make up one of the largest racially segregated concentrations of poor people in our nation.

Brook Avenue, the tenth stop on the local, lies in the center of Mott Haven, whose 48,000 people are the poorest in the South Bronx. Walking into St. Ann's Church in Mott Haven on a hot summer afternoon, one is immediately in the presence of small children. They seem to be everywhere: in the garden, in the hallways, in the kitchen, in the chapel, on the stairs. The first time I see the pastor, Martha Overall, she is carrying a newborn baby in her arms and is surrounded by three lively and excited little girls. In one of the most diseased and dangerous communities in any city of the Western world, the beautiful, old, stone church on St. Ann's Avenue is a gentle sanctuary from the terrors of the streets outside.

A seven-year-old body named Cliffie, whose mother has come to the church to talk with the Reverend Overall, agrees to take me for a walk around the neighborhood. Reaching up to take my hand the moment we leave the church, he starts a running commentary almost instantly, interrupting now and then to say hello to men and women on the street, dozens of whom are standing just outside the gateway to St. Ann's, waiting for a soup kitchen to open.

At a tiny park in a vacant lot less than a block away, he points to a number of stuffed animals that are attached to the branches of a tree.

"Bears," he says.

"Why are there bears in the tree?" I ask.

He doesn't answer me but smiles at the bears affectionately. "I saw a boy shot in the head right over there," he says a moment later. He looks up at me pleasantly. "Would you like a chocolate-chip cookie?"

"No, thank you," I say.

From Jonathan Kozol, "Poverty's Children: Growing Up in the South Bronx," *The Progressive* (October 1995). Copyright © 1995 by *The Progressive*. Reprinted by permission of *The Progressive*, 409 E. Main Street, Madison, WI 53703.

He has a package of cookies and removes one. He breaks it in half, returns half to the package, and munches on the other half as we are walking. We walk a long block to a rutted street called Cypress Avenue. He gestures down a hill toward what he calls "the bad place," and asks if I want to go see it.

I say, "OK."

"They're burning bodies down there," he announces ominously.

"What kind of bodies?" I ask.

"The bodies of people!" he says in a spooky voice, as if enjoying the opportunity to terrify a grownup.

The place Cliffie is referring to turns out to be a waste incinerator that went into operation recently over the objections of the parents in the neighborhood. The incinerator, I am later reassured by the Reverend Overall, does not burn entire "bodies." What it burns are so-called red-bag products, such as amputated limbs and fetal tissue, bedding, bandages, and syringes that are transported here from New York City hospitals.

Munching another cookie as we walk, Cliffie asks me, "Do you want to go on Jackson Avenue?" Although I don't know one street from another, I agree.

"Come on," he says. "I'll take you there. We have to go around this block." He pauses, however, and pulls an asthma inhaler from his pocket, holds it to his mouth, presses it twice, and then puts it away.

As confident and grown-up as he seems in some ways, he has the round face of a baby and is scarcely more than three-and-a-half feet tall. When he has bad dreams, he tells me, "I go in my mommy's bed and crawl under the covers." At other times, when he's upset, he says, "I sleep with a picture of my mother and I dream of her."

Unlike many children I meet these days, he has an absolutely literal religious faith. When I ask him how he pictures God, he says, "He has long hair and He can walk on the deep water." To make sure I understand how unusual this is, he says. "Nobody else can."

He seems to take the lessons of religion literally also. Speaking of a time his mother sent him to the store "to get a pizza"—"three slices, one for my mom, one for my dad, and one for me"—he says he saw a homeless man who told him he was hungry. "But he was too cold to move his mouth! He couldn't talk."

"How did you know that he was hungry if he couldn't talk?"

"He pointed to my pizza."

"What did you do?"

"I gave him some!"

"Were your parents mad at you?"

He looks surprised by this. "Why would they be mad?" he asks, "God told us, 'Share!'"

When I ask him who his heroes are he first says "Michael Jackson," and then, "Oprah!"—like that, with an exclamation on the word. I try to get him to speak about "important" persons as the schools tend to define them: "Have you read about George Washington?"

"I don't even know the man," he says.

We follow Jackson Avenue past several boarded buildings and a "flat-fix" shop, stop briefly in front of a fenced-in lot where the police of New York City bring impounded cars, then turn left and go two blocks to a highway with an elevated road above it, where a sign says BRUCKNER BOULEVARD. Crossing beneath the elevated road, we soon arrive at Locust Avenue.

The medical waste incinerator is a new-looking building, gun-metal blue on top of cinder blocks. From one of its metal sliding doors, a sourly unpleasant odor drifts into the street. Standing in front of the building, Cliffie grumbles slightly, but does not seem terribly concerned. "You sure that you don't want a cookie?"

Again I say, "No, thank you."

"I think I'll have another one," he says, and takes one for himself.

"You want to go the hard way or the easy way back to the church?"

"Let's go the easy way," I say.

Next to another vacant lot where someone has dumped a heap of auto tires and some rusted auto parts, he points to a hypodermic needle in the tangled grass and to the bright-colored caps of crack containers, then, for no reason that I can discern, starts puffing up his cheeks and blowing out the air, a curious behavior that seems whimsical and absent-minded and disconsolate at the same time.

"The day is coming when the world will be destroyed," he finally announces, "Everyone is going to be burned to crispy cookies." He reaches into the package for another cookie, only to discover they're all gone.

* * *

Cliffie's mother is a small, wiry woman wearing blue jeans and a baseball cap, a former cocaine addict who now helps addicted women and their kids.

Inside the church, when I return Cliffie to her, she looks at me with some amusement on her face and asks, "Did this child wear you out?"

"No," I say. "I enjoyed the walk." I mention, however, that he took me to the waste incinerator and I share with her his comment about "burning bodies." She responds by giving him a half-sarcastic look, hesitating, and then saying, "Hey!

You never know! Maybe this child knows something we haven't heard."

She gives him another pleasantly suspicious look and leans back in her chair. "The point is they put a *lot* of things into our neighborhood that no one wants," she says. "The waste incinerator is just one more lovely way of showing their affection."

I ask, "Does it insult you?"

"It used to," she replies. "The truth is, you get used to the offense. There's trashy things all over. There's a garbage dump three blocks away. Then there's all the trucks that come through stinking up the air, heading for the Hunts Point Market. Drivers get their drugs there and their prostitutes."

She tells me that 3,000 homeless families have been relocated by the city in this neighborhood during the past few years and asks a question I hear from many other people here. "Why do you want to put so many people with small children in a place with so much sickness? This is the *last* place in New York that they should put poor children. Clumping so many people, all with the same symptoms and same problems, in one crowded place with nothing they can grow on? Our children start to mourn themselves before their time."

Cliffie, who is listening to this while leaning on his elbow like a pensive grownup, offers his tentative approval to his mother's words. "Yes," he says. "I think that's probably true."

He says it with so much thought, and grown-up reserve, that his mother can't help smiling, even though it's not a funny statement. She looks at him hard, grabs him suddenly around the neck, and kisses him.

* * *

Alice Washington lives on a street called Boston Road, close to East Tremont Avenue, about two miles north of St. Ann's Church. Visibly fragile as a consequence of having AIDS and highly susceptible to chest infections, she lives with her son, who is a high-school senior, in a first-floor apartment with three steel locks on the door. A nurse comes once a month to take her temperature and check her heart and her blood pressure.

The nurse, says Mrs. Washington one evening when we're sitting in her kitchen, has another sixteen patients in the building. "Some are children born with AIDS. Some are older people. One is a child, twelve years old, shot in a crossfire at the bus stop on the corner. The bullet ricocheted and got her in the back. She's lost her hair. Can't go to school. She's paralyzed. I see her mother all the time. They wheel her outside in the summer.

"This happened last year, on the Fourth of July. Summer had just begun. I feel so sorry for that child."

I ask how many people in the building now have AIDS.

"In this building? Including the children, maybe twenty-seven people. That's just in this section. In the other building over there, there's maybe twenty more. Then there's lots of other people have it but don't know, afraid to know, and don't want to be tested. We're living in a bad time. What else can I say?"

She tells me that her food stamps and her welfare check have been cut off. It's a complicated story, but it seems that her food stamps and her welfare payment had been stolen from her in the street some months before. When she began the process of replacing them, there was a computer error that removed her from the rolls entirely.

She relates a story that I've heard many times from people in New York who have lost their welfare payments. "To get an emergency replacement for my check," she says, "I needed to bring three letters to the welfare office—one from my doctor, one from the hospital, and one from my social worker....

"I got the doctor's letter and the social worker's letter, but the hospital's letter didn't come. So I went back and forth from welfare to the hospital—it took a week and finally I got the letter. I brought in all the letters and I waited for another week and then I went to the computer. I put my card in, but it didn't work.... Then the man there said, 'Your card is dead. You've been cut off.'

"My doctor says, when it comes to the poor, they can't get nothin' right. Anyway, they got me runnin' uptown, downtown, to the hospital, to 34th Street, to the welfare, with the streets so hot and everyone at welfare so impatient. I've got no choice but I don't think I can go through it anymore. I feel like somebody beat me up."

* * *

Listening to her voice, which does sound like that of someone who is feeling beaten, I find myself thinking of the words of certain politicians who believe that we have got to get much tougher with unmarried, indigent, non-working women. How much tougher could we get with Mrs. Washington, I wonder, without settling for plain extermination?

"If poor people behaved rationally," says Lawrence Mead, a professor of political science at New York University, "they would seldom be poor for long in the first place." Many social scientists appear to hold this point of view today and argue that the largest portion of the suffering that poor people undergo has to be blamed upon their own behaviors.

But even from the most severe of academic viewpoints about "rationality" or "good" and "bad" behaviors, what has Mrs. Washington done wrong?

She was born in 1944 in New York City. She grew up in Harlem and the Bronx and went to segregated public schools, not something of her choosing, nor that of her mother and her father. She finished high school, studied bookkeeping at a secretarial college, and went to work when she was nineteen.

When she married, at the age of twenty-five, she had to choose her husband from that segregated "marriage pool," to which our social scientists sometimes quite icily refer, of frequently unemployable black men, some of whom have been involved in drugs or spent some time in prison. From her husband, after many years of what she thought to be monogamous matrimony, she contracted the AIDS virus.

She left her husband after he began to beat her. Cancer of her fallopian tubes was detected at this time, then cancer of her uterus. She had three operations. Too frail to keep on with the second of two jobs that she had held, in all, for nearly twenty years, she was forced to turn for mercy to the city of New York.

In 1983, at the age of thirty-nine, she landed with her children in a homeless shelter two blocks from Times Square, an old hotel in which the plumbing did not work and from which she and her son David and his sister had to carry buckets to a bar across the street in order to get water. After spending close to four years in three shelters in Manhattan, she was moved by the city to the neighborhood where she now lives in the South Bronx. It was at this time that she learned she carried the AIDS virus. Since the time I met Mrs. Washington, I have spent hundreds of hours talking with her in her kitchen. I have yet to figure out what she has done that was irrational.

* * *

The entire discussion of poor women and their children and their values seems to take place out of any realistic context that includes the physical surroundings of their lives.

The statement, for example, heard so often now as to assume the character of incantation, that low-income neighborhoods like the South Bronx have undergone a "breakdown of family structure" infuriates many poor women I have met, not because they think it is not true but because those who employ this phrase do so with no reference to the absolute collapse of almost every other form of life-affirming institution in the same communities.

"Nothing works here in my neighborhood," a mother named Elizabeth has told me. "Keeping a man is not the biggest problem. Keeping from being killed is bigger. Keeping your kids alive is bigger. If nothing else works, why should a marriage work? I'd rather have a peaceful little life just with my kids than live with somebody who knows that he's a failure. Men like that make everyone feel rotten."

Perhaps it is partly for this reason that so much of the debate about the breakdown of the family has a note of the unreal or incomplete to many of the poorest women I know, and to many of the priests and organizers who work with them. "Of course the family structure breaks down in a place like the South Bronx!" says a white minister who works in one of New York City's poorest neighborhoods. "Everything breaks down in a place like this. The pipes break down. The phone breaks down. The electricity and heat break down. The spirit breaks down. The body breaks down. The immune agents of the heart break down. Why wouldn't the family break down also?

"If we saw the children in these neighborhoods as part of the same human family to which we belong, we'd never put them in such places to begin with. But we do *not* think of them that way. That is one area of 'family breakdown' that the sociologists and the newspapers do not often speak of."

* * *

Mrs. Shirley Flowers, whose neighbors call her "Miss Shirley," sits for several hours every day at a table in the lobby of her building to keep out drug dealers.

When I visit, we talk for a while of some of the children I have met at St. Ann's Church, almost all of whom have relatives in prison. Mrs. Flowers speaks of one of these kids, a fourteen-year-old boy who used to live here in this building but whose mother has since died of cancer.

"The family lived upstairs. The daughter's out at Rikers Island. Been there several times. Had two of her babies there. Now a brother of hers is out there, too. Another brother's dead."

"What happens to the kids," I ask, "when mothers are in prison?"

"Some of them, their relatives take them in. Others go in foster care. Other times," she says, "a neighbor takes the baby."

She speaks of toddlers in the streets who sometimes don't know where their mothers are. "If it's dinnertime, I'll bring them in and feed them. If they're dirty, I'll give them their bath." Many of the kids, she says, have little bugs all over them. "*Piojos* is the word the Puerto Rican children use. They get into their hair and skin. I say to them, 'Stay here with me. I'll keep you safe until your mamma's home.' The children know me, so they know that they don't need to be afraid."

For the past seven years, a gang of murderers and dealers has been based four doors away from Mrs. Flower's home on Beekman Avenue. They marketed crack in a distinctive vial with a red and orange cap, and disciplined dishonest dealers by such terrifying means as mutilations. In one mid-day mutilation, *Newsday* reported, gang enforcers punished a refractory gang member by taking him to St. Mary's Park, right at the end of Beekman Avenue, where "they hacked at him with machetes" and a serrated knife, "opening wounds so severe that some of his organs spilled out." A crowd including children from a nearby junior high school watched the killing.

In one massacre that took place on the street two years before, a man and woman were shot dead for buying crack from the wrong dealer, the dealer was shot and killed as well, and a fourth person who had no drug involvement but was walking in the alley at the wrong time was chased down the street into St. Mary's Park and shot there fourteen times.

I ask Mrs. Flowers, "Have you ever seen a shooting victim die before your eyes?"

"I've seen a *generation* die," she answers. "Some of them were killed with guns. Some lost their minds from drugs. Some from disease. Now we have AIDS, the great plague, the plague of AIDS, the plague that can't be cured. It's true. I've seen it. I've been there. I've been here in this building twenty-four years and I've seen it all."

Despite the horrors she has seen, she seems a fearless person and almost serene. I ask, "How do you keep yourself composed?"

"I pray. I talk to God. I tell him, 'Lord, it is your work. Put me to rest at night and wake me in the morning.'"

"Do your children have the same belief in God that you do?"

"Yes," she says, nodding at her daughter and her son-in-law. "They do. This family talks to God."

Before I leave, she shows me a handful of photocopied clippings from newspapers that have sent reporters here to talk with her. It occurs to me that I must be one in a long line of people who have come to ask her questions. "Do you ever get sick of all these people knocking at your door year after year to pick your brain?" I ask her.

"No," she says. "I don't get sick of it because a lot of them have been nice people. The trouble is, you answer their questions and you give them your opinions. They collect your story from you. Then you see it and you read it. You think, 'Good.' But nothing happens. It's just 'there' and then it drops. It's like they put you in a bucket, like a wishing well. Only it's a wishing well where wishes don't come true." ...

* * *

Anthony meets me in the garden of St. Ann's and takes me for a walk to see the building where he lives, a few blocks to the west and north, and the building where his grandmother lives, which is close to the same neighborhood

and which he says he likes to visit because "my grandma feeds me."

His grandmother, he tells me, is "the happiest person that I know."

I ask him why he thinks that she is happy.

"I don't know why," he says. "I think that feeding people makes her happy." Children from the neighborhood, he says, come to her house and she makes ices for them and bakes cookies. "I think that she likes children more than grownups."

His uncle, however, who lives with his grandmother, is, he says, "not happy. He has many troubles."

His eyes look worried when he says this.

"Anthony," I ask. "What troubles does your uncle have?"

"Mr. Jonathan, my uncle is a sick man. He has AIDS."

"What does he do during the day?" I ask. "Is he well enough to go outside?"

"Yes, he goes out...." Then, in a grownup voice, he adds, "How can I say this? He goes out but he stays in. He stays inside himself. He does not look at people. He looks down. The man looks at the ground. I don't know why. I think that he's afraid to look up at the world."

"Anthony, is your uncle a drug-user?"

"That," he answers, "is something that I do not want to know."

"Do you cry for your uncle?"

"Yes, I cry. It's not a sin to cry."

"Do you know other children who cry?"

"Many cry."

"Do you know children who are happy?"

"Truly happy? No."

"Happy at all?"

"Not many.... Well, to tell the truth, not any who are happy for more than one day." Then he corrects himself. "No! Not for one day. For fifteen minutes." He thinks this over, as if to check that he is being accurate, then reports. "Not any. That's no lie."

I wonder at times if a sense of the dramatic might lead Anthony to overstate his answers to my questions, so I challenge him by telling him that I've met children in the schoolyard who seem cheerful.

"Cheerful? Yes. Happy is not the same as cheerful," he replies.

"I think there are certain children who are happy anywhere," I tell him. But he holds his ground.

"Whenever you see a child who enjoys life in this neighborhood, come and see me right away. I'll have to go and see a doctor."

He stops at that moment and waves his hand around him at the neighborhood. "Would you be happy if you had to live here?"

"No, Anthony. I wouldn't," I reply.

We walk as far as Alexander Avenue, then circle back. As we walk, we pass a painted memorial to a victim of gunfire that has been partly whited over in one of the periodic cleanups by the city. A name and date can still be read, however. Sometimes, the Reverend Overall has told me, the city needs to use sandblasters to remove these tributes to the dead.

"How old would you like to live to be?" I ask Anthony.

"That's easy," he replies. "One hundred and thirteen."

"That number's quite exact," I say. "How did you decide on that?"

"I'm thirteen. I'd like to live another 100 years."

"Why *exactly* 100 years?"

"I would like to live to see the human race grow up."

POSTSCRIPT

Are the Poor Responsible for Their Poverty?

The debate over the culture of poverty thesis is as strong today as it was over 25 years ago when Banfield drafted his version of it in *The Unheavenly City*. In fact, he did not judge it necessary to revise his chapter on the culture of poverty when he reissued his book 20 years later.

The poverty debate, however, constantly invokes new theories, such as the role of welfare in inducing a dysfunctional culture. In 1981 George Gilder incorporated the culture of poverty thesis in his book *Wealth and Poverty* (Basic Books). In it he argues that hard work is the tried and true path from poverty to wealth. He also argues that many welfare programs perpetuate poverty by breeding dependence and supporting the culture of poverty. This criticism of welfare has been addressed with ample statistics by Charles Murray in *Losing Ground* (Basic Books, 1984).

There are countless works that describe the adverse conditions of the poor. The nineteenth-century English novelist Charles Dickens was a crusader for the poor, and many of his novels, still in print and certainly considered classics, graphically depict the wretchedness of poverty. Michael Harrington described poverty in America in his influential nonfiction book *The Other America* (Macmillan, 1963) at a time when most of the country was increasingly affluent.

More recently, William Julius Wilson has written about the macroeconomic forces at work on the poor in *The Truly Disadvantaged* (University of Chicago Press, 1987). The most vigorous proponent of the culture of poverty thesis today is Lawrence E. Harrison, who wrote *Who Prospers? How Cultural Values Shape Economic and Political Success* (Basic Books, 1992). In *The Dream and the Nightmare: The Sixties' Legacy to the Underclass* (William Morrow, 1993), Myron Magnet blames the culture of the underclass for their poverty, but he also blames the upper classes for contributing greatly to the underclass's culture. The counter to the cultural explanation of poverty is the structural explanation. Its most current version focuses on the loss of unskilled jobs. If Jeremy Rifkin's analysis in *The End of Work: The Decline of the Global Labor Force and the Dawn of the Post-Market Era* (Putnam, 1995) is right, new technologies will lengthen unemployment lines unless the economy or the working world is radically restructured. For a similar view, see Stanley Aronowitz and William DiFazio, *The Jobless Future: Sci-Tech and the Dogma of Work* (University of Minnesota Press, 1994). For a review of a wide range of explanations of poverty, see William Kelso, *Poverty and the Underclass* (New York University Press, 1994).

ISSUE 10

Should Affirmative Action Policies Be Discontinued?

YES: Arch Puddington, from "What to Do About Affirmative Action," *Commentary* (June 1995)

NO: Roger Wilkins, from "The Case for Affirmative Action: Racism Has Its Privileges," *The Nation* (March 27, 1995)

ISSUE SUMMARY

YES: Policy analyst Arch Puddington argues that Americans support anti-discrimination laws but strongly oppose racial preference policies. In support of abandoning such policies, he attacks popular arguments that promote affirmative action.

NO: Professor of history Roger Wilkins defends affirmative action against those who claim that since the playing field is now level, affirmative action is unfair. Wilkins argues that racism and discrimination are still virulent and that the right kind of affirmative action will benefit whites as well as blacks.

In America, equality is a principle as basic as liberty. "All men are created equal" is perhaps the most well known phrase in the Declaration of Independence. More than half a century after the signing of the Declaration, the French social philosopher Alexis de Tocqueville examined democracy in America and concluded that its most essential ingredient was the equality of condition. Today we know that the "equality of condition" that Tocqueville perceived did not exist for women, blacks, Native Americans, and other racial minorities, nor for other disadvantaged social classes. Nevertheless, the ideal persisted.

When slavery was abolished after the Civil War, the Constitution's newly ratified Fourteenth Amendment proclaimed:

"No State shall ... deny to any person within its jurisdiction the equal protection of the laws."

Equality has been a long time coming. For nearly a century after the abolition of slavery, American blacks were denied equal protection by law in some states and by social practice nearly everywhere. One-third of the states either permitted or forced schools to become racially segregated, and segregation was achieved elsewhere through housing policy and social behavior. In 1954 the Supreme Court reversed a 58-year-old standard that had found "separate but equal" schools compatible with equal protection of the law. A unanimous decision in *Brown v. Board of Education* held that separate is *not* equal for the members of the discriminated-against group when the segregation "generates a feeling of inferiority as to their status in the community that may affect their hearts and minds in a way unlikely ever to be undone." The 1954 ruling on public elementary education has been extended to other areas of both governmental and private conduct, including housing and employment.

Even if judicial decisions and congressional statutes could end all segregation and racial discrimination, would this achieve equality—or simply perpetuate the status quo? Consider that the unemployment rate for blacks today is more than twice that of whites. Disproportionately higher numbers of blacks experience poverty, brutality, broken homes, physical and mental illness, and early deaths, while disproportionately lower numbers of them reach positions of affluence and prestige. It seems possible that much of this inequality has resulted from 300 years of slavery and segregation. Is termination of this ill treatment enough to end the injustices? No, say the proponents of affirmative action.

Affirmative action—the effort to improve the educational and employment opportunities for minorities—has had an uneven history in U.S. federal courts. In *Regents of the University of California v. Allan Bakke* (1978), which marked the first time the Supreme Court directly dealt with the merits of affirmative action, a 5–4 majority ruled that a white applicant to a medical school had been wrongly excluded in favor of a less qualified black applicant due to the school's affirmative action policy. Yet the majority also agreed that "race-conscious" policies may be used in admitting candidates—as long as they do not amount to fixed quotas. The ambivalence of *Bakke* has run through the Court's treatment of the issue since 1978. Recent decisions suggest that the Court is beginning to take a dim view of affirmative action. In 1989, for example, the Court ruled that a city council could *not* set aside a fixed percentage of public construction projects for minority contractors.

Affirmative action is hotly debated outside the courts, and white males have recently been vocal on talk shows and in print about being treated unjustly because of affirmative action policies. In the following selections, Arch Puddington and Roger Wilkins debate the merits of affirmative action. In Puddington's view, affirmative action has outlived its usefulness, and the government should follow a policy of strict race neutrality. Wilkins, on the other hand, considers affirmative action an essential means for undoing some of the effects of white racism.

YES

Arch Puddington

WHAT TO DO ABOUT
AFFIRMATIVE ACTION

The thinking behind the policy of racial preference which has been followed in America over the past quarter-century under the name of "affirmative action"[1] is best summed up by former Supreme Court Justice Harry Blackmun's famous dictum that, "In order to get beyond racism, we must first take race into account."

The Orwellian quality of Blackmun's admonition is obvious. Seldom has a democratic government's policy so completely contradicted the core values of its citizenry as racial preference does in violating the universally held American ideals of fairness and individual rights, including the right to be free from discrimination. Not surprisingly, then, where Americans regarded the original civil-rights legislation as representing a long-overdue fulfillment of the country's democratic promise, they overwhelmingly see racial preference as an undemocratic and alien concept, a policy implemented by stealth and subterfuge and defended by duplicity and legalistic tricks.

Americans do not believe that past discrimination against blacks in the workplace justifies present discrimination against whites. Nor do they accept the thesis that tests and standards are tainted, *en masse*, by cultural bias against minorities. Having been taught in high-school civics classes that gerrymandering to ensure party domination represents a defect in democracy, Americans are bewildered by the argument that gerrymandering is necessary to ensure the political representation of blacks and Hispanics. They are unimpressed by the contention that a university's excellence is enhanced by the mere fact of racial and ethnic diversity in its student body, especially when entrance requirements must be lowered substantially to achieve that goal.

Americans, in short, oppose racial preference in all its embodiments, and have signified their opposition in opinion poll after opinion poll, usually by margins of three to one or more, with women as strongly opposed as men, and with an impressive proportion of blacks indicating opposition as well. The contention, repeatedly advanced by advocates of preferential policies, that a national consensus exists in support of such policies has been true only at the level of political elites. Americans do support what might be called soft affirmative action, entailing special recruitment, training, and outreach efforts, and are willing to accept some short-term compensatory measures to rectify obvious cases of proven discrimination. But attitudes have, if anything, hardened against the kind of aggressive, numbers-driven preference schemes increasingly encountered in university admissions and civil-service hiring.

* * *

Nonetheless, up until this year, racial preference in its various manifestations has been impressively resistant to calls for reform, much less elimination. In fact, race consciousness has begun to insinuate itself into areas which, common sense alone would suggest, should be immune to intrusive government social engineering. To cite but one example of this disturbing trend: Congress has mandated that guidelines be established guaranteeing the involvement of minorities (and women) in clinical research—a form of scientific experimentation by quota.

There is, furthermore, reason to question whether the advocates of race-conscious social policy continue to take seriously the objective of getting "beyond race," a condition which presumably would warrant the elimination of all preferential programs. The late Thurgood Marshall, an outspoken champion of preference while on the Supreme Court, is reported to have blurted out during an in-chambers discussion that blacks would need affirmative action for a hundred years. A similar opinion has been expressed by Benjamin Hooks, the former director of the National Association for the Advancement of Colored People (NAACP). Hooks contends that affirmative action in some form should be accepted as one of those permanent, irritating features of American life—he cited as examples speeding laws and the April 15 income-tax deadline—which citizens tolerate as essential to the efficient and just functioning of society.

Neither Marshall nor Hooks is regarded as an extremist on race matters; their advocacy of a permanent regime of affirmative action falls within the mainstream of present-day liberal thought. The promotion of "diversity"—the latest euphemism for preferential representation—is as fundamental to liberal governance as was the protection of labor unions in an earlier era. And until very recently, liberal proponents of preference clearly believed that history was on their side....

* * *

In 1964, the year the Civil Rights Act was passed, an optimistic and morally confident America believed that the challenge posed by the "Negro revolution" could be met through a combination of anti-discrimination laws, economic growth, and the voluntary good will of corporations, universities, and other institutions. But by the decade's end, a crucial segment of elite opinion had concluded that America was deeply flawed, even sick, and that racism, conscious or otherwise, permeated every institution and government policy. Where individual prejudice had previously been identified as the chief obstacle to black progress, now a new target, "institutional racism," was seen as the principal villain. And where it was once thought that democratic guarantees against discrimination, plus the inherent fairness of the American people, were sufficient to overcome injustice, the idea now took hold that since racism was built into the social order, coercive measures were required to root it out.

In this view, moreover, the gradualist Great Society approach launched by Lyndon Johnson, which stressed education, training, and the strengthening of black institutions, could not alleviate the misery of the inner-city poor, at least not as effectively as forcing employers to hire them. Even Johnson himself began calling for affirmative action and issued an executive order directing that federal contractors adopt hiring policies which did not discriminate on the basis of race (or gender); in a process that would soon become all too familiar, court decisions and the guidelines of regulators subsequently interpreted the directive as mandating racial balance in the workforce, thus paving the way for demands that companies doing business with the government institute what often amounted to quotas in order to qualify for contracts.

Little noticed at the time—or, for that matter, later—was that black America was in the midst of a period of unprecedented economic progress, during which black poverty declined, the racial income gap substantially narrowed, black college enrollment mushroomed, and black advancement into the professions took a substantial leap forward. All this, it should be stressed, occurred *prior* to the introduction of government-mandated racial preference.

* * *

Once affirmative action got going, there was no holding it back. The civil-rights movement and those responsible for implementing civil-rights policy simply refused to accept an approach under which preference would be limited to cases of overt discrimination, or applied to a narrow group of crucial institutions, such as urban police departments, where racial integration served a pressing public need.

Instead, every precedent was exploited to further the permanent entrenchment of race consciousness.

For example, the Philadelphia Plan, the first preferential policy to enjoy presidential backing (the President being Richard Nixon), was a relatively limited effort calling for racial quotas in the Philadelphia building trades, an industry with a notorious record of racial exclusion. Yet this limited program was seized upon by the EEOC [Equal Employment Opportunity Commission] and other agencies as a basis for demanding hiring-by-the-numbers schemes throughout the economy, whether or not prior discrimination could be proved.

Similarly, once a race-conscious doctrine was applied to one institution, it inevitably expanded its reach into other arenas. The Supreme Court's decision in *Griggs* v. *Duke Power, Inc.*—that employment tests could be found to constitute illegal discrimination if blacks failed at a higher rate than whites—was ostensibly confined to hiring and promotion. But *Griggs* was used to legitimize the burgeoning movement against testing and standards in the educational world as well. Tracking by intellectual ability, special classes for high achievers, selective high schools requiring admissions tests, standardized examinations for university admissions—all were accused of perpetuating historic patterns of bias.

The campaign against testing and merit in turn gave rise to a series of myths about the economy, the schools, the workplace, about America itself. Thus, lowering job standards as a means of hiring enough blacks to fill a quota was justified on the grounds that merit had never figured prominently in the American workplace, that the dominant principles had always been nepotism, backscratching, and conformism. To explain the racial gap in Scholastic Aptitude Test scores, the concept of cultural bias was advanced, according to which disparities in results derived from the tests' emphasis on events and ideas alien to urban black children. Another theory claimed that poor black children were not accustomed to speaking standard English and were therefore placed at a disadvantage in a normal classroom environment. It was duly proposed that black children be taught much like immigrant children, with bilingual classes in which both standard English and black English would be utilized. A related theory stated that black children retained a distinct learning style which differed in significant respects from the learning styles of other children. As one educator expressed the theory, any test which stressed "logical, analytical methods of problem-solving" would *ipso facto* be biased against blacks.

* * *

The arguments which have lately been advanced in favor of retaining affirmative action are by and large the same arguments that were made more than twenty years ago, when the intellectual debate over preference began.

Probably the least compelling of these is the contention that the advantages extended by university admissions offices to athletes, the children of alumni, and applicants from certain regions of the country justify extending similar advantages on the basis of race. The answer to this contention is simple: race is different from other criteria. America acknowledged the unique nature of racial discrimination when it enacted the landmark civil-rights laws of the 1960's. Moreover, the suggestion cannot be sustained that outlawing preference based on race while permitting preference based on nonracial standards would leave blacks even farther behind. Blacks, in fact, benefit disproportionately from admissions preferences for athletes or those with talents in music and art. No one objects, or thinks it unusual or wrong for some groups to be overrepresented and others to be underrepresented on the basis of such criteria.

A similar, but even weaker, argument (already alluded to above) holds that America has never functioned as a strict meritocracy, and that white males have maintained their economic dominance through connections, pull, and family. Affirmative action, this theory goes, simply levels the playing field and actually strengthens meritocracy by expanding the pool of talent from which an employer draws. The problem is that those who advance this argument seem to assume that only white males rely on personal relationships or kinship. Yet as we have learned from the experience of immigrants throughout American history, every racial and ethnic group values family and group ties. Korean-American shop-owners enlist their families, Haitian-American taxi fleets hire their friends.

What about the claim that affirmative action has improved the racial climate by hastening the integration of the workplace and classroom? While the integration process has often been painful and disruptive, there is no question that more contact between the races at school and at work has made America a better society. But integration has not always succeeded, and the most signal failures have occurred under conditions of government coercion, whether through busing schemes or the imposition of workplace quotas. In case after case, the source of failed integration can be traced to white resentment over racial preference or the fears of blacks that they will be perceived as having attained their positions through the preferential track.[2]

There is, finally, the argument that, since black children suffer disproportionately from poor nutrition, crack-addicted parents, wrenching poverty, and outright discrimination, affirmative action rightly compensates for the burden of being born black in America. Yet affirmative action has been almost entirely irrelevant to these children, who rarely attend college or seek a professional career. The new breed of Republican conservatives may sometimes betray a disturbing ignorance of the history of racial discrimination in America. But on one crucial issue they are most certainly right: the march toward equality begins at birth, with the structure, discipline, and love of a family. The wide array of government-sponsored compensatory programs, including affirmative action, has proved uniformly ineffective in meeting the awesome challenge of inner-city family deterioration.

* * *

To advocate a policy of strict race neutrality is not to ignore the persistence of race consciousness, racial fears, racial solidarity, racial envy, or racial prejudice. It is, rather, to declare that government should not be in the business of preferring certain groups over others. Because it got into this business, the United States has been moved dangerously close to a country with an officially-sanctioned racial spoils system. Even Justice Blackmun was concerned about this kind of thing. In his [1978 *Regents of the University of California* v. *Allan*] *Bakke* opinion, Blackmun made it clear that preferential remedies should be regarded as temporary, and he speculated that race-conscious policies could be eliminated in ten years—that is, by the end of the 1980's.

Affirmative action's supporters grow uncomfortable when reminded of Blackmun's stipulation, which clashes with their secret conviction that preferences will be needed forever. Despite considerable evidence to the contrary, they believe that racism (and sexism) pervade American life, and they can always find a study, a statistic, or an anecdote to justify their prejudice.

If racial preference is not eliminated now, when a powerful national momentum favors resolving the issue once and for all, the result may well be the permanent institutionalization of affirmative action, though probably at a somewhat less expansive level than is the case right now. Alternatively, a cosmetic solution, which eliminates a few minor policies while leaving the foundation of racial preference in place, could trigger a permanent and much more divisive racial debate, with a mushrooming of state referenda on preference and the growing influence of extremists of both races.

It is clear that a bipartisan majority believes that the era of racial preference should be brought to a close. It will take an unusual amount of political determination and courage to act decisively on this belief. But the consequences of a failure to act could haunt American political life for years to come.

NOTES

1. Affirmative action has, of course, been extended to women and certain other groups, but I will confine the discussion here to race.

Affirmative action was devised primarily to promote the economic status of blacks, and the racial implications of the debate over this policy are far more significant than questions arising from preferences for women or other ethnic minorities. I should add that if preference for black Americans is unjustified, there is even less to be said for it when applied to women or to such immigrant groups as Hispanics, and Asians.

2. An important exception is the military, where affirmative action is applied to promotions but where standards have not been lowered to enlarge the pool of qualified black applicants.

NO

Roger Wilkins

THE CASE FOR AFFIRMATIVE ACTION: RACISM HAS ITS PRIVILEGES

The storm that has been gathering over affirmative action for the past few years has burst. Two conservative California professors are leading a drive to place an initiative on the state ballot in 1996 that will ask Californians to vote affirmative action up or down. Since the state is beloved in political circles for its electoral votes, advance talk of the initiative has put the issue high on the national agenda. Three Republican presidential contenders—Bob Dole, Phil Gramm and Lamar Alexander—have already begun taking shots at various equal opportunity programs. Congressional review of the Clinton Administration's enforcement of these programs has begun. The President has started his own review, promising adherence to principles of nondiscrimination and full opportunity while asserting the need to prune those programs that are unfair or malfunctioning.

It is almost an article of political faith that one of the major influences in last November's [1994] election was the backlash against affirmative action among "angry white men," who are convinced it has stacked the deck against them. Their attitudes are shaped and their anger heightened by unquestioned and virtually uncheckable anecdotes about victimized whites flooding the culture. For example, *Washington Post* columnist Richard Cohen recently began what purported to be a serious analysis and attack on affirmative action by recounting that he had once missed out on a job someplace because they "needed a woman."

Well, I have an anecdote too, and it, together with Cohen's, offers some important insights about the debate that has flared recently around the issues of race, gender and justice. Some years ago, after watching me teach as a visiting professor for two semesters, members of the history department at George Mason University invited me to compete for a full professorship and endowed chair. Mason, like other institutions in Virginia's higher education system, was under a court order to desegregate. I went through the appropriate application and review process and, in due course, was appointed. A few years later, not long after I had been honored as one of the university's distinguished professors, I was shown an article by a white historian asserting that he had been a candidate for that chair but that at the last moment the job had been whisked away and handed to an unqualified black. I checked the story and discovered that this fellow had, in fact, applied but had not even passed the first threshold. But his "reverse discrimination" story is out there polluting the atmosphere in which this debate is taking place.

Affirmative action, as I understand it, was not designed to punish anyone; it was, rather—as a result of a clear-eyed look at how America actually works—an attempt to enlarge opportunity for *everybody*. As amply documented in the 1968 Kerner Commission report on racial disorders, when left to their own devices, American institutions in such areas as college admissions, hiring decisions and loan approvals had been making choices that discriminated against blacks. That discrimination, which flowed from doing what came naturally, hurt more than blacks: It hurt the entire nation, as the riots of the late 1960s demonstrated. Though the Kerner report focused on blacks, similar findings could have been made about other minorities and women.

Affirmative action required institutions to develop plans enabling them to go beyond business as usual and search for qualified people in places where they did not ordinarily conduct their searches or their business. Affirmative action programs generally require some proof that there has been a good-faith effort to follow the plan and numerical guidelines against which to judge the sincerity and the success of the effort. The idea of affirmative action is *not* to force people into positions for which they are unqualified but to encourage institutions to develop realistic criteria for the enterprise at hand and then to find a reasonably diverse mix of people qualified to be engaged in it. Without the requirements calling for plans, good-faith efforts and the setting of broad numerical goals, many institutions would do what they had always done: assert that they had looked but "couldn't find anyone qualified," and then go out and hire the white man they wanted to hire in the first place.

Affirmative action has done wonderful things for the United States by enlarging opportunity and developing and utilizing a far broader array of the skills available in the American population than in the past. It has not outlived its usefulness. It was never designed to be a program to eliminate poverty. It has not always been used wisely, and some of its permutations do have to be reconsidered, refined or, in some cases, abandoned. It is not a quota program, and those cases where rigid numbers are used (except under a court or administrative order after a specific finding of discrimination) are a bastardization of an otherwise highly beneficial set of public policies.

President Clinton is right to review what is being done under present laws and to express a willingness to eliminate activities that either don't work or are unfair. Any program that has been in place for thirty years should be reviewed. Getting rid of what doesn't work is both good government and good politics. Gross abuses of affirmative action provide ammunition for its opponents and undercut the moral authority of the entire effort. But the President should retain—and strengthen where required—those programs necessary to enlarge social justice.

What makes the affirmative action issue so difficult is that it engages blacks and whites exactly at those points where they differ the most. There are some areas, such as rooting for the local football team, where their experiences and views are virtually identical. There are others —sometimes including work and school —where their experiences and views both overlap and diverge. And finally, there are areas such as affirmative action and inextricably related notions about the presence of racism in society where the divergences draw out almost all the points of difference between the races.

THIS LAND IS MY LAND

Blacks and whites experience America very differently. Though we often inhabit the same space, we operate in very disparate psychic spheres.

Whites have an easy sense of ownership of the country; they feel they are entitled to receive all that is best in it. Many of them believe that their country —though it may have some faults—is superior to all others and that, as Americans, they are superior as well. Many of them think of this as a white country and some of them even experience it that way. They think of it as a land of opportunity —a good place with a lot of good people in it. Some suspect (others *know*) that the presence of blacks messes everything up.

To blacks there's nothing very easy about life in America, and any sense of ownership comes hard because we encounter so much resistance in making our way through the ordinary occurrences of life. And I'm not even talking here about overt acts of discrimination but simply about the way whites intrude on and disturb our psychic space without even thinking about it.

A telling example of this was given to me by a black college student in Oklahoma. He said whites give him looks that say: "What are *you* doing here?"

"When do they give you that look?" I asked.

"Every time I walk in a door," he replied.

When he said that, every black person in the room nodded and smiled in a way that indicated recognition based on thousands of such moments in their own lives.

For most blacks, America is either a land of denied opportunity or one in which the opportunities are still grudgingly extended and extremely limited. For some—that one-third who are mired in poverty, many of them isolated in dangerous ghettos—America is a land of desperadoes and desperation. In places where whites see a lot of idealism, blacks see, at best, idealism mixed heavily with hypocrisy. Blacks accept America's greatness, but are unable to ignore ugly warts that many whites seem to need not to see. I am reminded here of James Baldwin's searing observation from *The Fire Next Time:*

> The American Negro has the great advantage of having never believed that collection of myths to which white Americans cling: that their ancestors were all freedom-loving heroes, that they were born in the greatest country the world has ever seen, or that Americans are invincible in battle and wise in peace, that Americans have always dealt honorably with Mexicans and Indians and all other neighbors or inferiors, that American men are the world's most direct and virile, that American women are pure.

It goes without saying, then, that blacks and whites remember America differently. The past is hugely important since we argue a lot about who we are on the basis of who we think we have been, and we derive much of our sense of the future from how we think we've done in the past. In a nation in which few people know much history these are perilous arguments, because in such a vacuum, people tend to weave historical fabled tailored to their political or psychic needs.

Blacks are still recovering the story of their role in America which so many white historians simply ignored or told in ways that made black people ashamed. But in a culture that batters us, learning the real history is vital in helping blacks feel fully human. It also helps us understand just how deeply American we are, how richly we have given, how much has been taken from us and how much has yet to be restored. Supporters of affirmative action believe that broad and deep damage has been done to American culture by racism and sexism over the whole course of American history and that they are still powerful forces today. We believe that minorities and women are still disadvantaged in our highly competitive society and that affirmative action is absolutely necessary to level the playing field.

Not all white Americans oppose this view and not all black Americans support it. There are a substantial number of whites in this country who have been able to escape our racist and sexist past and to enter fully into the quest for equal justice. There are other white Americans who are not racists but who more or less passively accept the powerful suggestions coming at them from all points in the culture that whites are entitled to privilege and to freedom from competition with blacks. And then there are racists who just don't like blacks or who actively despise us. There are still others who may or may not feel deep antipathy, but who know how to manipulate racism and white

anxiety for their own ends. Virtually all the people in the last category oppose affirmative action and some of them make a practice of preying upon those in the second category who are not paying attention or who, like the Post's Richard Cohen, are simply confused.

THE POLITICS OF DENIAL

One of these political predators is Senate majority leader Bob Dole. In his offhandedly lethal way, Dole delivered a benediction of "let me now forgive us" on *Meet the Press* recently. After crediting affirmative action for the 62 percent of the white male vote garnered by the Republicans, he remarked that slavery was "before we were born" and wondered whether future generations ought to have to continue "paying a price" for those ancient wrongs.

Such a view holds that whatever racial problems we once may have had have been solved over the course of the past thirty years and that most of our current racial friction is caused by racial and gender preferences that almost invariably work to displace some "qualified" white male. Words and phrases like "punish" or "preference" or "reverse discrimination" or "quota" are dropped into the discourse to buttress this view, as are those anecdotes about injustice to whites. Proponents of affirmative action see these arguments as disingenuous but ingenious because they reduce serious and complex social, political, economic, historical and psychological issues to bumper-sticker slogans designed to elicit Pavlovian responses.

The fact is that the successful public relations assault on affirmative action flows on a river of racism that is as broad, powerful and American as the

Mississippi. And, like the Mississippi, racism can be violent and deadly and is a permanent feature of American life. But while nobody who is sane denies the reality of the Mississippi, millions of Americans who are deemed sane—some of whom are powerful and some even thought wise—deny, wholly or in part, that racism exists.

It is critical to understand the workings of denial in this debate because it is used to obliterate the facts that created the need for the remedy in the first place. One of the best examples of denial was provided recently by the nation's most famous former history professor, House Speaker Newt Gingrich. According to *The Washington Post*, "Gingrich dismissed the argument that the beneficiaries of affirmative action, commonly African Americans, have been subjected to discrimination over a period of centuries. 'That is true of virtually every American,' Gingrich said, noting that the Irish were discriminated against by the English, for example."

That is breathtaking stuff coming from somebody who should know that blacks have been on this North American continent for 375 years and that for 245 the country permitted slavery. Gingrich should also know that for the next hundred years we had legalized subordination of blacks, under a suffocating blanket of condescension and frequently enforced by nightriding terrorists. We've had only thirty years of something else.

That something else is a nation trying to lift its ideals out of a thick, often impenetrable slough of racism. Racism is a hard word for what over the centuries became second nature in America-preferences across the board for white men and, following in their wake, white women. Many of these men

seem to feel that it is un-American to ask them to share anything with blacks —particularly their work, their neighborhoods or "their" women. To protect these things—apparently essential to their identity—they engage in all forms of denial. For a historian to assert that "virtually every American" shares the history I have just outlined comes very close to lying.

Denial of racism is much like the denials that accompany addictions to alcohol, drugs or gambling. It is probably not stretching the analogy too much to suggest that many racist whites are so addicted to their unwarranted privileges and so threatened by the prospect of losing them that all kinds of defenses become acceptable, including insistent distortions of reality in the form of hypocrisy, lying or the most outrageous political demagogy.

'THOSE PEOPLE' DON'T DESERVE HELP

The demagogues have reverted to a new version of quite an old trick. Before the 1950s, whites who were busy denying that the nation was unfair to blacks would simply assert that we didn't deserve dual treatment because we were *inferior*. These days it is not permissible in most public circles to say that blacks are inferior, but it is perfectly acceptable to target the *behavior* of blacks, specifically poor blacks. The argument then follows a fairly predictable line: The behavior of poor blacks requires a severe rethinking of national social policy, it is said. Advantaged blacks really don't need affirmative action anymore, and when they are the objects of such programs, some qualified white person (unqualified white people don't show up in these arguments) is

-sum game in which only the "vic-
s" benefit. But racist and sexist whites
o are not able to accept the full
manity of other people are them-
ves badly damaged—morally stunted
people. The principal product of a
cist and sexist society is damaged peo-
e and institutions—victims and victim-
rs alike....

Journalistic institutions often view the
tion through a lens that bends reality
support white privilege. A recent issue
U.S. News & World Report introduced a
ackage of articles on these issues with a
uestion on its cover: "Does affirmative
ction mean NO WHITE MEN NEED
APPLY?" The words "No white men
eed apply" were printed in red against
white background and were at least
our times larger than the other words
n the question. Inside, the lead story was
llustrated by a painting that carries out
he cover theme, with a wan white man
separated from the opportunity ladders
eagerly being scaled by women and
dark men. And the story yielded up the
following sentence: "Affirmative action
poses a conflict between two cherished
American principles: the belief that all
Americans deserve equal opportunities
and the idea that hard work and merit,
not race or religion or gender or birth-
right, should determine who prospers
and who does not."

Whoever wrote that sentence was in
the thrall of one of the myths that Baldwin
was talking about. The sentence suggests
—as many people do when talking
about affirmative action—that America
is a meritocratic society. But what kind
of meritocracy excludes women and
blacks and other minorities from all
meaningful competition? And even in the
competition among white men, money,
family and connections often count for
much more than merit, test results (for
whatever they're worth) and hard work.

The U.S. News story perpetuates and
strengthens the view that many of my
white students absorb from their parents:
that white men now have few chances in
this society. The fact is that white men still
control virtually everything in America
except the wealth held by widows.
According to the Urban Institute, 53
percent of black men aged 25–34 are
either unemployed or earn too little to
lift a family of four from poverty....

Seen only as a corrective for ancient
wrongs, affirmative action may be dismissed by the likes of Gingrich, Gramm
and Dole, just as attempts to federalize
decent treatment of the freed slaves were
dismissed after Reconstruction more than
a century ago. Then, striking down the
Civil Rights Act of 1875, Justice Joseph
Bradley wrote of blacks that "there must
be some stage in the progress of his ele-
vation when he takes the rank of a mere
citizen, and ceases to be the special fa-
vorite of the laws, and when his rights, as
a citizen or a man, are to be protected in
the ordinary modes by which other men's
rights are protected."

But white skin has made some citizens
—particularly white males—*the special
favorites of the culture.* It may be that we
will need affirmative action until most
white males are really ready for a color-
blind society—that is, when they are
ready to assume "the rank of a mere
citizen." As a nation we took a hard
look at that special favoritism thirty years
ago. Though the centuries of cultural
preference enjoyed by white males still
overwhelmingly skew power and wealth
their way, we have in fact achieved a
more meritocratic society as a result of
affirmative action than we have ever
previously enjoyed in this country.

(as Dole might put it) "punished." While it is possible that color-blind affirmative action programs benefiting all disadvantaged Americans are needed, those (i.e., blacks) whose behavior is so distressing must be punished by restricting welfare, shriveling the safety net and expanding the prison opportunity. All of that would presumably give us, in William Bennett's words, "what we want—a color-blind society," for which the white American psyche is presumably fully prepared.

There are at least three layers of unreality in these precepts. The first is that the United States is not now and probably never will be a color-blind society. It is the most color-conscious society on earth. Over the course of 375 years, whites have given blacks absolutely no reason to believe that they can behave in a color-blind manner. In many areas of our lives —particularly in employment, housing and education—affirmative action is required to counter deeply ingrained racist patterns of behavior

Second, while I don't hold the view that all blacks who behave badly are blameless victims of a brutal system, I do believe that many poor blacks have, indeed, been brutalized by our culture, and I know of *no* blacks, rich or poor, who haven't been hurt in some measure by the racism in this country. The current mood (and, in some cases like the Speaker's, the cultivated ignorance) completely ignores the fact that some blacks never escaped the straight line of oppression that ran from slavery through the semislavery of sharecropping to the late mid-century migration from Southern farms into isolated pockets of urban poverty. Their families have always been excluded, poor and without skills, and so they were utterly defenseless when the enormous American economic dislocations that be-

gan in the mid-1970s slammed communities, followed closely waves of crack cocaine. One wo that the double-digit unemploy fered consistently over the p decades by blacks who were *lo work* would be a permanent fe the discussions about race, respor welfare and rights.

But a discussion of the huge nt of black workers who are becomir nomically redundant would raise cult questions about the efficiency economy at a time when millions of men feel insecure. Any honest app of unemployment would reveal tha lions of low-skilled white men wer ing severely damaged by corporate Federal Reserve decisions; it might refocus the anger of those whites in middle ranks whose careers have b shattered by the corporate downsizi fad.

But people's attention is kept train on the behavior of some poor blacks b politicians and television news shows, re inforcing the stereotypes of blacks as dan gerous, as threats, as unqualified. Fright ened whites direct their rage at pushy blacks rather than at the corporations that export manufacturing operations to low wage countries, or at the Federal Reserve which imposes interest rate hikes tha slow down the economy.

WHO BENEFITS? WE ALL DO

There is one final denial that blar kets all the rest. It is that only s ciety's "victims"—blacks, other minor ties and women (who should, for God sake, renounce their victimological ou looks)—have been injured by white ma supremacy. Viewed in this light, aff mative action remedies are a kind

If we want to continue making things better in this society, we'd better figure out ways to protect and defend affirmative action against the confused, the frightened, the manipulators and, yes, the liars in politics, journalism, education and wherever else they may be found. In the name of longstanding American prejudice and myths and in the service of their own narrow interests, power-lusts or blindness, they are truly victimizing the rest of us, perverting the ideals they claim to stand for and destroying the nation they pretend to serve.

POSTSCRIPT

Should Affirmative Action Policies Be Discontinued?

Despite their basic disagreement, both Puddington and Wilkins desire a colorblind society. The authors' main disagreement is on the need for affirmative action today to achieve this goal. Wilkins suggests that in order to *bring about* color blindness, it may be necessary to become temporarily color conscious. But for how long? And is there a danger that this temporary color consciousness may become a permanent policy, as Puddington fears? Puddington observes that Americans support "soft affirmative action" but are opposed to more aggressive affirmative action. Could less aggressive affirmative action be the way to greater national unity on the race issue?

The writings on this subject are diverse and numerous. For a personal reading of black and white attitudes, see Studs Terkel, *Race: How Blacks and Whites Think and Feel About the American Obsession* (New Press, 1992). For a more academic reading of white racial attitudes, see Paul M. Sniderman and Thomas Piazza, *The Scar of Race* (Harvard University Press, 1993). One way to learn about racism is to read Gregory Howard Williams's story about living as a black after years as a white in *Life on the Color Line: The True Story of a White Boy Who Discovered He Was Black* (E. P. Dutton, 1995). Two works that portray the experiences of racism by the black middle class are Ellis Close, *The Rage of a Privileged Class* (HarperCollins, 1993) and Joe R. Feagin and Melvin P. Sikes, *Living With Racism: The Black Middle-Class Experience* (Beacon, 1994). Two personal accounts of this experience are Brent Staples, *Parallel Time: Growing Up in Black and White* (Pantheon, 1994) and Henry Louis Gates, *Colored People* (Free Press, 1994). Steven L. Carter's *Reflections of an Affirmative Action Baby* (Basic Books, 1991) is based on the author's own experiences under affirmative action. Andrew Hacker argues that affirmative action has relatively minor adverse consequences for whites in *Two Nations: Black and White, Separate, Hostile, Unequal* (Charles Scribner's Sons, 1992). Lee Sigleman and Susan Welch, in *Black Americans' Views of Racial Inequality: The Dream Deferred* (Cambridge University Press, 1991), argue that blacks and whites have basically different perspectives of the racial situation. Dinesh D'Souza, in *The End of Racism* (Free Press, 1995), argues that white racism has pretty much disappeared in the United States. The opposite is argued by Joe Feagin and Hernan Vera in *White Racism: The Basics* (Routledge, 1995) and by Stephen Steinberg in *Turning Back* (Beacon Press, 1995). Further support for the thesis of continuing racism is supplied by Douglas S. Massey and Nancy A. Denton in *American Apartheid: Segregation and the Making of the Underclass* (Harvard University Press, 1993).

ISSUE 11

Do Social and Mental Pathologies Largely Account for Homelessness?

YES: Myron Magnet, from *The Dream and the Nightmare: The Sixties' Legacy to the Underclass* (William Morrow, 1993)

NO: Jonathan Kozol, from *Rachel and Her Children: Homeless Families in America* (Crown Publishers, 1988)

ISSUE SUMMARY

YES: Essayist Myron Magnet argues that the vast majority of the permanently homeless are people who belong in institutions, not low-income housing.

NO: Social commentator Jonathan Kozol maintains that homelessness results from the lack of affordable housing, not from the personal problems of the homeless people themselves.

The number of America's homeless has become a national scandal. No one knows for certain exactly how many homeless there are—estimates have ranged from a low of 250,000 to a high of 3 million—but anyone walking through the streets of America's cities is likely to encounter them.

A generation ago, it was rare to see anyone begging and living on the streets of an American city. Why are there so many homeless people on the streets of America now? The answer seems to vary according to the ideology of the analyst. Leftists attribute homelessness to the structural failures of American capitalism. Liberals blame it on the Reagan and Bush administrations, which produced cutbacks in federal spending on low-income housing. Social conservatives say it comes from the breakdown of families and the unwise policy of "deinstitutionalizing" the mentally ill, which releases patients from institutional care and into the community. And fiscal conservatives blame rent control and similar government interventions in the market economy, which, as they see it, caused the deterioration and ultimate abandonment of residential buildings.

All these explanations may shed some light on the problem of homelessness. The U.S. economy has not been able to suppress its cyclical ups and downs, and during recession periods the homelessness problem gets worse. Even during good times, policymakers have not been able to find a satisfactory answer to the problem of the "underclass," or the chronically unemployed and dependent. Even for those who do work there is a shortage of affordable housing in some major American cities. But homelessness has other roots as well. The mentally ill have been deinstitutionalized in large numbers since the 1960s. The major purpose of this policy was to improve the quality of life of the patients, but for many of these former inmates the results turned out to be disastrous. Assumptions about the kind of care that they could receive in the community proved false, or the released patients failed to avail themselves of the services provided. Drug addicts also swelled the population of the homeless (some estimates put them at a third of New York City's homeless population), adding to the sense that homelessness is a kind of social disease and increasing much of the public's desire to solve the problem by "sweeping the streets" of the homeless.

There is no one simple solution to the tragedy of homelessness. The police could be ordered to sweep the streets of the homeless, but where would they be kept? In jail? In mental institutions? Both are overcrowded to begin with, and jailing or otherwise confining people who have committed no crime hardly seems just. At the other end of the spectrum is a seemingly compassionate solution: build more shelters and low-income housing. But the experiences of Washington, D.C., and New York City in this area indicate that shelter building and the policy of giving the homeless priority in getting low-income housing may cause even more homelessness. Moreover, many of the homeless are unable to afford even low-income housing, and others are unable to function without supervision even in free housing.

A clear-eyed, objective study of the varying needs of the homeless seems necessary. But even before that, perhaps researchers should listen to the many voices of those who are touched by homelessness—the homeless themselves, advocates for the homeless, local officials confronted with the problem, and people who are not homeless but who encounter homeless people every day.

Two of these voices are presented in the following selections. Myron Magnet argues that homelessness has become a national problem because of public shelter building and other forms of state-run charity. He maintains that these programs have encouraged a small minority of pathological individuals to live on the streets. Jonathan Kozol, however, contends that the homeless mostly consist not of weird social misfits but of individuals and families who are too poor to afford private housing. In Kozol's view, mass homelessness has resulted from a combination of market forces in the 1980s that forced the poor out of their neighborhoods and a cutback in government support for low-income housing. Perhaps the greatest difference between Magnet and Kozol is not what their heads think but what their hearts feel about the homeless.

YES   Myron Magnet

THE SIXTIES' LEGACY TO THE UNDERCLASS

Here is a man moving his bowels on the Seventy-ninth Street sidewalk in the pouring afternoon rain. Behind him rises the Beaux Arts splendor of the Apthorp Apartments, an opulent relic of New York's vanished age of civic confidence. The squatting man, his smile sheepishly vacant, slowly tears up a newspaper and wipes himself with great deliberateness. Passing along this busy thoroughfare, embarrassed and dismayed, I can't keep at bay a discordantly uncharitable thought: what a fitting end to years—years!—of preposterously muddleheaded reporting on the problem of homelessness.

This is not kind, I know. But the shocking actuality of homelessness is so utterly different from the picture journalists have drawn that it's hard to keep patience with their almost mystifying distortion and misrepresentation of the unsettling truth. Can all of today's reporters commute from the suburbs? If you live in a city, after all, you can't help glimpsing the painful reality, as here on Seventy-ninth Street, before averting your eyes in shame. You get used to reassuring children after they've seen such sights—after they've been startled by sleeping bundles of rags at first indistinguishable from the trash by which the sleeper lies, after they've been frightened by aggressively insistent beggars or implacably angry, wild-eyed mutterers pushing refuse-laden shopping carts.

We urban dwellers have had to meditate on sights like these black plastic garbage bags, laid out last night like rotund soldiers in neat platoons of twenty or thirty beside each apartment building. This morning, like so many mornings, they are slashed open, their contents wildly strewn all over the pavement in a sickening riot of rot and disorder.

Dogs? hazarded a visitor from out-of-town.

No. The homeless have been scavenging. Once I saw magazines I had thrown away spread out in rows on a busy sidewalk, offered for sale by a homeless entrepreneur.

Of course it's especially raw in my borderline neighborhood, by turns gentrifying and degentrifying. Here—one block from a park where the homeless live, three blocks from the mostly underclass housing project into whose windows my old apartment looked, around the corner from a crack house—the poor are real, not the figment of a reporter's or advocate's imagination. Just look: you can't help seeing the true texture of life at the bottom.

The evidence of your senses shows you firsthand what scientific studies have been revealing with ever-increasing insistence: the homeless are radically different from the picture the advocates and the press painted all through the eighties and beyond. The fictitious picture is, to be sure, a dramatic attention-grabber. For starters, its scale is heroic: homelessness is a big, big problem. The advocates claim that three million Americans—over 1 percent of the total population—have no roof over their heads. Many more are allegedly so precariously housed that they might find themselves out on the street tomorrow. Already urgent, the homelessness problem can only intensify.

But like so many of the "facts" about the homeless, these numbers are pure fantasy. They were pulled out of the air by the wildest of advocates, the late Mitch Snyder, a troubled, stubble-bearded radical activist who headed an antiquated Washington antiwar commune grandiosely styled the Community for Creative Non-Violence. The commune sheltered the homeless, and Snyder, available right down the street whenever legislators needed an "expert," was asked by a congressional committee in 1980 exactly how many Americans were homeless. He simply made up a number: exactly 2.2 million fellow citizens, one American out of every hundred, lacked homes, he pronounced. Two years later he upped his estimate to 3 million. Snyder always declined to debate these figures; getting numbers right, he haughtily remarked, could only concern "Americans with little Western minds that have to quantify everything in sight."

Networks, newsweeklies, and most national dailies readily swallowed this fabrication. For a decade, "three million homeless" became a journalistic mantra.

But this number isn't just false: it is grotesquely, outrageously false. Responsible scientific investigators went out looking for Snyder's huddled masses. Guided by experienced policemen, social workers, and local homeless people, researchers combed major cities after dark, searching out the homeless in alleys, cellars, vacant buildings, thickets, all-night movies, and parked cars, including those rented out at fifty cents a night by an enterprising Washington garage attendant. The evidence they turned up after such diligence suggests a number around *one tenth* of Snyder's—probably 300,000 to 360,000. This is a lot of people, but it is hardly the apocalyptic catastrophe requiring total national mobilization that Snyder and his fellow advocates, supported by a credulous press, have depicted.

It's not merely the size of the problem that the advocates have misrepresented. More important, they have hopelessly muddled the larger question of who the homeless are and how they landed in their deplorable plight. In particular, listening to the advocates' insistence that increasing numbers of the homeless are families rather than unattached individuals, you'd think that Ozzie and Harriet were out on the street with their frightened kids clinging to their knees. Turning on the TV news to see what congressional advocates for the homeless are up to only strengthens that impression. Says advocate Robert Hayes, an ex–Wall Street lawyer who heads the National Coalition for the Homeless: "I can't tell you how often a congressional committee has called and said, 'We need a witness for a hearing. Can you get us a homeless family: mother, father—father out of work in the past four months from an industrial plant—white?' " Though such families can be found among the homeless —and could especially be found in the very early eighties, when the first wave of America's successful industrial restructuring painfully dislocated Rust Belt, logging, and oil patch workers—they are most untypical and are never homeless for long.

The broad intention of this distortion is to make viewers sympathize by identification, even if that entails shading the truth. But within that general intention is a sharply focused political point. Here are mainstream citizens doing everything right but nevertheless struck down by the homelessness plague—as you could be. The advocates have no doubt whatever about the source of the contagion. Says Hayes: "The homeless are indeed the most egregious symbol of a cruel economy, an unresponsive government, a festering value system." They are the victims of a ferocious, unjust economic Darwinism that has made the rich opulently richer at the calamitous expense of the poor, that has swept away jobs through "deindustrialization," that has gentrified affordable housing off the face of the earth for the benefit of self-cherishing yuppies. Indeed, the homeless are a moral thermometer, registering in their numbers and degradation the rising heartlessness and inequality of the American social order.

By now even the homeless themselves have incorporated these sentiments into their begging jingles. One drug-wasted regular on my downtown subway wove it into a craftily up-to-the-minute fabric of rock music and "concerned" politics as he lurched through the train jingling his cup each morning.

> "We got a problem, [he rather woozily sang]
> We gotta address it,
> It needs a so-lu-tion—
> It could happen to you or meeee...."

Throughout the eighties, many turned the indictment explicitly partisan. A Case Western Reserve professor "of family and child welfare," to take only one example, confidently predicted in *The New York Times* a rash of Hoovervilles that he dubbed Reaganvilles. As an academic expert on the homeless, sociologist Peter Rossi, sums up: "The advocates want you to say, 'There but for the grace of God— and the fact that Reagan didn't look at me directly—go I.' "

And then it became George Bush's turn. As columnist Anna Quindlen pronounced: "If empty shelves became a symbol for the failure of Communism in the Soviet Union, people living in cardboard boxes are the most visible sign that America is on the skids. They are living, breathing symbols of an economy that, no matter what the Astigmatism president says, is a mess."

You don't have to live in my neighborhood to know that this whole farrago just isn't so. All you have to do is go home by train or subway and pay attention. What you see, if you stop to look, is craziness, drunkenness, dope, and danger. Far from being the index of the nation's turpitude, the homeless are an encyclopedia of social pathology and mental disorder.

And what has produced homelessness is by no means Reaganomics or yuppification or any other primarily economic dislocation. What the homeless encamped in the streets, parks, and train stations in the heart of our cities really embody is the most extreme and catastrophic failure of the cultural revolution of the Haves and the social policies that resulted from it.

Look at who the homeless really are. The various subgroups of them overlap, so that separating them into categories yields only approximations. But the overall picture is clear.

In outline, it looks like this. Homeless families account for a little over a quarter of all homeless persons. These aren't conventional or ordinary families: put aside the image of Beaver Cleaver and his folks scouring the country for work. Instead, homeless families—almost *all* of them—consist of a single mother and her children. Almost *all* such families are on welfare. Half of them, according to one authoritative study, are headed by women under twenty-five years old, many themselves the illegitimate daughters of single mothers.

Homeless families, in other words, are an extension of the underclass. For the most part, they are headed by a subgroup of welfare mothers who haven't succeeded in keeping a roof over their children's heads. They live in welfare hotels and shelters, and they are homeless not in the sense of having been living on the streets but rather having been evicted from their own apartments or having been thrown out by friends. Or they have declared themselves homeless —no one checks to see if they really are —in order to get bumped to the head of the waiting list for permanent subsidized housing.

By contrast with homeless families, single homeless individuals are mostly men—at least three of them for each single homeless woman. Not as young as homeless welfare mothers, they are still youngish, with an average age in the mid-

to late thirties. A majority of the single homeless are blacks and other minorities, with the proportion of minority persons ranging from 89 percent in New York to 23 percent in Portland, Oregon.

The single homeless are an even more pathological population than the underclass. Around one third of them are alcoholics, and the majority use drugs. In New York City shelters, 65 percent of the homeless singles tested by urinalysis showed positive results for drugs or alcohol, with 83 percent of that group testing positive for cocaine.

A startling number of them are criminals. Checking the records of several homeless beggars recently arrested for misdemeanors in New York's Pennsylvania Station, for example, police were taken aback to discover that two of the men were wanted for murder. Half of those arrested for rape in Santa Monica, California, in 1991 were homeless men. At least 40 percent of the single homeless nationwide have been in jail, for an average of two years. Somewhere between 13 and 26 percent of the incarcerated, depending on which study you pick, served their time for major crimes or felonies. While some of the criminal homeless landed in jail for crimes committed after they became homeless, the majority—63 percent—were criminals first and homeless second. So for most of this group, one can't argue that homelessness drove them to crime. Putting it mildly, all this adds up to something very different from the mainstream impression the advocates have tried to evoke.

It's a tough stretch to follow the advocates in seeing the criminal or drug-taking homeless as victims deserving compassion; but for one of the largest, most conspicuous groups of the homeless, those who are mentally ill, compassion is properly in order. These disturbing figures—the lumpish shopping-bag ladies, the muttering men in rags pushing grocery carts—did not create their deplorable fate. They are the involuntary victims not only of their disease but also of a society that mocks them with a benefit they don't need in place of one they need desperately.

Ten National Institute of Mental Health studies of different large cities consistently show that around one third of the homeless—well over 100,000 souls if the homeless total 350,000—suffer from serious mental illnesses. If anything, the number may be higher: a recent, authoritative psychiatric study of the homeless in Baltimore found that almost half the women and 42 percent of the men suffered from a major mental disorder. Add in alcohol and drug abuse, and you account for 80 percent of the homeless single women and 91 percent of the homeless men in Baltimore. A 1988 Los Angeles study showed that 44 percent of the single homeless in that city had been hospitalized for psychiatric reasons. Two thirds of the New York homeless who live on the streets, rather than in the shelters, are schizophrenic, another study found....

It shouldn't be possible to be so protected from the natural consequences of your own self-destructive actions as to have a taxpayer-provided roof over your head with no questions asked and no conditions imposed. Take your meals at the soup kitchen, panhandle unmolested at the railroad station for crack or wine money—you can usually make at least a tax-free twelve dollars in a few hours, not much worse than the minimum wage —and you have achieved the life of a significant fraction of the homeless. This life is squalid, to be sure, but it insulates those who live it from the most immediate bad consequences of their behavior and removes an extremely effective deterrent to such behavior.

Public shelters, open to all comers, may cause at least as much homelessness as they cure. They draw more people out of housing than off the street. It's not just that they give people the option of not paying rent; they also allow people who've been doubled up with family or friends to move out—or to be shoved out with less guilt. That's one reason why cities and counties with liberal shelter admissions policies have larger homeless populations than jurisdictions with less "generous" policies, and why homeless populations suddenly grow as provision for the homeless is liberalized. A scant two years after Washington voters passed Initiative 17, guaranteeing shelter to all District of Columbia residents, for instance, homeless families in D.C. shelters increased by 500 percent. One woman phoned from Hong Kong as soon as she heard of the guarantee to say that she had just enough money for plane fare, so would the authorities please reserve space for her and her children.

Right-to-shelter policies promote dependency. Take the case of Lowell, a twenty-seven-year-old I met in New York's Catherine Street family shelter. With winning smile and ingratiating manner, he formerly made $350 a week as a manager of a Burger King; his wife, who lived in the shelter with him, was earning $160 at one of the chain's other branches. He landed in the shelter when an aunt evicted him from his little apartment in her house. Within several weeks, after getting back from work late enough to be locked out of the shelter several times, he quit his job. Too much hassle.

He told me he could easily find another job, but the idea left him cold. "If you get a job, you're going to be abused financially," he said. "No one has ever paid me what I'm worth." So he was spending his time lettering signs for the shelter and feasting on grandiose fantasies of becoming a famous graphic artist. Alas, his signs plastered on every wall showed no trace of the requisite talent. Meanwhile, he had no complaints. "You know what we had for dinner last night?" he asked. "Steak! We have a TV, a video room. I see more movies here than I ever saw outside. You really can't ask for more." If he had less, he would bestir himself quickly and soon be neither homeless nor a dropout from the labor force.

I don't at all mean to say that you won't find genuine distress being relieved in shelters. Of course some of those taking refuge there have been driven from their homes by fire, job loss, domestic violence. People do suffer misfortunes that overwhelm them, or they lose their way, grow confused, lose heart, and temporarily stop struggling. I have talked to them in shelters, seen the fear and humiliation that breaks through the armor of rigid reserve and haughty impassivity. But such people are seldom homeless long, and they are a very small minority of the public shelter population.

Public shelters don't distinguish among the unfortunate, the malingerers like Lowell, and the truly asocial. At Catherine Street, for instance, you look in one large, messy, fourteen-bed room housing four or five families and discover a malevolent-looking young man and his sixteen- or seventeen-year-old wife lying in adjoining beds at noon. A few doors down the hall you come upon four beds drawn close together to mark out one family's turf, each bed made up with military precision, each pillow surmounted

by a handmade stuffed animal, a goldfish swimming in a bowl on the nightstand—all this betokening a far different mode of life, far higher aspirations. But to the shelter, all are equally homeless, all equally deserving of being housed at the taxpayers' cost.

At the very least, it would make sense for public shelter systems to institute much more discriminating admissions policies and house far fewer people. They would create less dependency if they also offered only temporary, not open-ended, shelter.

Even so, privately supported and privately run shelters are vastly preferable to public ones. Private shelters resist turning into huge, ravenously expensive, permanent bureaucracies with specious "entitlements" that continually expand the clientele and sink clients into permanent dependency. What's more, private shelters have a purposefulness that public ones lack. They have standards and values. They aim to change lives and save souls, to rescue the sinner and redeem the irredeemable. Laudable and necessary in a humane community, these goals nevertheless move beyond the scope of the state.

Suppose the following reversals occurred: what would happen? Picture for a moment the public shelters of the great cities shrunk or closed, the mentally ill in appropriate treatment, private shelters relieving temporary distress and trying to rehabilitate such drunks, drug takers, and dropouts as they deem salvageable, public places swept of beggars and sleepers, and a sense of public order restored. Would the sum total of distress be greater? Would thousands upon thousands of the homeless who formerly slept in the public shelters or in the subways now be freezing under bridges and starving on skid rows?

I think not. Were it to stop being so easy to drop out into a truly dead-end life—were compassionate citizens to stop sympathetically viewing the alcoholic, the drug-addicted, and the idle as poor, downtrodden victims to whom giving handouts is a public necessity—this variety of homelessness would become far less attractive. And in an intact social order, where petty lawlessness and self-destructive irresponsibility are not suffered to flourish in the heart of the city, many fewer would feel tempted to fall into such a fate.

We have misconceived every part of the homelessness problem—who the homeless are, how they got that way, what our own responsibility for their plight really is, what help to give them. We have abandoned the mad to the streets in the name of a liberty that mocks them. We take the sympathy we owe them and lavish it indiscriminately upon those who happen to look like them and be standing near them. If our public spaces are hijacked and despoiled, that somehow helps assuage the vague guilt we feel but can't quite bring into focus. If that erodes our social order, who are we —the guilty—to call others to account?

Enough. It's time to stop kidding ourselves and clean up the mess that a specious liberation has made.

NO

Jonathan Kozol

HOMELESS FAMILIES IN AMERICA

OVERVIEW: A CAPTIVE STATE

Since 1980 homelessness has changed its character. What was once a theater of the grotesque (bag ladies in Grand Central Station, winos sleeping in the dusty sun outside the Greyhound station in El Paso) has grown into the common misery of millions.

"This is a new population," said a homeless advocate in Massachusetts. "Many are people who were working all their lives. When they lose their jobs they lose their homes. When they lose their homes they start to lose their families too."

Even in New York City, with its permanent population of the long-term unemployed, 50 percent of individuals served at city shelters during 1984 were there for the first time. The same percentage holds throughout the nation.

The chilling fact, from any point of view, is that small children have become the fastest-growing sector of the homeless. At the time of writing there are 28,000 homeless people in emergency shelters in the city of New York. An additional 40,000 are believed to be unsheltered citywide. Of those who are sheltered, about 10,000 are homeless individuals. The remaining 18,000 are parents and children in almost 5,000 families. The average homeless family includes a parent with two or three children. The average child is six years old, the average parent twenty-seven.

In Massachusetts, three fourths of all homeless people are now children and their parents. In certain parts of Massachusetts (Plymouth, Attleboro, and Northampton) 90 to 95 percent of those who have no homes are families with children.

Homeless people are poor people. Four out of ten poor people in America are children, though children make up only one fourth of our population. The number of children living in poverty has grown to 14 million—an increase of 3 million over 1968—while welfare benefits to families with children have declined one third.

Seven hundred thousand poor children, of whom 100,000 have no health insurance, live in New York City. Approximately 20 percent of New York City's children lived in poverty in 1970, 33 percent in 1980, over 40 percent by 1982....

How Many Are Homeless in America?
The U.S. Department of Health and Human Services (HHS), relying on groups that represent the homeless, suggested a figure of 2 million people in late 1983. Diminished numbers of low-income dwelling units and diminished welfare grants during the four years since may give credence to a current estimate, accepted by the Coalition for the Homeless, of 3 to 4 million people.

There is much debate about the numbers; the debate has a dreamlike quality for me because it parallels exactly the debates about the numbers of illiterate Americans. Government agencies again appear to contradict each other and attempt to peg the numbers low enough to justify inaction—or, in this case, negative action in the form of federal cuts.

Officials in the U.S. Department of Housing and Urban Development (HUD) puzzled congressional leaders during hearings held in 1984 by proposing a low estimate of 250,000 to 350,000 homeless people nationwide. The study from which HUD's estimate was drawn had contemplated as many as 586,000 people, but this number was discredited in its report.

A House subcommittee revealed serious flaws in the HUD study. Subsequent investigations indicated HUD had "pressured its consultants to keep the estimates low." HUD's researchers, for example, suggested a "reliable" low estimate of 12,000 homeless persons in New York City on a given night in January 1984. Yet, on the night in question, over 16,000 people had been given shelter in New York; and this, of course, does not include the larger number in the streets who had received no shelter. U.S. Representative Henry Gonzalez termed HUD's study intentionally deceptive.

Estimates made by shelter operators in twenty-one selected cities in October 1986 total about 230,000 people. This sampling does not include Chicago, San Francisco, Houston, Cleveland, Philadelphia, Baltimore, Atlanta, Pittsburgh, St. Paul, San Diego, or Detroit. With estimates from these and other major cities added, the total would exceed 400,000.

Even this excludes the metropolitan areas around these cities and excludes those middle-sized cities—Lawrence, Lowell, Worcester, Brockton, Attleboro, for example, all in Massachusetts—in which the loss of industrial jobs has marginalized hundreds of thousands of the working poor. Though technically not unemployed, most of these families live in economic situations so precarious that they cannot meet the basic costs of life, particularly rent, which in all these cities has skyrocketed. Nor does this include the rural areas of the Midwest and the Plains states, the oil towns of the Southwest, the southern states from which assembly plants and textile industries have fled, lumber counties such as those in Oregon and their New England counterparts in northern Maine. The homeless in these areas alone, if added to the major-city totals, would bring a cautious national count above 1.5 million.

We would be wise, however, to avoid the numbers game. Any search for the "right number" carries the assumption that we may at last arrive at an acceptable number. There is no acceptable number. Whether the number is 1 million or 4 million or the administration's estimate of less than a million, there are too many homeless people in America.[1]

Homeless people are, of course, impossible to count because they are so difficult to find. That is intrinsic to their plight. They have no address beyond a shelter bed, room number, tent or cave. In this book I follow my own sense that the number is between 2 and 3 million. If we include those people housing organizers call the "hidden homeless"— families doubled up illegally with other families, with the consequent danger that both families may be arbitrarily evicted— we are speaking of much larger numbers.

In 1983, 17,000 families were doubled up illegally in public housing in New York City. The number jumped to 35,000 by spring of 1986. Including private as well as public housing, the number had risen above 100,000 by November 1986. If we accept the New York City estimate of three to four family members in each low-income household, the total number of people (as opposed to families) doubled up in public and private housing in New York is now above 300,000.

The line from "doubling up" to homelessness is made explicit in a study by Manhattan's borough president: At least 50 percent of families entering New York City shelters (1986) were previously doubled up. Nationwide, more than 3 million families now are living doubled up.

It is, however, not only families doubled up or tripled up who are in danger of eviction. Any poor family paying rent or mortgage that exceeds one half of monthly income is in serious danger. Over 6 million American households pay half or more of income for their rent. Of these, 4.7 million pay 60 percent or more. Of mortgaged homeowners, 2 million pay half or more of income for their hous-

ing. Combining these households with those who are doubled up, it appears that well above 10 million families may be living near the edge of homelessness in the United States.

Why Are They Without Homes?

Unreflective answers might retreat to explanations with which readers are familiar: "family breakdown," "drugs," "culture of poverty," "teen pregnancies," "the underclass," etc. While these are precipitating factors for some people, they are not the cause of homelessness. *The cause of homelessness is lack of housing.*

Half a million units of low-income housing are lost every year to condominium conversion, abandonment, arson, demolition. Between 1978 and 1980, median rents climbed 30 percent for those in the lowest income sector. Half these people paid nearly three quarters of their income for their housing. Forced to choose between housing and food, many of these families soon were driven to the streets. That was only a beginning. After 1980, rents rose at even faster rates. In Boston, between 1982 and 1984, over 80 percent of housing units renting below $300 disappeared, while the number of units renting above $600 more than doubled.

Hard numbers, in this instance, may be of more help than social theory in explaining why so many of our neighbors end up in the streets. By the end of 1983, vacancies averaged 1 to 2 percent in San Francisco, Boston and New York. Vacancies in *low-income* rental units averaged less than 1 percent in New York City by 1987. In Boston they averaged .5 percent. Landlords saw this seller's market as an invitation to raise rents. Evictions grew. In New York City, with a total of nearly 2 million rental units, there were half a million legal actions for eviction during 1983.[2] Half of these actions were against people on welfare, four fifths of whom were paying rents above the maximum allowed by welfare. Rent ceilings established by welfare in New York were frozen for a decade at the levels set in 1975. They were increased by 25 percent in 1984; but rents meanwhile had nearly doubled.

During these years the White House cut virtually all federal funds to build or rehabilitate low-income housing. Federal support for low-income housing dropped from $28 billion to $9 billion between 1981 and 1986. "We're getting out of the housing business. Period," said a HUD deputy assistant secretary in 1985.

The consequences now are seen in every city of America.

What Distinguishes Housing from Other Basic Needs of Life? Why, of Many Essentials, Is It the First to Go?

Housing has some unique characteristics, as urban planning specialist Chester Hartman has observed. One pays for housing well in advance. The entire month's rent must be paid on the first day of any rental period. One pays for food only a few days before it is consumed, and one always has the option of delaying food expenditures until just prior to eating. Housing is a nondivisible and not easily adjustable expenditure. "One cannot pay less rent for the next few months by not using the living room," Hartman observes. By contrast, one can rapidly and drastically adjust one's food consumption: for example, by buying less expensive food, eating less, or skipping meals. "At least in the short run," Hartman notes, "the consequences of doing so are not severe." The cost of losing housing and then paying for re-

entry to the housing system, on the other hand, is very high, involving utility and rent deposits equal sometimes to twice or three times the cost of one month's rent. For these reasons, one may make a seemingly "rational" decision to allocate scarce funds to food, clothing, health care, transportation, or the search for jobs— only to discover that one cannot pay the rent. "Some two and a half million people are displaced annually from their homes," writes Hartman. While some find other homes and others move in with their friends or relatives, the genesis of epidemic and increasing homelessness is there.

Is This a Temporary Crisis?

As families are compelled to choose between feeding their children or paying their rent, homelessness has taken on the characteristics of a captive state. Economic recovery has not relieved this crisis. Adults whose skills are obsolete have no role in a revived free market. "The new poor," according to the U.S. Conference of Mayors, "are not being recalled to their former jobs, because their former plants are not being reopened.... Their temporary layoffs are from dying industries."

Two million jobs in steel, textiles, and other industries, according to the AFL-CIO, have disappeared each year since 1979. Nearly half of all new jobs created from 1979 to 1985 pay poverty-level wages.

Increased prosperity among the affluent, meanwhile, raises the profit motive for conversion of low-income properties to upscale dwellings. The Conference of Mayors reported in January 1986 that central-city renewal has accelerated homelessness by dispossession of the poor. The illusion of recovery, therefore, has the ironic consequence of worsening the status of the homeless and near-homeless, while diluting explanations for their presence and removing explanations for their indigence.

But it is not enough to say that this is not a "temporary" crisis: Congressional research indicates that it is likely to grow worse. The House Committee on Government Operations noted in April 1985 that, due to the long advance-time needed for a federally assisted housing program to be terminated, the United States has yet to experience the full impact of federal cuts in housing aid. "The committee believes that current federal housing policies, combined with the continuing erosion of the private inventory of low-income housing, will add to the growth of homelessness...." The "harshest consequences," the committee said, are "yet to come."...

DISTANCING OURSELVES FROM PAIN AND TEARS

... "A Cold-Blooded Assault on Poor People." This headline in the *Washington Post* precedes an article by William Raspberry. "Programs for low-income Americans," he writes, represent "just over a tenth of the federal budget," but are "ticketed" for one third of the 1987 Reagan budget cuts. "Are appropriations for low-income housing so excessively generous," he asks, "that it makes sense to cut them by a third?" Do indigent people waste so many of our dollars on "imagined illness," he asks, "that a $20 billion cut in Medicaid over the next five years" is justified? "Do housing repair grants, rural housing programs, emergency food assistance, legal services and the Work Incentive Program" represent such foolishly misguided policies that

"they should be terminated altogether, as the president proposes?"...

"A continuously rising level of child abuse and homelessness," writes New York City Council President Andrew Stein, "is not a force of nature...." This is a point he is compelled to make because we tend so easily to speak of homelessness as an unauthored act: something sad, perhaps the fault of those who have no homes, more likely that of chance. Homelessness "happens," like a flood or fire or a devastating storm—what legal documents, insurance forms, might call "an act of God." But homelessness is not an act of God. It is an act of man. It is done by people like ourselves....

Phrases such as "no quick fix" do more than to dilute a sense of urgency; they also console us with the incorrect impression that we are, no matter with what hesitation, moving in the right direction. All available statistics make it clear that this is not the case.

"Federal housing assistance programs have been cut a full 64 percent since 1980," according to Manhattan Borough President David Dinkins in a study released in March of 1987, "from $32 billion to $9 billion in the current fiscal year."

In 1986, the Department of Housing and Urban Development subsidized construction of only 25,000 housing units nationwide. When Gerald Ford was president, 200,000 units were constructed. Under President Carter, 300,000 units were constructed.

"For each dollar authorized for national defense in 1980, nineteen cents were authorized for subsidized housing programs," according to another recent study. In 1984, only *three* cents were authorized for housing for each military dollar. This is neither a "quick fix" nor a "slow fix." It is an aggressive fix against the life and health of undefended children.

Mr. Stein poses a challenging scenario. "Imagine the mayor of New York calling an urgent news conference," he writes, "to announce that the crisis of the city's poor children had reached such proportions that he was mobilizing the city's talents for a massive rescue effort...." Some such drastic action, he asserts, is warranted "because our city is threatened by the spreading blight of a poverty even crueler in some ways than that of the Great Depression half a century ago."

We hear this voice of urgency too rarely. Instead, we are told that all these children we have seen—those who cannot concentrate in school because they are too hungry and must rest their heads against their desks to stifle stomach pains, those who sleep in "pigpens," those who travel sixty miles twice a day to glean some bit of education from a school at which they will arrive too late for breakfast and may find themselves denied a lunch because of presidential cuts—must wait a little while and be patient and accept the fact that there is "no quick fix" for those who are too young to vote and whose defeated parents have no lobbyists in Washington or City Hall.

There is a degree of cruelty at stake when those who aren't in pain assume the privilege to counsel moderation in addressing the despair of those who are, or when those who have resources to assuage such pain urge us to be patient in denial of such blessings to the poor. It is still more cruel when those who make such judgments are, as they are bound to be, articulate adults and those who are

denied are very frail and very small and very young....

The debate persists as to how many homeless people are the former patients of large mental hospitals, deinstitutionalized in the 1970s. Many homeless *individuals* may have been residents of such institutions. In cities like New York, however, where nearly half the homeless people are small children, with an average age of six, such suppositions obviously make little sense. Six-year-olds were not deinstitutionalized before their birth. Their parents, with an average age of twenty-seven, are not likely to have been the residents of mental hospitals when they were still teenagers. But there is a reason for the repetition of such arguments in face of countervailing facts. In a sense, when we refer to "institutions"—those from which we think some of the homeless come, those to which we think they ought to be consigned—we are creating a new institution of our own: the abstract institution of an airtight capsule ("underclass," "behavioral problem," "nonadaptive" or "psychotic") that will not allow their lives to touch our own. Few decent people or responsible physicians wish to do this; but the risk is there. The homeless are a nightmare.... It is natural to fear and try to banish nightmares. It is not natural to try to banish human beings.

The distancing we have observed receives its most extreme expression in the use of language such as "undeserving." This is, in some sense, the ultimate act of disaffiliation and the most decisive means of placing all these families and their children in a category where they can't intrude upon our dreams....

[Charles Murray] argues that a thorough extirpation of the social benefactions that evolved from Franklin Roosevelt's time into our own would remove unnatural incentives to unadmirable behavior: "Take away all governmentally-sponsored subsidies for irresponsible behavior.... The natural system will produce the historically natural results."

Murray's ideas have been received well in the [Reagan] White House. The harshness of the wording he employs reflects a mood that may be dangerous for our society. "Some people are better than others," he writes. "They deserve more of society's rewards...." The obverse of this statement, when applied to children such as Benjamin, is chilling.

Why is it that views like these, so alien to our American tradition and Judeo-Christian roots, should have received acceptance in this decade? Weariness and frustration, I have said, may lead some people to impatience and, at length, to anger at some of the mothers whom we have described. The fear of seeing our own nightmares acted out upon the sidewalk right before our eyes may be another reason for our willingness to place the indigent at a safe distance from our lives.

NOTES

1. One reason for discrepancies in estimates derives from various ways of counting. Homeless advocates believe that all who ask for shelter during any extended period of time ought to be termed homeless. The government asks: "How many seek shelter on a given day?" If the HUD study, cited above, had considered those who asked for shelter in the course of one full year, its upper estimate would have exceeded 1.7 million.

2. Half a million families, of course, were not evicted in one year. Many of these legal actions are "repeats." Others are unsuccessful. Still others are settled with payment of back rent.

POSTSCRIPT

Do Social and Mental Pathologies Largely Account for Homelessness?

Part of the argument between Kozol and Magnet concerns the number of homeless. Is it, as Kozol thinks, 2 to 3 million, or 360,000 at the most, as Magnet claims? The numbers issue ties in with the larger question of whether most of the homeless are ordinary people victimized by the economy or pathological types who have been motivated by misplaced compassion to live on the streets. If the number of people living in the streets is in the millions, then that would indicate that the American economy has indeed gone awry. But if the number of homeless is relatively small, it is more plausible to think of them as a pathological fringe element.

It is not easy to resolve this numbers argument. Much research has been done, so far without producing a consensus. Two articles on how estimates of the homeless are done are Peter H. Rossi, "The Urban Homeless: Estimating Size and Composition," *Science* (March 13, 1987) and Constance Holden, "Homelessness: Experts Differ on Root Causes," *Science* (May 2, 1986). For a review of the literature and empirical studies on homelessness, see Anne B. Shlay and Peter H. Rossi, "Social Science Research and Contemporary Studies of Homelessness," *Annual Review of Sociology* (vol. 18, 1992).

Some of the major efforts to explain the causes of homelessness are Peter H. Rossi, *Down and Out in America: The Origins of Homelessness* (University of Chicago Press, 1988); James D. Wright, *Address Unknown: The Homeless in America* (Aldine de Gruyter, 1989); Karin Ringheim, *At Risk of Homelessness: The Role of Income and Rent* (Praeger, 1990); David A. Snow and Leon Anderson, *Down on Their Luck: A Study of Homeless Street People* (University of California Press, 1992); Joel Blau, *The Visible Poor: Homelessness in the United States* (Oxford University Press, 1992); Martha R. Burt, *Over the Edge: The Growth of Homelessness in the 1980s* (Russell Sage Foundation, 1992); Alice S. Baum and Donald W. Burnes, *A Nation in Denial: The Truth About Homelessness* (Westview, 1993); David Wagner, *Checkerboard Square: Culture and Resistance in a Homeless Community* (Westview, 1993); Jennifer Wolch and Michael Dean, *Malign Neglect: Homelessness in an American City* (Jossey-Bass, 1993); Doug A. Timmer, D. Stanley Eitzen, and Kathryn D. Talley, *Paths to Homelessness* (Westview, 1994); Rob Rosenthal, *Homeless in Paradise* (Temple University Press, 1994); and Christopher Jencks, *The Homeless* (Harvard University Press, 1994). Charles Hoch and Robert A. Slayton carefully examine the differences between homelessness today and homelessness in the 1960s in *New Homelessness and Old: Community and the Skid Row Hotel* (Temple University Press, 1989). For a sensitive examination of the ambivalent feelings that Americans have about the homeless, see Peter Marin, "Helping and Hating the Homeless," *Harper's* (January 1987). Finally, for two deeply moving portrayals of the lives of the homeless, see the award-winning *Rachel and Her Children: Homeless Families in America* by Jonathan Kozol (Anchor Press, 1985) and *Tell Them Who I Am: The Lives of Homeless Women* by Elliot Liebow (Free Press, 1993).

PART 4

Political Economy

Are political power and economic power merged within a "power elite" that dominates the U.S. political system? The first issue in this part explores that debate. The second issue concerns the proper role of government in the economy. Some believe that the government must correct for the many failures of the market, while others think that the government usually complicates the workings of the free market. The next debate concerns public policy: How should we assess the impact and efficacy of welfare programs? Finally, the last issue in this part examines the role of the government in public education.

- Is Government Dominated by Big Business?

- Should Government Intervene in a Capitalist Economy?

- Does Welfare Do More Harm Than Good?

- Is Choice a Panacea for the Ills of Public Education?

ISSUE 12

Is Government Dominated by Big Business?

YES: John C. Berg, from *Unequal Struggle: Class, Gender, Race, and Power in the U.S. Congress* (Westview Press, 1994)

NO: Jeffrey M. Berry, from "Citizen Groups and the Changing Nature of Interest Group Politics in America," *The Annals of the American Academy of Political and Social Science* (July 1993)

ISSUE SUMMARY

YES: John C. Berg, a professor at Suffolk University, argues that the U.S. government takes care of the interests of big business quickly and effectively while largely ignoring the interests of the working class and other middle and lower groups. The inordinate political influence of big business, he contends, is observable in the outcomes of the political process.

NO: Jeffrey M. Berry, a professor of political science, contends that public interest pressure groups that have entered the political arena since the end of the 1960s have effectively challenged the political power of big business.

Since the framing of the U.S. Constitution in 1787, there have been periodic charges that America is unduly influenced by wealthy financial interests. Richard Henry Lee, a signer of the Declaration of Independence, spoke for many Anti-Federalists (those who opposed ratification of the Constitution) when he warned that the proposed charter shifted power away from the people and into the hands of the "aristocrats" and "moneyites."

Before the Civil War, Jacksonian Democrats denounced the eastern merchants and bankers who, they charged, were usurping the power of the people. After the Civil War, a number of radical parties and movements revived this theme of antielitism. The ferment—which was brought about by the rise of industrial monopolies, government corruption, and economic hardship for western farmers—culminated in the founding of the People's Party at the beginning of the 1890s. The Populists, as they were more commonly called, wanted economic and political reforms aimed at transferring power away from the rich and back to "the plain people."

By the early 1900s the People's Party had disintegrated, but many writers and activists have continued to echo the Populists' central thesis: that the U.S. democratic political system is in fact dominated by business elites. Yet the thesis has not gone unchallenged. During the 1950s and the early 1960s, many social scientists subscribed to the *pluralist* view of America.

Pluralists argue that because there are many influential elites in America, each group is limited to some extent by the others. There are some groups, like the business elites, that are more powerful than their opponents, but even the more powerful groups are denied their objectives at times. Labor groups are often opposed to business groups; conservative interests challenge liberal interests, and vice versa; and organized civil libertarians sometimes fight with groups that seek government-imposed bans on pornography or groups that demand tougher criminal laws. No single group, the pluralists argue, can dominate the political system.

Pluralists readily acknowledge that American government is not democratic in the full sense of the word; it is not driven by the majority. But neither, they insist, is it run by a conspiratorial "power elite." In the pluralist view, the closest description of the American form of government would be neither majority rule nor minority rule but *minorities* rule. (Note that in this context, "minorities" does not necessarily refer to race or ethnicity but to any organized group of people with something in common—including race, religion, or economic interests—not constituting a majority of the population.) Each organized minority enjoys some degree of power in the making of public policy. In extreme cases, when a minority feels threatened, its power may take a negative form: the power to derail policy. When the majority—or, more accurately, a coalition of other minorities—attempts to pass a measure that threatens the vital interests of an organized minority, that group may use its power to obstruct their efforts. (Often cited in this connection is the use of the Senate filibuster, which is the practice of using tactics during the legislative process that cause extreme delays or prevent action, thus enabling a group to "talk to death" a bill that threatens its vital interests.) But in the pluralist view negative power is not the only driving force: when minorities work together and reach consensus on certain issues, they can institute new laws and policy initiatives that enjoy broad public support. Pluralism, though capable of producing temporary gridlock, ultimately leads to compromise, consensus, and moderation.

Critics of pluralism argue that pluralism is an idealized depiction of a political system that is in the grip of powerful elite groups. Critics fault pluralist theory for failing to recognize the extent to which big business dominates the policy-making process. In the selections that follow, John C. Berg supports this view and argues that the government is dedicated to furthering the interests of business. He contends that corporate dominance is built into the basic legal order and into the structure of the government. It is also reinforced by the electoral system and the weakness of anticapitalist ideologies. Jeffrey M. Berry, in opposition, argues that, thanks to new consumer, environmental, and other citizen groups, big business no longer enjoys the cozy relationship it once had with Washington policymakers.

YES

John C. Berg

UNEQUAL STRUGGLE

CONGRESS AND THE POWERFUL

Money talks. Everyone knows that. It talks a lot to Congress. Well-heeled lobbyists, political action committees (PACs), expense-paid junkets, multimillion-dollar campaigns, and juicy honoraria are abiding elements of American political lore. Everyone knows, too, that the rich do better than other people at getting their opinions heard and their interests accommodated by legislators. Average citizens, political scientists, and the members of Congress themselves join in bewailing the excessive importance of money in politics.

Although everyone may know these things, not everyone explains them in the same way. I believe that the most common explanations—those derived from the pluralist and institutionalist models of Congress—are superficial, and that the most commonly proposed solutions, such as banning PACs or providing public funds for congressional campaigns, would improve the character of Congress only slightly.

Pluralist theory, on the one hand, treats money as one weapons—albeit the major one—that interest groups deploy in the political battle. Some groups may enter the battlefield more heavily armed than others, but there are other weapon—votes, enthusiasm, publicity, moral righteousness, and information —that can be used by groups with less money; moreover, the battlefield itself is expected to be level. One implication of pluralism is that groups with less money but possessed of some other resource, such as a large membership or the perception that they stand for the public interest, may be able to hold their own in the conflict. A second implication is that if we can just eliminate money as a political resource, then interest group conflict will become fair and equal once again. Herbert Alexander describes this position as follows: "The reform efforts of recent years, in addition to seeking to limit both real and perceived corruption, have attempted to smooth out the impact of political money—or, in current lingo, to 'level the playing field' " (1992, 4).

CONGRESS AND BIG BUSINESS

The American economy is not just capitalist; it is dominated by a small number of gigantic capitalist corporations. In 1988, the 500 largest industrial corporations in the United States—the so-called Fortune 500—had total sales of over $2 trillion. One-fifth of this amount, $402,183,000,000, was produced by just five companies: General Motors (GM), Ford, Exxon, International Business Machines (IBM), and General Electric (GE) ("The Biggest Blowout Ever" 1989, 349–401). In the same year, there were about 3.5 million corporations, and 14 million nonfarm proprietorships and partnerships, in the United States (U.S. Department of Commerce 1989). The three major automobile makers alone employed 1,270,000 people, had assets of $356 billion, and earned profits of $11.2 billion ("The Biggest Blowout Ever" 1989, 349–401). The ten largest commercial banks—all but one of them located in New York City—had assets of $860 billion, with nearly one-quarter of that, $207 billion, held by one bank, New York's Citicorp ("At Last, Profits Worth Savoring" 1989, 364).

These giants are so big that the rest of the country needs them to be healthy. When Chrysler Corporation, only the third largest automobile maker, faced possible bankruptcy, the federal government stepped in to save it. It stepped in again to avert the failure of Chicago-based Continental Bank Corporation, the fourteenth largest commercial bank. As this practice has become more common, it has acquired a name, the "too big to fail" doctrine. It is one example of *hegemony*.

When Charles E. ("Engine Charlie") Wilson went from president of General Motors to secretary of defense in the Eisenhower administration, he told a Senate committee that he was not worried about any possible conflict of interest because he had always believed that "what was good for our country was good for General Motors, and vice versa. The difference did not exist. Our company is too big. It goes with the welfare of the country."

The implication of biased pluralism would be that we may need to go further, eliminating the influence of wealth on public opinion as well; and that even then, the privileged position of business would force other groups to fight their way uphill. But to the extent that it stops short of economic determinism in the last instance, biased pluralism seems to imply that the power of money can be overcome "through tiresome sequences of increments" (Lindblom 1983, 385).

Institutionalists, on the other hand, emphasize Congress's success in insulating its members from outside pressure. Institutionalists see the role of money in one of two ways. Some argue that it is largely irrelevant to the policy process, in that members of Congress can always get along without any particular contribution and often find that the vote that loses one contribution will gain another at the same time. Others believe that contributions are important, but that the direction of causality is reversed from that in common understanding. In other words, Congress is thought to have developed procedures that allow its members to extract the greatest possible amount of money from interest groups while doing more or less what they would have done anyway. Campaign finance limitations, then, would make members of Congress more honest, make the public less cynical about politics, and perhaps remove a burdensome cost from businesses; but they would not have much effect on policy output.

The view of *Marxist* theory is that Congress looks out for the interests of wealth not only as a result of bribery and campaign spending but also because the economic structure of our society requires it. Bribes and campaign spending might be controlled by new regulations; changing our economic structure is a larger and much more difficult task.

Congressional politics is part of the fundamental social conflict in America. Congress is one arena in which this conflict takes place, but it is not an independent arena. Forces outside Congress influence what goes on inside it; in particular, if the Marxist theory is correct, Congress is influenced heavily by the economic structure of our society. Those who dominate the American economy dominate Congress as well. But Congress is also the most democratic part of our national government. Thus, oppressed social groups have found it the most permeable part of the state, often seeking to use congressional politics to advance their cause....

We can see the effect of economic structure when we compare the way Congress handles different issues. In 1977, with the nation suffering from an energy shortage that restricted economic growth, hurt the balance of trade, inflated the cost of living, and forced many poor people to go without heat in winter, President Jimmy Carter presented a comprehensive national energy plan to Congress. After two years of hearings, backroom negotiations, and public debate, Congress managed to pass only one part of the plan: It removed price controls from natural gas, thus making energy even more expensive.

In 1989 the wreck of the oil tanker Exxon Valdez killed thousands of waterfowl, fish, marine mammals, and plants, threatened the ecological balance of Prince William Sound, and infuriated the public. Individual members of Congress responded with thousands of dramatic public speeches; but it was sixteen months before Congress as a legislative body managed to pass a bill raising the limits on liability of negligent oil shippers from $150 to $1,200 per ton of oil. Although the final bill was considered a victory by environmental lobbyists, several concessions had to be made to the oil industry before it could be passed. Double-hull requirements for oil tankers were deferred until 2010 (and to 2015 for most barges and for ships unloading offshore to lighters), oil companies shipping oil in tankers owned by others were exempted, and state governors lost any power to determine when a cleanup was complete (Congressional Quarterly 1991a, 283–87).

In the early 1980s a large number of savings and loan associations—known as thrift institutions, or simply "thrifts" —began to lose money; by 1987 many were in danger of failing. The Federal Savings and Loan Insurance Corporation (FSLIC), which insured thrift deposits of $100,000 or less, warned that it might not be able to pay all the claims. Congress gave the FSLIC another $10 billion in 1987, but otherwise did nothing until after the 1988 election. Then, in early 1989, Congress moved with remarkable speed to enact a complicated —and expensive—reorganization plan for the thrift industry. President George Bush proposed a plan on February 6 and signed a new law on August 9. The S&L Bailout—as it became known— would cost $50 billion by the end of 1991, and at least $110 billion by 1999; some of the money would be paid to the holders of insured accounts, but much of it would be used to subsidize healthier, more profitable banks and thrifts in taking over unhealthy ones (Congressional Quarterly 1990, 14–15, 117–19)....

In the largest sense, Wilson was dead wrong. GM has been a cumbersome, inefficient enterprise that has contributed greatly to a whole range of national problems, from low productivity to air pollution to worker alienation. But in the short run—that is, given that GM already existed—Wilson was right. GM's huge labor force, its annual sales, and its impact as a customer on other major industries were so great that a failure of GM—or of another giant corporation—might well have plunged the whole economy into recession.

Corporate Hegemony

Until sometime in the early 1970s the giant financial and industrial corporations were able to dominate America and much of the rest of the world. This domination gave them a sense of security and led some to conclude that they were more interested in stability than in profits (Galbraith 1985). Since that time, however, their dominance has been threatened by growing international competition. The best-known example is the auto industry, in which the big three U.S. automakers have lost market share to Japanese and European competitors both at home and abroad; but the same thing has occurred in many other industries as well.

This new global competition has changed both the composition and the interests of the hegemonic bloc. By reviving the emphasis on profits it has reinforced the dominance of finance capital over industrial corporations. Such once-mighty giants as IBM have learned that Wall Street would rather shift its investments to other companies and industries than support them in fighting to preserve their corporate position. The willingness of many corporations to accept high wages and benefits and a certain amount of government regulation is likewise falling before international competitive pressure. These changes in the economic position of U.S. big business have had important political results...; but the basic division between hegemonic and nonhegemonic sectors of the capitalist class remains.

Politics and ideology tend to reflect economics. Thus, the state (including Congress) tends to further the interests of the giant corporations; and public debate tends to be carried on in terms that incorporate those interests—as in 1990, when President Bush referred to protection of Exxon's oil supplies in the Persian Gulf as a defense of "our way of life." This is not automatically so. The nonhegemonic classes can and do organize themselves to contend for political power, and to change the terms of public discourse. But they find it harder to win; and unless they succeed in changing the economic structure as well, such political and ideological reforms are likely to be only temporary. Let us look at some concrete examples.

The crisis in the savings and loan industry threatened to destabilize the whole financial system, endangering giant banks along with small thrift institutions. It thus struck at the heart of corporate hegemony. The nature of this hegemony is missed by much left rhetoric. For example, Manning Marable has written recently:

> Is it right for a government to spend billions and billions for bailing out fat

cats who profited from the savings and loan scam while millions of jobless Americans stand in unemployment lines desperate for work? Is it fair that billions of our dollars are allocated for the Pentagon's permanent war economy to obliterate the lives of millions of poor people from Panama to Iraq to Grenada to Vietnam, while two million Americans sleep in the streets and 37 million Americans lack any form of medical coverage? (1993, 12)

The policies Marable decries are indeed neither right nor fair; but even those members of Congress who agree with this characterization fear that allowing the savings and loan industry to collapse, or (more debatably) cutting the military budget, would send even more millions to the unemployment lines or into the streets. For this reason, debate within Congress about the savings and loan crisis has centered on who should take the blame, not on whether to act.

By contrast, the crisis in education strikes at the U.S. working class, and cholera threatens workers and peasants in other countries. Millions of lives may be blighted, neighborhoods destabilized, and great human suffering caused, but most members of Congress still see a solution as optional—something *we* certainly ought to do if we can just find the money. Even the advocates of school reform find it useful to base their arguments on the need of capitalism for a more skilled labor force.

This is the theory of hegemony in its bare bones. Hegemonic interests are privileged in that Congress and the state act quickly and effectively to protect them; they find it more difficult to promote other interests that are equally vital in human terms. But students of politics must ask how this privilege is

maintained. What is it about our political system—what is it about Congress—that makes it more responsive to hegemonic interests than to others?

In fact, the interests of the great corporations are well entrenched in the structure of American government This structure is itself the product of past political struggles, dating back at least to the drafting of the Constitution. Some of these struggles have been won by the working class, farmers, and petty bourgeoisie; by women; by racial minorities; and by other democratizing forces. But on the whole, the trend has been toward the kind of state envisioned by Alexander Hamilton, a state dedicated to furthering business interests (Hamilton [1791] 1966).

Corporate hegemony is built into the structure of Congress on at least three levels. First, it has become part of our basic legal order. Second, it is built into the separation of powers, which places the most crucial decisions outside of Congress's reach. Finally, it is part of the internal structure of Congress itself. The end result of decades of conflict is that Congress finds it easy to act on behalf of corporate interests and difficult to act against them. These structural features are reinforced by the nature of the American electoral system, and by the weakness of anticapitalist ideology....

These three structural factors—the basic legal order, the division of powers among the branches of government, and the power of the hegemonic committees within Congress—provide the terrain on which pluralist conflict takes place. This conflict is fought out with the usual weapons of democratic politics—namely, votes and money; but the giant corporations enter the battle already in possession of the commanding heights and are therefore much more likely to win. We can see the difference this makes by looking more closely at one of the examples mentioned above.

The Savings and Loan Crisis

PAC spending and corrupt politics certainly played a part in the collapse of the thrift industry. Charles Keating's contributions to five senators and the shady role of President Bush's son Neal have entered the national consciousness. Keating and Bush are not atypical, either; the entire thrift industry has been a major player in the PAC game (Jackson 1988; Marcus 1989).

A common view is that the crisis was the result of pluralism run amok, distorted into what Theodore Lowi (1979) has called "interest group liberalism." The nation's savings and loan companies lobbied so well that they won control of the agencies charged with regulating them. They then used that control to remove important restraints on their activity and proceeded to swindle the taxpayer out of hundreds of billions of dollars. Their proceeds included such other plums as private jets, sports cars, vacation homes, and even Rubens's *Portrait of a Man as Mars*, which was purchased at auction for $13.2 million by Centrust, a Florida savings and loan, for its chief executive officer David Paul to keep at home and use while entertaining customers (Mayer 1990, 77).

Upon looking at the overall contours of the crisis, however, we find an interesting contrast between some of the details and the larger picture. In many particular cases, crooked thrift owners were able to buy political influence and use it to keep shaky institutions going while they milked them for a few more millions. But the net result of the crisis was that thrifts and their owners lost their niche in the American economy and were often swallowed up by large commercial banks.

Thrifts take their name from the virtue that they were designed to encourage. They were intended to pool the savings of local community residents to provide capital for housing and other consumer purchases. Two rules were necessary to bring about this objective. First, thrifts were not allowed to make certain kinds of investment, such as commercial loans, so that their funds would be available for long-term mortgages. And to make sure that such loans would be possible, savings account interest was limited by the Federal Reserve Board's Regulation Q, so that the thrifts would not have to pay their depositors more than they received from their borrowers. Other banks were held to a rate slightly below that allowed to the thrifts, so that thrift-based savings accounts would be attractive to small savers—those who did not have enough money to buy common stocks, U.S. Treasury notes, or other more profitable investment vehicles popular among the rich.

These regulations protected the thrift industry from the big banks, which otherwise could have undercut and ultimately acquired them. But they could not withstand the political and economic assaults of Wall Street in the 1960s and 1970s. Driven by their own competitive pressures, large financial institutions devised new ways to attract the money of small savers; most notable among the options they offered was the money market mutual fund. Anyone with $1,000 —for some funds, only $250—could now get a better rate than the thrifts paid on passbook savings accounts.

The thrifts were left with two choices, neither viable in the long run. They could sit back and watch their deposits dwindle as depositors pursued the higher rates on Wall Street, although this option would leave them with no money for housing and other consumer loans, and no real reason to exist. Alternatively, they could invent their own ways to pay higher rates—through daily compounding, certificates of deposit, and a bevy of special accounts. This latter course staved off disaster for the moment, but it also left the thrifts in danger of being whipsawed as the rates they were paying out on short-term deposits approached, and sometimes surpassed, those they were collecting on long-term mortgage loans.

That was precisely what happened, of course. The thrifts tried to save themselves through deregulation—that is, through changes in the rules that let them make ever more desperate attempts to pay higher rates and attract deposits, or to convert to joint stock corporations and attract equity capital from investors.

The Garn-St Germain Depository Institutions Act of 1982 was the biggest step in this deregulation. Immortalized by President Reagan's comment, "I think we hit a home run," as he signed it, Garn-St Germain is sometimes portrayed as the mistake that brought on the thrift crisis. As pluralists would have expected, the bill was the focus of heavy lobbying, particularly by the United States Savings and Loan League; but in reality Garn-St Germain was not so much the cause of the crisis as the beginning of the end—the last desperate attempt by the thrifts to beat back the assault from Wall Street. This attempt failed miserably.

Every reform just dug the thrifts' hole a little deeper, while opening the door to abuses and fraud by the unscrupulous investors who are so abundant on the American financial scene. The sight of this open door inspired a stampede of embezzlement and theft; but this was the result, not the cause, of the thrift crisis.

As the dust from the collapse of the thrift industry begins to settle, we can begin to make out the outlines of the banking system of the twenty-first century. There will be fewer, larger banks, which will compete nationally and internationally; and regionally based banks will either expand, merge, or die. All banks, whether they began life as savings and loan associations, savings banks, or commercial banks, will compete on the same terms; consequently, homebuyers will have to compete with commercial borrowers for credit, and interest rates will rise accordingly. And, of course, the American taxpayer will pay the cost of salvaging the industry, a cost variously estimated at $200 to $500 billion over the next few decades.

If we applied the pluralist model, we might expect the thrifts to have benefited according to their PAC spending and political activity. However, this is only half the story. Both individual thrifts and their interest group, the United States Savings and Loan League, were indeed active lobbyists; but this lobbying must be seen in the larger context of the thrift industry's inability to defend itself from the giant national and international commercial banks. The thrifts won some political battles but lost the most important ones —not because they were outspent but because of the hegemonic structural position of their opponents.

The important points for our analysis are as follows.

1. The cause of the thrifts' decline was economic, not political; they were

unable to resist the competition of larger financial institutions.

2. Intensive lobbying won them deregulation and the Garn-St Germain Act; but these political measures only delayed their economic defeat, while opening the door to and exacerbating their ultimate collapse.

3. Once the crisis appeared to threaten hegemonic financial interests, Congress moved quickly and almost effortlessly to solve the problem. The interest of the big banks, the investment houses, and big depositors (those with deposits above the insurance limit) were protected at the expense of the thrifts and the tax-paying public. In this stage of the crisis, lobbying and PAC contributions by the thrifts had little impact.

4. In confronting the crisis, Congress chose to limit its own future influence on the matter by creating the Resolution Trust Corporation (RTC), a quasi-governmental agency not directly answerable to Congress. Dissident members of Congress could then complain freely about the RTC's practices without interfering seriously with its operations.

In this case, business interests in the nonhegemonic sector (the thrifts) lost out despite their intensive political activity. If smaller business always lost out, the U.S. political system would be less stable than it is. However, most of the time smaller businesses are able to get much of what they need from Congress and, accordingly, continue to align themselves with the hegemonic interests as part of the power bloc....

* * *

The giant corporations may rule America, but they do not rule alone....

Conclusion

... Neither the pluralist claim that Congress responds to group pressures nor the institutionalist claim that Congress has won the ability to act autonomously provides a satisfactory explanation of congressional action. Each appears to be true in some instances but not in others, so a more general theory is needed. Marxism provides such a theory: Congress acts autonomously when the views of its leaders correspond with the interests of the hegemonic interests in the capitalist economic structure, as in the case of the savings and loan bailout; it responds to group pressure when different nonhegemonic capitalist interests contend for advantage...; and it responds more slowly and less strongly than pluralist pressure would suggest when action is sought by the working class, women, or African Americans.

NO
Jeffrey M. Berry

CITIZEN GROUPS AND THE CHANGING NATURE OF INTEREST GROUP POLITICS IN AMERICA

ABSTRACT: The rise of liberal citizen groups that began in the 1960s has had a strong impact on the evolution of interest group advocacy. The success of these liberal organizations was critical in catalyzing the broader explosion in the numbers of interest groups and in causing the collapse of many subgovernments. New means of resolving policy conflicts had to be established to allow for the participation of broader, more diverse policy communities. Citizen groups have been particularly important in pushing policymakers to create new means of structuring negotiations between large numbers of interest group actors. The greater participation of citizen groups, the increased numbers of all kinds of interest groups, and change in the way policy is made may be making the policymaking process more democratic.

Many protest movements have arisen in the course of American history, each affecting the political system in its own way. The social movements that took hold in the 1960s had their own unique set of roots but seemed to follow a conventional life span. The civil rights and antiwar groups that arose to protest the injustices they saw were classic social movements. Their views were eventually absorbed by one of the political parties, and, after achieving their immediate goals, their vitality was sapped. The antiwar movement disappeared, and black civil rights organizations declined in power. The most enduring and vital citizen groups born in this era of protest were never protest oriented. Consumer groups, environmental groups, and many other kinds of citizen lobbies have enjoyed unprecedented prosperity in the last 25 years. Never before have citizen groups been so prevalent in American politics, and never before have they been so firmly institutionalized into the policymaking process.

The rise of citizen groups has not only empowered many important constituencies, but it has altered the policymaking process as well. This article

From Jeffrey M. Berry, "Citizen Groups and the Changing Nature of Interest Group Politics in America," *The Annals of the American Academy of Political and Social Science*, vol. 528 (July 1993). Copyright © 1993 by The American Academy of Political and Social Science. Reprinted by permission of Sage Publications, Inc. Notes omitted.

focuses on how citizen groups have affected interest group politics in general and how these organizations have contributed to the changing nature of public policymaking. A first step is to examine the initial success of liberal advocacy organizations as well as the conservative response to this challenge. Next, I will look at the impact of this growth of citizen group politics on the policymaking process. Then I will turn to how Congress and the executive branch have tried to cope with a dense population of citizen groups and the complex policymaking environment that now envelops government.

Finally, I will speculate as to how all of this has affected policymaking in terms of how democratic it is. The popular perception is that the rise of interest groups along with the decline of political parties has had a very negative impact on American politics. Analysis of the decline of parties will be left to others, but a central point here is that the growth in the numbers of citizen groups and of other lobbying organizations has not endangered the political system. There are some unfortunate developments, such as the increasing role of political action committees in campaign financing, but the rise of citizen groups in particular has had a beneficial impact on the way policy is formulated. The overall argument may be stated succinctly: the rise of liberal citizen groups was largely responsible for catalyzing an explosion in the growth of all types of interest groups. Efforts to limit the impact of liberal citizen groups failed, and the policymaking process became more open and more participatory. Expanded access and the growth in the numbers of competing interest groups created the potential for gridlock, if not chaos. The government responded, in turn, with institutional changes that have helped to rationalize policymaking in environments with a large number of independent actors.

THE RISE OF CITIZEN GROUPS

The lobbying organizations that emerged out of the era of protest in the 1960s are tied to the civil rights and antiwar movements in two basic ways. First, activism was stimulated by the same broad ideological dissatisfaction with government and the two-party system. There was the same feeling that government was unresponsive, that it was unconcerned about important issues, and that business was far too dominant a force in policymaking. Second, the rise of liberal citizen groups was facilitated by success of the civil rights and antiwar movements. More specifically, future organizers learned from these social movements. They learned that aggressive behavior could get results, and they saw that government could be influenced by liberal advocacy organizations. Some activists who later led Washington-based citizen lobbies cut their teeth as volunteers in these earlier movements.

For liberal consumer and environmental groups, an important lesson of this era was that they should not follow the protest-oriented behavior of the civil rights and antiwar movements. There was a collective realization that lasting influence would come from more conventional lobbying inside the political system. For consumer and environmental organizers, "power to the people" was rejected in favor of staff-run organizations that placed little emphasis on participatory democracy. This is not to say that these new organizations were simply copies of business lobbies; leaders of these groups like Ralph Nader and John Gardner placed themselves above politics-as-usual with their moralistic rhetoric and their attacks against the established political order.

While there was significant support for these groups from middle-class liberals, a major impetus behind their success was financial backing from large philanthropic foundations. The foundations wanted to support social change during a time of political upheaval, but at the same time they wanted responsible activism. This early support, most notably from the Ford Foundation's program in public interest law, was largely directed at supporting groups relying on litigation and administrative lobbying. The seed money for these organizations enabled them to flourish and provided them with time to establish a track record so that they could appeal to individual donors when the foundation money ran out. Other groups emerged without the help of foundations, drawing on a combination of large donors, dues-paying memberships, and government grants. Citizen lobbies proved remarkably effective at raising money and at shifting funding strategies as the times warranted.

Citizen groups emerged in a variety of areas. In addition to consumer and environmental groups, there were organizations interested in hunger and poverty, governmental reform, corporate responsibility, and many other issues. A number of new women's organizations soon followed in the wake of the success of the first wave of citizen groups, and new civil rights groups arose to defend other groups such as Hispanics and gays. As has been well documented, the rise of citizen groups was the beginning of an era of explosive growth in interest groups in national politics. No precise baseline exists,

so exact measurement of this growth is impossible. Yet the mobilization of interests is unmistakable. One analysis of organizations represented in Washington in 1980 found that 40 percent of the groups had been started since 1960, and 25 percent had begun after 1970.

The liberal citizen groups that were established in the 1960s and 1970s were not simply the first ripples of a new wave of interest groups; rather, they played a primary role in catalyzing the formation of many of the groups that followed. New business groups, which were by far the most numerous of all the groups started since 1960, were directly stimulated to organize by the success of consumer and environmental groups. There were other reasons why business mobilized, but much of their hostility toward the expanded regulatory state was directed at agencies strongly supported by liberal citizen groups. These organizations had seemingly seized control of the political agenda, and the new social regulation demanded increased business mobilization. New conservative citizen lobbies, many focusing on family issues such as abortion and the Equal Rights Amendment, were also begun to counter the perceived success of the liberal groups.

The swing of the ideological pendulum that led to a conservative takeover of the White House in 1980 led subsequently to efforts to limit the impact of liberal citizen groups. The Reagan administration believed that the election of 1980 was a mandate to eliminate impediments to economic growth. Environmental and consumer groups were seen as organizations that cared little about the faltering American economy; President Reagan referred to liberal public interest lawyers as "a bunch of ideological ambulance chasers." Wherever possible, liberal citizen groups were to be removed from the governmental process....

The Reagan administration certainly succeeded in reducing the liberal groups' access to the executive branch. On a broader level, however, the conservative counterattack against the liberal groups was a failure. The reasons go far beyond the more accommodating stance of the Bush administration or the attitude of any conservative administrations that may follow. These organizations have proved to be remarkably resilient, and they are a strong and stable force in American politics. Most fundamentally, though, the Reagan attempt failed because the transformation of interest group politics led to large-scale structural changes in the public policymaking process.

CONSEQUENCES

The rise of citizen groups and the rapid expansion of interest group advocacy in general have had many important long-term consequences for the way policy is formulated by the national government. Most important, policymaking moved away from closed subgovernments, each involving a relatively stable and restricted group of lobbyists and key government officials, to much broader policymaking communities. Policymaking in earlier years is typically described as the product of consensual negotiations between a small number of back-scratching participants.

Policymaking is now best described as taking place within issue networks rather than in subgovernments. An issue network is a set of organizations that share expertise in a policy area and interact with each other over time as relevant issues are debated. As sociologist Barry Wellman states, "The world is composed of networks, not groups." This is certainly descriptive of Washington policymaking. Policy formulation cannot be portrayed in terms of what a particular group wanted and how officials responded to those demands. The coalitions within networks, often involving scores of groups, define the divisions over issues and drive the policymaking process forward. Alliances are composed of both old friends and strange bedfellows; relationships are built on immediate need as well as on familiarity and trust. Organizations that do not normally work in a particular issue network can easily move into a policymaking community to work on a single issue. The only thing constant in issue networks is the changing nature of the coalitions.

The result of issue network politics is that policymaking has become more open, more conflictual, and more broadly participatory. What is crucial about the role of citizen groups is that they were instrumental in breaking down the barriers to participation in subgovernments. Building upon their own constituency support and working with allies in Congress, citizen groups made themselves players. They have not been outsiders, left to protest policies and a system that excluded them. Rather, they built opposition right into the policymaking communities that had previously operated with some commonality of interest. Even conservative administrators who would prefer to exclude these liberal advocacy groups have recognized that they have to deal with their opponents in one arena or another. The Nuclear Regulatory Commission, the epitome of an agency hostile to liberal advocacy groups, cannot get away with ignoring groups like the Union of Concerned Scientists. The consensus over nuclear power has long been broken. Critics and advocacy groups like the Union of Concerned Scientists have the technical expertise to involve themselves in agency proceedings, and they have the political know-how to get themselves heard on Capitol Hill and in the news media.

Issue networks are not simply divided between citizen groups on one side and business groups on another. Organizations representing business usually encompass a variety of interests, many of which are opposed to each other. As various business markets have undergone rapid change and become increasingly competitive, issue networks have found themselves divided by efforts of one sector of groups to use the policymaking process to try to gain market share from another sector of the network. Citizen groups, rather than simply being the enemy of business, are potential coalition partners for different business sectors. A characteristic of the culture of interest group politics in Washington is that there are no permanent allies and no permanent enemies.

Citizen groups are especially attractive as coalition partners because they have such a high level of credibility with the public and the news media. All groups claim to represent the public interest because they sincerely believe that the course of action they are advocating would be the most beneficial to the country. Since they do not represent any vocational or business interest, citizen groups may be perceived by some to be less biased—though certainly not unbiased— in their approach to public policy problems. This credibility is also built around the high-quality research that many citizen groups produce and distribute to journalists and policymakers in Washington. Reports from advocacy organiza-

tions such as Citizens for Tax Justice or the Center for Budget and Policy Priorities are quickly picked up by the media and disseminated across the country. Most business groups would love to have the respect that these citizen groups command in the press. For all the financial strength at the disposal of oil lobbyists, no representative of the oil industry has as much credibility with the public as a lobbyist for the Natural Resources Defense Council.

Despite the growth and stability of citizen groups in national politics, their reach does not extend into every significant policymaking domain. In the broad area of financial services, for example, citizen groups have played a minor role at best. There are some consumer groups that have been marginally active when specific issues involving banks, insurance companies, and securities firms arise, but they have demonstrated little influence or staying power. There is, however, a vital consumer interest at stake as public policymakers grapple with the crumbling walls that have traditionally divided different segments of the financial services market. Defense policy is another area where citizen groups have been relatively minor actors. But if citizen groups are conspicuous by their absence in some important areas, their overall reach is surprisingly broad. They have become major actors in policy areas where they previously had no presence at all. In negotiations over a free trade agreement with Mexico, for example, environmental groups became central players in the bargaining. These groups were concerned that increased U.S. investment in Mexico would result in increased pollution there from unregulated manufacturing, depleted groundwater supplies, and other forms of environmental degradation. To its dismay, the Bush White House found that the only practical course was to negotiate with the groups.

The increasing prominence of citizen groups and the expanding size of issue networks change our conception of the policymaking process. The basic structural attribute of a subgovernment was that it was relatively bounded with a stable set of participants. Even if there was some conflict in that subgovernment, there were predictable divisions and relatively clear expectations of what kind of conciliation between interest groups was possible. In contrast, issue networks seem like free-for-alls. In the health care field alone, 741 organizations have offices in Washington or employ a representative there. Where subgovernments suggested control over public policy by a limited number of participants, issue networks suggest no control whatsoever. Citizen groups make policymaking all the more difficult because they frequently sharpen the ideological debate; they have different organizational incentive systems from those of the corporations and trade groups with which they are often in conflict; and they place little emphasis on the need for economic growth, an assumption shared by most other actors.

This picture of contemporary interest group politics may make it seem impossible to accomplish anything in Washington. Indeed, it is a popular perception that Congress has become unproductive and that we are subject to some sort of national gridlock. Yet the policymaking system is adaptable, and the relationship between citizen groups and other actors in issue networks suggests that there are a number of productive paths for resolving complicated policy issues.

COMPLEX POLICYMAKING

The growth of issue networks is not, of course, the only reason why the policymaking process has become more complex. The increasingly technical nature of policy problems has obviously put an ever higher premium on expertise. Structural changes are critical, too. The decentralization of the House of Representatives that took place in the mid-1970s dispersed power and reduced the autonomy of leaders. Today, in the House, jurisdictions between committees frequently overlap and multiple referrals of bills are common. When an omnibus trade bill passed by both houses in 1987 was sent to conference, the House and the Senate appointed 200 conferees, who broke up into 17 subconferences. The growth of the executive branch has produced a similar problem of overlapping jurisdictions. In recent deliberations on proposed changes in wetlands policy, executive branch participants included the Soil Conservation Service in the Agriculture Department, the Fish and Wildlife Service in Interior, the Army Corps of Engineers, the Environmental Protection Agency (EPA), the Office of Management and Budget, the Council on Competitiveness, and the President's Domestic Policy Council.

Nevertheless, even though the roots of complex policymaking are multifaceted, the rise of citizen groups has been a critical factor in forcing the Congress and the executive branch to focus more closely on developing procedures to negotiate settlements of policy disputes. The quiet bargaining of traditional subgovernment politics was not an adequate mechanism for handling negotiations between scores of interest groups, congressional committees, and executive branch agencies.

Citizen groups have been particularly important in prompting more structured negotiations for a number of reasons. First, in many policy areas, citizen groups upset long-standing working arrangements between policymakers and other interest groups. Citizen groups were often the reason subgovernments crumbled; under pressure from congressional allies and public opinion, they were included in the bargaining and negotiating at some stage in the policymaking process.

Second, citizen groups could not be easily accommodated in basic negotiating patterns. It was not a matter of simply placing a few more chairs at the table. These groups' entrance into a policymaking community usually created a new dividing line between participants. The basic ideological cleavage that exists between consumer and environmental interests and business is not easy to bridge, and, consequently, considerable effort has been expended to devise ways of getting mutual antagonists to negotiate over an extended period. As argued above, once accepted at the bargaining table, citizen groups could be attractive coalition partners for business organizations.

Third, . . . citizen groups typically have a great deal of credibility with the press. Thus, in negotiating, they often have had more to gain by going public to gain leverage with other bargainers. This adds increased uncertainty and instability to the structure of negotiations.

Fourth, citizen groups are often more unified than their business adversaries. The business interests in an issue network may consist of large producers, small producers, foreign producers, and companies from other industries trying to expand into new markets. All these business interests may be fiercely divided as each tries to defend or encroach upon established market patterns. The environmentalists in the same network, while each may have its own niche in terms of issue specialization, are likely to present a united front on major policy disputes. In a perverse way, then, the position of citizen groups has been aided by the proliferation of business groups. (Even without the intrusion of citizen lobbies, this sharp rise in the number of business groups would have irretrievably changed the nature of subgovernments.) . . .

CONCLUSION

Citizen groups have changed the policymaking process in valuable an enduring ways. Most important, they have broadened representation in our political system. Many previously unrepresented or underrepresented constituencies now have a powerful voice in Washington politics. The expanding numbers of liberal citizen groups and their apparent success helped to stimulate a broad mobilization on the part of business. The skyrocketing increase in the numbers of interest groups worked to break down subgovernments and led to the rise of issue networks.

Issue networks are more fragmented, less predictable policymaking environments. Both Congress and the executive branch have taken steps to bring about greater centralized control and coherence to policymaking. Some of these institutional changes seem aimed directly at citizen groups. Negotiated regulations, for example, are seen as a way of getting around the impasse that often develops between liberal citizen groups and business organizations. Centralized regulatory review has been used by Republican administrations as a means of ensuring that business interests are given primacy; regulators are seen as too sympathetic to the citizen groups that are clients of their agencies.

Although government has established these and other institutional mechanisms for coping with complex policymaking environments, the American public does not seem to feel that the government copes very well at all. Congress has been portrayed as unproductive and spineless, unwilling to tackle the tough problems that require discipline or sacrifice. At the core of this criticism is that interest groups are the culprit. Washington lobbies, representing every conceivable interest and showering legislators with the political action committee donations they crave, are said to be responsible for this country's inability to solve its problems.

Although it is counterintuitive, it may be that the increasing number of interest groups coupled with the rise of citizen groups has actually improved the policymaking system in some important ways. More specifically, our policymaking process may be more democratic today because of these developments. Expanded interest group participation has helped to make the policymaking process more open and visible. The closed nature of subgovernment politics meant not only that participation was restricted but that public scrutiny was minimal. The proliferation of interest groups, Washington media that are more aggressive, and the willingness and ability of citizen groups in particular to go public as part of their advocacy strategy have worked to open up policymaking to the public eye.

The end result of expanded citizen group advocacy is policy communities that are highly participatory and more broadly representative of the public. One can argue that this more democratic policymaking process is also one that is less capable of concerted action; yet there is no reliable evidence that American government is any more or less responsive to pressing policy problems than it has ever been. There are, of course, difficult problems that remain unresolved, but that is surely true of every era. Democracy requires adequate representation of interests as well as institutions capable of addressing difficult policy problems. For policymakers who must balance the demand for representation with the need for results, the key is thinking creatively about how to build coalitions and structure negotiations between large groups of actors.

POSTSCRIPT

Is Government Dominated by
Big Business?

One of the problems for any pluralist is the danger that many people may not be properly represented. Suppose, for example, that business and environmental groups in Washington compromise their differences by supporting environmental legislation but passing the costs along to consumers. The legislation may be good, even necessary, but have the consumer's interests been taken into account? There are, of course, self-styled consumer groups, but it is hard to determine whether or not they really speak for the average consumer. The same is true of other activist organizations that claim to represent different groups in our society. The challenge for pluralists is to make their system as inclusive as possible.

Social science literature contains a number of works on the issues of pluralism and corporate power. Political scientist Charles E. Lindblom supported pluralism in the 1950s, but he later changed his mind and concluded that big business dominates American policy making. Lindblom takes the pluralist perspective in his early book *Politics, Economics, and Welfare* (Harper, 1953), written with political scientist Robert A. Dahl. His repudiation of pluralism was complete by the time he published *Politics and Markets: The World's Political-Economic Systems* (Basic Books, 1977). Lindblom may have been influenced by some of the critiques of pluralism that appeared in the 1960s, including Peter Bachrach, *The Theory of Democratic Elitism* (Little, Brown, 1976) and Theodore Lowi, *The End of Liberalism* (W. W. Norton, 1969). More recent works arguing that corporate elites possess inordinate power in American society are Michael Schwartz, ed., *The Structure of Power in America* (Holmes & Meier, 1987); G. William Domhoff, *The Power Elite and the State* (Aldine de Gruyter, 1990) and *Who Rules America Now?* (Prentice Hall, 1983); Michael Useem, *The Inner Circle* (Oxford University Press, 1984); Beth Mintz and Michael Schwartz, *The Power Structure of American Business* (University of Chicago Press, 1985); Robert R. Alford and Roger Friedland, *Powers of Theory: Capitalism, the State, and Democracy* (Cambridge University Press, 1985); Dan Clawson et al., *Money Talks: Corporate PACs and Political Influence* (Basic Books, 1992); and Mark S. Mizruchi, *The Structure of Corporate Political Action: Interfirm Relations and Their Consequences* (Harvard University Press, 1992).

For some pluralist arguments, see Andrew M. Greeley, *Building Coalitions* (Franklin Watts, 1974); David Vogel, *Fluctuating Fortunes: The Political Power of Business in America* (Basic Books, 1989); John P. Heinz, Edward O. Laumann,

Robert L. Nelson, and Robert H. Salisbury, *The Hollow Core: Private Interests in National Policy Making* (Harvard University Press, 1993); Lawrence S. Rothenberg, *Linking Citizens to Government: Interest Group Politics at Common Cause* (Cambridge University Press, 1992); and Susan Herbst, *Numbered Voices: How Opinion Polls Shape American Politics* (University of Chicago Press, 1993).

ISSUE 13

Should Government Intervene in a Capitalist Economy?

YES: Ernest Erber, from "Virtues and Vices of the Market: Balanced Correctives to a Current Craze," *Dissent* (Summer 1990)

NO: Milton and Rose Friedman, from *Free to Choose: A Personal Statement* (Harcourt Brace Jovanovich, 1980)

ISSUE SUMMARY

YES: Author Ernest Erber argues that capitalism creates serious social problems that need to be redressed by an activist government.

NO: Economists Milton and Rose Friedman maintain that market competition, when permitted to work unimpeded, protects citizens better than government regulations intended to correct for failures of the market.

The expression "That government is best which governs least" sums up a deeply rooted attitude of many Americans. From early presidents Thomas Jefferson and Andrew Jackson to America's most recent leaders, Ronald Reagan, George Bush, and Bill Clinton, American politicians have often echoed the popular view that there are certain areas of life best left to the private actions of citizens.

One such area is the economic sphere, where people make their living by buying and selling goods and services. The tendency of most Americans is to regard direct government involvement in the economic sphere as both unnecessary and dangerous. The purest expression of this view is the economic theory of *laissez-faire*, a French term meaning "let be" or "let alone." The seminal formulation of *laissez-faire* theory was the work of eighteenth-century Scottish philosopher Adam Smith, whose treatise *The Wealth of Nations* appeared in 1776. Smith's thesis was that each individual, pursuing his or her own selfish interests in a competitive market, will be "led by an invisible hand to promote an end which was no part of his intention." In other words, when people single-mindedly seek profit, they actually serve the community because sellers must keep prices down and quality up if they are to meet the competition of other sellers.

Laissez-faire economics was much honored (in theory, if not always in practice) during the nineteenth and early twentieth centuries. But as the nineteenth century drew to a close, the Populist Party sprang up. The Populists denounced eastern bankers, Wall Street stock manipulators, and rich "moneyed interests," and they called for government ownership of railroads, a progressive income tax, and other forms of state intervention. The Populist Party died out early in the twentieth century, but the Populist message was not forgotten. In fact, it was given new life after 1929, when the stock market collapsed and the United States was plunged into the worst economic depression in its history.

By 1932 a quarter of the nation's workforce was unemployed, and most Americans were finding it hard to believe that the "invisible hand" would set things right. Some Americans totally repudiated the idea of a free market and embraced socialism, the belief that the state (or "the community") should run all major industries. Most stopped short of supporting socialism, but they were now prepared to welcome some forms of state intervention in the economy. President Franklin D. Roosevelt, elected in 1932, spoke to this mood when he pledged a "New Deal" to the American people. "New Deal" has come to stand for a variety of programs that were enacted during the first eight years of Roosevelt's presidency, including business and banking regulations, government pension programs, federal aid to the disabled, unemployment compensation, and government-sponsored work programs. Side by side with the "invisible hand" of the marketplace was now the very visible hand of an activist government.

Government intervention in the economic sphere increased during World War II as the government fixed prices, rationed goods, and put millions to work in government-subsidized war industries. Activist government continued during the 1950s, but the biggest leap forward occurred during the late 1960s and early 1970s, when the federal government launched a variety of new welfare and regulatory programs: the multibillion-dollar War on Poverty, new civil rights and affirmative action mandates, and new laws protecting consumers, workers, disabled people, and the environment. These, in turn, led to a proliferation of new government agencies and bureaus, as well as shelves and shelves of published regulations. Proponents of the new activism conceded that it was expensive, but they insisted that activist government was necessary to protect Americans against pollution, discrimination, dangerous products, and other effects of the modern marketplace. Critics of government involvement called attention not only to its direct costs but also to its effect on business activity and individual freedom.

In the following selections, Ernest Erber argues that although competitive markets are very productive, they bring about a variety of negative consequences, and he concludes that business regulation and other forms of government intervention are necessary to counter some of the harmful effects of the marketplace. Milton and Rose Friedman argue that the "invisible hand" of the market will work effectively if it is allowed to do so without government interference.

YES

Ernest Erber

VIRTUES AND VICES OF THE MARKET: BALANCED CORRECTIVES TO A CURRENT CRAZE

Not since they encountered it in nursery rhymes have references to the market so intruded into the consciousness of Americans as in recent months. There is now a virtual consensus that the market is the natural state of economic affairs, and its creation in nations not yet blessed with it is the prescription for every economic ailment. This makes vague good sense to most Americans, for whom the market has pleasant associations. Not surprisingly, for the market has long since come to determine their tastes and values, their very lives....

This worldwide consensus would not exist if it did not reflect a body of evidence that links the market with economic growth, increased productivity, and improved living standards. That this historical progress has been facilitated by the market's competitive and entrepreneurial incentives cannot be contested. Neither can the beliefs that the market's function as a pricing mechanism has historically contributed to economic stability conducive to growth, even if plagued by a persistent tendency toward inflation in recent years, nor that the market's negative, even self-destructive, side effects have been largely diminished by state intervention through regulation, credit-budget-tax policies, price supports, and social welfare programs....

NATURE OF THE MARKET

... The market as we know it today is the historically specific product of industrial capitalism and can only be understood if perceived as such....

The Market is, essentially, an economic decision-making process that determines the allocation of society's resources by deciding what and how much is produced and how and to whom it is distributed. Those who participate in this process are buyers and sellers who "meet" in the "marketplace," though they are not only individuals, since buyers and sellers also include businesses of all sizes, farmers and professionals as groups, governments at all levels.

As an alternative to the Market, society's resources can also be directly allocated by political decisions of government (that is, by "command"). Government can also act deliberately to influence indirectly how the Market functions indirectly. Those who determine a government's economic role are citizens, governing officials, and administrators (including, sometimes, planners, though every governmental impact upon the economy should not be called "planning" and, in the United States, it almost never is that). Within capitalist economies, the purpose of governmental intervention in the Market is twofold: (1) to facilitate the functioning of the Market by protecting it from its shortcomings, including tendencies toward self-destructiveness; (2) to supplement the Market by providing those goods and services that the Market has no incentive to supply because they do not entail a profit (public schools, social welfare, low-cost housing, infrastructure, and so on).

The extent to which government should influence the economy is an issue that has been fought over for a very long time. Charles E. Lindblom begins his definitive *Politics and Markets* by observing that "the greatest distinction between one government and another is in the degree to which market replaces government or government replaces market. Both Adam Smith and Karl Marx knew this."

* * *

The word "degree" is used by Lindblom deliberately, for neither the market nor government replaces the other completely. Thus all economies are a mix of the Market and political decision making. Even the totally mad Stalinist effort to eliminate the Market in Soviet-type societies fell short of complete success, for these societies had to tolerate market operations in corners of the economy, either by compromise, as in permitted sales from garden plots of collective farmers and *kolkhoz* "surplus" production, or through black market sales of scarce commodities, tolerated because they were considered helpful to the economy.

Another variant of madness, though largely rhetorical, is the Thatcherite and Reaganite pronouncements about getting government out of the economy and "letting the market decide." After a decade of such huffing and puffing, the role of government vis-à-vis the economy, both in Great Britain and in the United States, remains essentially unchanged, some privatizations notwithstanding....

* * *

A final aspect of the Market's historical context is the largely forgotten role played by the state in getting market-based economies off the ground in various parts of the world. Japan, Prussia, and Czarist Russia are outstanding examples of the state's role in "jump starting" both capitalist production and market relations through generous credit, subsidies, enactment of special rights, licenses, and so on. Government construction of infrastructure often played a key role.

What we can conclude is that the prevailing view that attributes the material progress of human societies during the last century or two *solely* to the Market is fallacious, because the Market's contribution cannot be sufficiently separated from that of the Industrial Revolution, the capitalist mode of production, or the nourishing role of the state. To the extent that references to the Market are euphemistic in order to advocate capitalism under another name, there is an implied admission that the market cannot be separated from capitalism, that is, private property in the means of production, labor as a commodity, unearned income, accumulation, and so forth. But insofar as there now exists an effort to utilize the Market's virtues, while straining out its vices, in order to serve the common welfare, an assessment of its feasibility cannot be made until we have clearer insights into how it would resolve a number of contradictions that seem to make this objective unworkable.

THE MARKET'S SIDE EFFECTS AND POLITICAL REMEDIES

The following descriptions of the Market's side effects are valid, on the whole, though in some cases not entirely separable from other causes. The rationale of the Market is competition—for survival and gain. It pits each against all in social Darwinian "survival of the fittest": worker against worker and entrepreneur against entrepreneur, capital against labor and producer against consumer. The weak are eliminated and the strong survive, resulting in the trend toward concentration and monopolies. Businesses live by the "bottom line," with an incentive toward price gouging, adulteration, misrepresentation, environmental degradation. Product or service promotion caters to every human weakness. Advertising seduces consumers to develop endless wants. The central effect is to subvert human solidarity and civic responsibility.

The multitudinous buy/sell decisions that drive the market process are made in total ignorance of their collective impact, as expressed in Adam Smith's now hoary "unseen hand." Its social impact causes society to "fly blind," as when millions of individually bought automobiles collectively spell traffic gridlock and death-dealing air pollution. Government seeks to overcome these destructive results by regulating the manufacture of automobiles and gasoline. If this fails, as is likely, government will have to turn to long-range planning of alternate transportation, replacing private automobile trips with public conveyances. This will be a political decision to allocate resources from the private sector's automobile solution to the public sector's rail and bus solution. This is only one example of the choices between decisions by the Market and by the political process (made with or without planning).

The nineteenth-century laissez-faire market process, almost total economic determination by consumer demand, eventually proved unworkable. This was capitalism as Karl Marx knew it, and unworkable as he had predicted. During the course of the twentieth century, laissez-faire gave way to large-scale political intervention, resulting in state-guided and, increasingly, state-managed capitalism, with the state's control of money flow through central banks (Federal Reserve in the United States), credit control, tariffs and quotas, subsidies, tax policy, industrial and agricultural loans, price supports, wages policy, loan guarantees, savings incentives, marketing assistance, stockpiling, and various regulatory controls. This continuing transformation of market-based economies, which has come to be known as the Keynesian Revolution, is likely to be viewed by historians as of greater significance than the Soviet Revolution.

* * *

The proportions of market vs. political decision making in economic affairs does not necessarily reflect the proportions of private vs. state ownership of the economy. State-owned industries in countries such as Austria, Italy, and France, where they form a high proportion of the economy, are largely indistinguishable from the private sector in operating by the rules of the Market to produce in response to consumer demand. On the other hand, despite a relatively small nationalized sector, the state in Sweden is omnipresent in managing economic affairs. *The current widespread tilt toward privatization does not, therefore, diminish the trend toward an increased role of the state in economic affairs.*

The Market process demands that those who wish to participate pay admission. Those who cannot afford to get in—or who drop out—fall through the cracks; if lucky, into a social safety net. As the burden increased beyond private charities' resources, government was forced to assume it and the twentieth century's "welfare state" emerged. Its "transfer" programs of public goods and services exist outside the Market for those who cannot make it within.

The insecurity of various categories of entrepreneurs (such as farmers, oil drillers, ship owners, owners of small businesses, bank depositors), caused by the instability and unpredictability of the market process, led these entrepreneurs to use their political power to seek public assistance through subsidies, loans, insurance, "bailouts," and so forth, eventually becoming entitlements. The latter, together with welfare state transfer payments, proliferated and grew enormously, in part because they reflected the universal transition within affluent societies from satisfying needs to meeting wants. Adding these to the cost of traditional categories of public goods and services (such as national defense, public schools, parks, libraries, streets and roads) resulted in ballooning governmental budgets and the diversion through taxation of increasing proportions of the GNPs of industrial nations to their public sectors.

This had the effect of cutting into the availability of accumulated capital for investment in direct wealth-producing enterprise. Government response differed sharply, depending upon whether it followed a national economic policy or relied upon the Market. Sweden, an example of the former, tapped its Supplementary Pension Program to create the so-called fourth fund for targeted industrial investment, creating and sustaining employment that yielded a flow of payroll deductions back into the fund. The United States, on the other hand, permitted Market forces to drive up interest rates, bringing an inflow of foreign capital and an outflow of dividends and interest.

But, regardless of how the problem is managed, there are political limits to the diversion of funds from the private sector to the public sector via taxation. This can be seen in the "tax revolts" in Europe and the United States in the last two decades, which also had repercussions in the Scandinavian countries, including Sweden. This diversion also triggered the resurgence of laissez-faire ideology and right-wing politics.

Even for those countries in which the Market successfully accumulates the "wealth of nations," there results a lopsided inequality of distribution within the population, resulting in recurring economic instability and social confrontation. (Brazil, a country with the eighth largest Market-based economy in the world, leads all others in polarization between rich and poor.) The Market process generates cyclical and chronic unemployment, bankruptcies, mass layoffs, over- and underproduction, strikes and lockouts, and many other kinds of economic warfare and social tension. There is good reason to believe that the sharp shift in income from earned to unearned during the 1980s will be reflected in rising class conflict in the 1990s.

The Market is not a surefire prescription for the "wealth of nations" because its acclaimed incentives, acting as a spur to economic development, are also historically specific. Just because eighteenth-century England used the Market process to turn itself into a "nation of shopkeepers" and nineteenth-century England used it to lead the way in the Industrial Revolution to become the "world's workshop," is no assurance that, at any other time in history, people of any other culture and level of development can similarly use the Market to the same end—notwithstanding the examples of Western Europe, the United States, Canada, and Japan. (South Korea and Taiwan, judged by their per capita incomes, have not yet made it.)

Internationally, the Market has resulted in hierarchical ranking of nations by wealth, grouping a fortunate few as the rich nations and the rest as relatively or absolutely poor. Market-process relations between the industrially developed nations and the rest take the form of the developed responding to the consumer-driven demands of the underdeveloped for investments, loans, goods, and services, thereby aggravating their dependency, and frustrating their ability to accumulate enough capital to significantly improve their productivity (Argentina, Brazil, Mexico, Egypt, India, to name some).

* * *

In summarizing the Market's negative side effects we have noted that it flies blindly; that its growth becomes destruc-

tive of communitarian values and institutions and of the natural environment; that its "work ethic" becomes exploitation, even of children (child labor is again on the rise in the United States according to the Department of Labor); that it reduces the cost of production but also triggers inflation; that it produces a cornucopia of goods but also mountains of waste; that its pharmaceutical research lengthens lifespans, but its chemicals (pesticides and herbicides) shorten them; that it makes feverish use of humankind's growing power over nature, born of scientific and technological progress, but puts profits above ecology and market share above the need to conserve natural resources; that it provides conveniences, comforts, and luxuries for an increasing number but shows no ability to close the widening gap between haves and have nots, neither within nor between nations. But, above all, the Market, despite Keynesianism, operates in cycles of boom and bust, victimizing businesses, large and small, farmers, professionals, and wage workers. Left to its own devices, the Market is inherently self-destructive.

Though the Market's negative side effects can be countered through government intervention and largely have been, such countering tends to be ameliorative rather than curative, and often raises new problems requiring additional intervention, thus reinforcing the overall tendency for the state to backstop the Market. But, despite this, Market economies still move blindly, though increasingly within broad channels marked out by government. The Market economy still overheats and runs out of fuel, but government now acts to cool it and then to fuel it (and even attempts to "fine tune" it). Will it prove a viable arrangement in the long term for government to treat the

Market as if it were an elemental force of nature?

The people seem to want the benefits of the Market, but look to government to minimize the dreadful side effects that come with it. But one person's "dreadful side effects" are another person's sweet accumulation of capital. Translated into social relations, this conflict of interests expresses itself as interest-group confrontations and social-class struggles. And as decision making in economic affairs continues to shift from the Market to the political process, an ever fiercer political resistance is mounted by the interest groups and classes whose power is far greater and more direct in the Market than in the political arena—for instance, the resurgence of the new right in waging ideological and political warfare on behalf of laissez-faire policies.

THE MARKET'S THRUST VS. SOCIETAL GUIDANCE

Understanding the direction in which the Market is likely to move in the next few decades is critically important to an assessment of its capacity to accommodate solutions for outstanding problems. In the past, especially since World War II, the Market's contribution to easing the great problems of civilization has been in the form of economic growth. The nature of the problems that now loom, however, makes them less subject to solution through economic growth. The rising tide that once raised all boats now leaves many stuck on muddy bottoms.

Market-based growth has not demonstrated an ability to reduce the glaring inequality in living standards and in educational/cultural levels within and between nations. In the United States during the last decade the gap between the bottom and the top of the income quintiles has widened. And growth solutions now generate new problems: the degradation of the natural environment on earth and in space; the exhaustion of natural resources; the emergence of *social* limits to growth, caused by the level at which acquisition of goods, services, and facilities by enough people spoils the advantages of possessing them; the puzzle of insatiable wants after basic needs have been satisfied (when is enough enough?). There are also the growth of private affluence and public squalor; an individualistic society's reluctance to resort to collective solutions (national health care) before first going through the agony of postponing the inevitable, and other looming problems sensed but seemingly too elusively complex to articulate. These problems join a long list of old problems that go unsolved to become a leaden weight on progress.

* * *

Is there reason to believe that the Market's failure to cope with these problems will (or can) be remedied in the future? Is there anything in the nature and function of the Market that is likely to redirect its performance to be able to solve these problems? Are any of its negative side effects going to be eliminated, except insofar as governmentally applied correctives can curb them without altering the overall thrust of the Market? Left to its own devices, the Market's current trends are likely to expand and exacerbate problems. Are any countervailing forces in view? Yes.

One is the sharpening competition in the world market. The latter is being badly misread. True, a coded message on a computer or fax machine can transfer billions of dollars overseas at the end of the business day and retrieve it first thing in the morning—with earnings added. True, multinationals no longer fly a single flag. But national interests are as sharply defined as ever. And waging war with economic weapons has not reduced competitiveness and aggressiveness. The competitors are dividing into several major blocs: North America (the United States plus Canada and Mexico), Japan (plus the Asian rim countries) and a united Europe. The goal: market share. As Japan has shown (and also Europe to a lesser extent), this warfare requires maximum mobilization of economic resources: capital, management, knowledge-industry, and labor. Japan has shown that the way to bring these together is by making them all part of the corporate state. The power of Japan, Inc. is recognized in all American boardrooms, though a much smaller nation, Sweden, has also used the corporate strategy brilliantly. The striking similarity of Japanese and Swedish economic strategies, though for different social ends, is largely overlooked because the former is dominated by corporations and the latter by organized labor acting through the Social Democratic party.

The corporate state strategy has anti-market overtones. Rather than letting the market decide, it operates through strategic planning and a national industrial (investment) policy. If global market share is the goal, the nation's consumers had better not be permitted to decide on the allocation of resources. Laissez-faire America illustrates why not. The consumers opt for second homes, third cars, snowmobiles, Jacuzzis, and Torneau watches, thereby short-changing education at all levels, skill retraining of the labor force, housing, and health care—all essential ingredients in mobilizing resources to fight for market share.

The last thing any nation needs or will ever want after the debacle of the Stalinist model is an administrative-command economy (misnamed "planning"). Let the Market process determine the number, style, size, and color of shoes. And similarly for other basic needs and reasonable wants. But the nation also has collective needs, and the polity should determine the allocation of resources to supply them. Because this cannot be determined by the blind outcomes of the Market, the latter must be subordinated to strategically planned priorities designed to serve an overriding common purpose.

If coping with the major problems facing humankind in both its social and natural environments requires societal guidance, it necessitates setting goals and choosing strategies to achieve them; in short, strategic planning. This calls for conscious, deliberate, and coordinated measures to mobilize a nation's resources. The American people with its Market-instilled value system is decidedly averse to this (except in time of war, when by political decision a goal-oriented government controlled wages, employment, prices, profits, manufacturing, and construction).

The twenty-first is not likely to be an American Century. Clinging to the Market, the negation of societal guidance, we might not even come in second. More likely we will be third, after a united Europe and an Asian-rim dominant Japan operating with strategic planning. Americans are more likely to be content with nursery reveries of

To market, to market, to buy a fat pig,
Home again, home again, to dance a fast
jig.

NO

Milton and Rose Friedman

FREE TO CHOOSE

THE POWER OF THE MARKET

The Role of Prices

The key insight of Adam Smith's *Wealth of Nations* is misleadingly simple: if an exchange between two parties is voluntary, it will not take place unless both believe they will benefit from it. Most economic fallacies derive from the neglect of this simple insight, from the tendency to assume that there is a fixed pie, that one party can gain only at the expense of another.

This key insight is obvious for a simple exchange between two individuals. It is far more difficult to understand how it can enable people living all over the world to cooperate to promote their separate interests.

The price system is the mechanism that performs this task without central direction, without requiring people to speak to one another or to like one another. When you buy your pencil or your daily bread, you don't know whether the pencil was made or the wheat was grown by a white man or a black man, by a Chinese or an Indian. As a result, the price system enables people to cooperate peacefully in one phase of their life while each one goes about his own business in respect of everything else.

Adam Smith's flash of genius was his recognition that the prices that emerged from voluntary transactions between buyers and sellers—for short, in a free market—could coordinate the activity of millions of people, each seeking his own interest, in such a way as to make everyone better off. It was a startling idea then, and it remains one today, that economic order can emerge as the unintended consequence of the actions of many people, each seeking his own interest.

The price system works so well, so efficiently, that we are not aware of it most of the time. We never realize how well it functions until it is prevented from functioning, and even then we seldom recognize the source of the trouble.

The long gasoline lines that suddenly emerged in 1974 after the OPEC oil embargo, and again in the spring and summer of 1979 after the revolution in Iran, are a striking recent example. On both occasions there was a sharp disturbance in the supply of crude oil from abroad. But that did not lead to gasoline lines in Germany or Japan, which are wholly dependent on imported oil. It led to long gasoline lines in the United States, even though we produce much of our own oil, for one reason and one reason only: because legislation, administered by a government agency, did not permit the price system to function. Prices in some areas were kept by command below the level that would have equated the amount of gasoline available at the gas stations to the amount consumers wanted to buy at that price. Supplies were allocated to different areas of the country by command, rather than in response to the pressures of demand as reflected in price. The result was surpluses in some areas and shortages plus long gasoline lines in others. The smooth operation of the price system —which for many decades had assured every consumer that he could buy gasoline at any of a large number of service stations at his convenience and with a minimal wait—was replaced by bureaucratic improvisation....

The Role of Government
Where does government enter into the picture?...

[W]hat role should be assigned to government?

It is not easy to improve on the answer that Adam Smith gave to this question two hundred years ago:

... According to the system of natural liberty, the sovereign has only three duties to attend to; three duties of great importance, indeed, but plain and intelligible to common understandings: first, the duty of protecting the society from the violence and invasion of other independent societies; secondly, the duty of protecting, as far as possible, every member of the society from the injustice or oppression of every other member of it, or the duty of establishing an exact administration of justice; and thirdly, the duty of erecting and maintaining certain public works and certain public institutions, which it can never be for the interest of any individual, or small number of individuals, to erect and maintain; because the profit could never repay the expence to any individual or small number of individuals, though it may frequently do much more than repay it to a great society.

... A fourth duty of government that Adam Smith did not explicitly mention is the duty to protect members of the community who cannot be regarded as "responsible" individuals. Like Adam Smith's third duty, this one, too, is susceptible of great abuse. Yet it cannot be avoided....

Adam Smith's three duties, or our four duties of government, are indeed "of great importance," but they are far less "plain and intelligible to common understandings" than he supposed. Though we cannot decide the desirability or undesirability of any actual or proposed government intervention by mechanical reference to one or another of them, they provide a set of principles that we can use in casting up a balance sheet of pros and cons. Even on the loosest interpretation, they rule out much existing government intervention—all those "systems either of preference or of restraint" that Adam Smith fought against, that were subsequently destroyed, but have since reappeared in the form of today's tariffs, governmentally fixed prices and wages, restrictions on entry into various occupations, and numerous other departures from his "simple system of natural liberty."...

CRADLE TO GRAVE

... At the end of the war [World War II] it looked as if central economic planning was the wave of the future. That outcome was passionately welcomed by some who saw it as the dawn of a world of plenty shared equally. It was just as passionately feared by others, including us, who saw it as a turn to tyranny and misery. So far, neither the hopes of the one nor the fears of the other have been realized.

Government has expanded greatly. However, that expansion has not taken the form of detailed central economic planning accompanied by ever widening nationalization of industry, finance, and commerce, as so many of us feared it would. Experience put an end to detailed economic planning, partly because it was not successful in achieving the announced objectives, but also because it conflicted with freedom....

The failure of planning and nationalization has not eliminated pressure for an ever bigger government. It has simply altered its direction. The expansion of government now takes the form of welfare programs and of regulatory activities. As W. Allen Wallis put it in a somewhat different context, socialism, "intellectually bankrupt after more than a century of seeing one after another of its arguments for socializing the *means* of production demolished—now seeks to socialize the *results* of production."

In the welfare area the change of direction has led to an explosion in recent decades, especially after President Lyndon Johnson declared a "War on Poverty" in 1964. New Deal programs of Social Security, unemployment insurance, and direct relief were all expanded to cover new groups; payments were increased; and Medicare, Medicaid, food stamps, and numerous other programs were added. Public housing and urban renewal programs were enlarged. By now there are literally hundreds of government welfare and income transfer programs. The Department of Health, Education and Welfare, established in 1953 to consolidate the scattered welfare programs, began with a budget of $2 billion, less than 5 percent of expenditures on national defense. Twenty-five years later, in 1978, its budget was $160 billion, one and a half times as much as total spending on the army, the navy, and the air force. It had the third largest budget in the world, exceeded only by the entire budget of the U.S. government and of the Soviet Union....

No one can dispute two superficially contradictory phenomena: widespread dissatisfaction with the results of this explosion in welfare activities; continued pressure for further expansion.

The objectives have all been noble; the results, disappointing. Social Security expenditures have skyrocketed, and the system is in deep financial trouble. Public housing and urban renewal programs have subtracted from rather than added to the housing available to the poor. Public assistance rolls mount despite growing employment. By general agreement, the welfare program is a "mess" saturated with fraud and corruption. As government has paid a larger share of the nation's medical bills, both patients and physicians complain of rocketing costs and of the increasing impersonality of medicine. In education, student performance has dropped as federal intervention has expanded....

The repeated failure of well-intentioned programs is not an accident. It is not simply the result of mistakes of execution. The failure is deeply rooted in the use of bad means to achieve good objectives.

Despite the failure of these programs, the pressure to expand them grows. Failures are attributed to the miserliness of Congress in appropriating funds, and so are met with a cry for still bigger programs. Special interests that benefit from specific programs press for their expansion—foremost among them the massive bureaucracy spawned by the programs....

CREATED EQUAL

Capitalism and Equality

Everywhere in the world there are gross inequities of income and wealth. They offend most of us. Few can fail to be moved by the contrast between the luxury enjoyed by some and the grinding poverty suffered by others.

In the past century a myth has grown up that free market capitalism—equality of opportunity as we have interpreted that term—increases such inequalities, that it is a system under which the rich exploit the poor.

Nothing could be further from the truth. Wherever the free market has been permitted to operate, wherever anything approaching equality of opportunity has existed, the ordinary man has been able to attain levels of living never dreamed of before. Nowhere is the gap between rich and poor wider, nowhere are the rich richer and the poor poorer, than in those societies that do not permit the free market to operate. That is true of feudal societies like medieval Europe, India before independence, and much of modern South America, where inherited status determines position. It is equally true of centrally planned societies, like Russia or China or India since independence, where access to government determines position. It is true even where central planning was introduced, as in all three of these countries, in the name of equality....

WHO PROTECTS THE CONSUMER?

... The pace of intervention quickened greatly after the New Deal—half of the thirty-two agencies in existence in 1966 were created after FDR's election in 1932. Yet intervention remained fairly moderate and continued in the single-industry mold. The *Federal Register*, established in 1936 to record all the regulations, hearings, and other matters connected with the regulatory agencies, grew, at first rather slowly, then more rapidly. Three volumes, containing 2,599 pages and taking six inches of shelf space, sufficed for 1936; twelve volumes, containing 10,528 pages and taking twenty-six inches of shelf space, for 1956; and thirteen volumes, containing 16,850 pages and taking thirty-six inches of shelf space, for 1966.

Then a veritable explosion in government regulatory activity occurred. No fewer than twenty-one new agencies were established in the next decade. Instead of being concerned with specific industries, they covered the waterfront: the environment, the production and distribution of energy, product safety, occupational safety, and so on. In addition to concern with the consumer's pocketbook, with protecting him from exploitation by sellers, recent agencies are primarily concerned with things like the consumer's safety and well-being, with protecting him not only from sellers but also from himself.

Government expenditures on both older and newer agencies skyrocketed —from less than $1 billion in 1970 to roughly $5 billion estimated for 1979. Prices in general roughly doubled, but these expenditures more than quintupled. The number of government bureaucrats employed in regulatory activities tripled, going from 28,000 in 1970 to 81,000 in 1979; the number of pages in the *Federal Register*, from 17,660 in 1970 to 36,487 in 1978, taking 127 inches of shelf space—a veritable ten-foot shelf....

This revolution in the role of government has been accompanied, and largely produced, by an achievement in public persuasion that must have few rivals. Ask yourself what products are currently least satisfactory and have shown the least improvement over time. Postal service, elementary and secondary schooling, railroad passenger transport would surely be high on the list. Ask yourself which products are most satisfactory and have improved the most. Household appliances, television and radio sets, hi-fi equipment, computers, and, we would add, supermarkets and shopping centers would surely come high on that list.

The shoddy products are all produced by government or government-regulated industries. The outstanding products are all produced by private enterprise with little or no government involvement. Yet the public—or a large part of it—has been persuaded that private enterprises produce shoddy products, that we need ever vigilant government employees to keep business from foisting off unsafe, meretricious products at outrageous prices on ignorant, unsuspecting, vulnerable customers. That public relations campaign has succeeded so well that we are in the process of turning over to the kind of people who bring us our postal service the far more critical task of producing and distributing energy....

Government intervention in the marketplace is subject to laws of its own, not legislated laws, but scientific laws. It obeys forces and goes in directions that may have little relationship to the intentions or desires of its initiators or supporters. We have already examined this process in connection with welfare activity. It is present equally when government intervenes in the marketplace, whether to protect consumers against high prices or shoddy goods, to promote their safety, or to preserve the environment. Every act of intervention establishes positions of power. How that power will be used and for what purposes depends far more on the people who are in the best position to get control of that power and what their purposes are than on the aims and objectives of the initial sponsors of the intervention....

Environment

The environmental movement is responsible for one of the most rapidly growing areas of federal intervention. The Environmental Protection Agency, established in 1970 "to protect and enhance the physical environment," has been granted increasing power and authority. Its budget has multiplied sevenfold from 1970 to 1978 and is now more than half a billion dollars. It has a staff of about 7,000. It has imposed costs on industry and local and state governments to meet its standards that total in the tens of billions of dollars a year. Something between a tenth and a quarter of total net investment in new capital equipment by business now goes for antipollution purposes. And this does not count the costs of requirements imposed by other agencies, such as those designed to control emissions of motor vehicles, or the costs of land-use planning or wilderness preservation or a host of other federal, state, and local government activities undertaken in the name of protecting the environment.

The preservation of the environment and the avoidance of undue pollution are real problems and they are problems concerning which the government has an important role to play. When all the costs and benefits of any action, and the people hurt or benefited, are readily identifiable, the market provides an excellent means for assuring that only those actions are undertaken for which the benefits exceed the costs for all participants. But when the costs and benefits or the people affected cannot be identified, there is a market failure....

Government is one means through which we can try to compensate for "market failure," try to use our resources more effectively to produce the amount of clean air, water, and land that we are willing to pay for. Unfortunately, the very factors that produce the market failure also make it difficult for government to achieve a satisfactory solution. Generally, it is no easier for government to identify the specific persons who are hurt and benefited than for market participants, no easier for government to assess the amount of harm or benefit to each. Attempts to use government to correct market failure have often simply substituted government failure for market failure.

Public discussion of the environmental issue is frequently characterized more by emotion than reason. Much of it proceeds as if the issue is pollution versus no pollution, as if it were desirable and possible to have a world without pollution. That is clearly nonsense. No one who contemplates the problem seriously will regard zero pollution as either a desirable or a possible state of affairs. We could have zero pollution from automobiles, for example, by simply abolishing all automobiles. That would also make the kind of agricultural and industrial productivity we now enjoy impossible, and so condemn most of us to a drastically lower standard of living, perhaps many even to death. One source of atmospheric pollution is the carbon dioxide that we all exhale. We could stop that very simply. But the cost would clearly exceed the gain.

It costs something to have clean air, just as it costs something to have other good things we want. Our resources are limited and we must weigh the gains from reducing pollution against the costs. Moreover, "pollution" is not an objective phenomenon. One person's pollution may be another's pleasure. To some of us rock music is noise pollution; to others of us it is pleasure.

The real problem is not "eliminating pollution," but trying to establish arrangements that will yield the "right" amount of pollution: an amount such that the gain from reducing pollution a bit more just balances the sacrifice of the other good things—houses, shoes, coats, and so on—that would have to be given up in order to reduce the pollution. If we go farther than that, we sacrifice more than we gain....

The Market
Perfection is not of this world. There will always be shoddy products, quacks, con artists. But on the whole, market competition, when it is permitted to work, protects the consumer better than do the

alternative government mechanisms that have been increasingly superimposed on the market.

As Adam Smith said..., competition does not protect the consumer because businessmen are more soft-hearted than the bureaucrats or because they are more altruistic or generous, or even because they are more competent, but only because it is in the self-interest of the businessman to serve the consumer.

If one storekeeper offers you goods of lower quality or of higher price than another, you're not going to continue to patronize his store. If he buys goods to sell that don't serve your needs, you're not going to buy them. The merchants therefore search out all over the world the products that might meet your needs and might appeal to you. And they stand back of them because if they don't, they're going to go out of business. When you enter a store, no one forces you to buy. You are free to do so or go elsewhere. That is the basic difference between the market and a political agency. You are free to choose. There is no policeman to take the money out of your pocket to pay for something you do not want or to make you do something you do not want to do.

But, the advocate of government regulation will say, suppose the FDA weren't there, what would prevent business from distributing adulterated or dangerous products? It would be a very expensive thing to do.... It is very poor business practice—not a way to develop a loyal and faithful clientele. Of course, mistakes and accidents occur—but... government regulation doesn't prevent them. The difference is that a private firm that makes a serious blunder may go out of business. A government agency is likely to get a bigger budget.

Cases will arise where adverse effects develop that could not have been foreseen—but government has no better means of predicting such developments than private enterprise. The only way to prevent all such developments would be to stop progress, which would also eliminate the possibility of unforeseen favorable developments....

What about the danger of monopoly that led to the antitrust laws? That is a real danger. The most effective way to counter it is not through a bigger antitrust division at the Department of Justice or a larger budget for the Federal Trade Commission, but through removing existing barriers to international trade. That would permit competition from all over the world to be even more effective than it is now in undermining monopoly at home. Freddie Laker of Britain needed no help from the Department of Justice to crack the airline cartel. Japanese and German automobile manufacturers forced American manufacturers to introduce smaller cars.

The great danger to the consumer is monopoly—whether private or governmental. His most effective protection is free competition at home and free trade throughout the world. The consumer is protected from being exploited by one seller by the existence of another seller from whom he can buy and who is eager to sell to him. Alternative sources of supply protect the consumer far more effectively than all the Ralph Naders of the world.

Conclusion

... [T]he reaction of the public to the more extreme attempts to control our behavior —to the requirement of an interlock system on automobiles or the proposed ban of saccharin—is ample evidence that we want no part of it. Insofar as the government has information not generally available about the merits or demerits of the items we ingest or the activities we engage in, let it give us the information. But let it leave us free to choose what chances we want to take with our own lives.

POSTSCRIPT

Should Government Intervene in a Capitalist Economy?

Erber concedes that the market should not be abolished. He writes that a "body of evidence... links the market with economic growth, increased productivity, and improved living standards," and that this linkage "cannot be contested." Nevertheless, he calls for an activist government to subordinate the market to "planned priorities designed to serve an overriding common purpose." The Friedmans believe that such subordination can only destroy the market. The question, then, is whether or not we can successfully graft the market's "invisible hand" to the arm of the state. Would the graft take? Has the experiment perhaps already proven successful in post–New Deal America? Or is the American government in the process of destroying what gave the nation its growth, prosperity, and living standards?

Erber calls the market a "blind" force. The Friedmans seem to agree that the market in itself is amoral, though they feel that it produces good results. But philosopher Michael Novak goes further, contending that the ethic of capitalism transcends mere moneymaking and is (or can be made) compatible with Judeo-Christian morality. See *The Spirit of Democratic Capitalism* (Madison Books, 1991) and *The Catholic Ethic and the Spirit of Capitalism* (Free Press, 1993). No such claim is made by the Friedmans in *Free to Choose* or in Milton Friedman's earlier *Capitalism and Freedom* (University of Chicago Press, 1962), which portrays capitalism as supportive of democracy and freedom. Another broad-based defense of capitalism is Peter L. Berger's *The Capitalist Revolution: Fifty Propositions About Prosperity, Equality and Liberty* (Basic Books, 1988). For an attack on capitalism, see Victor Perlo, *Superprofits and Crisis: Modern U.S. Capitalism* (International Publishers, 1988). For a mixed view of capitalism, see Charles Wolf, Jr., *Markets or Governments: Choosing Between Imperfect Alternatives* (MIT Press, 1993). Andrew Shonfield's *In Defense of the Mixed Economy* (Oxford University Press, 1984) takes a similar position to Erber and commends Japan for steering the right course between *laissez-faire* and socialism. Ralph Miliband, in *Socialism for a Skeptical Age* (Verso, 1995), argues that socialism is still applicable today. Two works that attack government interventions in the market are William C. Mitchell and Randy T. Simmons, *Beyond Politics: Markets, Welfare, and the Failure of Bureaucracy* (Westview, 1994) and Jonathan Rauch, *Demosclerosis: The Silent Killer of American Government* (Times Books, 1994).

ISSUE 14

Does Welfare Do More Harm Than Good?

YES: Charles Murray, from "What to Do About Welfare," *Commentary* (December 1994)

NO: Mark Robert Rank, from *Living on the Edge: The Realities of Welfare in America* (Columbia University Press, 1994)

ISSUE SUMMARY

YES: Researcher and social critic Charles Murray argues that welfare contributes to dependency, illegitimacy, and absent fathers, and he maintains that workfare, enforced child support, and the abolition of welfare will greatly reduce these problems.

NO: Sociologist Mark Robert Rank asserts that most welfare recipients fall into welfare because of an economic crisis and that welfare is not financially lucrative enough to entice people to its way of life.

Long before Ronald Reagan's campaign for the presidency in 1980, the welfare problem had become a national issue. As far back as the Nixon administration, plans had been made to reform the system by various means. One idea involved the institution of modest cash payments based upon a negative income tax in place of the crazy quilt of services, commodities, checks, and in-kind payments provided by the existing welfare system. The Carter administration also tried to interest Congress in a reform plan that would simplify, though probably not reduce, welfare.

Currently, there is a backlash against welfare recipients, often voiced in mean-spirited jibes such as "Make the loafers work" and "I'm tired of paying them to breed." Such attitudes ignore the idea that most people on welfare are not professional loafers but women with dependent children or elderly or disabled persons. Petty fraud may be common, but "welfare queens" who cheat the system for spectacular sums are extremely rare. The majority of people on welfare are those whose condition would become desperate if payments were cut off. Although many people believe that women on welfare commonly bear children in order to increase their benefits, there is no conclusive evidence that child support payments have anything to do with conception; the costs of raising children far exceed the payments. Also, payments to families with dependent children have eroded considerably relative to the cost of living over the last two decades, so the incentive to get off welfare has increased.

This does not mean that all objections to welfare can be dismissed. There does seem to be evidence that welfare in some cases reduces work incentives and increases the likelihood of family breakups. Concern about the problem of incentives is being addressed by recent proposed changes in welfare programs that limit the amount of time one can be on welfare, provide training, or require welfare recipients to work. As a result, the issue of incentives might be less of a problem in the future.

What should be done about welfare? Broadly speaking, the suggestions fall into three categories: (1) *trim* the program; (2) *monitor* it carefully to make sure that the truly needy are receiving a fair share of it and that work incentives are not lost; and (3) *abolish* welfare outright except for the aged and the physically handicapped.

The *trim* approach was a central tenet in the philosophy of the Reagan administration. When Reagan first campaigned for the presidency in 1980, he promised to "get government off our backs." His contention was that government welfare programs tend to stifle initiative, depress the economy, and do the poor more harm than good. After eight years in office, Reagan's conservative critics claimed that he had not really fulfilled his promises to trim welfare; his liberal critics claimed that he had indeed carried out his promises, albeit with disastrous results.

The radical approach of abolishing welfare is advocated by writer Charles Murray in his influential 1984 book *Losing Ground.* Conservatives hailed it as a masterful critique, and even writers on the Left paid it a kind of backhanded homage by refuting it at length. In the following selections, Murray updates his recommendation of abolishing welfare, this time limiting the reform to unmarried women. He believes that such radical action is needed because of welfare's severely negative consequences. Mark Robert Rank asserts that women on welfare are driven to seek welfare by economic crises and that most of the women seek work while on welfare. In most cases the welfare is desperately needed, and the consequences of abolishing welfare would be horrendous.

YES

Charles Murray

WHAT TO DO ABOUT WELFARE

In the 1992 campaign, Bill Clinton's television ad promising to "end welfare as we know it" was one of his best vote-getters, so effective that it was the first choice for a heavy media buy in closely contested states at the end of the campaign. This should come as no surprise. No American social program has been so unpopular, so consistently, so long, as welfare. But why? What is wrong with welfare that evokes such a widespread urge to "do something about it"?

One obvious candidate is size and cost. Bill Clinton campaigned during a surging increase in the welfare rolls. By the end of his first year in office, more than fourteen million people would be enrolled in Aid to Families with Dependent Children (AFDC), representing more than 7 percent of American families and two million more recipients than had been on the rolls in 1989.

With so many working-aged people being supported by government, the amounts of money involved have mounted accordingly. But, as with so many other questions involving welfare, there is no uncontroversial answer as to exactly how much, because few can agree about where the definition of "welfare" begins and ends.

In 1990, before the most recent increase in the rolls had gotten well under way, figures cited by various parties in the welfare debate ranged from $21 billion to $210 billion. The lower figure, used by those who claim that welfare is really a piddling part of the budget, represents just AFDC. But no serious student of the issue denies that Medicaid, food stamps, and public housing are also part of welfare. That brings the total to $129 billion. But this number covers only part of the array of programs for low-income families. The upper-end figure of $210 billion is the bottom line for the Congressional Research Service's report of state and federal expenditures on "cash and non-cash benefits for persons with limited income" in 1990. Of that, $152 billion came from the federal government.

Two hundred and ten billion dollars works out to $6,270 for every man, woman, and child under the poverty line in 1990, only a few hundred dollars less than the official poverty threshold ($6,652 for a single unrelated individual in 1990). Statements such as "We could eliminate poverty tomorrow if we just gave the money we're already spending directly to poor people" may be oversimplified, but they are not so far off the mark either.

One approach to the topic of "what to do about welfare" could thus reasonably involve ways to reduce expenditures. Yet, though complaints about wasting money on welfare loafers are commonly heard, and though the country truly does spend a lot of money on welfare, it is not obvious that money is really the problem. Suppose that for $210 billion we were buying peaceful neighborhoods and happy, healthy children in our low-income neighborhoods. Who would say that the nation could not afford it? Money may well become a decisive issue as the dependent population continues to grow, but it has not yet.

Instead, I will proceed from the assumption that the main source of the nationwide desire to do something about welfare is grounded in concerns about what welfare is doing to the health of the society. Judging from all that can be found in the press, on talk shows, and in the technical literature, an unusually broad consensus embracing just about everyone except the hard-core Left now accepts that something has gone drastically wrong with the family, that the breakdown is disproportionately found in poor neighborhoods, and that the welfare system is deeply implicated.

Different people put different emphases on just what has gone wrong. There are so many choices. In many welfare families, no one has ever held a regular job. This is bad for the taxpayer who supports such families, bad for the women who are trapped into poverty, and, most portentously in the long run, bad for children who need to be socialized to the world of work. In many wel-

fare families, the mother works, but only sporadically and surreptitiously in the illegal economy. The welfare system becomes an instrument for teaching her children all the wrong lessons about how to get along in life.

In the vast majority of welfare homes, there is no biological father in the house. In many, there has never been a father. The male figure in the home is instead likely to consist of a series of boyfriends who do not act as fathers but as abusive interlopers.

* * *

These circumstances are damaging to children in so many ways that to list them individually would be to trivialize them. On this issue, the intellectual conventional wisdom has changed remarkably in just the last few years. The visible turning point was Barbara Dafoe Whitehead's 1993 *Atlantic* article, "Dan Quayle Was Right," but the groundwork had been laid in the technical journals in preceding years, as more and more scholars concluded that single parenthood was bad for children independently of poverty and other markers of socioeconomic disadvantage.

Statistically, measures of child well-being tend to order families by their structure: conditions are best for children in intact families, next best for children of divorce (it does not seem to help if the custodial parent remarries), and worst for children born out of wedlock (even if the woman later marries another man). This ordering applies to a wide variety of outcomes, from emotional development to school performance to delinquency to family formation in the next generation.

But the evidence accumulated so far tells only part of the story. Families that have been on welfare for long periods of time are overwhelmingly concentrated in communities where many other welfare families live. While it is unfortunate when a child must grow up in a family without a father, it is a disaster when a generation of children—especially male children—grows up in a neighborhood without fathers. The proof of this is before our eyes in the black inner city, where the young men reaching twenty in 1994 came of age in neighborhoods in which about half the children were born out of wedlock. Social science is only beginning to calibrate the extent and nature of the "neighborhood effects" that compound the problems associated with illegitimacy.

If these results were confined to the inner cities of our major cities, the effects on American society would still be grim enough. A look at the national mood about crime shows how a problem that is still localized (as the most severe crime rates still are, impressions notwithstanding) can nonetheless impinge on American life as a whole. But there is no reason to think that the effects will remain within the black inner city. The white illegitimacy ratio, which stood at 22 percent for all whites in 1991, is approaching the 50-percent mark in a number of working-class American cities. There is no good reason to assume that white communities with extremely high illegitimacy ratios will escape the effects of an unsocialized new generation.

These observations have led me to conclude that illegitimacy is the central social problem of our time, and that its spread threatens the underpinning of a free society. We cannot have a free society, by this reasoning, unless the great majority of young people come of age having internalized norms of self-restraint, self-reliance, and commitment to a civic order, and receive an upbringing that prepares them to transmit these same values to their children. We cannot achieve that kind of socialization without fathers playing a father's role in the great majority of homes where children grow up.

For those who accept this pessimistic reasoning, extreme measures to change the welfare system are justified; for those who still consider illegitimacy to be one problem among many, more incremental reforms seem called for. Put broadly, four types of welfare reform are being considered in various combinations: workfare; the substitution of work for welfare; penalties for fathers; and the complete abolition of welfare....

* * *

... [T]he fourth option, scrapping welfare altogether, [is] a proposal with which I have been associated for some years. I am under no illusions that Congress is about to pass such a plan nationally. But... a state can do what the federal government cannot. And it is conceivable that Congress will pass reforms permitting the states wide discretion in restructuring the way they spend their welfare budgets.

The main reason for scrapping welfare is to reduce the number of babies born to single women. The secondary reason is to maximize the chance that children born to single women are raised by mature adults who are able and willing to provide a loving, stable, nurturing environment—a result that will ensue because more children will be given up for adoption at birth, and because single mothers who choose to keep their babies in a no-welfare society will be self-selected and thus their number will be limited to those who have the most resources for caring for children.

These goals presume that ending welfare will have a drastic effect on behavior. One must ask whether there is good reason to believe that it will.

One way of approaching the question is to ask whether welfare causes illegitimacy in the first place. I have written two reviews of this debate in the past two years—one long and technical, the other shorter and nontechnical[1]—and will not try to cover all of the ground here. These are the highlights plus a few new points:

Academics have focused almost exclusively on comparisons of illegitimacy based on the differences in welfare payments across states. It is now generally if reluctantly acknowledged by these scholars that the generosity of welfare benefits has a relationship to extramarital fertility among whites. More recent work is showing that a relationship exists among blacks as well. The size of the effect for whites seems to be in the region of a 50-percent change in extramarital fertility for a 10-percent change in benefits, with some of the estimates substantially larger than that....

Last summer [1994], 76 social scientists signed a statement saying that the relationship of welfare to illegitimacy was small. When I replied that the very studies they had in mind were consistent with something in the neighborhood of a 5-percent drop in white illegitimacy if welfare were eliminated, there were cries of outrage—but not because my statement was technically inaccurate. It was a straightforward extrapolation of the 5-percent (or more) change in white fertility per 10-percent change in welfare benefits that has been found in recent research.

I should add that I do not place much faith in such linear extrapolations in this case. Indeed, I argue from other evidence that the effects would most likely steepen as the reductions in welfare approached 100 percent. But this is speculative—no one has any empirical way to estimate how the curve might be shaped.

* * *

Meanwhile, two characteristics of illegitimate births imply a stronger relationship to welfare than that indicated by the cross-state analyses.

The first of these characteristics is that the illegitimate birth rate has been increasing while the legitimate birth rate has been decreasing. The *rate* in this case refers to the production of babies per unit of population, in contrast to the more commonly used statistic, the illegitimacy *ratio*, representing the proportion of live births that are extramarital.

The logic goes like this: birth rates are driven by broad historic forces that are so powerful and so consistent that they have applied everywhere in the West. Put simply, birth rates fall wherever women have an option to do something besides have babies. The options are brought about by better medical care (so more babies survive to adulthood), increased wealth and educational opportunities, and the opening of careers to women. Improved technology for birth control and access to abortion facilitate the effects of these forces.

Thanks to all this, among both blacks and whites in America, the number of legitimate babies per unit of population has been falling steeply. But during this same period, concentrated in the post-1960's, the number of illegitimate babies per unit of population has been rising. In other words, something is increasing the production of one kind of baby (that born to single women) at the same time that the production of the other kind of baby (that born to married women) is dropping.

The scholars who say that welfare cannot be an important cause of the breakdown of marriage and the encouragement of illegitimacy have yet to offer an explanation of what this mysterious something might be. The existence of a welfare system that pays single women to have babies meets the test of parsimony.

Perhaps, however, the "mysterious something" is the lack of these new options for disadvantaged women. But why specify *single* disadvantaged women? That brings us to one of the most provocative features of illegitimacy, its relationship to poverty—not poverty after the baby is born, but before. It is one of the stronger reasons for believing that the welfare system is implicated in the production of illegitimate babies.

Begin with young single women from affluent families or women in high-paying jobs. For them, the welfare system is obviously irrelevant. They are restrained from having babies out of wedlock by moral considerations, by fear of the social penalties (both of which still exist, though weakened, in middle-class circles), by a concern that the child have a father around the house, and because having a baby would interfere with their plans for the future.

In most of the poorest communities, having a baby out of wedlock is no longer subject to social stigma, nor do moral considerations still appear to carry much weight. But the welfare system is very much part of the picture. For a poor young woman, the welfare system is highly relevant to her future if she has a child, easing the short-term economic penalties that might ordinarily restrain

her childbearing. The poorer she is, the more attractive the welfare package, and the more likely that she will think herself enabled by it to have a baby.

The implication of this logic is that illegitimate births will be concentrated among poor young women—and they are. This may be inferred from the information about family income from the Bureau of the Census data, showing that in 1992, women with incomes of less than $20,000 contributed 73 percent of all illegitimate babies, while women with incomes above $75,000 contributed just 2 percent.

But these data are imprecise, because income may have fallen after the baby was born (and the woman had to quit work, for example). The logic linking welfare to illegitimacy specifically refers to women who are poor before the baby is born. For data on this point, I turn to one of the best available bases, the National Longitudinal Survey of Youth (NLSY),[2] and ask: of women of all races who were below the poverty line in the year prior to giving birth, how many of their children were born out of wedlock? The answer is 56 percent. Among women who were anywhere above the poverty line, only 11 percent of babies were born out of wedlock.

* * *

Why should illegitimate births be so much more likely to occur among women who are already poor? The common argument that young women with few prospects "want something to love" may be true, but it has no answer to the obvious rejoinder, that single poor young women in the years before the welfare system began probably wanted something to love as well, and yet the vast majority of them nonetheless made sure they were married before bearing a child. Other things being equal, poor single young women face the most daunting prospects if they have a baby without a man to help take care of it, and that reality used to govern the behavior of such young women. Of course the sexual revolution has changed the behavior of young women at all levels of society, but why has it produced babies predominantly in just one economic class?

Once again, an answer based on a welfare system that offers incentives only to poor women meets the test of parsimony. Once again, the scholarly literature has yet to offer an alternative explanation, or even to acknowledge that an alternative explanation is called for.

There is one additional characteristic of women who are at most risk of giving birth to children out of wedlock: they generally have low intelligence. This point is new to the welfare debate. Richard Herrnstein and I discuss it at length in *The Bell Curve*, again using the National Longitudinal Survey of Youth, which administered a high-quality cognitive test to its subjects when the study began. The chances that a poor young woman's baby would be born out of wedlock were 68 percent if she had an IQ of 85, but only 26 percent if she had an IQ of 115.

Lest it be thought that this result is conflated with racial complications, it should be noted that the relationship held among whites as powerfully as among the population as a whole. Lest it be thought that the result is conflated with the opportunity that smart women have to go to college, it should also be noted that the relationship holds as powerfully among women who never got beyond high school as it does for the popula-

tion as a whole. Lest it be thought that this is a reflection of socioeconomic background, the independent importance of IQ is still great after holding socioeconomic status constant. Conversely, the independent importance of socioeconomic background after holding the effects of IQ constant is severely attenuated.

Summarizing the overall picture: women in the NLSY (in their mid-twenties to early thirties when this observation applies) who remained childless or had babies within marriage had a mean IQ of 102. Those who had an illegitimate baby but never went on welfare had a mean IQ of 93. Those who went on welfare but did not become chronically dependent on welfare had a mean IQ of 89. Those who became chronic welfare recipients had a mean IQ of 85.

* * *

Now back to the first and most crucial goal of welfare reform, that it drastically reduce the number of children conceived by unmarried women. In trying to develop methods for accomplishing this goal, we know from the outset that both sex and the cuddliness of babies are going to continue to exert their powerful attractions. We know that decisions about whether to have sex and whether to use birth control are not usually made in moments of calm reflection.

Therefore, any reform must somehow generate a situation in which a young woman, despite not being calm and reflective, and often despite not being very bright, is so scared at the prospect of getting pregnant that she will not have intercourse, or will take care not to get pregnant if she does.

This means that the welfare reform will have accomplished one of two things. Either the change has been so big, so immediate, and so punishing that even a young, poor, and not very smart girl has been affected by it; or else the change has directly motivated people around that young woman to take an active role in urging her not to have the baby.

Bill Clinton's program, based on the threat of "two years and out, if you've had a reasonable chance at job training and a reasonable chance to find a job," is not calculated to meet this criterion. Two years is an eternity to a young girl. The neighborhood is filled with single women who have been on welfare for ages and have not gotten thrown off. Is a sixteen-year-old going to believe that she will really be cut off welfare two years down the road, or will she believe the daily evidence around her?

Other commonly urged recommendations—sex education, counseling, and the like—are going to be just as futile. A major change in the behavior of young women and the adults in their lives will occur only when the prospect of having a child out of wedlock is once again so immediately, tangibly punishing that it overrides everything else—the importuning of the male, the desire for sex, the thoughtlessness of the moment, the anticipated cuddliness of the baby. Such a change will take place only when young people have had it drummed into their heads from their earliest memories that having a baby without a husband entails awful consequences. Subtle moral reasoning is not the response that works. "My father would kill me" is the kind of response that works.

From time immemorial, fathers and mothers raised the vast majority of their daughters, bright ones and dull ones, to understand these lessons. Somehow, in the last half-century, they began to lose their capacity to do so—curiously, just as social-welfare benefits for single women expanded. I want to press the argument that the overriding threat, short-term and tangible, which once sustained low illegitimacy ratios was the economic burden that the single woman presented to her parents and to the community. I do not mean to deny the many ways in which noneconomic social stigma played a role or to minimize the importance of religious belief, but I would argue that much of their force was underwritten by economics.

... [T]he overriding theme of what we do about welfare [is to treat] the human drama of "having a child" as the deeply solemn, responsibility-laden act that it is, and treating all parents the same in their obligation to be good parents. The government does not have the right to prescribe how people shall live or to prevent women from having babies. It should not have the right even to encourage certain women to have babies through the granting of favors. But for 60 years the government has been granting those favors, and thereby intervening in a process that human communities know how to regulate much better than governments do. Welfare for single mothers has been destructive beyond measure, and should stop forthwith.

NOTES

1. "Welfare and the Family: The American Experience," *Journal of Labor Economics* (January 1993), and "Does Welfare Bring More Babies?," *Public Interest* (Spring 1994).

2. The NLSY is a very large (originally 12,686 persons), nationally representative sample of American youths who were aged 14 to 22 in 1979, when the study began, and have been followed ever since.

NO
Mark Robert Rank

LIVING ON THE EDGE: THE REALITIES OF WELFARE IN AMERICA

For most Americans, receiving welfare represents a failure to provide for oneself and one's family (Kluegel and Smith 1986). It is thus a highly stigmatized behavior.... Most applicants typically felt two emotions when applying for public assistance—embarrassment and anxiety (in some cases, fear)....

When asked why they had turned to public assistance, many female heads of households mentioned either a divorce or a separation that had caused severe economic distress. Often they had limited job experience and skills at the time of the separation. Most of the women interviewed could see no other choice but to turn to the welfare system, which they saw as a stopgap solution until they got back on their feet....

For other female heads of household, and particularly for black female heads, the family structural change involves having a child out of wedlock. Much has been written about the unfavorable marriage market for low-income black women (e.g., Guttentag and Secord 1983; Wilson 1987; Jaynes and Williams 1989; Lichter, LeClere, and McLaughlin 1991; Hacker 1992), and indeed a much larger percentage of black women interviewed were not married when they had children. An example is Ruth Miller. A long-term welfare recipient, she was asked why she began receiving public assistance in Chicago.

> Well, I had two little bitty babies. And I was working at the time I got pregnant. So I tried going back to work when Stacy was about—say two months old. And the lady that I got to babysit for me just didn't come up to par for me. And with me having the two babies, one was just walking and one was an arm baby, I made the decision that it's best for me to try to be here with them. And I know they were taken care of like I would have wanted to be taken care of. So that's when I applied for aid....

DAY-TO-DAY LIVING

... Perhaps most apparent when one listens to welfare recipients describe their daily lives and routines is the constant economic struggle that they face. This includes difficulties paying monthly bills, not having enough food, worrying about health care costs, and so on. The amount of income received each month is simply insufficient to cover all these necessary expenses. Having talked with dozens of families, having seen the daily hardships of recipients, having felt their frustrations and pain, I have no doubt that these families are indeed living on the edge.

This economic struggle is typified by the experience of Mary Summers. A fifty-one-year-old divorced mother, Mary and her two teenage daughters have been on public assistance for eleven months. She receives $544 a month from AFDC [Aid to Families with Dependent Children] and $106 a month worth of Food Stamps. After paying $280 for rent (which includes heat and electricity), she and her daughters are left with $370 a month (including Food Stamps) to live on. This comes to approximately $12 a day, or $4 per family member. While this may seem like an implausibly small income for any household to survive on, it is quite typical of the assistance that those on welfare receive....

Food Stamp and AFDC benefits, received monthly, are usually not enough to provide adequately throughout a particular month. Many recipients find that their Food Stamps routinely run out by the end of the third week. Even with the budgeting and stretching of resources that recipients try to do, there is simply not enough left....

Borrowing from friends or relatives is [one] end-of-the-month strategy. We asked Rosa and Alejandro Martinez, an elderly married couple, about this. Rosa responded, "Sometimes we're short of money to pay for everything. We have to pay life insurance, mine and his. We have to pay for the car. We have to pay the light.

And we have to pay the telephone. And there are a lot of expenses that we have to pay. And sometimes we can't meet them all. And between the month, I borrow, but I borrow from my friends to make ends meet."

Others deal with the financial squeeze at the end of the month differently. For example, Clarissa and John Wilson, a married couple in their thirties, rely on extra money from a blood plasma center to help them through....

For welfare recipients, there is little financial leeway should any unanticipated expenses occur. When nothing out of the ordinary happens, recipients may be able to scrape by. However, when the unexpected occurs (as it often does), it can set in motion a domino effect touching every other aspect of recipients' lives. One unanticipated expense can cause a shortage of money for food, rent, utilities, or other necessary items. The dominoes begin to fall one by one.

Unanticipated expenses include items such as medical costs and needed repairs on a major appliance or an automobile. During these crises, households must make difficult decisions regarding other necessities in their lives....

Much has been written about the negative consequences of poverty. The poor suffer from higher rates of disease and crime, experience more chronic and acute health problems, pay more for particular goods and services, have higher infant mortality rates, encounter more dangerous environmental effects, face a greater probability of undernourishment, and have higher levels of psychological stress....

[H]unger is a real consequence of poverty. Many of the families I talked to admitted that there were times when they and their children were forced to go hungry and/or significantly alter their diets. Running out of food is not uncommon among those who rely on public assistance.

In addition to suffering from hunger, recipients may let health problems go unattended until they became serious, live in undesirable and dangerous neighborhoods, or face various types of discrimination as a result of being poor. But perhaps the most ubiquitous consequence of living in poverty and on public assistance is the sheer difficulty of accomplishing various tasks most of us take for granted: not being able to shop at larger and cheaper food stores because of lack of transportation and so paying more for groceries; having to take one's dirty clothing on the bus to the nearest laundromat with three children in tow; being unable to afford to go to the dentist even though the pain is excruciating; not purchasing a simple meal at a restaurant for fear it will disrupt the budget; never being able to go to a movie; having no credit, which in turn makes getting a future credit rating difficult; lacking a typewriter or personal computer on which to improve secretarial skills for a job interview. The list could go on and on.

WORKING

... [M]any policymakers believe that welfare recipients lack positive attitudes, particularly toward work (see, e.g., Gilder 1981). The attitudes expressed by the recipients I interviewed contrast sharply with this viewpoint. Welfare recipients repeatedly emphasized their desires to work, often regardless of the working conditions.... Judy Griffin had experienced a serious back injury while loading and unloading heavy goods in a warehouse. Her attitudes were typical: "Well,

I dislike NOT being able to work at all. I mean, I'm used to doing work (*pounds hand on table*). Sure, I don't like every day I go to work. But I don't like sitting home every day. The first week is just wonderful, but after that, you know, you can have it. No, I'm not used to sittin.' That's hard." Variations on these sentiments were often expressed; the general attitudes toward work were strong and positive....

Virtually every welfare recipient interviewed in this study had a background of employed work. For some (e.g., recently divorced women with children), that history was limited; for others (e.g., married husbands), it was quite extensive. Yet in practically every case, recipients had had various experiences in the labor force, usually in a series of low-wage jobs, often in several different occupations that required either semi-skilled or unskilled labor and carried little status....

Only one-quarter to one-third of welfare recipients work, and they generally work only part-time. Both of these facts cause considerable anger among the general public. True, anyone working full-time cannot receive much in the way of public assistance, so it is not surprising that many on welfare work less than forty hours a week. Still, the question remains, why do not more welfare recipients find full-time work and get off welfare altogether? The reasons are several.

First, the majority of welfare recipients (under age sixty-five) are either working or actively looking for work.... [A]pproximately 30 percent of those receiving public assistance are employed. Many of these people would prefer full-time jobs but have been unable to find them. Other recipients are regularly looking for work or are receiving some kind of job training. Within the in-depth interview sample, 71 percent of households whose members were under age sixty-five were characterized by the head or spouse employed or actively looking or preparing for work. Such activity involves participating in job training programs, responding to want ads, attending technical college, or pursuing various other job-related activities (detailed below). Indeed, one of the requirements for continued eligibility in most public assistance programs is that able-bodied adults must actively look for work. But, like Ellen Harris, many recipients are lacking in human capital and consequently face stiff competition in the job market. As a result, it can often take a long time to locate permanent employment.

For the remaining one-quarter of recipients who are neither employed nor looking for work, what barriers are preventing employment? For some, physical injuries and other health problems are important factors....

For others, particularly female heads of household with young children, the lack of affordable child care coupled with concerns regarding their children's upbringing, can present a major barrier to employed work. The dilemma is whether to pay a significant sum for child care in order to work at a low-paying job, lacking in benefits, or to stay at home with one's children and receive public assistance. Janice Winslow elaborates, "I don't think of myself as being unfortunate for being on AFDC. My choice was I could send the kids to day care, the babies, and go work and make about what I'm making now, if I made that much, once you pay for day care for three kids or two. That's just not much of a choice to make."

A related obstacle to working is that welfare benefits are often reduced by a dollar for every dollar a recipient earns. This is in effect a 100 per cent tax rate....

Finally, a few people do appear half-hearted when it comes to working. A prime example is Scott Meyer, who was receiving eighty dollars a month in Food Stamps. Twenty years old, Scott was fired several times for using drugs on the job. He has been severely addicted to cocaine and has also dealt drugs. When interviewed, Scott was on probation. His probation officer had found him a job as a janitor. Without such pressure, Scott would probably not be working....

Attitudes like Scott's were very atypical, but they do exist and represent yet another barrier to working....

MYTHS AND REALITIES

Surviving on Welfare Is Difficult

Perhaps most apparent... is the sheer difficulty and pain associated with living on welfare. The notion that public assistance programs provide for a good life, or for even a modest life-style, sharply contrasts with reality.

Severe economic hardship is ever present for those trying to survive on public assistance.... Recipients and their children are often forced to go hungry. All reported forgoing many of the necessities that most of us take for granted. The assistance provided by the government routinely runs out before the end of each month. To be on welfare is by definition to live in poverty. And to live in poverty translates into a day-to-day struggle for survival.

Existing on welfare is also psychologically difficult. Most recipients experience firsthand the stigma associated with receiving welfare.... The general public tends to view people who rely on public assistance as failures and parasites.

Recipients encounter such attitudes routinely and ... often share them.

Finally, there is the social burden that welfare recipients carry. Largely as a result of the economic and psychological strains of living in poverty, relations within and outside the family are under constant pressure.... Relations between spouses, between parents and children, and with outsiders are frequently strained.

Given all this, it seems implausible that anyone would choose such a life. And, in fact, this is precisely what recipients told us. As [a] fifty-one-year-old divorced mother ... said, "I can't see anybody that would ever settle for something like this just for the mere fact of getting a free ride, because it's not worth it." Living on welfare is a trying experience that virtually all wish to leave far behind.

Frequently Assumed Negative Behavioral Effects Are Negligible

Many assume that the welfare system induces severe negative behavioral changes in its participants, breaking up families, causing women to have more children, encouraging recipients to remain on the rolls for long periods of time, influencing people to drop out of the labor market, and so on.

With an important exception, there is little support for these notions.... [W]omen on welfare actually have a lower birthrate than women in the general population. In addition, welfare programs appear to have little effect on the likelihood of marriage or divorce.... [T]hose on public assistance tend to remain on the rolls temporarily.

One reason for the lack of an effect on the above types of behavior is that, as noted, no one enjoys living on welfare. The idea that people would desire such a life by having more children, dropping out of the labor market, and becoming female heads of households, is a stretch of the imagination, as most recipients will tell you. Furthermore, a significant number of those on welfare receive fairly small amounts of assistance.... For example, singles and married couples often receive only modest amounts of in-kind assistance from the Food Stamp program. Such amounts are simply too low to impact behavior in any noticeable way.

Economic hardship, far more than welfare recipience, influences family interaction and behavior among welfare families.... Public assistance is a by-product of that economic adversity. It alone does little to explain family dynamics.

It should be noted that the setting for this study represents a very conservative test of these findings. Wisconsin is ranked above most states in terms of its ratio of average welfare payments to average earnings and in terms of average and maximum allowed state welfare payments. In view of the strong support for a lack of negative behavioral effects in this setting, it is unlikely that recipients in states with lower welfare benefits would behave substantially differently.

The single negative behavioral effect is the work disincentives embedded in these programs, particularly AFDC and Medicaid. For each dollar a person earns, a dollar is lost from the grant ... in effect a 100 percent tax rate. Equally important is that although a job at minimum wage may pay slightly more than welfare, it often lacks medical coverage. Particularly for families with children, this is a very strong disincentive. Yet in spite of it, many on welfare work or eventually will find work....

Larger Factors Are Important

To understand why people find themselves in the position of needing welfare, one must recognize the important influence of larger factors that lie beyond people's immediate control. This is not to suggest that individual characteristics are irrelevant. They are simply best understood within a wider context.

For female-headed families, divorce or separation, lack of child-support payments, shortage of affordable child care, and the difficulty of finding work with livable wages and benefits combine to make assistance necessary. For married couples, layoffs, low-paying wages, and the lack of benefits are key. For singles, incapacitation and/or recurring health problems are usually behind the need for help. For the elderly, dwindling resources coupled with medical expenses lead to economic insecurity.

Certainly, there are some recipients at whom we could point our finger and say, "It's your fault." Yet for most recipients, this explanation is inadequate. Consider Joe Hall, who worked with the same company for twenty years, was laid off, and has over a hundred job applications out. Can we honestly say that it is his fault? ...

Those on Welfare Hold Fundamental Values

The values welfare recipients hold are for the most part fundamental, bedrock American values. What do I mean by this? Simply that what most welfare recipients value, the majority of other Americans value as well. They value their independence, specifically their economic independence. They do not enjoy living off the taxpayers' dollars. They want to get ahead in their lives and to improve their lot. They stress the importance of work. They understand the significance of education. They want to see their sons and daughters successful in their own lives. They believe in persevering and struggling despite the odds against them. They have faith that such efforts will eventually be rewarded.

There is scant evidence that those on welfare somehow believe in a set of values different from those of mainstream America. Rather, what I heard and saw was a reaffirmation of the bedrock values of middle America. This is not to say that welfare recipients are modern-day saints. Far from it. They simply share many of the fundamental principles and values that their fellow Americans cherish. No more, no less.

Recipients Are Not Much Different from the Rest of Us

Perhaps the most salient theme to emerge from this study is that the welfare recipient is fundamentally not much different from you or me. [T]here is a tendency to view welfare recipients and the poor as significantly different from the rest of us—they just do not work hard enough; they are not concerned about their future; they lack the right motivation. In short, they get what they deserve.

After spending ten years on this project, I have come to a much different conclusion. These are people who work just as hard as the rest of us, care just as much about their future and their children's future, and hope to get ahead just as much as the next fellow. The difference lies not within them, but primarily within their position in relation to the larger forces found in our society....

Explanations Lacking Support

The general public favors the attitudinal/motivational explanation for people being poor and on welfare. This explanation argues that people on welfare do not have the right attitudes, drive, or motivation. Were they to exert themselves, they would rise from the ranks of poverty and welfare dependency. It is appealing because it is simple makes intuitive sense, and does not question the status quo of the society we live in. It assumes that there is a sense of justice or fairness at play. People are by and large accountable and hence deserving of their fate of impoverishment.

Unfortunately, there is little support for such an explanation.... [T]he research findings in this study indicate that welfare recipients are just as motivated as the next fellow, if not more so. If motivation were all that mattered, 95 percent of the families in this book would no longer be poor and on welfare.

A similar explanation, but of a more structural nature, is what Schiller (1989) has referred to as the "Big Brother argument." The thesis here is that the current welfare system creates dramatic behavioral changes in people who are exposed to it. Such changes then foster welfare dependency and long-term poverty (see, e.g., Murray 1984; Mead 1986).

Again, I find little support for such an explanation. Welfare payments are just too meager to motivate most people to alter their behavior radically. This is not to say that welfare recipients do not divorce, have children, and so on, just that public assistance has little to do with these behavioral vicissitudes.

It is important to note that when I say there is little support for a motivational or a Big Brother argument, this is not to imply that there is absolutely no support. Stereotypes endure because they accrete some grain of truth. I have indeed encountered people who were obviously lazy or perhaps corrupted by the welfare system. But they represent a very small minority of the total welfare population. Moreover, they certainly have not cornered the market on laziness or corruption. One can find such people throughout society—rich and poor. My earlier point bears repeating: welfare recipients are our fellow Americans—no better, no worse....

Clarifying the Focus: A Structural Vulnerability Explanation

... Human capital characteristics are important to understanding the lives of welfare recipients. Household heads on welfare are to varying degrees lacking in marketable skills and training. Education is often limited. So too are family resources and assets. In addition, factors such as race and gender can be understood as components of human capital, in that employers may use such characteristics to screen and/or limit potential employees. In short, the basket of goods and resources necessary to compete effectively within our economic system often comes up short.

... [O]ne key to understanding why people are on public assistance is to recognize the vulnerability created by a lack of human capital, which, when coupled with a severe crisis, can push people into economic tailspins. The events precipitating these crises are often a result of, or at least exacerbated by, structural changes and forces in our society. Thus, the economic tailspin leading to welfare utilization results from both individual and structural factors....

It follows that many of the families in this study lacked human capital not because they failed to work hard or were unmotivated but because of the structural constraints imposed by the reproduction of social class.... [T]he childhoods of the sampled recipients were characterized by substantially reduced life chances and options. Although some children in such positions can conceivably become bankers or lawyers, most will not. The decks are simply stacked against them, and this increases the likelihood that their accumulation of human capital will be limited....

To summarize, the structural vulnerability perspective helps explain why a large proportion of those receiving welfare find themselves in the position of relying on public assistance. The explanation combines aspects of human capital theory with the more detrimental outcomes of various structural forces in our society. It argues that people lacking human capital are more economically vulnerable if a crisis occurs. Such crises are often the result of broader economic, social, and political forces in our society. In addition, the lack of human capital is largely a result of the reproduction of social class. Children from lower-class backgrounds begin with fewer resources and opportunities, which in turn limits their future life chances and outcomes, including the accumulation of human capital. Finally, although lack of human capital and the vulnerability this leads to explain who the losers of the economic game are, the more structural components of our economic, social, and political systems explain why there are losers in the first place.

POSTSCRIPT

Does Welfare Do More Harm Than Good?

Welfare is an ambiguous term. In the popular sense it usually means "aid to the poor," which would include programs like Aid to Families with Dependent Children (AFDC) and food stamps. But these programs constitute a small percentage of "welfare" in the broadest sense of "government assistance to individuals." In that sense, some would argue, the largest welfare program is Social Security, which dispenses almost $300 billion annually (compared to $25 billion for AFDC), much of it to people who are not poor. It could also be argued that there are other forms of middle- and upper-class "welfare," including farm subsidies and homeowners' tax breaks.

Murray argues that welfare not only costs a lot but it hurts its own intended beneficiaries by contributing to the breakup of the family and reducing individuals' incentive to become responsible wage earners. His argument is contrary to the picture of welfare recipients that emerges from Rank's interviews. Rank finds that most welfare recipients do not want to be on welfare, are seeking work, and have mainstream American values.

Sar A. Levitan and Clifford M. Johnson conclude that the current welfare system is a rational and necessary response to emerging societal needs in *Beyond the Safety Net: Reviving the Promise of Opportunity in America* (Ballinger, 1984). Michael B. Katz, in *The Undeserving Poor: From the War on Poverty to the War on Welfare* (Pantheon Books, 1989), traces the evolution of welfare policies in the United States from the 1960s through the 1980s. Writers who criticize the welfare program for going too far include Lawrence M. Mead, *The New Politics of Poverty* (Basic Books, 1992) and Jack D. Douglas, *The Myth of the Welfare State* (Transaction, 1989). Mary Jo Bane and David T. Ellwood do not join Mead or Douglas in blaming the adverse consequences of welfare on overly generous benefits—they blame the organization and administration of welfare. See their *Welfare Realities: From Rhetoric to Reform* (Harvard University Press, 1994). Mickey Kaus, in *The End of Equality* (Basic Books, 1992), reviews welfare's negative effects and advocates workfare as the best reform of welfare. Fred Block and his colleagues respond to attacks on welfare in *The Mean Season: The Attack on the Welfare State* (Pantheon Books, 1987). Two works that offer explanations of why welfare provision is so minimal in the United States and that bring in race and gender factors are Linda Gordon, *Pitied but Not Entitled: Single Mothers and the History of Welfare* (Free Press, 1994) and Joel F. Handler and Yeheskel Hasenfeld, *The Moral Construction of Poverty: Welfare Reform in America* (Sage Publications, 1991).

ISSUE 15

Is Choice a Panacea for the Ills of Public Education?

YES: John E. Chubb and Terry M. Moe, from "America's Public Schools: Choice *Is* a Panacea," *The Brookings Review* (Summer 1990)

NO: Bill Honig, from "Why Privatizing Public Education Is a Bad Idea," *The Brookings Review* (Winter 1990/1991)

ISSUE SUMMARY

YES: Political scientists John E. Chubb and Terry M. Moe attribute the failure of public schools to bureaucratic controls that imprison the expertise and professional judgment of principals and teachers. The authors contend that school choice will liberate school personnel from these controls and enhance performance through competition.

NO: Public school superintendent Bill Honig maintains that the reforms of the 1980s have largely overcome the problems of stifling bureaucracy and that they make risky, radical changes unnecessary. Furthermore, he argues, the school choice program would greatly increase educational inequality.

The quality of American public schooling has been criticized for several decades. Secretary of Education Richard Riley said in 1994 that some American schools are so bad that they "should never be called schools at all." The average school year in the United States is 180 days, while Japanese children attend school 240 days of the year. American schoolchildren score lower than the children of many other Western countries on certain standardized achievement tests. In 1983 the National Commission on Excellence in Education published *A Nation at Risk,* which argued that American education was a failure. Critics of *A Nation at Risk* maintain that the report produced very little evidence to support its thesis, but the public accepted it anyway. Now, 13 years and several reforms later, the public still thinks that the American school system is failing and needs to be fixed. The solution most frequently proposed today is school choice.

The U.S. educational system has a proud record of achievement over the last two centuries. The present system began to take shape in the nineteenth century, when the states set up locally controlled school districts providing free elementary and high school education. Over time the states also passed compulsory schooling laws, which usually were applicable through elementary school and later were raised to age 16. With free and compulsory education, America has always been and still is the world leader in providing mass education. In the twentieth century the expansion of mass education was phenomenal. Today 99 percent of children aged 6 to 13 are in school. In 1900 only about 7 percent of the appropriate age group graduated from high school, but in 1990, 86 percent did. Another success is the extraordinary improvement in the graduation rates for blacks since 1964, when it was 45 percent, to 1987, when it was 83 percent. Now this rate is almost at parity with white graduation rates. And over two-thirds of the present American population have a high school degree. No other nation comes close to these accomplishments.

American education reforms of the past 40 years have focused on quality and on what is taught. In the late 1950s the Soviet Union's launch of the first space satellite convinced the public of the need for more math and science in the curriculum. In the late 1960s and 1970s schools were criticized for rigid authoritarian teaching styles, and schools were made less structured. They became more open, participatory, and individualized in order to stimulate student involvement, creativity, and emotional growth. In the 1980s a crusade for the return to basics was triggered by the announcement that SAT scores had declined since the early 1960s. More recently, the continued problems of public schools have led many to call for their restructuring by means of school choice.

Two questions on the current situation in American schools serve as background for the school choice issue. First, is there really a school performance crisis? David C. Berliner and Bruce J. Biddle, in *The Manufactured Crisis: Myths, Fraud, and the Attack on America's Public Schools* (Addison-Wesley, 1995), argue that school performance has not declined. They point out that the decline in SAT scores since 1960 was due to the changing composition of the sample of students taking the tests, and better indicators of school performance over time show gains, not losses. Second, is the current structure of schools the main reason why schools seem to be failing? Many other trends have also affected school performance. For example, curricula changes away from basics, new unstructured teaching techniques, and the decline of discipline in the classroom have contributed to perceived problems. The relatively poor quality of teachers may be another factor. There is evidence that those who go into teaching score far lower on SATs than the average college student. In addition, societal trends outside the school may significantly impact on school performance. Increasing breakdown of the family, more permissive childrearing, the substantial decline in the amount of time that parents spend with children, and the increased exposure of children to television are trends that are affecting school performance.

In the following selections, John E. Chubb and Terry M. Moe promote school choice as a way to improve public education, while Bill Honig attacks school choice as unnecessary and dangerous.

YES

John E. Chubb and
Terry M. Moe

AMERICA'S PUBLIC SCHOOLS: CHOICE *IS* A PANACEA

For America's public schools, the last decade has been the worst of times and the best of times. Never before have the public schools been subjected to such savage criticism for failing to meet the nation's educational needs—yet never before have governments been so aggressively dedicated to studying the schools' problems and finding the resources for solving them.

The signs of poor performance were there for all to see during the 1970s. Test scores headed downward year after year. Large numbers of teenagers continued to drop out of school. Drugs and violence poisoned the learning environment. In math and science, two areas crucial to the nation's success in the world economy, American students fell far behind their counterparts in virtually every other industrialized country. Something was clearly wrong.

During the 1980s a growing sense of crisis fueled a powerful movement for educational change, and the nation's political institutions responded with aggressive reforms. State after state increased spending on schools, imposed tougher requirements, introduced more rigorous testing, and strengthened teacher certification and training. And, as the decade came to an end, creative experiments of various forms—from school-based management to magnet schools—were being launched around the nation.

We think these reforms are destined to fail. They simply do not get to the root of the problem. The fundamental causes of poor academic performance are not to be found in the schools, but rather in the institutions by which the schools have traditionally been governed. Reformers fail by automatically relying on these institutions to solve the problem—when the institutions are the problem.

The key to better schools, therefore, is institutional reform. What we propose is a new system of public education that eliminates most political and bureaucratic control over the schools and relies instead on indirect control through markets and parental choice. These new institutions naturally function to promote and nurture the kinds of effective schools that reformers have wanted all along.

SCHOOLS AND INSTITUTIONS

Three basic questions lie at the heart of our analysis. What is the relationship between school organization and student achievement? What are the conditions that promote or inhibit desirable forms of organization? And how are these conditions affected by their institutional settings?

Our perspective on school organization and student achievement is in agreement with the most basic claims and findings of the "effective schools" literature, which served as the analytical base of the education reform movement throughout the 1980s. We believe, as most others do, that how much students learn is not determined simply by their aptitude or family background—although, as we show, these are certainly influential—but also by how effectively schools are organized. By our estimates, the typical high school student tends to learn considerably more, comparable to at least an extra year's worth of study, when he or she attends a high school that is effectively organized rather than one that is not.

Generally speaking, effective schools— be they public or private—have the kinds of organizational characteristics that the mainstream literature would lead one to expect: strong leadership, clear and ambitious goals, strong academic programs, teacher professionalism, shared influence, and staff harmony, among other things. These are best understood as integral parts of a coherent syndrome of organization. When this syndrome is viewed as a functioning whole, moreover, it seems to capture the essential features of what people normally mean by a team—principals and teachers working together, cooperatively and informally, in pursuit of a common mission.

How do these kinds of schools develop and take root? Here again, our own perspective dovetails with a central theme of educational analysis and criticism: the dysfunctions of bureaucracy, the value of autonomy, and the inherent tension between the two in American public education. Bureaucracy vitiates the most basic requirements of effective organization. It imposes goals, structures, and requirements that tell principals and teachers what to do and how to do it—denying them not only the discretion they need to exercise their expertise and professional judgment but also the flexibility they need to develop and operate as teams. The key to effective education rests with unleashing the productive potential already present in the schools and their personnel. It rests with granting them the autonomy to do what they do best. As our study of American high schools documents, the freer schools are from external control the more likely they are to have effective organizations.

Only at this late stage of the game do we begin to part company with the mainstream. While most observers can agree that the public schools have become too bureaucratic and would benefit from substantial grants of autonomy, it is also the standard view that this transformation can be achieved within the prevailing framework of democratic control. The implicit assumption is that, although political institutions have acted in the past to bureaucratize, they can now be counted upon to reverse course, grant the schools autonomy, and support and nurture this new population of autonomous schools. Such an assumption, however, is not based on a systematic understanding of how these institutions operate and what their consequences are for schools.

POLITICAL INSTITUTIONS

Democratic governance of the schools is built around the imposition of higher-order values through public authority. As long as that authority exists and is available for use, public officials will come under intense pressure from social groups of all political stripes to use it. And when they do use it, they cannot blithely assume that their favored policies will be faithfully implemented by the heterogeneous population of principals and teachers below—whose own values and professional views may be quite different from those being imposed. Public officials have little choice but to rely on formal rules and regulations that tell these people what to do and hold them accountable for doing it.

These pressures for bureaucracy are so substantial in themselves that real school autonomy has little chance to take root throughout the system. But they are not the only pressures for bureaucracy. They are compounded by the political uncertainty inherent in all democratic politics: those who exercise public authority know that other actors with different interests may gain authority in the future and subvert the policies they worked so hard to put in place. This knowledge gives them additional incentive to embed their policies in protective bureaucratic arrangements—arrangements that reduce the discretion of schools and formally insulate them from the dangers of politics.

These pressures, arising from the basic properties of democratic control, are compounded yet again by another special feature of the public sector. Its institutions provide a regulated, politically sensitive setting conducive to the power of unions, and unions protect the interests of their members through formal constraints on the governance and operation of schools—constraints that strike directly at the schools' capacity to build well-functioning teams based on informal cooperation.

The major participants in democratic governance—including the unions —complain that the schools are too bureaucratic. And they mean what they say. But they are the ones who bureaucratized the schools in the past, and they will continue to do so, even as they tout the great advantages of autonomy and professionalism. The incentives to bureaucratize the schools are built into the system.

MARKET INSTITUTIONS

This kind of behavior is not something that Americans simply have to accept, like death and taxes. People who make decisions about education would behave differently if their institutions were different. The most relevant and telling comparison is to markets, since it is through democratic control and markets that American society makes most of its choices on matters of public importance, including education. Public schools are subject to direct control through politics. But not all schools are controlled in this way. Private schools—representing about a fourth of all schools—are subject to indirect control through markets.

What difference does it make? Our analysis suggests that the difference is considerable and that it arises from the most fundamental properties that distinguish the two systems. A market system is not built to enable the imposition of higher-order values on the schools, nor is it driven by a democratic struggle to exercise public authority. Instead, the authority to make educational choices is radically decentralized to those most immediately involved. Schools compete for the support of parents and students, and parents and students are free to choose among schools. The system is built on decentralization, competition, and choice.

Although schools operating under a market system are free to organize any way they want, bureaucratization tends to be an unattractive way to go. Part of the reason is that virtually everything about good education—from the knowledge and talents necessary to produce it, to what it looks like when it is produced—defies formal measurement through the standardized categories of bureaucracy.

The more basic point, however, is that bureaucratic control and its clumsy efforts to measure the unmeasurable are simply *unnecessary* for schools whose primary concern is to please their clients. To do this, they need to perform as effectively as possible, which leads them, given the bottom-heavy technology of education, to favor decentralized forms of organization that take full advantage of strong leadership, teacher professionalism, discretionary judgment, informal cooperation, and teams. They also need to ensure that they provide the kinds of services parents and students want and that they have the capacity to cater and adjust to their clients' specialized needs and interests, which this same syndrome of effective organization allows them to do exceedingly well.

Schools that operate in an environment of competition and choice thus have strong incentives to move toward the kinds of "effective-school" organizations that academics and reformers would like to impose on the public schools. Of course, not all schools in the market will respond equally well to these incentives. But those that falter will find it more difficult to attract support, and they will tend to be weeded out in favor of schools that are better organized. This process of natural selection complements the incentives of the marketplace in propelling and supporting a population of autonomous, effectively organized schools....

EDUCATIONAL CHOICE

It is fashionable these days to say that choice is "not a panacea." Taken literally, that is obviously true. There are no panaceas in social policy. But the message this aphorism really means to get across is that choice is just one of many reforms with something to contribute. School-based management is another. So are teacher empowerment and professionalism, better training programs, stricter accountability, and bigger budgets. These and other types of reforms all bolster school effectiveness in their own distinctive ways—so the reasoning goes—and the best, most aggressive, most comprehensive approach to transforming the public school system is therefore one that wisely combines them into a multifaceted reformist package.

Without being too literal about it, we think reformers would do well to entertain the notion that choice *is* a panacea. Of all the sundry education reforms that attract attention, only choice has the capacity to address the basic institutional problem plaguing America's schools. The other reforms are all system-preserving. The schools remain subordinates in the structure of public authority—and they remain bureaucratic.

In principle, choice offers a clear, sharp break from the institutional past. In practice, however, it has been forced into the same mold with all the other reforms. It has been embraced half-heartedly and in bits and pieces—for example, through magnet schools and limited open enrollment plans. It has served as a means of granting parents and students a few additional options or of giving schools modest incentives to compete. These are popular moves that can be accomplished without changing the existing system in any fundamental way. But by treating choice like other system-preserving reforms that presumably make democratic control work better, reformers completely miss what choice is all about.

Choice is not like the other reforms and should not be combined with them. Choice is a self-contained reform with its own rationale and justification. It has the capacity *all by itself* to bring about the kind of transformation that reformers have been seeking to engineer for years in myriad other ways. Indeed, if choice is to work to greatest advantage, it must be adopted *without* these other reforms, since they are predicated on democratic control and are implemented by bureaucratic means. The whole point of a thoroughgoing system of choice is to free the schools from these disabling constraints by sweeping away the old institutions and replacing them with new ones. Taken seriously, choice is not a system-preserving reform. It is a revolutionary reform that introduces a new system of public education.

A PROPOSAL FOR REAL REFORM

... Our guiding principle in the design of a choice system is this: public authority must be put to use in creating a system that is almost entirely beyond the reach of public authority. Because states have primary responsibility for American public education, we think the best way to achieve significant, enduring reform is for states to take the initiative in withdrawing authority from existing institutions and vesting it directly in the schools, parents, and students. This restructuring cannot be construed as an exercise in delegation. As long as authority remains "available" at higher levels within state government, it will eventually be used to control the schools. As far as possible, all higher-level authority must be eliminated.

What we propose, more specifically, is that state leaders create a new system of public education with the following properties.

The Supply of Schools

The state will be responsible for setting criteria that define what constitutes a "public school" under the new system. These criteria should be minimal, roughly corresponding to the criteria many states now use in accrediting private schools—graduation requirements, health and safety requirements, and teacher certification requirements. Any educational group or organization that applies to the state and meets these minimal criteria must then be chartered as a public school and granted the right to accept students and receive public money.

Existing private schools will be among those eligible to participate. Their participation should be encouraged, because they constitute a supply of already effective schools. Our own preference would be to include religious schools too, as long as their sectarian functions can be kept clearly separate from their educational functions. Private schools that do participate will thereby become public schools, as such schools are defined under the new choice system.

YES Chubb and Moe / 273

School districts can continue running their present schools, assuming those schools meet state criteria. But districts will have authority over only their own schools and not over any of the others that may be chartered by the state....

Choice Among Schools
Each student will be free to attend any public school in the state, regardless of district, with the student's scholarship —consisting of federal, state, and local contributions—flowing to the school of choice. In practice most students will probably choose schools in reasonable proximity to their homes. But districts will have no claim on their own residents.

To the extent that tax revenues allow, every effort will be made to provide transportation for students who need it. This provision is important to help open up as many alternatives as possible to all students, especially the poor and those in rural areas....

Schools will make their own admissions decisions, subject only to nondiscrimination requirements. This step is absolutely crucial. Schools must be able to define their own missions and build their own programs in their own ways, and they cannot do that if their student population is thrust on them by outsiders.

Schools must be free to admit as many or as few students as they want, based on whatever criteria they think relevant— intelligence, interest, motivation, special needs—and they must be free to exercise their own, informal judgments about individual applicants....

CHOICE AS A PUBLIC SYSTEM

... Once this structural framework is democratically determined,... governments would continue to play important roles within it. State officials and agencies would remain pivotal to the success of public education and to its ongoing operation. They would provide funding, approve applications for new schools, orchestrate and oversee the choice process, elicit full information about schools, provide transportation to students, monitor schools for adherence to the law, and (if they want) design and administer tests of student performance. School districts, meantime, would continue as local taxing jurisdictions, and they would have the option of continuing to operate their own system of schools.

The crucial difference is that direct democratic control of the schools—the very *capacity* for control, not simply its exercise—would essentially be eliminated. Most of those who previously held authority over the schools would have their authority permanently withdrawn, and that authority would be vested in schools, parents, and students. Schools would be legally autonomous: free to govern themselves as they want, specify their own goals and programs and methods, design their own organizations, select their own student bodies, and make their own personnel decisions. Parents and students would be legally empowered to choose among alternative schools, aided by institutions designed to promote active involvement, well-informed decisions, and fair treatment.

NO
Bill Honig

WHY PRIVATIZING PUBLIC EDUCATION IS A BAD IDEA

One of the loudest salvos in the ongoing battle over "choice" in public schools came this year from theoreticians John E. Chubb and Terry M. Moe in *The Brookings Review* ("America's Public Schools: Choice *Is* a Panacea," summer issue). Chubb and Moe propose to transform our public schools from democratically regulated to market-driven institutions. They argue that the past decade has seen the most ambitious period of school reform in the nation's history, but that gains in test scores or graduation rates are nil. Their explanation: government, with its politics and bureaucracy, so hampers schools' ability to focus on academic achievement that improvement efforts are doomed.

Using data from the early eighties, Chubb and Moe contend that freeing schools from democratic control boosts performance a full grade level. Thus, they would give students scholarships for any public, private, or newly formed school; prohibit states or school districts from establishing organizational or effective curricular standards or assessing school performance; and allow schools to restrict student entry. They assert that parent choice alone will assure quality.

What's wrong with this proposal to combine vouchers with radical deregulation? Everything.

In the first place, Chubb and Moe's basic charge that current reform efforts have not succeeded is dead wrong and, consequently, the need for risky and radical change unjustified. While their data say something useful about the dangers of rigid bureaucracy and the overpoliticization of education, their findings cannot be used to judge the reform effort, since the students in their study were tested before reforms began. Evidence gathered more recently points to substantial gains.

For example, in 1983 California began refocusing on academic excellence, reducing bureaucracy, enhancing professional autonomy, and moving away from a rule-based to a performance-driven system. We raised standards; strengthened curriculum and assessment; invested in teacher and principal training; established accountability, including performance targets and incentives for good results and penalties for bad; provided funds for team building at the school; pushed for better textbooks; and forged alliances with parents, higher education, and the business community.

The result of this comprehensive approach has been real progress. In 1989, in reading and math, California high school seniors scored *one year* ahead of seniors in 1983, the exact improvement that Chubb and Moe say their proposal would achieve and just what they argue could not be accomplished within the existing system.

Since 1986, California eighth grade scores have risen 25 percent, the pool of dropouts has decreased 18 percent, and the number of high school graduates meeting the University of California entrance requirements has risen 20 percent. Since 1983, the number of seniors scoring about 450 in the verbal section of the Scholastic Aptitude Test has grown 19 percent, the number scoring above 500 has increased 28 percent, and the rate of seniors passing Advanced placement tests has jumped 114 percent—to more than 50,000 students a year.

California educators achieved these results even though the number of students in poverty doubled, the number of those who do not speak English doubled to one out of five, and California's student population grew explosively.

Impressive gains were also made nationally during the 1980s. The dropout pool shrunk by a third; the number of graduates attending college grew 18 percent; and on the National Assessment of Educational Progress, the number of 17-year-olds able to solve moderately complex problems increased 22 percent in mathematics, and 18 percent in science. Reading and writing scores, however, grew less.

Further evidence of improvement in the performance of college-bound American youngsters is that Advanced Placement courses taken have nearly doubled since 1982. The number of students taking the more demanding curriculum, suggested by *A Nation at Risk*, of four years of English; three years of social studies, science, and math; and two years of foreign languages more than doubled between 1982 and 1987, from 13 percent to 29 percent of high school graduates. In science, the number of graduates taking chemistry grew 45 percent to nearly one of every two students, and the number taking physics expanded 44 percent to one of every five students.

Certainly, these gains are not sufficient to prepare American youngsters for the changing job market, to reach their potential, to participate in our democracy, or to keep up with international competition. We still have a long way to go. But that is not the issue. Educators are being challenged on whether we have a strategy that can produce results. We do, and this nation should be discussing how best to build on this record and accelerate the pace of reform—not how to dismantle public education.

* * *

It is no exaggeration to say that Chubb and Moe's ideas for change would jeopardize our youngsters and this democracy. Any one of the following objections should be enough to sink their plan.

First, the proposal risks creating elite academies for the few and second-rate schools for the many. It allows schools to exclude students who do not meet their standards—almost guaranteeing exacerbation of existing income and racial stratification. We had such a two-tiered system in the 19th century before mass public education helped make this country prosperous and free. We should not go back 100 years in search of the future.

Second, cult schools will result. Nearly 90 percent of American youngsters attend public schools, which are the major institutions involved in transmitting our democratic values. By prohibiting common standards, Chubb and Moe enshrine the rights of parents over the needs of children and society and encourage tribalism. Is it good public policy to use public funds to support schools that teach astrology or creationism instead of science, inculcate antiminority or antiwhite attitudes, or prevent students from reading *The Diary of Anne Frank* or *The Adventures of Huckleberry Finn*? Absent democratic controls, such schools will multiply.

Third, their plan violates the constitutional prohibition against aiding religious schools.

Fourth, the lack of accountability and the naivete of relying on the market to protect children is alarming. In the 19th century the slogan was "let the buyer beware," and meat packers sold tainted meat to consumers. In the 20th century deregulation produced the savings and loan debacle. Nobody seriously proposes rescinding environmental safeguards—why should our children not be similarly protected? Look at private trade schools. Regulation is weak, and scholarships are available. The results: widespread fraud and misrepresentation. Similar problems occurred when New York decentralized its school system. Corruption and patronage surfaced in its local boards of education. All across the nation there are calls for *more* accountability from our schools, not less.

Fifth, the plan would be tremendously chaotic. Vast numbers of new schools would have to be created for this plan to succeed; yet most new enterprises fail. Many youngsters will suffer during the transition period, and with no accountability we will not even know if the experiment was successful.

Sixth, taxpayers will have to pay more. Chubb and Moe maintain that competition will produce savings, but they offer no proof. A potent counter-example: colleges compete, yet costs are skyrocketing. Furthermore, if this plan is adopted nationwide, a substantial portion of the cost of private school students—about $17 billion a year—currently paid for by their parents will be picked up by taxpayers (unless public school expenditures are reduced 10 percent, which would make the plan doubly disastrous). In addition, the proposal includes expensive transportation components and the creation of a new level of bureaucracy—Choice Offices. These offices will include Parent Information Centers, where liaisons will meet with parents and students to advise them on what schools to choose. But how many employees will be necessary for this process if parents are to receive the information they need in a timely manner?

* * *

If this country is willing to spend billions to improve education, there are much better investments with proven returns than Chubb and Moe's fanciful idea. One is providing funds to bring teachers up to speed in math, science, and history. Investing in team-building efforts, technology, improving assessment, Headstart programs, or prenatal care also offers proven returns for the dollar spent.

Chubb and Moe misread the evidence on choice and claim it is the only answer. We *should* give public school parents more choice, either through magnet schools or through open-enrollment plans. Choice builds commitment of parents and students and keeps the system honest. But limits are necessary to prevent skimming of the academic or athletically talented or furthering racial segregation. More important, where choice has been successful, such as in East Harlem, it has been one component of a broader investment in quality.

This country has an incredible opportunity to build a world-class school system. Public schools have turned the corner, educators have developed an effective game plan for the nineties, and promising ideas to encourage further flexibility within a context of vision and accountability are being implemented. If our leaders support that plan instead of chasing will-o'-the-wisp panaceas, come the year 2000, America's children will enjoy the schools they deserve.

POSTSCRIPT

Is Choice a Panacea for the Ills of Public Education?

Chubb and Moe hypothesize that bureaucratic control is the main cause of poor school performance, so reducing bureaucratic control through school choice would greatly improve American education. Americans are generally sympathetic to antibureaucratic arguments because bureaucracies are often perceived as demanding conformity to mandates from the top, which may be unsuited to situations at the bottom. Therefore, choice is attractive because it takes the power of decision making away from the officials and gives it to the parents. School choice advocates believe that schools will have to provide an education that parents want in order to stay in business and that bad schools will go out of business. Honig contends that schools have improved in the 1980s, making radical reform unnecessary. This point is supported with data by David C. Berliner and Bruce J. Biddle in *The Manufactured Crisis: Myths, Fraud, and the Attack on America's Public Schools* (Addison-Wesley, 1995). Honig also argues that school choice would increase school inequalities for the rich and the poor, expand the growth of cult schools, create chaos in the school system, and increase the costs of education. Finally, Honig states that the market has a sordid record of shoddy products and services and considerable misrepresentation in advertising.

With a great deal of public attention focused on school choice, the literature on it has mushroomed. The choice proposal first gained public attention in 1955 when Milton Friedman wrote about vouchers in "The Role of Government in Education," in Robert Solo, ed., *Economics and the Public Interest* (Rutgers University Press). More recent school choice advocates include David Harmer, *School Choice: Why You Need It, How You Get It* (Cato Institute, 1994); Bruce W. Wilkinson, *Educational Choice: Necessary but Not Sufficient* (Renouf Publishing, 1994); James R. Rinehart and Jackson F. Lee, Jr., *American Education and the Dynamics of Choice* (Praeger, 1991); and Myron Lieberman, *Public Education: An Autopsy* (Harvard University Press, 1993). Some advocates of choice would limit the choices in major ways. Timothy W. Young and Evans Clinchy, in *Choice in Public Education* (Teachers College Press, 1992), contend that there is already considerable choice in public education in that there are alternative and magnet schools, intradistrict choice plans, "second chance" options, postsecondary options, and interdistrict choice plans. Research shows that these options work well, so the authors recommend that they be expanded. They argue against a voucher system, which they feel will divert badly needed financial resources from the public schools to give further support to parents who can already afford private schools. In the end they promote a limited choice plan rather than a fully free market plan. For another proposal of a limited choice plan, see Peter W. Cookson, Jr., *School Choice: The Struggle for the Soul of American Education* (Yale University Press, 1994).

Important critiques of school choice include Albert Shanker and Bella Rosenberg, *Politics, Markets, and America's Schools: The Fallacies of Private School Choice* (American Federation of Teachers, 1991); Jeffrey R. Henig, *Rethinking School Choice: Limits of the Market Metaphor* (Princeton University Press, 1994); and Judith Pearson, *Myths of Educational Choice* (Praeger, 1993). Three works that cover the issue broadly or from several points of view are William L. Boyd and Herbert J. Walberg, eds., *Choice in Education: Potential and Problems* (McCutchan, 1990); Ruth Randall and Keith Geiger, *School Choice: Issues and Answers* (National Educational Service, 1991); and Simon Hakim et al., *Privatizing Education and Educational Choice: Concepts, Plans, and Experiences* (Praeger, 1994). On the issue of the impact of choice on the equalization of opportunity, see Stanley C. Trent, "School Choice for African-American Children Who Live in Poverty: A Commitment to Equality or More of the Same?" *Urban Education* (October 1992) and Charles V. Willie, "Controlled Choice: An Alternative Desegregation Plan for Minorities Who Feel Betrayed," *Education and Urban Society* (February 1991).

PART 5

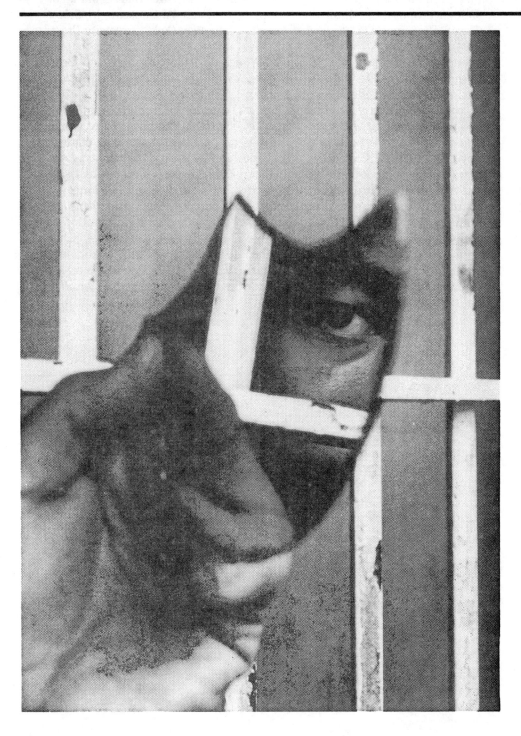

Crime and Social Control

All societies label certain hurtful actions as crimes and punish those who commit the crimes. Other harmful actions, however, are not defined as crimes, and the perpetrators are not punished. Today the definition of crime and the appropriate treatment of criminals is widely debated. Some of the major questions are: Does street crime pose more of a threat to the public's well-being than white-collar crime? Billions of dollars have been spent on the "war on drugs," but who is winning? Would legalizing some drugs free up money that could be directed to other types of social welfare programs, such as the rehabilitation of addicts? And is imprisonment an effective means of reducing crime by removing criminals from the streets, or is it, in the long run, costly and inhumane?

- Is Street Crime More Harmful Than White-Collar Crime?

- Should Drugs Be Legalized?

- Is Incapacitation the Answer to the Crime Problem?

ISSUE 16

Is Street Crime More Harmful Than White-Collar Crime?

YES: John J. DiIulio, Jr., from "The Impact of Inner-City Crime," *The Public Interest* (Summer 1989)

NO: Jeffrey Reiman, from *The Rich Get Richer and the Poor Get Prison: Ideology, Class, and Criminal Justice,* 3rd ed. (Macmillan, 1990)

ISSUE SUMMARY

YES: John J. DiIulio, Jr., an associate professor of politics and public affairs, analyzes the enormous harm done—especially to the urban poor and, by extension, to all of society—by street criminals and their activities.

NO: Professor of philosophy Jeffrey Reiman argues that the dangers posed by negligent corporations and white-collar criminals are a greater menace to society than are the activities of typical street criminals.

The word *crime* entered the English language (from the Old French) around A.D. 1250, when it was identified with "sinfulness." Later, the meaning of the word was modified: crime became the kind of sinfulness that was rightly punishable by law. Even medieval writers, who did not distinguish very sharply between church and state, recognized that there were some sins for which punishment was best left to God; the laws should punish only those that cause harm to the community. Of course, their concept of harm was a very broad one, embracing such offenses as witchcraft and blasphemy. Modern jurists, even those who deplore such practices, would say that the state has no business punishing the perpetrators of these types of offenses.

What, then, should the laws punish? The answer depends in part on our notion of harm. We usually limit the term to the kind of harm that is tangible and obvious: taking a life, causing bodily injury or psychological trauma, and destroying property. For most Americans today, particularly those who live in cities, the word *crime* is practically synonymous with street crime. Anyone who has ever been robbed or beaten by street criminals will never forget the experience. The harm that these criminals cause is tangible, and the connection between the harm and the perpetrator is very direct.

But suppose the connection is not so direct. Suppose, for example, that A hires B to shoot C. Is that any less a crime? B is the actual shooter, but is A any less guilty? Of course not, we say; he may even be more guilty, since he is the ultimate mover behind the crime. A would be guilty even if the chain of command were much longer, involving A's orders to B, and B's to C, then on to D, E, and F to kill G. Organized crime kingpins go to jail even when they are far removed from the people who carry out their orders. High officials of the Nixon administration, even though they were not directly involved in the burglary attempt at the Democratic National Committee headquarters at the Watergate Hotel complex in 1972, were imprisoned.

This brings us to the topic of white-collar crime. The burglars at the Watergate Hotel were acting on orders that trickled down from the highest reaches of political power in the United States. Other white-collar criminals are as varied as the occupations from which they come. They include stockbrokers who make millions through insider trading, as Ivan Boesky did; members of Congress who take payoffs; and people who cheat on their income taxes, like hotel owner and billionaire Leona Helmsley. Some, like Helmsley, get stiff prison sentences when convicted, though many others (like most of the officials in the Watergate scandal) do little or no time in prison. Do they deserve stiffer punishment, or are their crimes less harmful than the crimes of street criminals?

Although white-collar criminals do not directly cause physical harm or relieve people of their wallets, they can still end up doing considerable harm. The harm done by Nixon's aides threatened the integrity of the U.S. electoral system. Every embezzler, corrupt politician, and tax cheat exacts a toll on our society. Individuals can be hurt in more tangible ways by decisions made in corporate boardrooms: Auto executives, for example, have approved design features that have caused fatalities. Managers of chemical companies have allowed practices that have polluted the environment with cancer-causing agents. And heads of corporations have presided over industries wherein workers have been needlessly killed or maimed.

Whether or not these decisions should be considered crimes is debatable. A crime must always involve "malicious intent," or what the legal system calls *mens rea*. This certainly applies to street crime—the mugger obviously has sinister designs—but does it apply to every decision made in a boardroom that ends up causing harm? And does that harm match or exceed the harm caused by street criminals? In the following selections, John J. DiIulio, Jr., focuses on the enormous harm done—especially to the poor—by street criminals. Not only does street crime cause loss, injury, terror, and death for individuals, he argues, but it also causes neighborhood decline, community disintegration, loss of pride, business decline and failure, hampered schools, and middle-class flight to the suburbs. According to Jeffrey Reiman, white-collar crime also does more harm than is commonly recognized. By his count, white-collar crime causes far more deaths, injuries, illnesses, and financial loss than street crime. In light of this, he argues, we must redefine our ideas about what crime is and who the criminals are.

YES

John J. DiIulio, Jr.

THE IMPACT OF INNER-CITY CRIME

My grandmother, an Italian immigrant, lived in the same Philadelphia row house from 1921 till her death in 1986. When she moved there, and for the four decades thereafter, most of her neighbors were Irish and Italian. When she died, virtually all of her neighbors were black. Like the whites who fled, the first blacks who moved in were mostly working-class people living just above the poverty level.

Until around 1970, the neighborhood changed little. The houses were well-maintained. The children played in the streets and were polite. The teenagers hung out on the street corners in the evenings, sometimes doing mischief, but rarely—if ever—doing anything worse. The local grocers and other small businesspeople (both blacks and the few remaining whites) stayed open well past dark. Day or night, my grandmother journeyed the streets just as she had during the days of the Great Depression, taking the bus to visit her friends and relatives, going shopping, attending church, and so on.

She was a conspicuous and popular figure in this black community. She was conspicuous for her race, accent, and advanced age; she was popular for the homespun advice (and home-baked goods) she dispensed freely to the teenagers hanging out on the corners, to the youngsters playing ball in the street in front of her house, and to their parents (many of them mothers living without a husband).

Like the generations of ethnics who had lived there before them, these people were near the bottom of the socioeconomic ladder. I often heard my grandmother say that her new neighbors were "just like us," by which she meant that they were honest, decent, law-abiding people working hard to advance themselves and to make a better life for their children.

But in the early 1970s, the neighborhood began to change. Some, though by no means all, of the black families my grandmother had come to know moved out of the neighborhood. The new neighbors kept to themselves. The exteriors of the houses started to look ratty. The streets grew dirty. The grocery and variety stores closed or did business only during daylight hours. The children played in the schoolyard but not in front of their homes. The teenagers on the corners were replaced by adult drug dealers and their "runners." Vandalism

Excerpted from John J. DiIulio, Jr., "The Impact of Inner-City Crime," *The Public Interest*, no. 96 (Summer 1989), pp. 28–46. Copyright © 1989 by National Affairs, Inc. Reprinted by permission of *The Public Interest* and the author.

and graffiti became commonplace. My grandmother was mugged twice, both times by black teenagers; once she was severely beaten in broad daylight.

In the few years before she died at age eighty-four, and after years of pleading by her children and dozens of grandchildren, she stopped going out and kept her doors and windows locked at all times. On drives to visit her, when I got within four blocks of her home, I instinctively checked to make sure that my car doors were locked. Her house, where I myself had been raised, was in a "bad neighborhood," and it did not make sense to take any chances. I have not returned to the area since the day of her funeral.

My old ethnic and ghetto neighborhood had become an underclass neighborhood. Why is it that most readers of this article avoid, and advise their friends and relatives to avoid, walking or driving through such neighborhoods? Obviously we are not worried about being infected somehow by the extremely high levels of poverty, joblessness, illiteracy, welfare dependency, or drug abuse that characterize these places. Instead we shun these places because we suppose them to contain exceedingly high numbers of predatory street criminals, who hit, rape, rob, deal drugs, burglarize, and murder.

This supposition is absolutely correct. The underclass problem, contrary to the leading academic and journalistic understandings, is mainly a crime problem. It is a crime problem, moreover, that can be reduced dramatically (although not eliminated) with the human and financial resources already at hand.

Only two things are required: common sense and compassion. Once we understand the underclass problem as a crime problem, neither of those two qualities

should be scarce. Until we understand the underclass problem as a crime problem, policymakers and others will continue to fiddle while the underclass ghettos of Philadelphia, Newark, Chicago, Los Angeles, Miami, Washington, D.C., and other cities burn....

THE TRULY DEVIANT

Liberals ... have understood the worsening of ghetto conditions mainly as the by-product of a complex process of economic and social change. One of the latest and most influential statements of this view is William Julius Wilson's *The Truly Disadvantaged: The Inner City, the Underclass, and Public Policy* (1987).

Wilson argues that over the last two decades a new and socially destructive class structure has emerged in the ghetto. As he sees it, the main culprit is deindustrialization. As plants have closed, urban areas, especially black urban areas, have lost entry-level jobs. To survive economically, or to enjoy their material success, ghetto residents in a position to do so have moved out, leaving behind them an immobilized "underclass." ...

Wilson has focused our attention on the socioeconomic straits of the truly disadvantaged with an elegance and rhetorical force that is truly admirable.[1] But despite its many strengths, his often subtle analysis of the underclass problem wrongly deemphasizes one obvious possibility: "The truly disadvantaged" exist mainly because of the activities of "the truly deviant"—the large numbers of chronic and predatory street criminals—in their midst. One in every nine adult black males in this country is under some form of correctional supervision (prison, jail, probation, or parole).[2] Criminals come disproportionately from underclass neighborhoods. They victimize their neighbors directly through crime, and indirectly by creating or worsening the multiple social and economic ills that define the sad lot of today's ghetto dwellers.

PREDATORY GHETTO CRIMINALS

I propose [another] way of thinking about the underclass problem. The members of the underclass are, overwhelmingly, decent and law-abiding residents of America's most distressed inner cities. Fundamentally, what makes them different from the rest of us is not only their higher than normal levels of welfare dependency and the like, but their far higher than normal levels of victimization by predatory criminals.

This victimization by criminals takes several forms. There is *direct victimization* —being mugged, raped, or murdered; being threatened and extorted; living in fear about whether you can send your children to school or let them go out and play without their being bothered by dope dealers, pressured by gang members, or even struck by a stray bullet. And there is *indirect victimization*—dampened neighborhood economic development, loss of a sizable fraction of the neighborhood's male population to prison or jail, the undue influence on young people exercised by criminal "role models" like the cash-rich drug lords who rule the streets, and so on.

Baldly stated, my hypothesis is that this victimization causes and perpetuates the other ills of our underclass neighborhoods. Schools in these neighborhoods are unable to function effectively because of their disorderly atmosphere and because of the violent behavior of the criminals (especially gang members) who hang around their classrooms. The truly deviant are responsible for a high percentage of teen pregnancies, rapes, and sexual assaults. Similarly, many of the chronically welfare-dependent, female-headed households in these neighborhoods owe their plights to the fact that the men involved are either unable (because they are under some form of correctional supervision) or unwilling (because it does not jibe well with their criminal lifestyles) to seek and secure gainful employment and live with their families. And much of the poverty and joblessness in these neighborhoods can be laid at the door of criminals whose presence deters local business activity, including the development of residential real estate.

Blacks are victims of violent crimes at much higher rates than whites. Most lone-offender crime against blacks is committed by blacks, while most such crimes against whites are committed by whites; in 1986, for instance, 83.5 percent of violent crimes against blacks were committed by blacks, while 80.3 percent of violent crimes against whites were committed by whites. This monochrome picture of victim-offender relationships also holds for multiple-offender crimes. In 1986, for example, 79.6 percent of multiple-offender violent crimes against blacks were committed by blacks; the "white-on-white" figure was 59.4 percent.

Criminals are most likely to commit crimes against people of their own race. The main reason is presumably their physical proximity to potential victims. If so, then it is not hard to understand why underclass neighborhoods, which have more than their share of would-be criminals, have more than their share of crime.

Prison is the most costly form of correctional supervision, and it is normally reserved for the most dangerous felons —violent or repeat offenders. Most of my readers do not personally know anyone in prison; most ghetto dwellers of a decade or two ago probably would not have known anyone in prison either. But most of today's underclass citizens do; the convicted felons were their relatives and neighbors—and often their victimizers.

For example, in 1980 Newark was the street-crime capital of New Jersey. In the Newark area, there were more than 920 violent crimes (murders, non-negligent manslaughters, forcible rapes, robberies, and aggravated assaults) per 100,000 residents; in the rest of the state the figure was under 500, and in affluent towns like Princeton it was virtually nil. In the same year, New Jersey prisons held 5,866 criminals, 2,697 of them from the Newark area.[3] In virtually all of the most distressed parts of this distressed city, at least one of every two hundred residents was an imprisoned felon.[4] The same basic picture holds for other big cities.[5]

Correlation, however, is not causation, and we could extend and refine this sort of crude, exploratory analysis of the relationship between crime rates, concentrations of correctional supervisees, and the underclass neighborhoods from which they disproportionately come. But except to satisfy curiosity, I see no commanding need for such studies. For much the same picture emerges from the anecdotal accounts of people who have actually spent years wrestling with—as opposed to merely researching —the problem.

For example, in 1988 the nation's capital became its murder capital. Washington, D.C., had 372 killings, 82 percent of them committed on the streets by young black males against other young black males. The city vied with Detroit for the highest juvenile homicide rate in America. Here is part of the eloquent testimony on this development given by Isaac Fulwood, a native Washingtonian and the city's police-chief designate:

> The murder statistics don't capture what these people are doing. We've had in excess of 1,260 drug-related shootings.... People are scared of these kids. Someone can get shot in broad daylight, and nobody saw anything.... Nobody talks. And that's so different from the way it was in my childhood.

The same thing can be said about the underclass neighborhoods of other major cities. In Detroit, for instance, most of the hundreds of ghetto residents murdered over the last six years were killed within blocks of their homes by their truly deviant neighbors.

To devise meaningful law-enforcement and correctional responses to the underclass problem, we need to understand why concentrations of crime and criminals are so high in these neighborhoods, and to change our government's criminal-justice policies and practices accordingly.

UNDERSTANDING THE PROBLEM

We begin with a chicken-and-egg question: Does urban decay cause crime, or does crime cause urban decay?

In conventional criminology, which derives mainly from sociology, ghettos are portrayed as "breeding grounds" for predatory street crime. Poverty, joblessness, broken homes, single-parent families, and similar factors are identified as the "underlying causes" of crime.[6] These conditions cause crime, the argument goes; as they worsen—as the ghetto community becomes the underclass neighborhood—crime worsens. This remains the dominant academic perspective on the subject, one that is shared implicitly by most public officials who are close to the problem.

Beginning in the mid-1970s, however, a number of influential studies appeared that challenged this conventional criminological wisdom.[7] Almost without exception, these studies have cast grave doubts on the classic sociological explanation of crime, suggesting that the actual relationships between such variables as poverty, illiteracy, and unemployment, on the one hand, and criminality, on the other, are far more ambiguous than most analysts freely assumed only a decade or so ago....

LOCKS, COPS, AND STUDIES

Camden, New Jersey, is directly across the bridge from Philadelphia. Once-decent areas have become just like my grandmother's old neighborhood: isolated, crime-torn urban war zones. In February 1989 a priest doing social work in Camden was ordered off the streets by drug dealers and threatened with death if he did not obey. The police chief of Camden sent some extra men into the area, but the violent drug dealers remained the real rulers of the city's streets.

The month before the incident in Camden, the Rockefeller Foundation announced that it was going to devote some of its annual budget (which exceeds $100 million) to researching the underclass problem. Other foundations, big and small, have already spent (or misspent) much money on the problem. But Rockefeller's president was quoted as follows: "Nobody knows who they are, what they do.... The underclass is not a topic to pursue from the library. You get out and look for them."

His statement was heartening, but it revealed a deep misunderstanding of the problem. Rather than intimating that the underclass was somehow hard to locate, he would have done better to declare that his charity would purchase deadbolt locks for the homes of ghetto dwellers in New York City who lacked them, and subsidize policing and private-security services in the easily identifiable neighborhoods where these poor people are concentrated.

More street-level research would be nice, especially for the networks of policy intellectuals (liberal and conservative) who benefit directly from such endeavors. But more locks, cops, and corrections officers would make a more positive, tangible, and lasting difference in the lives of today's ghetto dwellers.

NOTES

1. In addition, he has canvassed competing academic perspectives on the underclass; see William Julius Wilson, ed., "The Ghetto Underclass: Social Science Perspectives," *Annals of the American Academy of Political and Social Science* (January 1989). It should also be noted that he is directing a $2.7 million research project on poverty in Chicago that promises to be the most comprehensive study of its kind yet undertaken.

2. According to the Bureau of Justice Statistics, in 1986 there were 234,430 adult black males in prison, 101,000 in jail, an estimated 512,000 on probation, and 133,300 on parole. There were 8,985,000 adult black males in the national residential population. I am grateful to Larry Greenfeld for his assistance in compiling these figures.

3. I am grateful to Hank Pierre, Stan Repko, and Commissioner William H. Fauver of the New Jersey

Department of Corrections for granting me access to these figures and to related data on density of prisoner residence; to Andy Ripps for his heroic efforts in organizing them; and to my Princeton colleague Mark Alan Hughes for his expert help in analyzing the data.

4. Ten of the thirteen most distressed Newark census tracts were places where the density of prisoner residence was that high. In other words, 76.9 percent of the worst underclass areas of Newark had such extremely high concentrations of hardcore offenders. In most of the rest of Newark, and throughout the rest of the state, such concentrations were virtually nonexistent.

5. In 1980 in the Chicago area, for example, in 182 of the 1,521 census tracts at least one of every two hundred residents was an imprisoned felon. Fully twenty of the thirty-five worst underclass tracts had such extraordinary concentrations of serious criminals; in several of them, more than one of every hundred residents was behind prison bars. I am grateful to Wayne Carroll and Commissioner Michael Lane of the Illinois Department of Corrections for helping me with these data.

6. For example, see the classic statement by Edwin H. Sutherland and Donald R. Cressey, *Principles of Criminology*, 7th rev. ed. (Philadelphia: J. P. Lippincott, 1966).

7. See, for example, James Q. Wilson, *Thinking About Crime* (New York: Basic Books, 1975), especially the third chapter.

NO

Jeffrey Reiman

A CRIME BY ANY OTHER NAME

If one individual inflicts a bodily injury upon another which leads to the death of the person attacked we call it manslaughter; on the other hand, if the attacker knows beforehand that the blow will be fatal we call it murder. Murder has also been committed if society places hundreds of workers in such a position that they inevitably come to premature and unnatural ends. Their death is as violent as if they had been stabbed or shot.... Murder has been committed if society knows perfectly well that thousands of workers cannot avoid being sacrificed so long as these conditions are allowed to continue. Murder of this sort is just as culpable as the murder committed by an individual.

—Frederick Engels
The Condition of the Working Class in England

WHAT'S IN A NAME?

If it takes you an hour to read this chapter, by the time you reach the last page, two of your fellow citizens will have been murdered. *During that same time, at least four Americans will die as a result of unhealthy or unsafe conditions in the workplace!* Although these work-related deaths could have been prevented, they are not called murders. Why not? Doesn't a crime by any other name still cause misery and suffering? What's in a name?

The fact is that the label "crime" is not used in America to name all or the worst of the actions that cause misery and suffering to Americans. It is primarily reserved for the dangerous actions of the poor.

In the March 14, 1976 edition of the *Washington Star*, a front-page article appeared with the headline: "Mine Is Closed 26 Deaths Late." The article read in part:

> Why, the relatives [of the twenty-six dead miners] ask, did the mine ventilation fail and allow pockets of volatile methane gas to build up in a shaft 2,300 feet below the surface?
>
> Why wasn't the mine cleared as soon as supervisors spotted evidence of methane gas near where miners were driving huge machines into the 61-foot-high coal seam? ...

From Jeffrey Reiman, *The Rich Get Richer and the Poor Get Prison: Ideology, Class, and Criminal Justice*, 3rd ed. (Macmillan, 1990). Copyright © 1990 by Jeffrey Reiman. Reprinted by permission of Macmillan College Publishing Company. Notes omitted.

[I]nvestigators of the Senate Labor and Welfare Committee... found that there have been 1,250 safety violations at the 13-year-old mine since 1970. Fifty-seven of those violations were serious enough for federal inspectors to order the mine closed and 21 of those were in cases where federal inspectors felt there was imminent danger to the lives of the miners working there....

Federal inspectors said the most recent violations found at the mine were three found in the ventilation system on Monday—the day before 15 miners were killed.

Next to the continuation of this story was another, headlined: "Mass Murder Claims Six in Pennsylvania." It described the shooting death of a husband and wife, their three children, and a friend in a Philadelphia suburb. This was murder, maybe even mass murder. My only question is, "Why wasn't the death of the miners also murder?"

Why do twenty-six dead miners amount to a "disaster" and six dead suburbanites a "mass murder"? "Murder" suggests a murderer, whereas "disaster" suggests the work of impersonal forces. If more than 1,000 safety violations had been found in the mine—three the day before the first explosion—was no one responsible for failing to eliminate the hazards? Was no one responsible for *preventing* the hazards? If someone could have prevented the hazards and did not, does that person not bear responsibility for the deaths of twenty-six men? Is he less evil because he did not want them to die although he chose to leave them in jeopardy? Is he not a murderer, perhaps even a *mass* murderer?

These questions are at this point rhetorical. My aim is not to discuss this case but rather to point to the blinders we wear when we look at such a "disaster." Perhaps there will be an investigation. Perhaps someone will be held responsible. Perhaps he will be fined. But will he be tried for *murder?* Will anyone think of him as a murderer? *And if not, why not?* Would the miners not be safer if such people were treated as murderers? Might they not still be alive? ... Didn't those miners have a right to protection from the violence that took their lives? *And if not, why not?*

Once we are ready to ask this question seriously, we are in a position to see that the reality of crime—that is, the acts we label crime, the acts we think of as crime, the actors and actions we treat as criminal—is *created:* It is an image shaped by decisions as to *what* will be called crime and *who* will be treated as a criminal.

THE CARNIVAL MIRROR

... The American criminal justice system is a mirror that shows a distorted image of the dangers that threaten us—an image created more by the shape of the mirror than by the reality reflected. What do we see when we look in the criminal justice mirror?

On the morning of September 16, 1975, the *Washington Post* carried an article in its local news section headlined "Arrest Data Reveal Profile of a Suspect." The article reported the results of a study of crime in Prince George's County, a suburb of Washington, D.C. It read in part that

The typical suspect in serious crime in Prince George's County is a black male, aged 14 to 19....

This is the Typical Criminal feared by most law-abiding Americans. His crime, according to former Attorney General John Mitchell (who was by no means a typical criminal), is forcing us "to change the fabric of our society,... forcing us, a free people, to alter our pattern of life,... to withdraw from our neighbors, to fear all strangers and to limit our activities to 'safe' areas." These poor, young, urban (disproportionately) black males comprise the core of the enemy forces in the war against crime. They are the heart of a vicious, unorganized guerrilla army, threatening the lives, limbs, and possessions of the law-abiding members of society—necessitating recourse to the ultimate weapons of force and detention in our common defense. They are the "career criminals" President Reagan had in mind when he told the International Association of Chiefs of Police, assuring them of the tough stance that the federal government would take in the fight against crime, that "a small number of criminals are responsible for an enormous amount of the crime in American society."

... The acts of the Typical Criminal are not the only acts that endanger us, nor are they the acts that endanger us the most. We have a greater chance... of being killed or disabled, for example, by an occupational injury or disease, by unnecessary surgery, or by shoddy emergency medical services than by aggravated assault or even homicide! Yet even though these threats to our well-being are graver than that posed by our poor, young, urban, black males, they do not show up in the FBI's Index of serious crimes. The individuals who are responsible for them do not turn up in arrest records or prison statistics. *They never become part of the reality reflected in the criminal justice mirror, although the danger they pose is at least as great and often greater than those who do!*

Similarly, the general public loses more money *by far*... from price-fixing and monopolistic practices and from consumer deception and embezzlement than from all the property crimes in the FBI's Index combined. Yet these far more costly acts are either not criminal, or if technically criminal, not prosecuted, or if prosecuted, not punished, or if punished, only mildly. In any event, although the individuals responsible for these acts take more money out of the ordinary citizen's pocket than our Typical Criminal, they rarely show up in arrest statistics and almost never in prison populations. *Their faces rarely appear in the criminal justice mirror, although the danger they pose is at least as great and often greater than those who do.*

The inescapable conclusion is that the criminal justice system does not simply *reflect* the reality of crime; it has a hand in *creating* the reality we see.

The criminal justice system is like a mirror in which society can see the face of the evil in its midst. Because the system deals with some evil and not with others, because it treats some evils as the gravest and treats some of the gravest evils as minor, the image it throws back is distorted like the image in a carnival mirror. Thus, the image cast back is false, not because it is invented out of thin air, but because the proportions of the real are distorted: Large becomes small and small large; grave becomes minor and minor grave. Like a carnival mirror, although nothing is reflected that does not exist in the world, the image is more a creation of the mirror than a picture of the world....

This is my point. Because we accept the belief... that the model for crime is one person specifically intending to harm another, we accept a legal system that leaves us unprotected against much greater dangers to our lives and well-being than those threatened by the Typical Criminal....

Work May Be Dangerous to Your Health

Since the publication of *The President's Report on Occupational Safety and Health* in 1972, numerous studies have documented both the astounding incidence of disease, injury, and death due to hazards in the workplace *and* the fact that much or most of this carnage is the consequence of the refusal of management to pay for safety measures and of government to enforce safety standards.

In that 1972 report, the government estimated the number of job-related illnesses at 390,000 per year and the number of annual deaths from industrial disease at 100,000. For 1986, the Bureau of Labor Statistics [BLS] of the U.S. Department of Labor estimates 136,800 job-related illnesses and 3,610 work-related deaths. Note that the latter figure applies only to private-sector work environments with eleven or more employees. It is not limited to death from occupational disease but includes all work-related deaths, including those resulting from accidents on the job.

Before considering the significance of these figures, it should be pointed out that there is wide agreement that occupational diseases are seriously underreported. *The Report of the President to the Congress on Occupational Safety and Health* for 1980 stated that

> recording and reporting of illnesses continue to present measurement problems, since employers (and doctors) are of-

ten unable to recognize some illnesses as work-related. The annual survey includes data only on the visible illnesses of workers. To the extent that occupational illnesses are unrecognized and, therefore, not recorded or reported, the illness survey estimates may understate their occurrence.

... For these reasons, plus the fact that BLS's figures on work-related deaths are only for private workplaces with eleven or more employees, we must supplement the BLS figures with other estimates. In 1982, then U.S. Secretary of Health and Human Services Richard Schweiker stated that "current estimates for overall workplace-associated cancer mortality vary within a range of five to fifteen percent." With annual cancer deaths currently running more than 460,000, that translates into between 23,000 and 69,000 job-related cancer deaths per year. In testimony before the Senate Committee on Labor and Human Resources, Dr. Philip Landrigan, director of the Division of Environmental and Occupational Medicine at the Mount Sinai School of Medicine in New York City, stated that

> Recent data indicate that occupationally related exposures are responsible each year in New York State for 5,000 to 7,000 deaths and for 35,000 new cases of illness (not including work-related injuries). These deaths due to occupational disease include 3,700 deaths from cancer....

Crude national estimates of the burden of occupational disease in the United States may be developed by multiplying the New York State data by a factor of 10. New York State contains slightly less than 10 percent of the nation's workforce, and it includes a broad mix of employment in the manufacturing, service and agricultural sectors. Thus, it may be calculated that occupational disease is responsible each year in the United States for 50,000 to 70,000 deaths, and for approximately 350,000 new cases of illness.

It is some confirmation of Dr. Landrigan's estimates that they imply work-related cancer deaths of approximately 37,000 a year—a figure that is squarely in the middle of the range implied in Secretary Schweiker's statement on this issue. Thus, even if we discount OSHA's [Occupational Safety and Health Administration's] 1972 estimate of 100,000 deaths a year due to occupational disease or Dr. Landrigan's estimate of between 50,000 to 70,000, we would surely be erring in the other direction to accept the BLS figure of 3,610. We can hardly be overestimating the actual toll if we set it at 25,000 deaths a year resulting from occupational disease.

As for the BLS estimate of 136,800 job-related illnesses, here, too, there is reason to assume that the figure considerably understates the real situation. Dr. Landrigan's estimates suggest that the BLS figure represents less than half of the actual number. However, the BLS figure is less accurate than its figure for job-related deaths for at least two reasons: It is not limited to firms with eleven or more employees and symptoms of illness generally can be expected to appear sooner after contracting an illness than does death. To stay on the conservative side, then, I shall assume that there are annually in the United States approximately 150,000 job-related illnesses and 25,000 deaths from occupational diseases. How does this compare to the threat posed by crime? Before jumping to any conclusions, note that the risk of occupational disease and death falls only on members of the labor force, whereas the risk of crime falls on the whole population, from infants to the elderly. Because the labor force is less than half the total population (110,000,000 in 1986, out of a total population of 241,000,000), to get a true picture of the *relative* threat posed by occupational diseases compared to that posed by crime we should *halve* the crime statistics when comparing them to the figures for industrial disease and death. Using the 1986 statistics, this means that the *comparable* figures would be:

	Occupational Disease	Crime (halved)
Death	25,000	10,000
Other physical harm	150,000	400,000

... It should be noted further that the statistics given so far are *only* for occupational *diseases* and deaths from those diseases. They do not include death and disability from work-related injuries. Here, too, the statistics are gruesome. The National Safety Council reported that in 1986, work-related accidents caused 10,700 deaths and 1.8 million disabling work injuries, at a total cost to the economy of $34.8 billion. This brings the number of occupation-related deaths to 36,700 a year. If, on the basis of these additional figures, we recalculated our chart comparing occupational to criminal dangers, it would look like this:

	Occupational Hazard	Crime (halved)
Death	36,700	10,000
Other physical harm	1,950,000	400,000

Can there be any doubt that workers are more likely to stay alive and healthy in the face of the danger from the underworld than in the face of what their employers have in store for them on the job?...

[T]he vast majority of occupational deaths result from disease, not accident, and disease is generally a function of conditions outside a worker's control. Examples of such conditions are the level of coal dust in the air (about 10 percent of all active coal miners have black lung disease) or textile dust (some 85,000 American cotton textile workers presently suffer breathing impairments caused by acute byssinosis or brown lung, and another 35,000 former mill workers are totally disabled with chronic brown lung) or asbestos fibers (a study of 632 asbestos-insulation workers between 1943 and 1971 indicates that 11 percent have died of asbestosis and 38 percent of cancer; two doctors who have studied asbestos workers conclude "we can anticipate three thousand excess respiratory, cardiopulmonary deaths and cancers of the lung—three thousand excess deaths *annually* for the next twenty or thirty years"), or coal tars ("workers who had been employed five or more years in the coke ovens died of lung cancer at a rate three and a half times that for all steelworkers"; coke oven workers also develop cancer of the scrotum at a rate five times that of the general population). Also, some 800,000 people suffer from occupationally related skin disease each year (according to a 1968 estimate by the U.S. surgeon general), and "the number of American workers experiencing noise conditions that may damage their hearing is estimated [in a 1969 Public Health Service publication of the Department of Health, Education and Welfare] to be in excess of 6 million, and may even reach 16 million."

To blame the workers for occupational disease and deaths is simply to ignore the history of governmental attempts to compel industrial firms to meet safety standards that would keep dangers (such as chemicals or fibers or dust particles in the air) that are outside of the worker's control down to a safe level. This has been a continual struggle, with firms using everything from their own "independent" research institutes to more direct and often questionable forms of political pressure to influence government in the direction of loose standards and lax enforcement. So far, industry has been winning because OSHA has been given neither the personnel nor the mandate to fulfill its purpose....

When inspectors do find violations, the penalties they can assess are severely limited by the OSHA law that Congress has not updated since it established the agency. The maximum penalty for a serious OSHA violation is $1,000; an employer who acts willfully can be fined up to $10,000 for each incident....

Even when the agency hits employers hard, however, the sting does not often last very long. The big proposed fines that grab headlines are seldom paid in full. The two record-breaking citations of last year, against Union Carbide Corporation for $1.37 million and Chrysler for $910,000, were each settled this year for less than a third of the original amounts.

According to *Occupational Hazards*,

... NIOSH's [National Institute for Occupational Safety and Health's] budget, rather than being increased, had continued to be cut—by as much as 47 percent since 1980, when adjusted for inflation. And that while nations such as Finland spend approximately $2 per worker each year on occupational disease surveillance, the United States spends about 2¢ per worker.

... Is a person who kills another in a bar brawl a greater threat to society than a business executive who refuses to cut into his profits in order to make his plant a safe place to work? By any measure of death and suffering the latter is by far a greater danger than the former. Because he wishes his workers no harm, because he is only indirectly responsible for death and disability, while pursuing legitimate economic goals, his acts are not called "crimes." Once we free our imagination from the irrational shackle of the one-on-one model of crime, can there be any doubt that the criminal justice system does *not* protect us from the gravest threats to life and limb? It seeks to protect us when danger comes from a young, lower-class male in the inner city. When a threat comes from an upper-class business executive in an office, the criminal justice system looks the other way. This is in the face of growing evidence that for every American citizen murdered by some thug, two American workers are killed by their bosses.

Health Care May Be Dangerous to Your Health

... On July 15, 1975, Dr. Sidney Wolfe of Ralph Nader's Public Interest Health Research Group testified before the House Commerce Oversight and Investigations Subcommittee that there "were 3.2 million cases of unnecessary surgery performed each year in the United States." These unneeded operations, Dr. Wolfe added, "cost close to $5 billion a year and kill as many as 16,000 Americans." Wolfe's estimates of unnecessary surgery were based on studies comparing the operations performed and surgery recommended by doctors who are paid for the operations they do with those performed and recommended by salaried doctors who receive no extra income from surgery.

... In an article on an experimental program by Blue Cross and Blue Shield aimed at curbing unnecessary surgery, *Newsweek* reports that

a Congressional committee earlier this year [1976] estimated that more than 2 million of the elective operations performed in 1974 were not only unnecessary—but also killed about 12,000 patients and cost nearly $4 billion.

... In fact, if someone had the temerity to publish a *Uniform Crime Reports* that really portrayed the way Americans are murdered, the FBI's statistics on the *type of weapon used* in murder would have to be changed for 1986, from those shown in Table 1 to something like those shown in Table 2.

The figures shown in Table 2 would give American citizens a much more honest picture of what threatens them. We are not likely to see it broadcast by the criminal justice system, however, because it would also give American citizens a more honest picture of *who* threatens them.

We should not leave this topic without noting that, aside from the other losses it imposes, unnecessary surgery was estimated to have cost between $4 and $5 billion in 1974. The price of medical care has nearly tripled between 1974 and 1986. Thus, assuming that the same number of unneeded operations were performed in 1986, the cost of unnecessary surgery would be between $12 and $15 billion. To this we should add the unnecessary 22 percent of the 6 billion administered doses of medication. Even at the extremely conservative estimate of $3 a dose, this adds about $4 billion. In short, assuming that earlier trends

Table 1

How Americans Are Murdered

Total	Firearms	Knife or Other Cutting Instrument	Other Weapon: Club, Arson, Poison, Strangulation, etc.	Personal Weapon: Hands, Fists, etc.
19,257[a]	11,381	3,957	2,609	1,310

[a] Note that this figure diverges somewhat from the figure of 20,613 murders and nonnegligent manslaughters used elsewhere in the FBI *Uniform Crime Reports*, 1987; see for example, p. 7.

Source: FBI *Uniform Crime Reports*, 1987: "Murder Victims: Weapons Used, 1986."

have continued, there is reason to believe that unnecessary surgery and medication cost the public between $16 and $19 billion annually—far outstripping the $11.6 billion taken by thieves that concern the FBI. This give us yet another way in which we are robbed of more money by practices that are not treated as criminal than by practices that are.

Waging Chemical Warfare Against America

… "A 1978 report issued by the President's Council on Environmental Quality (CEQ) unequivocally states that 'most researchers agree that 70 to 90 percent of cancers are caused by environmental influences and are hence theoretically preventable.'" This means that a concerted national effort could result in saving 300,000 or more lives a year and reducing each individual's chances of getting cancer in his or her lifetime from one in four to one in twelve or less. …

The simple truth is that the government that strove so mightily to protect us against a guerrilla war 10,000 miles from home [the Vietnam War, in which the United States spent around $165 billion] is doing next to nothing to protect us against the chemical war in our midst.

This war is being waged against us on three fronts:

• Air pollution
• Cigarette smoking
• Food additives

Not only are we losing on all three fronts, but it looks like we do not even have the will to fight. …

In 1970, Lester B. Lave and Eugene P. Seskin reviewed more than fifty scientific studies of the relationship between air pollution and morbidity and mortality rates for lung cancer, nonrespiratory tract cancers, cardiovascular disease, bronchitis, and other respiratory diseases. They found in every instance a *positive quantifiable relationship*. Using sophisticated statistical techniques, they concluded that a 50 percent reduction in air pollution in major urban areas would result in:

• A 25 percent reduction in mortality from lung cancer (using 1974 mortality rates, this represents a potential saving of 19,500 lives per year)
• A 25 percent reduction in morbidity and mortality due to respiratory disease (a potential saving of 27,000 lives per year)
• A 20 percent reduction in morbidity and mortality due to cardiovascular

Table 2

How Americans Are (Really) Murdered

Total	Occupational Hazard & Disease	Inadequate Emergency Medical Care	Knife or Other Cutting Instrument Including Scalpel	Firearms	Other Weapon: Club, Poison, Hypodermic, Prescription Drug	Personal Weapon: Hands, Fists, etc.
114,957	61,700	20,000	15,957[a]	11,381	4,609[a]	1,310

[a] these figures represent the relevant figures in Table 1 plus the most conservative figures for the relevant categories discussed in the text.

disease (a potential saving of 52,000 lives per year)....

A more recent study, done in 1978 by Robert Mendelsohn of the University of Washington and Guy Orcutt of Yale University, estimates that air pollution causes a total of 142,000 deaths a year....

Based on the knowledge we have, there can be no doubt that air pollution, tobacco, and food additives amount to a chemical war that makes the crime wave look like a football scrimmage. Quite conservatively, I think we can estimate the death toll in this war as at least a quarter of a million lives a year—*more than ten times the number killed by criminal homicide!* ...

Summary

Once again, our investigations lead to the same result. The criminal justice system does not protect us against the gravest threats to life, limb, or possessions. Its definitions of crime are not simply a reflection of the objective dangers that threaten us. The workplace, the medical profession, the air we breathe... lead to far more human suffering, far more death and disability, and take far more dollars from our pockets than the murders, aggravated assaults, and thefts reported annually by the FBI. What is more, this human suffering is preventable. A government really intent on protecting our well-being could enforce work safety regulations, police the medical profession, [and] require that clean air standards be met,... but it does not. Instead we hear a lot of cant about law and order and a lot of rant about crime in the streets. It is as if our leaders were not only refusing to protect us from the major threats to our well-being but trying to cover up this refusal by diverting our attention to crime—as if this were the only real threat. As we have seen, the criminal justice system is a carnival mirror that presents a distorted image of what threatens us.... All the mechanisms by which the criminal justice system comes down more frequently and more harshly on the poor criminal than on the well-off criminal take place *after* most of the dangerous acts of the well-to-do have been excluded from the definition of crime itself.

POSTSCRIPT

Is Street Crime More Harmful Than White-Collar Crime?

DiIulio implies that much of the social misery of America, including the persistence of poverty, can be traced to the "truly depraved" street criminals in our central cities. Is this focus too narrow? Surely there are many other sources of the social crisis that afflicts our central cities. Reiman's focus, on the other hand, may be overly broad. He claims that more people are killed and injured by "occupational injury or disease, by unnecessary surgery, and by shoddy emergency medical services than by aggravated assault or even homicide!" Can shoddy medical services be categorized as a crime? And could the residents of city ghettos, where most of the violent crime occurs, ever be convinced that they face a greater risk from occupational injury or disease than from street criminals? In the end, the questions remain: What is a crime? Who are the criminals?

A set of readings that support Reiman's viewpoint is *Corporate Violence: Injury and Death for Profit* edited by Stuart L. Hills (Rowman & Littlefield, 1987). Further support is provided by Marshall B. Clinard, *Corporate Corruption: The Abuse of Power* (Praeger, 1990). *White-Collar Crime* edited by Gilbert Geis and Robert F. Meier (Free Press, 1977) is a useful compilation of essays on corporate and political crime, as is Gary Green's *Occupational Crime* (Nelson-Hall, 1990). Four other books that focus on crime in high places are J. Douglas and J. M. Johnson, *Official Deviance* (J. B. Lippincott, 1977); J. Anthony Lukas, *Nightmare: The Underside of the Nixon Years* (Viking Press, 1976); Marshall B. Clinard, *Corporate Elites and Crime* (Sage Publications, 1983); and David R. Simon and Stanley Eitzen, *Elite Deviance* (Allyn & Bacon, 1982). A work that deals with the prevalence and fear of street crime is Elliott Currie, *Confronting Crime: An American Challenge* (Pantheon Books, 1985). Two works on gangs, which are often connected with violent street crime, are Martin Sanchez Jankowski, *Islands in the Street: Gangs and American Urban Society* (University of California Press, 1991) and Felix M. Padilla, *The Gang as an American Enterprise* (Rutgers University Press, 1992). One interesting aspect of many corporate, or white-collar, crimes is that they involve crimes of obedience, as discussed in Herman C. Kelman and V. Lee Hamilton, *Crimes of Obedience: Toward a Social Psychology of Authority and Responsibility* (Yale University Press, 1989).

UE 17

Should Drugs Be Legalized?

YES: Ethan A. Nadelmann, from "Should We Legalize Drugs? Yes," *American Heritage* (February/March 1993)

NO: David T. Courtwright, from "Should We Legalize Drugs? No," *American Heritage* (February/March 1993)

ISSUE SUMMARY

YES: Ethan A. Nadelmann, an assistant professor of politics and public affairs, argues that history shows that not only is drug prohibition costly but it also exacerbates the drug problem. He maintains that controlled legalization would reduce the drug problem in the United States.

NO: Professor of history David T. Courtwright argues that legalizing drugs would not eliminate drug-related criminal activity and that it would increase drug use. Therefore, the government should continue the war against drugs.

A century ago, drugs of every kind were freely available to Americans. Laudanum, a mixture of opium and alcohol, was popularly used as a painkiller. One drug company even claimed that it was a very useful substance for calming hyperactive children, and the company called it Mother's Helper. Morphine came into common use during the Civil War. Heroin, developed as a supposedly less addictive substitute for morphine, began to be marketed at the end of the nineteenth century. By that time, drug paraphernalia could be ordered through Sears and Roebuck catalogues, and Coca-Cola, which contained small quantities of cocaine, had become a popular drink.

Public concerns about addiction and dangerous patent medicines, and an active campaign for drug laws waged by Dr. Harvey Wiley, a chemist in the U.S. Department of Agriculture, led Congress to pass the first national drug regulation act in 1906. The Pure Food and Drug Act required that medicines containing certain drugs, such as opium, must say so on their labels. The Harrison Narcotic Act of 1914 went much further and cut off completely the supply of legal opiates to addicts. Since then, ever stricter drug laws have been passed by Congress and by state legislatures.

Drug abuse in America again came to the forefront of public discourse during the 1960s, when heroin addiction started growing rapidly in inner-city neighborhoods. Also, by the end of the decade, drug experimentation had spread to the middle-class, affluent baby boomers who were then attending college. Indeed, certain types of drugs began to be celebrated by some of the leaders of the counterculture. Heroin was still taboo, but other drugs, notably marijuana and LSD (a psychedelic drug), were regarded as harmless and even spiritually transforming. At music festivals like Woodstock in 1969, marijuana and LSD were used openly and associated with love, peace, and heightened sensitivity. Much of this enthusiasm cooled over the next 20 years as baby boomers entered the workforce full-time and began their careers. But even among the careerists, certain types of drugs enjoyed high status. Cocaine, noted for its highly stimulating effects, became the drug of choice for many hard-driving young lawyers, television writers, and Wall Street bond traders.

The high price of cocaine put it out of reach for many people, but in the early 1980s, cheap substitutes began to appear on the streets and to overtake poor urban communities. Crack cocaine, a potent, highly addictive, smokable form of cocaine, came into widespread use. By the end of the 1980s, the drug known as "ice," or as it is called on the West Coast, "L.A. glass," a smokable form of amphetamine, had hit the streets. These stimulants tend to produce very violent, disorderly behavior. Moreover, the street gangs who sell them are frequently at war with one another and are well armed. Not only gang members but also many innocent people have become victims of contract killings, street battles, and drive-by shootings.

This new drug epidemic prompted President George Bush to declare a "war on drugs," and in 1989 he asked Congress to appropriate $10.6 billion for the fight. Although most Americans support such measures against illegal drugs, some say that in the years since Bush made his declaration, the drug situation has not showed any signs of improvement. Some believe that legalization would be the best way to fight the drug problem.

The drug legalization issue is especially interesting to sociologists because it raises basic questions about what should be socially sanctioned or approved, what is illegal or legal, and what is immoral or moral. An aspect of the basic value system of America is under review. The process of value change may be taking place in front of our eyes. As part of this debate, Ethan A. Nadelmann argues that the present policy does not work and that it is counterproductive. Legalization, he contends, would stop much of the violence and crime associated with illegal drugs. Although Nadelmann concedes that it may increase the use of lower-potency drugs, he believes that legalization would reduce the use of the worst drugs. David T. Courtwright agrees that the current policy is not solving the problem, but he argues that drug use and addiction would surge disastrously with legalization. He also believes that drug-related crime would persist and that drug rings would continue operating under a policy of controlled legalization.

YES   Ethan A. Nadelmann

SHOULD WE LEGALIZE DRUGS?

Most opponents of "drug legalization" assume that it would involve making cocaine and heroin available the way alcohol and tobacco are today. But most legalization supporters favor nothing of the kind; in fact, we disagree widely as to which drugs should be legalized, how they should be controlled, and what the consequences are likely to be. Where drug-policy reformers do agree is in our critique of the drug-prohibition system that has evolved in the United States—a system, we contend, that has proved ineffective, costly, counterproductive, and immoral.

Efforts to reverse drug prohibition face formidable obstacles. Americans have grown accustomed to the status quo. Alcohol prohibition was overturned before most citizens had forgotten what a legal alcohol policy was like, but who today can recall a time before drug prohibition? Moreover, the United States has succeeded in promoting its drug-prohibition system throughout the world. Opponents of alcohol prohibition could look to successful foreign alcohol-control systems, in Canada and much of Europe, but contemporary drug anti-prohibitionists must look further—to history.

The principal evidence, not surprisingly, is Prohibition. The dry years offer many useful analogies, but their most important lesson is the need to distinguish between the harms that stem from drugs and the harms that arise from outlawing them. The Americans who voted in 1933 to repeal Prohibition differed greatly in their reasons for overturning the system. They almost all agreed, however, that the evils of alcohol consumption had been surpassed by those of trying to suppress it.

Some pointed to Al Capone and rising crime, violence, and corruption; others to the overflowing courts, jails, and prisons, the labeling of tens of millions of Americans as criminals and the consequent broadening disrespect for the law, the dangerous expansions of federal police powers and encroachments on individual liberties, the hundreds of thousands of Americans blinded, paralyzed, and killed by poisonous moonshine and industrial alcohol, and the increasing government expenditure devoted to enforcing the Prohibition laws and the billions in forgone tax revenues. Supporters of Prohibition blamed the consumers, and some went so far as to argue that those who violated the laws deserved whatever ills befell them. But by 1933 most Americans blamed Prohibition.

If there is a single message that contemporary anti-prohibitionists seek to drive home, it is that drug prohibition is responsible for much of what Americans identify today as the "drug problem." It is not merely a matter of the direct costs—twenty billion dollars spent this year on arresting, prosecuting, and incarcerating drug-law violators. Choked courts and prisons, an incarceration rate higher than that of any other nation in the world, tax dollars diverted from education and health care, law-enforcement resources diverted from investigating everything from auto theft to savings-and-loan scams—all these are just a few of the costs our current prohibition imposes.

* * *

Consider also Capone's successors—the drug kingpins of Asia, Latin America, and the United States. Consider as well all the murders and assaults perpetrated by young drug dealers not just against one another but against police, witnesses, and bystanders. Consider the tremendous economic and social incentives generated by the illegality of the drug market—temptations so overwhelming that even "good kids" cannot resist them. Consider the violent drug dealers becoming the heroes of boys and young men, from Harlem to Medellín. And consider tens of millions of Americans being labeled criminals for doing nothing more than smoking a marijuana cigarette. In all these respects the consequences of drug prohibition imitate—and often exceed—those of alcohol prohibition.

Prohibition reminds us, too, of the health costs of drug prohibition. Sixty years ago some fifty thousand Americans were paralyzed after consuming an adulterated Jamaica ginger extract known as "jake." Today we have marijuana made more dangerous by government-sprayed paraquat and the chemicals added by drug dealers, heroin adulterated with poisonous powders, and assorted pills and capsules containing everything from antihistamines to strychnine. Indeed, virtually every illicit drug purchased at the retail level contains adulterants, at least some of which are far more dangerous than the drug itself. And restrictions on the sale of drug paraphernalia has, by encouraging intravenous drug addicts to share their equipment, severely handicapped efforts to stem the transmission of AIDS. As during Prohibition, many Americans view these ills as necessary and even desirable, but others, like their forebears sixty years ago, reject as perverse a system that degrades and destroys the very people it was designed to protect.

Prohibition's lessons extend in other directions as well. The current revisionist twist on that "Great Experiment" now claims that "Prohibition worked," by reducing alcohol consumption and alcohol-related ills ranging from cirrhosis to public drunkenness and employee absenteeism. There is some truth to this claim. But in fact, the most dramatic decline in American alcohol consumption occurred not between 1920 and 1933, while the Eighteenth Amendment was in effect, but rather between 1916 and 1922. During those years the temperance movement was highly active and successful in publicizing the dangers of alcohol. The First World War's spirit of self-sacrifice extended to temperance as a means of grain conservation, and there arose, as the historian David Kyvig puts it, "an atmosphere of hostility toward all things German, not the least of which was beer." In short, a great variety of factors coalesced in this brief time to substantially reduce alcohol consumption and its ills.

The very evidence on which pro-prohibition historians rely provides further proof of the importance of factors other than prohibition laws. One of these historians, John Burnham, has noted that the admission rate for alcohol psychoses to New York hospitals shrank from 10 percent between 1909 and 1912 to 1.9 percent in 1920—a decline that occurred largely before national prohibition and in a state that had not enacted its own prohibition law.

At best one can argue that Prohibition was most effective in its first years, when temperance norms remained strong and illicit sources of production had yet to be firmly established. By all accounts, alcohol consumption rose after those first years—despite increased resources devoted to enforcement. The pre-Prohibition decline in consumption, like the recent decline in cigarette consumption, had less to do with laws than with changing norms and the imposition of non-criminal-justice measures.

Perhaps the most telling indictment of Prohibition is provided by the British experience with alcohol control during a similar period. In the United States the death rate from cirrhosis of the liver dropped from as high as 15 per 100,000 population between 1910 and 1914 to 7 during the twenties only to climb back to pre-1910 levels by the 1960s, while in Britain the death rate from cirrhosis dropped from 10 in 1914 to 5 in 1920 and then gradually declined to a low of 2 in the 1940s before rising by a mere point by 1963. Other indicators of alcohol consumption and misuse dropped by similar magnitudes, even though the United Kingdom never enacted prohibition. Instead wartime Britain restricted

the amount of alcohol available, taxed it, and drastically reduced the hours of sale. At war's end the government dropped restrictions on quantity but made taxes even higher and set hours of sale at only half the pre-war norm.

* * *

Britain thus not only reduced the negative consequences of alcohol consumption more effectively than did the United States, but did so in a manner that raised substantial government revenues. The British experience—as well as Australia's and most of continental Europe's—strongly suggests not only that our Prohibition was unsuccessful but that more effective post-Repeal controls might have prevented the return to high consumption levels.

But no matter how powerful the analogies between alcohol prohibition and contemporary drug prohibition, most Americans still balk at drawing the parallels. Alcohol, they insist, is fundamentally different from everything else. They are right, of course, insofar as their claims rest not on health or scientific grounds but are limited to political and cultural arguments. By most measures, alcohol is more dangerous to human health than any of the drugs now prohibited by law. No drug is as associated with violence in American culture—and even in illicit-drug-using subcultures—as is alcohol. One would be hard pressed to argue that its role in many Native American and other aboriginal communities has been any less destructive than that of illicit drugs in America's ghettos.

The dangers of all drugs vary greatly, of course, depending not just on their pharmacological properties and how they are consumed but also on the attitudes and beliefs of their users and the settings in which they use them. Alcohol by and large plays a benign role in Jewish and Asian-American cultures but a devastating one in some Native American societies, and by the same token the impact of cocaine among Yuppies during the early 1980s was relatively benign compared with its impact a few years later in impoverished ghettos.

* * *

The culture helps determine the setting of drug use, but so do the laws. Prohibitions enhance the dangers not just of drugs but of the settings in which they are used. The relationship between prohibition and dangerous adulterations is clear. So too is its impact on the potency and forms of drugs. For instance, Prohibition caused a striking drop in the production and sale of beer, while that of hard liquor increased as bootleggers from Al Capone on down sought to maximize their profits and minimize the risks of detection. Similarly, following the Second World War, the enactment of anti-opium laws in many parts of Asia in which opium use was traditional—India, Hong Kong, Thailand, Laos, Iran—effectively suppressed the availability of opium at the cost of stimulating the creation of domestic heroin industries and substantial increases in heroin use. The same transition had occurred in the United States following Congress's ban on opium imports in 1909. And when during the 1980s the U.S. government's domestic drug-enforcement efforts significantly reduced the availability and raised the price of marijuana, they provided decisive incentives to producers, distributors, and consumers to switch to cocaine. In each case, prohibition forced switches from drugs that were bulky and relatively be-

nign to drugs that were more compact, more lucrative, more potent, and more dangerous.

In the 1980s the retail purity of heroin and cocaine increased, and highly potent crack became cheaply available in American cities. At the same time, the average potency of most legal psychoactive substances declined: Americans began switching from hard liquor to beer and wine, from high-tar-and-nicotine to lower-tar-and-nicotine cigarettes, and even from caffeinated to decaffeinated coffee and soda. The relationship between prohibition and drug potency was, if not indisputable, still readily apparent.

In turn-of-the-century America, opium, morphine, heroin, cocaine, and marijuana were subject to few restrictions. Popular tonics such as Vin Mariani and Coca-Cola and its competitors were laced with cocaine, and hundreds of medicines —Mrs. Winslow's Soothing Syrup may have been the most famous—contained psychoactive drugs. Millions, perhaps tens of millions of Americans, took opiates and cocaine. David Courtwright estimates that during the 1890s as many as one-third of a million Americans were opiate addicts, but most of them were ordinary people who would today be described as occasional users.

Careful analysis of that era—when the very drugs that we most fear were widely and cheaply available throughout the country—provides a telling antidote to our nightmare legalization scenarios. For one thing, despite the virtual absence of any controls on availability, the proportion of Americans addicted to opiates was only two or three times greater than today. For another, the typical addict was not a young black ghetto resident but a middle-aged white Southern woman or a West Coast Chinese immigrant. The violence, death, disease, and crime that we today associate with drug use barely existed, and many medical authorities regarded opiate addiction as far less destructive than alcoholism (some doctors even prescribed the former as treatment for the latter). Many opiate addicts, perhaps most, managed to lead relatively normal lives and kept their addictions secret even from close friends and relatives. That they were able to do so was largely a function of the legal status of their drug use.

But even more reassuring is the fact that the major causes of opiate addiction then simply do not exist now. Late-nineteenth-century Americans became addicts principally at the hands of physicians who lacked modern medicines and were unaware of the addictive potential of the drugs they prescribed. Doctors in the 1860s and 1870s saw morphine injections as a virtual panacea, and many Americans turned to opiates to alleviate their aches and pains without going through doctors at all. But as medicine advanced, the levels of both doctor- and self-induced addiction declined markedly.

In 1906 the first Federal Pure Food and Drug Act required over-the-counter drug producers to disclose whether their products contained any opiates, cocaine, cannabis, alcohol, or other psychoactive ingredients. Sales of patent medicines containing opiates and cocaine decreased significantly thereafter—in good part because fewer Americans were interested in purchasing products that they now knew to contain those drugs.

Consider the lesson here. Ethical debates aside, the principal objection to all drug legalization proposals is that they invite higher levels of drug use and misuse by making drugs not just legal but more available and less expensive. Yet the late-nineteenth-century experience suggests the opposite: that in a legal market most consumers will prefer lower-potency coca and opiate products to the far more powerful concoctions that have virtually monopolized the market under prohibition. This reminds us that opiate addiction per se was not necessarily a serious problem so long as addicts had ready access to modestly priced opiates of reliable quality—indeed, that the opiate addicts of late-nineteenth-century America differed in no significant respects from the cigarette-addicted consumers of today. And it reassures us that the principal cause of addiction to opiates was not the desire to get high but rather ignorance —ignorance of their addictive qualities, ignorance of the alternative analgesics, and ignorance of what exactly patent medicines contained. The antidote to addiction in late-nineteenth-century America, the historical record shows, consisted primarily of education and regulation— not prohibition, drug wars, and jail.

Why, then, was drug prohibition instituted? And why did it quickly evolve into a fierce and highly punitive set of policies rather than follow the more modest and humane path pursued by the British? In part, the passage of the federal Harrison Narcotic Act, in 1914, and of state and local bans before and after that, reflected a belated response to the recognition that people could easily become addicted to opiates and cocaine. But it also was closely intertwined with the increasingly vigorous efforts of doctors and pharmacists to professionalize their disciplines and to monopolize the public's access to medicinal drugs. Most of all, though, the institution of drug prohibition reflected the changing nature of the opiate- and cocaine-using population. By

1914 the number of middle-class Americans blithely consuming narcotics had fallen sharply. At the same time, however, opiate and cocaine use had become increasingly popular among the lower classes and racial minorities. The total number of consumers did not approach that of earlier decades, but where popular opinion had once shied from the notion of criminalizing the habits of elderly white women, few such inhibitions impeded it where urban gamblers, prostitutes, and delinquents were concerned.

The first anti-opium laws were passed in California in the 1870s and directed at the Chinese immigrants and their opium dens, in which, it was feared, young white women were being seduced. A generation later reports of rising cocaine use among young black men in the South—who were said to rape white women while under the influence —prompted similar legislation. During the 1930s marijuana prohibitions were directed in good part at Mexican and Chicano workers who had lost their jobs in the Depression. And fifty years later draconian penalties were imposed for the possession of tiny amounts of crack cocaine—a drug associated principally with young Latinos and African-Americans.

But more than racist fears was at work during the early years of drug prohibition. In the aftermath of World War I, many Americans, stunned by the triumph of Bolshevism in Russia and fearful of domestic subversion, turned their backs on the liberalizing reforms of the preceding era. In such an atmosphere the very notion of tolerating drug use or maintaining addicts in the clinics that had arisen after 1914 struck most citizens as both immoral and unpatriotic. In 1919 the mayor of New York created the Committee on Public Safety to investigate two ostensibly related problems: revolutionary bombings and heroin use among youth. And in Washington that same year, the Supreme Court effectively foreclosed any possibility of a more humane policy toward drug addicts when it held, in *Webb et al.* v. *U.S.*, that doctors could not legally prescribe maintenance supplies of narcotics to addicts.

*   *   *

But perhaps most important, the imposition of drug prohibition cannot be understood without recalling that it occurred almost simultaneously with the advent of alcohol prohibition. Contemporary Americans tend to regard Prohibition as a strange quirk in American history—and drug prohibition as entirely natural and beneficial. Yet the prohibition against alcohol, like that against other drugs, was motivated in no small part by its association with feared and despised ethnic minorities, especially the masses of Eastern and Southern European immigrants.

Why was Prohibition repealed after just thirteen years while drug prohibition has lasted for more than seventy-five? Look at whom each disadvantaged. Alcohol prohibition struck directly at tens of millions of Americans of all ages, including many of society's most powerful members. Drug prohibition threatened far fewer Americans, and they had relatively little influence in the halls of power. Only the prohibition of marijuana, which some sixty million Americans have violated since 1965, has come close to approximating the Prohibition experience, but marijuana smokers consist mostly of young and relatively powerless Americans. In the final analysis alcohol prohibition was repealed, and opiate, cocaine, and marijuana prohibition retained, not because scientists had concluded that alcohol was the least dangerous of the various psychoactive drugs but because of the prejudices and preferences of most Americans.

There was, of course, one other important reason why Prohibition was repealed when it was. With the country four years into the Depression, Prohibition increasingly appeared not just foolish but costly. Fewer and fewer Americans were keen on paying the rising costs of enforcing its laws, and more and more recalled the substantial tax revenues that the legal alcohol business had generated. The potential analogy to the current recession is unfortunate but apt. During the late 1980s the cost of building and maintaining prisons emerged as the fastest-growing item in many state budgets, while other costs of the war on drugs also rose dramatically. One cannot help wondering how much longer Americans will be eager to foot the bills for all this.

Throughout history the legal and moral status of psychoactive drugs has kept changing. During the seventeenth century the sale and consumption of tobacco were punished by as much as death in much of Europe, Russia, China, and Japan. For centuries many of the same Muslim domains that forbade the sale and consumption of alcohol simultaneously tolerated and even regulated the sale of opium and cannabis.

Drug-related moralities have always been malleable, and their evolution can in no way be described as moral progress. Just as our moral perceptions of particular drugs have changed in the past, so will they in the future, and people will continue to circumvent the legal and moral barriers that remain. My confidence in this prediction stems

from one other lesson of civilized human history. From the dawn of time humans have nearly universally shown a desire to alter their states of consciousness with psychoactive substances, and it is this fact that gives the lie to the declared objective of creating a "drug-free society" in the United States.

Another thing common to all societies, as the social theorist Thomas Szasz argued some years ago, is that they require scapegoats to embody their fears and take blame for whatever ails them. Today the role of bogeyman is applied to drug producers, dealers, and users. Just as anti-Communist propagandists once feared Moscow far beyond its actual influence and appeal, so today anti-drug proselytizers indict marijuana, cocaine, heroin, and assorted hallucinogens far beyond their actual psychoactive effects and psychological appeal. Never mind that the vast majority of Americans have expressed—in one public-opinion poll after another—little interest in trying these substances, even if they were legal, and never mind that most of those who have tried them have suffered few, if any, ill effects. The evidence of history and of science is drowned out by today's bogeymen. No rhetoric is too harsh, no penalty too severe.

*　*　*

Lest I be accused of exaggerating, consider the following. On June 27, 1991, the Supreme Court upheld, by a vote of five to four, a Michigan statute that imposed a mandatory sentence of life without possibility of parole for anyone convicted of possession of more than 650 grams (about 1.5 pounds) of cocaine. In other words, an activity that was entirely legal at the turn of the century, and that poses a danger to society roughly comparable to that posed by the sale of alcohol and tobacco, is today treated the same as first-degree murder.

The cumulative result of our prohibitionist war is that roughly 20 to 25 percent of the more than one million Americans now incarcerated in federal and state prisons and local jails, and almost half of those in federal penitentiaries, are serving time for having engaged in an activity that their great-grandparents could have pursued entirely legally.

Examples of less striking, but sometimes more deadly, penalties also abound. In many states anyone convicted of possession of a single marijuana joint can have his or her driver's license revoked for six months and be required to participate in a drug-treatment program. In many states anyone caught cultivating a marijuana plant may find all his or her property forfeited to the local police department. And in all but a few cities needle-exchange programs to reduce the transmission of AIDS among drug addicts have been rejected because they would "send the wrong message" —as if the more moral message is that such addicts are better off contracting the deadly virus and spreading it.

Precedents for each of these penalties scarcely exist in American history. The restoration of criminal forfeiture of property—rejected by the Founding Fathers because of its association with the evils of English rule—could not have found its way back into American law but for the popular desire to give substance to the rhetorical war on drugs.

Of course, changes in current policy that make legally available to adult Americans many of the now prohibited psychoactive substances are bound to entail a litany of administrative problems and certain other risks.

* * *

During the last years of the Volstead Act, the Rockefeller Foundation commissioned a study by the leading police scholar in the United States, Raymond Fosdick, to evaluate the various alternatives to Prohibition. Its analyses and recommendations ultimately played an important role in constructing post-Prohibition regulatory policies. A comparable study is currently under way at Princeton University, where the Smart Family Foundation has funded a working group of scholars from diverse disciplines to evaluate and recommend alternative drug-control policies. Its report will be completed late in 1993.

History holds one final lesson for those who cannot imagine any future beyond drug prohibition. Until well into the 1920s most Americans regarded Prohibition as a permanent fact of life. As late as 1930 Sen. Morris Shepard of Texas, who had coauthored the Prohibition Amendment, confidently asserted: "There is as much chance of repealing the Eighteenth Amendment as there is for a humming-bird to fly to the planet Mars with the Washington Monument tied to its tail."

History reminds us that things can and do change, that what seems inconceivable today can seem entirely normal, and even inevitable, a few years hence. So it was with Prohibition, and so it is—and will be—both with drug prohibition and the ever-changing nature of drug use in America.

NO

David T. Courtwright

SHOULD WE LEGALIZE DRUGS?

One thing that all parties in the American drug-policy debate agree on is that they want to eliminate the traffic in illicit drugs and the criminal syndicates that control it. There are two divergent strategies for achieving this end: the drug war and drug legalization, or, more precisely, controlled legalization, since few people want the government to simply abandon drug control and proclaim laissez faire.

The drug war was launched during the Reagan administration. It is actually the fourth such campaign, there having been sustained legislative and governmental efforts against drug abuse between 1909 and 1923, 1951 and 1956, and 1971 and 1973. What distinguishes the current war is that it is more concerned with stimulants like cocaine than with opiates, it is larger, and— no surprise in our age of many zeros—it is much more expensive.

The war against drugs has included the treatment of addicts and educational programs designed to discourage new users, but the emphasis has been on law enforcement, with interdiction, prosecution, imprisonment, and the seizure of assets at the heart of the campaign. The news from the front has been mixed. Price and purity levels, treatment and emergency-room admissions, urinalyses, and most other indices of drug availability showed a worsening of the problem during the 1980s, with some improvement in 1989 and 1990. The number of casual cocaine users has recently declined, but cocaine addiction remains widespread, affecting anywhere from about 650,000 to 2.4 million compulsive users, depending on whose definitions and estimates one chooses to accept. There has been some success in stopping marijuana imports—shipments of the drug are relatively bulky and thus easier to detect—but this has been offset by the increased domestic cultivation of high-quality marijuana, which has more than doubled since 1985. Heroin likewise has become both more available and more potent than it was in the late 1970s.

But cocaine has been the drug of greatest concern. Just how severe the crisis has become may be gauged by federal cocaine seizures. Fifty years ago the annual haul for the entire nation was 1 or 2 pounds, an amount that could easily be contained in the glove compartment of a car. As late as 1970 the total was under 500 pounds, which would fit in the car's trunk. In fiscal year

From David T. Courtwright, "Should We Legalize Drugs? No," *American Heritage*, vol. 44, no. 1 (February/March 1993). Copyright © 1993 by Forbes, Inc. Reprinted by permission of American Heritage, a division of Forbes, Inc.

1990 it was 235,000 pounds—about the weight of 60 mid-size cars. And this represented a fraction, no more than 10 percent, of what went into the nostrils and lungs and veins of the approximately seven million Americans who used cocaine during 1990. Worse may be in store. Worldwide production of coca surged during 1989 to a level of 225,000 metric tons, despite U.S. efforts to eradicate cultivation. Global production of opium, marijuana, and hashish has likewise increased since President Reagan formally declared war on drugs in 1986.

* * *

The greatest obstacle to the supply-reduction strategy is the enormous amount of money generated by the illicit traffic. Drug profits have been used to buy off foreign and domestic officials and to secure protection for the most vulnerable stages of the drug-cultivation, -manufacturing, and -distribution process. These profits also hire various specialists, from assassins to money launderers to lawyers, needed to cope with interlopers; they pay for technological devices ranging from cellular phones to jet planes; and they ensure that should a trafficker die or land in jail, there will be no shortage of replacements.

It is hardly surprising that these stubborn economic realities, together with the drug war's uneven and often disappointing results, have led several commentators to question the wisdom of what they call the prohibition policy. What is unprecedented is that these disenchanted critics include mayors, prominent lawyers, federal judges, nationally syndicated columnists, a congressman, a Princeton professor, and a Nobel laureate in economics. They espouse variations of

a position that is often called controlled legalization, meaning that the sale of narcotics should be permitted under conditions that restrict and limit consumption, such as no sales to minors, no advertising, and substantial taxation. They cite the numerous advantages of this approach: several billion dollars per year would be realized from tax revenues and savings on law enforcement; crime would diminish because addicts would not have to hustle to keep themselves supplied with drugs; the murders associated with big-city drug trafficking would abate as lower-cost, legal drugs drive the traffickers out of business. Because these drugs would be of known quality and potency, and because they would not have to be injected with shared needles, the risk of overdose and infection would drop. The issue of foreign complicity in the drug traffic, which has complicated American diplomatic relations with many countries, would disappear. Under a policy of controlled legalization, it would be no more criminal or controversial to import coca from Colombia than to import coffee.

The more candid of the legalization proponents concede that these advantages would be purchased at the cost of increased drug abuse. Widespread availability, lower prices, and the elimination of the criminal sanction would result in more users, some of whom would inevitably become addicts. But how many more? Herbert Kleber, a treatment specialist and former deputy director of the Office of National Drug Control Policy, has argued that there would be between twelve and fifty-five million addicted users if cocaine and heroin were legally available. While it is impossible to anticipate the exact magnitude of the increase, history does support Kleber's argument. In countries like Iran or Thailand, where narcotics have long been cheap, potent, and readily available, the prevalence of addiction has been and continues to be quite high. Large quantities of opium sold by British and American merchants created a social disaster in nineteenth-century China; that Chinese sailors and immigrants subsequently introduced opium smoking to Britain and America is a kind of ironic justice. Doctors, who constantly work with and around narcotics, have historically had a very serious addiction problem: estimates of the extent of morphine addiction among American physicians at the turn of the century ran from 6 percent to an astonishing 23 percent. In a word, exposure matters.

Kleber has also attacked the crime-reduction rationale by pointing out that addicts will generally use much more of an illicit substance if the cost is low. They would spend most of their time using drugs and little of it working, thus continuing to resort to crime to acquire money. If the total number of addicts rose sharply as availability increased, total crime would also increase. There would be less crime committed by any single addict but more crime in the aggregate.

The debate over decriminalization is, in essence, an argument about a high-stakes gamble, and so far the opponents represent the majority view. At the close of the 1980s, four out of every five Americans were against the legalization of marijuana, let alone cocaine. But if the drug war produces another decade of indifferent results, growing disillusionment could conceivably prompt experiments in controlled legalization.

* * *

The controlled-legalization argument rests on the assumption that legal sales would largely eliminate the illicit traffic and its attendant evils. The history of drug use, regulation, and taxation in the United States suggests otherwise. The very phrase *controlled legalization* implies denying certain groups access to drugs. Minors are the most obvious example. No one advocates supplying narcotics to children, so presumably selling drugs to anyone under twenty-one would remain a criminal offense, since that is the cut-off point for sales of beverage alcohol. Unfortunately, illicit drug abuse in this century has become concentrated among the young—that is, among the very ones most likely to be made exceptions to the rule of legal sales.

Until about 1900 the most common pattern of drug dependence in the United States was opium or morphine addiction, brought about by the treatment of chronic diseases and painful symptoms. Addicts were mainly female, middle-class, and middle-aged or older; Eugene O'Neill's mother, fictionalized as Mary Tyrone in *Long Day's Journey into Night*, was one. Habitual users of morphine, laudanum, and other medicinal opiates in their adolescence were extremely rare, even in big cities like Chicago.

Another pattern of drug use was nonmedical and had its roots in marginal, deviant, and criminal subcultures. The "pleasure users," as they were sometimes called, smoked opium, sniffed cocaine, injected morphine and cocaine in combination, or, after 1910, sniffed or injected heroin. Nonmedical addicts began much younger than their medical counterparts. The average age of addiction (not first use, which would have been lower still) for urban heroin addicts studied in the 1910s was only nineteen or twenty years. They were also more likely to be male than those whose addiction was of medical origin, and more likely to have been involved in crime.

Initially the pleasure users were the smaller group, but during the first two decades of this century—the same period when the police approach to national drug control was formulated—the number of older, docile medical addicts steadily diminished. There were several reasons: doctors became better educated and more conservative in their use of narcotics; the population grew healthier; patent-medicine manufacturers were forced to reveal the contents of their products; and the numerous morphine addicts who had been created in the nineteenth century began to age and die off. Drug use and addiction became increasingly concentrated among young men in their teens and twenties, a pattern that continues to this day.

In 1980, 44 percent of drug arrests nationwide were of persons under the age of twenty-one. There were more arrests among teen-agers than among the entire population over the age of twenty-five; eighteen-year-olds had the highest arrest rate of any age group. By 1987 the proportion of those arrested under twenty-one had declined to 25 percent. This was partly due to the aging of the population and to the effects of drug education on students. But when large numbers of "echo boomers" —the children of the baby boomers— become adolescents during the 1990s, the percentage of under-twenty-one drug arrests will likely increase.

So, depending on timing and demographic circumstances, at least a quarter and perhaps more than a third of all drug buyers would be underage, and there would be a great deal of money to be made by selling to them. The primary source of supply would likely be diversion—adults legally purchasing drugs and selling them to customers below the legal age. The sellers (or middlemen who collected and then resold the legal purchases) would make a profit through marking up or adulterating the drugs, and there might well be turf disputes and hence violence. Some of the dealers and their underage purchasers would be caught, prosecuted, and jailed, and the criminal-justice system would still be burdened with drug arrests. The black market would be altered and diminished, but it would scarcely disappear.

* * *

Potential for illegal sales and use extends far beyond minors. Pilots, police officers, fire fighters, drivers of buses, trains, taxis, and ambulances, surgeons, active-duty military personnel, and others whose drug use would jeopardize public safety would be denied access to at least some drugs, and those of them who did take narcotics would be liable to criminal prosecution, as would their suppliers. Pregnant women would also pose a problem. Drugs transmitted to fetuses can cause irreversible and enormously costly harm. Federal and local governments may soon be spending billions of dollars a year just to prepare the impaired children of addicts for kindergarten. Society has the right and the obligation to stop this neurological carnage, both because it cruelly handicaps innocents and because it harms everyone else through higher taxes and health-insurance premiums. Paradoxically, the arguments for controlled legalization might lead to denying alcohol and tobacco to pregnant women along with narcotics. Alcohol and tobacco can also harm fetal development, and several legalization proponents have observed that it is both inconsistent and unwise to treat them as if they were not dangerous because they are legal. If cocaine is denied to pregnant women, why not alcohol too? The point here is simply that every time one makes an exception for good and compelling reasons—every time one accents the "controlled" as opposed to the "legalization"—one creates the likelihood of continued illicit sales and use.

The supposition that this illegal market would be fueled by diversion is well founded historically. There has always been an undercurrent of diversion, especially in the late 1910s and 1920s, when black-market operators like Legs Diamond got their supplies not so much by smuggling as by purchases from legitimate drug companies. One possible solution is to require of all legal purchasers that which is required of newly enrolled methadone patients: consumption of the drug on the premises. Unfortunately, unlike methadone, heroin and cocaine are short-acting, and compulsive users must administer them every few hours or less. The dayrooms of drug-treatment clinics set up in Britain after 1968 to provide heroin maintenance were often clogged with whining addicts. Frustrated and angry, the clinic staffs largely abandoned heroin during the 1970s, switching instead to methadone, which, having the advantages of oral administration and twenty-four-hour duration, is far more suitable for clinic-based distribution. Confining the use of heroin or cocaine or other street drugs to clinics would be a logistical nightmare. But the alternative, take-home supplies, invites illegal sales to excluded groups.

Another historical pattern of black-market activity has been the smuggling of drugs to prisoners. Contraband was one of the reasons the government built specialized narcotic hospitals in Lexington, Kentucky, and Fort Worth, Texas, in the 1930s. Federal wardens wanted to get addicts out of their prisons because they were constantly conniving to obtain smuggled drugs. But when drug-related arrests multiplied after 1965 and the Lexington and Fort Worth facilities were closed, the prisons again filled with inmates eager to obtain drugs. Birch Bayh, chairing a Senate investigation of the matter in 1975, observed that in some institutions young offenders had a more plentiful supply of drugs than they did on the outside.

Since then more jails have been crammed with more prisoners, and these prisoners are more likely than ever to have had a history of drug use. In 1989, 60 to 80 percent of male arrestees in twelve large American cities tested positive for drugs. It is hard to imagine a controlled-legalization system that would permit sales to prisoners. Alcohol, although a legal drug, is not sold licitly in prisons, and for good reason, as more than 40 percent of prisoners were under its influence when they committed their crimes. If drugs are similarly denied to inmates, then the contraband problem will persist. If, moreover, we insist that our nearly three million parolees and probationers remain clean on the theory that drug use aggravates recidivism, the market for illegal sales would be so much the larger.

By now the problem should be clear. If drugs are legalized, but not for those under twenty-one, or for public-safety officers, or transport workers, or military personnel, or pregnant women, or prisoners, or probationers, or parolees, or psychotics, or any of several other special groups one could plausibly name, then just exactly who is going to buy them? Noncriminal adults, whose drug use is comparatively low to begin with? Controlled legalization entails a dilemma. To the extent that its controls are enforced, some form of black-market activity will persist. If, on the other hand, its controls are not enforced and drugs are easily diverted to those who are underage or otherwise ineligible, then it is a disguised form of wholesale legalization and as such morally, politically, and economically unacceptable.

One of the selling points of controlled legalization was also one of the decisive arguments for the repeal of Prohibition: taxation. Instead of spending billions to suppress the illicit traffic, the government would reap billions by imposing duties on legitimate imports and taxes on domestically manufactured drugs. Not only could these revenues be earmarked for drug treatment and education programs, but they would also increase the prices paid by the consumer, thus discouraging consumption, especially among adolescents.

The United States government has had extensive historical experience with the taxation of legal narcotics. In the nineteenth and early twentieth centuries, opium was imported and subject to customs duties. The imports were assigned to one of three categories. The first was crude opium, used mainly for medicinal purposes and for the domestic manufacture of morphine. Foreign-manufactured morphine, codeine, and heroin made up the second class of imports, while the third was smoking opium, most of it prepared in Hong Kong and shipped to San Francisco.

* * *

The imposts [taxes] on these imported drugs fluctuated over the years, but they were generally quite stiff. From 1866 to 1914 the average ad valorem duty [calculated according to value] on crude opium was 33 percent; for morphine or its salts, 48 percent. From 1866 to 1908 the average duty on smoking opium was an extraordinarily high 97 percent. This last was in the nature of a sin tax; congressmen identified opium smoking with Chinese coolies, gamblers, pimps, and prostitutes and wished to discourage its importation and use.

These customs duties produced revenue; they also produced widespread smuggling, much of it organized by violent criminal societies like the Chinese tongs. The smugglers were as ingenious as their latter-day Mafia counterparts. They hid their shipments in everything from hollowed-out lumber to snake cages. Avoiding the customs collectors, they saved as much as three dollars a pound on crude opium, three dollars an ounce on morphine, and twelve dollars a pound on smoking opium. Twelve dollars seems a trifling sum by modern standards, hardly worth the risk of arrest, but in the nineteenth century it was more than most workers earned in a week. Someone who smuggled in fifty pounds of smoking opium in 1895 had gained the equivalent of a year's wages. One knowledgeable authority estimated that when the duty on smoking opium was near its peak, the amount smuggled into the United States was nearly twice that legally imported and taxed. Something similar happened with eighteenth-century tobacco imports to the British Isles. More than a third of the tobacco consumed in England and Scotland circa 1750 had been clandestinely imported in order to avoid a duty of more than five pence per pound. The principle is the same for domestically produced drugs: if taxes are sufficiently onerous, an illegal supply system will spring up. Moonshining existed before and after, as well as during, Prohibition.

The obvious solution is to set taxes at a sufficiently low level to discourage smuggling and illegal manufacturing. But again there is a dilemma. The most important illicit drugs are processed agricultural products that can be grown in several parts of the world by peasant labor. They are not, in other words, intrinsically expensive. Unless they are heavily taxed, legal consumers will be able to acquire them at little cost, less than ten dollars for a gram of cocaine. If drugs are that cheap, to say nothing of being 100 percent pure, the likelihood of a postlegalization epidemic of addiction will be substantially increased. But if taxes are given a stiff boost to enhance revenues and limit consumption, black marketeers will reenter the picture in numbers proportionate to the severity of the tax.

Tax revenues, like drugs themselves, can be addictive. In the twelve years after the repeal of Prohibition, federal liquor tax revenues ballooned from 259 million to 2.3 billion dollars. The government's dependence on this money was one important reason anti-liquor forces made so little progress in their attempts to restrict alcohol consumption during World War II. Controlled drug legalization would also bring about a windfall in tax dollars, which in an era of chronic deficits would surely be welcomed and quickly spent. Should addiction rates become too high, a conflict between public health and revenue concerns would inevitably ensue.

When both proponents and opponents of controlled legalization talk about drug taxes, they generally assume a single level of taxation. The assumption is wrong. The nature of the federal system permits state and local governments to levy their own taxes on drugs in addition to the uniform federal customs and excise taxes. This means that total drug taxes, and hence the prices paid by consumers, will vary from place to place. Variation invites interstate smuggling, and if the variation is large enough, the smuggling can be extensive and involve organized crime.

The history of cigarette taxation serves to illustrate this principle. In 1960 state taxes on cigarettes were low, between zero and eight cents per pack, but after 1965 a growing number of states sharply increased cigarette taxes in response to health concerns and as a politically painless way of increasing revenue. Some states, mainly in the Northeast, were considerably more aggressive than others in raising taxes. By 1975 North Carolina purchasers were paying thirty-six cents per pack while New Yorkers paid fifty-four cents. The price was higher still in New York City because of a local levy that reached eight cents per pack (as much as the entire federal tax) at the beginning of 1976.

Thus was born an opportunity to buy cheap and sell dear. Those who bought in volume at North Carolina prices and sold at New York (or Connecticut, or Massachusetts) prices realized a substantial profit, and by the mid-1970s net revenue losses stood at well over three hundred million dollars a year. Much of this went to organized crime, which at one point was bootlegging 25 percent of the cigarettes sold in New York State and *half* of those sold in New York City. The pioneer of the illegal traffic, Anthony Granata, established a trucking company with thirty employees operating vehicles on a six-days-a-week basis. Granata's methods—concealed cargoes, dummy corporations, forged documents, fortresslike warehouses, bribery, hijacking, assault, and homicide—were strikingly similar to those used by illicit drug traffickers and Prohibition bootleggers.

* * *

Although high-tax states like Florida or Illinois still lose millions annually to cigarette bootleggers, the 1978 federal Contraband Cigarette Act and stricter law enforcement and accounting procedures have had some success in reducing over-the-road smuggling. But it is relatively easy to detect illegal shipments of cigarettes, which must be smuggled by the truckload to make a substantial amount of money. Cocaine and heroin are more compact, more profitable, and very easy to conceal. Smuggling these drugs to take advantage of state tax differentials would consequently be much more difficult to detect and deter. If, for example, taxed cocaine retailed in Vermont for ten dollars a gram and in New York for twelve dollars a gram, anyone who bought just five kilograms at Vermont prices, transported them, and sold them at New York prices would realize a profit of ten thousand dollars. Five kilograms of cocaine can be concealed in an attaché case.

* * *

Of course, if all states legalized drugs and taxed them at the same rate, this sort of illegal activity would not exist, but it is constitutionally and politically unfeasible to ensure uniform rates of state taxation. And federalism poses other challenges. Laws against drug use and trafficking have been enacted at the local, state, and federal levels. It is probable that if Congress repeals or modifies the national drug laws, some states will go along with controlled legalization while others will not. Nevada, long in the legalizing habit, might jettison its drug laws, but conservative Mormon-populated Utah might not. Alternately, governments could experiment with varying degrees of legalization. Congress might decide that anything was better than the current mayhem in the capital and legislate a broad legalization program for the District of Columbia. At the same time, Virginia and Maryland might experiment with the decriminalization of marijuana, the least risky legalization option, but retain prohibition of the nonmedical use of other drugs. The result would again be smuggling, whether from Nevada to Utah or, save for marijuana, from the District of Columbia to the surrounding states. It is hard to see how any state that chose to retain laws against drugs could possibly stanch the influx of prohibited drugs from adjacent states that did not. New York City's futile attempts to enforce its strict gun-control laws show how difficult it is to restrict locally that which is elsewhere freely available.

I referred earlier to the legalization debate as an argument about a colossal gamble, whether society should risk an unknown increase in drug abuse and addiction to eliminate the harms of drug prohibition, most of which stem from illicit trafficking. "Take the crime out of it" is the rallying cry of the legalization advocates. After reviewing the larger history of narcotic, alcohol, and tobacco use and regulation, it appears that this debate should be recast. It would be more accurate to ask whether society should risk an unknown but possibly substantial increase in drug abuse and addiction in order to bring about an unknown *reduction* in illicit trafficking and other costs of drug prohibition. Controlled legalization would take some, but by no means all, of the crime out of it. Just how much and what sort of crime would be eliminated would depend upon which groups were to be denied which drugs, the overall level of taxation, and differences in state tax and legalization policies. If the excluded groups were few *and* all states legalized all drugs *and* all governments taxed at uniformly low levels, then the black market would be largely eliminated. But these are precisely the conditions that would be most likely to bring about an unacceptably high level of drug abuse. The same variables that would determine how successful the controlled-legalization policy would be in eliminating the black market would also largely determine how unsuccessful it was in containing drug addiction.

POSTSCRIPT

Should Drugs Be Legalized?

The analogy often cited by proponents of drug legalization is the ill-fated attempt to ban the sale of liquor in the United States, which lasted from 1919 to 1933. Prohibition has been called "an experiment noble in purpose," but it was an experiment that greatly contributed to the rise of organized crime. The repeal of Prohibition brought about an increase in liquor consumption and alcoholism, but it also deprived organized crime of an important source of income. Would drug decriminalization similarly strike a blow at the drug dealers? Possibly, and such a prospect is obviously appealing. But would drug decriminalization also exacerbate some of the ills associated with drugs? Would there be more violence, more severe addiction, and more crack babies born to addicted mothers?

There are a variety of publications and theories pertaining to drug use and society. Ronald L. Akers, in *Drugs, Alcohol, and Society* (Wadsworth, 1992), relates drug patterns to social structure. For a comprehensive overview of the history, effects, and prevention of drug use, see Weldon L. Witters, Peter J. Venturelli, and Glen R. Hanson, *Drugs and Society*, 3rd ed. (Jones & Bartlett, 1992). Terry Williams describes the goings-on in a crackhouse in *Crackhouse: Notes from the End of the Zone* (Addison-Wesley, 1992). James A. Inciardi, Ruth Horowitz, and Anne El Pottieger focus on street kids and drugs in *Street Kids, Street Drugs, Street Crime: An Examination of Drug Use and Serious Delinquency in Miami* (Wadsworth, 1993). For an excellent study of how users of the drug ecstasy perceive the experience, see Jerome Beck and Marsha Rosenbaum, *Pursuit of Ecstasy: The MDMA Experience* (SUNY Press, 1994). For studies of female drug-using groups, see Carl S. Taylor, *Girls, Gangs, Women and Drugs* (Michigan State University Press, 1993) and Avril Taylor, *Women Drug Users: An Ethnography of a Female Injecting Community* (Clarendon Press, 1993). Erich Goode, in *Drugs in American Society* (McGraw-Hill, 1988), provides a sociological perspective on drugs. For a relatively balanced yet innovative set of drug policies, see Elliott Carrie, *Reckoning: Drugs, the Cities, and the American Future* (Hill & Wang, 1993). Franklin E. Zimring and Gordon Hawkins, in *The Search for Rational Drug Control* (Cambridge University Press, 1992), criticize the current antidrug crusades. William O. Walker III, ed., *Drug Control Policy* (Pennsylvania State University Press, 1992) critically evaluates drug policies from historical and comparative perspectives. The connection between drugs and crime is explored in *Drugs and Crime* edited by Michael Toney and James Q. Wilson (University of Chicago Press, 1990). A work on the legalization debate, biased toward the legalization side, is *The Drug Legalization Debate* edited by James A. Inciardi (Sage Publications, 1991).

ISSUE 18

Is Incapacitation the Answer to the Crime Problem?

YES: Morgan O. Reynolds, from "Crime Pays, But So Does Imprisonment," *Journal of Social, Political, and Economic Studies* (Fall 1990)

NO: D. Stanley Eitzen, from "Violent Crime: Myths, Facts, and Solutions," *Vital Speeches of the Day* (May 15, 1995)

ISSUE SUMMARY

YES: Professor of economics Morgan O. Reynolds argues that the decline in the cost of crime for criminals has contributed greatly to the increase in crime and that catching, convicting, and imprisoning more criminals would greatly reduce the crime rate.

NO: Professor emeritus of sociology D. Stanley Eitzen argues that the "get tough with criminals" approach to reducing crime does not work, costs too much, keeps many people who would otherwise go straight imprisoned, and does not deal with the fundamental causes of crime.

Not a day passes in America without reports of murders, rapes, or other violent crimes. As crime has increasingly captured the headlines, public indignation has intensified—particularly when spectacular cases have been brought to light about paroled convicts committing new felonies, light sentences being handed down for serious crimes, and cases being thrown out of court on legal technicalities. The perception that Michael Dukakis was soft on criminals seriously hurt his bid for the presidency in 1988. (As governor of Massachusetts, Dukakis approved a prison furlough program that released a convict named Willie Horton, who subsequently went on to commit a widely publicized violent crime in another state.) Over the past three decades, there has been a dramatic increase in the number of Americans who think that the authorities should be tougher on criminals. For example, while a majority of Americans in the 1960s favored the abolition of the death penalty, today more than 70 percent favor its use for certain crimes.

Even in the intellectual community there has been a turnaround. When the southern Democrat and presidential candidate George Wallace and other politicians raised the issue of "law and order" at the end of the 1960s, the term was called "a code word for racism" in academic and literary circles. This is understandable because Wallace *had* previously identified himself with white racism. The attitude toward crime that was popular in academic circles during the 1960s might be briefly summarized under two headings: the prevention of crime and the treatment of criminals.

To prevent crime, some academics argued, government must do more than rely upon police, courts, and jails. It must do something about the underlying social roots of crime, especially poverty and racism. It was assumed that, once these roots were severed, crime would begin to fade away or at least cease to be a major social problem.

The prescription for treating criminals followed much the same logic. The word *punishment* was avoided in favor of *treatment* or *rehabilitation*, for the purpose was not to inflict pain or to "pay back" the criminal but to bring about a change in his behavior. If that could be done by lenient treatment— short prison terms, education, counseling, and, above all, understanding— then so much the better.

By the late 1970s the intellectual community itself showed signs that it was reassessing its outlook toward crime. Criminologist and political scientist James Q. Wilson's views on crime became widely respected in universities and in the mass media. He argued that society's attempts to change social conditions had met with little success and that locking up criminals remained the best way to deal with the crime problem in the short term. Wilson's view is carried forward by Morgan O. Reynolds, who, after examining data collected on crimes and time in prison, has found that "crime pays" because most crimes do not result in significant jail time for the criminal. According to Reynolds, the way to reverse the increasing crime rate is to increase deterrence to at least the level of the 1950s, and this requires more prisons. Because the main objection is the high costs of imprisoning criminals, he discusses a number of ways to reduce these costs.

D. Stanley Eitzen argues that America already puts too many people in prison at too high a cost. The answer, he claims, is not cost reduction policies such as those that Reynolds recommends but to change the social conditions that are known to contribute greatly to violent crimes. We must break the cycle of poverty, strengthen the family, improve employment opportunities, and improve education for poor children. These are long-term solutions that even he admits are difficult to achieve. In the short run Eitzen recommends imprisoning the predatory sociopaths but otherwise imprisoning fewer criminals, enforcing stringent gun control laws and keeping guns away from juveniles, making laws more fair, rehabilitating criminals, and legalizing drugs.

YES

Morgan O. Reynolds

CRIME PAYS, BUT SO DOES IMPRISONMENT

America is burdened by an appalling amount of crime. Even though the crime rate is not soaring as it did during the 1960s and 1970s, we still have more crimes per capita than any other developed country.

- Every year nearly 6 million people are victims of violent crimes—murder, rape, robbery or assault.
- Another 29 million Americans each year are victims of property crimes—arson, burglary and larceny-theft.
- There is a murder every 25 minutes, a rape every six minutes, a robbery every minute and an aggravated assault every 35 seconds.
- There is a motor vehicle theft every 22 seconds, a burglary every ten seconds, and a larceny-theft every four seconds.

Although the number of crimes reported to the police each year has leveled off somewhat in the 1980s, our crime rate today is still enormously high—411 percent higher, for example, than it was in 1960.

Why is there so much crime?

THE EXPECTED PUNISHMENT FOR COMMITTING A CRIME

The economic theory of crime is a relatively new field of social science. According to this theory, most crimes are not irrational acts. Instead, crimes are freely committed by people who compare the expected benefits of crime with the expected costs. The reason we have so much crime is that, for many people, the benefits outweigh the costs. For some people, a criminal career is more attractive than their other career options. Put another way, the reason we have so much crime is that crime pays.

Because criminals and potential criminals rarely have accurate information about the probabilities of arrest, conviction and imprisonment, a great deal of uncertainty is involved in the personal assessment of the expected punishment from committing crimes. Individuals differ in skill and intellect. The more skillful and more intelligent criminals have better odds of commit-

From Morgan O. Reynolds, "Crime Pays, But So Does Imprisonment," *Journal of Social, Political, and Economic Studies* (Fall 1990). Copyright © 1990 by The Council for Social and Economic Studies, P.O. Box 35070, NW Washington, DC 20043. Reprinted by permission. Notes omitted.

ting successful crimes. Some people overestimate their probability of success, while others underestimate theirs.

Despite the element of subjectivity, the economic theory of crime makes one clear prediction: Crime will increase if the expected cost of crime to criminals declines. This is true for "crimes of passion" as well as economic crimes such as burglary or auto theft. The less costly crime becomes, the more often people fail to control their passions.

The economic theory of crime is consistent with public opinion, and with the perceptions of potential criminals. It is supported by considerable statistical research. According to the theory, the amount of crime is inversely related to expected punishment. What follows is a brief summary of the punishment criminals can expect.

EXPECTED TIME IN PRISON

What is the expected punishment for committing major types of serious crime in the United States today?... [T]he expected punishment is shockingly low.

- Even for committing the most serious crime—murder—an individual can expect to spend only 2.3 years in prison.
- On the average, an individual who commits an act of burglary can expect to spend only 7.1 days in prison.
- Someone considering an auto theft can expect to spend only 6.3 days in prison.

THE DECLINE IN EXPECTED IMPRISONMENT AND THE RISE IN CRIME

... On the average, those crimes with the longest expected prison terms (murder, rape, robbery and assault) are the crimes

Figure 1

Crime and Punishment

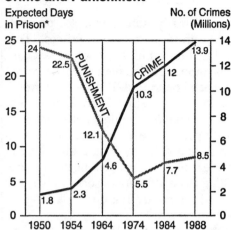

*Median prison sentence for all serious crimes, weighted by probabilities of arrest, prosecution, conviction, and imprisonment.

least frequently committed, comprising only about 10 percent of all serious crime. The remaining 90 percent carry an expected prison term of only a few days. When expected punishment is weighted by the frequency of types of crimes, the picture is even more shocking: On the average, a perpetrator of a serious crime in the United States can expect to spend about eight days in prison.... [T]his overall expectation has changed over time.

- Since the early 1950s, the expected punishment for committing a serious crime in the United States (measured in terms of expected time in prison) has been reduced by two-thirds.

- Over the same period, the total number of serious crimes committed has increased sevenfold.

THE "PRICES" WE CHARGE FOR CRIME

It is virtually impossible to prevent people from committing crimes. The most that the criminal justice system can do is impose punishment after the crime has been committed. People are largely free to commit almost any crime they choose. What the criminal justice system does is construct a list of prices (expected punishments) for various criminal acts. People commit crimes so long as they are willing to pay the prices society charges, just as many of us might risk parking or speeding tickets.

Viewed in this way, the expected prison sentences... are the prices we charge for various crimes. Thus, the price of murder is about 2.3 years in prison; the price of burglary is 7.7 days; the price for stealing a car is 4.2 days. Since these prices are so low, it is small wonder so many people are willing to pay them.

CALCULATING THE EXPECTED PUNISHMENT FOR CRIME

Five adverse events must occur before a criminal actually ends up in prison. The criminal must be arrested, indicted, prosecuted, convicted and sent to prison. As a result, the expected punishment for crime depends upon a number of probabilities: The probability of being arrested, given that a crime is committed; the probability of being prosecuted, given an arrest; the probability of conviction, given prosecution; and the probability of being sent to prison, given a conviction. As Table 1 shows, the overall probability of being punished is the result of multiplying four probabilities.

Even if each of the separate probabilities is reasonably high, their product can be quite low. For example, suppose that each of these probabilities were 0.5. That is, one-half of crimes result in an arrest, one-half of arrests lead to prosecution, one-half of prosecutions lead to a conviction, and one-half of convictions lead to a prison term. In this case, the overall probability that a criminal will spend time in prison is only 6.25 percent.

Table 1 also depicts recent probabilities in the case of burglary. Note that burglars who are sent to prison stay there for about 17 months, on the average.... But someone considering an act of burglary will surely be influenced by the fact that the probability of being arrested is only 14 percent. Although the probabilities of prosecution and conviction following an arrest are high, the criminal's probability of going to prison is less than one in three after being convicted. When all factors are taken into account (including the probability that the crime will never be reported), the overall probability that a burglar will end up in prison is less than one percent. The expected punishment prior to committing the crime is only 7.1 days.

PROBABILITY OF ARREST

... The striking fact... is the degree to which arrest rates have declined over the past 40 years, even for the most serious crimes. For example:

- Since 1950, the probability of being arrested after committing a murder has fallen by 25 percent.
- The probability of arrest for rapists has fallen 35 percent, for robbers 42 percent and for burglars 53 percent.

On the average, during the 1980s, only about 21 percent of all crimes in the United States were cleared by arrest.

Table 1

Calculating the Expected Punishment for Potential Criminals

Expected Time in Prison	=	Probability of arrest	×	Probability of prosecution, given arrest
	×	Probability of conviction, given prosecution	×	Probability of imprisonment, given conviction
	×	median sentence		

Example: Expected punishment for burglary

Expected Time in Prison	=	14% (Probability of arrest)	×	88% (Probability of prosecution, given arrest)
	×	81% (Probability of conviction, given prosecution)	×	28% (Probability of imprisonment, given conviction)
	×	1/2 (Adjustment for unreported crimes)*	×	17 months (median sentence)
	=	7.1 days		

* Approximately one-half of all burglaries are not reported to the police. Law enforcement agencies "clear" (or solve) an offense when at least one person is arrested, charged with the offense, and turned over for prosecution.

In Japan, by contrast, the clearance-by-arrest rate is 50 percent. Moreover, Japan with a population of 122 million has fewer murders each year than New York City with a population of seven million.

PROBABILITY OF PROSECUTION, CONVICTION AND IMPRISONMENT

Although there are 13 million arrests each year in the United States, including 2.8 million for serious (Index) crimes, annual admissions to prison only topped 200,000 in 1986. In other words, only eight of every 100 arrests for Index crimes results in imprisonment after defense attorneys, prosecutors and courts complete their work.

OVERALL PROBABILITY OF GOING TO PRISON

A criminal's overall probability of imprisonment has fallen dramatically since 1950 . . . :

- Since 1950, the percent of crimes resulting in a prison sentence has declined by at least 60 percent for every major category of crime.

- This includes a 60 percent drop for murder, a 79 percent decrease for rape, an 83 percent reduction for robbery and a 94 percent plunge for auto theft.

UNREPORTED CRIMES

Based on the number of crimes reported to the police, 1.66 percent of all serious crimes are punished by imprisonment; therefore 98.34 percent of serious crimes are not. According to the National Crime Survey, however, only 37 percent of serious crimes are actually reported. If there are two unreported crimes for every one reported, then the overall probability of going to prison for the commission of a serious crime falls to about 0.61 percent (.37 × 1.66%). This amounts to one prison term for every 164 felonies committed.

A POSSIBLE EXPLANATION: THE ROLE OF THE WARREN COURT

The main factor in the decline in expected punishment over the last three decades was a virtual collapse in the probability of imprisonment. Why? We cannot point to a shrinkage in law enforcement personnel as an explanation.... [T]he number of full-time police employees has risen steadily over the past three decades. Further, total employment in the criminal justice sector increased from 600,000 in 1965 to nearly 1.5 million in 1986. Government spending on the criminal justice sector doubled as a share of GNP, rising from less than 0.6 percent to nearly 1.2 percent. During the same period, private employment in detective and protection services grew rapidly, reaching half a million persons by the end of 1989. Apparently, more people now produce less justice.

The 1960s was a turbulent decade—the Vietnam War, the counterculture, urban riots. But one policy change that lasted well into the 1970s and 1980s was the change in the criminal justice system caused by the Supreme Court. Influenced by sociologists and other intellectuals, there was a growing reluctance to apprehend and punish criminals during the 1960s. In particular, 1961 brought the first landmark decision of the U.S. Supreme Court expanding the rights of criminal defendants and making it more costly for police and prosecutors to obtain criminal convictions.

Mapp v. Ohio (1961) declared that illegally obtained evidence could not be admitted in any state criminal prosecution, imposing the so-called "exclusionary rule" on all state judicial systems. A series of related decisions followed: *Gideon v. Wainwright* (1963) required taxpayer-funded counsel for defendants; *Escobedo v. Illinois* (1964) and *Malloy v. Hogan* (1964) expanded privileges against self-incrimination, thereby impeding interrogation by the police; and *Miranda v. Arizona* (1966) went further and made confessions, even if voluntary, inadmissible as evidence unless the suspect had been advised of certain rights.

The enforcement system was transformed by these decisions. Under the exclusionary rule, according to Justice Cardozo, "The criminal is to go free because the constable has blundered." Justice White, dissenting in the *Miranda* case, warned that the decision would have "a corrosive effect on the criminal laws as an effective device to prevent crime." It appears that the "pursuit of perfect justice," as Judge Macklin put it, changed the rules and increased the time and effort required to apprehend, convict and punish the guilty....

THE COST OF CRIME DETERRENCE

If America is to succeed in lowering the crime rate to, say, the level that prevailed in the 1950s, we must create at least as much crime deterrence as existed in the 1950s. For example, [there are] three ways of raising the expected prison sentence for burglary to its 1950 level. Since the probabilities of prosecution and conviction, given an arrest, are already high, the options are:

- Increase the proportion of burglaries cleared by arrest from 14 to 42 percent; or
- Increase the percent of convicted burglars sent to prison from 28 to 84 percent; or
- Increase the median prison sentence for burglars from 17 to 51 months.

All three alternatives are expensive. A higher arrest rate requires that more money be spent on criminal investigation. A higher sentencing rate requires more court and litigation costs. All three alternatives require more prison space. Unless prison space can be expanded, little else in the way of deterrence will be of much value.

America is in the midst of the biggest prison building boom in its history. On December 30, 1989, prisons held 673,565 convicts, up from 438,830 prisoners at the beginning of 1984 and at 110 percent of design capacity. In 1988 the system added 42,967 inmates, or enough to fill 86 new 500-bed prisons.

- Today, one out of every 364 Americans is in prison—not jail, probation or parole but in prison.
- With an additional 296,000 in local jails, 362,000 on parole and 2.4 million on probation, one out of every 69

Americans is under the supervision of the corrections establishment, or one of every 52 adults.

At an annual cost exceeding $20,000 per prisoner, the total prison tab is more than $15 billion a year. That cost will surely rise. Thirty-five states are under court orders to relieve prison overcrowding and others face litigation. To increase capacity, more than 100 new state and federal prisons currently are under construction around the country. California alone is spending $3.5 billion on new prison beds and has added 21,000 beds since 1984. State governments spent some $9 billion in 1989 on new prisons. In most cases, the construction cost per prison bed exceeds $50,000.

HOW TO REDUCE PRISON COSTS

Much could be done to reduce the high costs of constructing and operating prisons. The most promising ways to reduce taxpayer costs exploit private sector competition and efficiency in constructing and operating prisons and employing prisoners. Contracting out construction and remodeling is a proven economizer. Short of full privatization, government-operated correctional facilities should be corporatized and required to operate like private businesses, with profit and loss statements. Even within the existing system, economies are possible. What follows is a brief summary of ways to economize.

OPPORTUNITIES FOR REDUCING COSTS WITHIN THE PUBLIC SECTOR

Better Management Practices. Although entrepreneurship in the public sector is rare, opportunities for innovation in prison construction abound. For example:

- Florida expanded an existing facility by 336 beds for only $16,000 per cell.
- South Carolina used inmate labor to reduce construction costs by an estimated 50 percent with no quality loss and some delay.
- New York City has begun using renovated troop barges and a ferry boat for detention facilities.

Early Release of Elderly Prisoners. Although the recidivism rate is about 22 percent for prisoners age 18 to 24, among prisoners over 45 years old the recidivism rate is only 2.1 percent. Nationwide, there are at least 20,000 inmates over the age of 55. Moreover, the average maintenance cost of an elderly prisoner is about $69,000—three times the cost of a younger prisoner. Early release of elderly prisoners to make room for younger criminals makes sense and would improve crime deterrence.

Boot Camp Therapy for Young Prisoners. Called "shock incarceration" by federal drug Czar William Bennett, boot camp therapy as an alternative to prison for youngsters (not yet hardened criminals) is being used in Georgia, Alabama, Florida, Louisiana, Mississippi, New York, Oklahoma, South Carolina and Texas. Costs are lower, although the recidivism rate is about the same as for the prison system as a whole.

Electronic Ankle Bracelets. The cost of punishment would be greatly reduced if ways were found of punishing criminals without imprisonment. Few people would deny that imprisonment is necessary and desirable for violent crimes such as homicide, rape, robbery and assault. But less than half of U.S. prisoners have been incarcerated for such crimes. A mid-1980s survey found that:

- One-third of the prisoners were imprisoned for property offenses and another 20 percent for crimes against public order (including drug offenses).
- In Arkansas, nonviolent offenders outnumbered violent ones by a ratio of three to one.
- In Mississippi, Kentucky, Missouri and Wyoming the ratio was two to one.

A recent alternative to imprisonment is the electronic monitoring device that is worn by parolees. Judges can impose conditions of parole, including restrictions on the range and timing of activities, and they can be enforced by monitoring companies....

PRODUCTIVE WORK
FOR PRISONERS

A recent survey commissioned by the National Institute of Justice identified more than 70 companies which employ inmates in 16 states in manufacturing, service and light assembly operations. Prisoners work as reservations clerks for TWA and Best Western, sew leisure wear, manufacture water-bed mattresses, and assemble electronic components. PRIDE, a state-sponsored private corporation that runs Florida's 46 prison industries from furniture-making to optical glass grinding, made a $4 million profit in 1987. This work benefits nearly everyone. It enables prisoners to earn wages, acquire skills, and subtly learn individual responsibility and the value of productive labor. It also insures that they can contribute to victim compensation, and to their own and their families' support....

THE COST OF NOT BUILDING PRISONS

Although the cost of building and maintaining prisons is high, the cost of not creating more prisons appears to be much higher. A study by the National Institute of Justice concluded that the "typical" offender let loose in society will engage in a one-man crime wave, creating damage to society more than 17 times as costly than imprisonment. Specifically:

- Sending someone to prison for one year costs the government about $25,000.

- A Rand Corporation survey of 2190 professional criminals found that the average criminal committed 187 to 287 crimes a year, at an average cost per crime of $2,300.

- On the average, then, a professional criminal out of prison costs society $430,000 per year, or $405,000 more than the cost of a year in prison.

The failure to keep offenders in prison once they are there is also a hazard of too little prison space, and early release often leads to much more crime. A Rand Corporation survey of former inmates found that:

- In California, 76 percent were arrested within three years of their release and 60 percent were convicted of new crimes.

- In Texas, 60 percent of former inmates were arrested within three years and 40 percent were reconvicted.

- A survey of 11 states showed that 62.5 percent of all released prisoners were arrested within 3 years, 46.8 percent were reconvicted and 41.1 percent were reincarcerated.

In California, a comparison between ex-convicts and criminals who received probation rather than a prison sentence showed a disheartening rate of failure for both. Each ex-convict committed an estimated 20 crimes. Each probationer committed 25 crimes.

A Bureau of Justice Statistics study of 22 states found that 69 percent of young adults (ages 17 to 22) released from prison in 1978 were arrested within six years—each committing an average of 13 new crimes.

CONCLUSION

While crime continues on the high plateau, there are grounds for optimism. The number of young males began to decline in the 1980s and will continue to do so through the 1990s. Further, the odds of imprisonment for a serious offense increased in the 1980s as legislators responded to the public's "get tough" attitude. Yet we remained plagued with crime rates (per capita) triple those of the 1950s.

What can be done to build on this relatively promising recent trend? At a minimum the analysis in this report suggests three things. First, the U.S. Supreme Court should continue to reestablish the rule of law by restricting application of the exclusionary rule and other expansions of criminal privileges inherited from the Warren Court. Second, the public sector must continue raising the odds of imprisonment toward those of the 1950s in order to improve personal security. Deterrence of criminals implies building prisons and reducing prison costs by privatization. Third, the laws hampering productive employment of prisoners must be relaxed to take full advantage of the benefits of privatization.

ACKNOWLEDGMENT

My thanks to Dr. John Goodman, President, National Center for Policy Analysis, Dallas, Texas, for his help on this paper and his permission to reprint material from NCPA Report No. 149. Author.

NO

D. Stanley Eitzen

VIOLENT CRIME: MYTHS, FACTS, AND SOLUTIONS

My remarks are limited to violent street crimes (assault, robbery, rape, and murder). We should not forget that there are other types of violent crimes that are just as violent and actually greater in magnitude than street crimes: corporate, political, organized, and white collar. But that is another subject for another time. Our attention this morning is on violent street crime, which has made our cities unsafe and our citizens extremely fearful. What are the facts about violent crime and violent criminals and what do we, as a society, do about them?

I am going to critique the prevailing thought about violent crime and its control because our perceptions about violent crime and much of what our government officials do about it is wrong. My discipline—sociology—knows a lot about crime but what we know does not seem to affect public perceptions and public policies. Not all of the answers, however, are always crystal clear. There are disagreements among reasonable and thoughtful people, coming from different theoretical and ideological perspectives. You may, difficult as it seems to me, actually disagree with my analysis. That's all right. The key is for us to address this serious problem, determine the facts, engage in dialogue, and then work toward logical and just solutions.

What do criminologists know about violent crime? Much of what we know is counter intuitive; it flies in the face of the public's understanding. So, let me begin with some demythologizing.

Myth 1: As a Christian nation with high moral principles, we rank relatively low in the amount of violent crime.   Compared with the other industrialized nations of the world, we rank number one in belief in God, "the importance of God in our lives," and church attendance. We also rank first in murder rates, robbery rates, and rape rates. Take homicide, for example: the U.S. rate of 10 per 100,000 is three times that of Finland, five times that of Canada, and nine times greater than found in Norway, the Netherlands, Germany, and Great Britain. In 1992, for example, Chicago, a city about one-fifth the population of the Netherlands had nine times more gun-related deaths than occurred in the Netherlands.

Myth 2: We are in the midst of a crime wave. When it comes to crime rates we are misled by our politicians, and the media. Government data indicate that between 1960 and 1970 crime rates doubled, then continued to climb through the 1970s. From 1970 to 1990 the rates remained about the same. The problem is with violent crime by youth, which has increased dramatically. Despite the rise in violent crime among youth, however, the *overall* violent crime rate actually has decreased in the 1990s.

Our perceptions are affected especially by the media. While crime rates have leveled and slightly declined during the 1990s, the media have given us a different picture. In 1993, for example, the three major networks doubled their crime stories and tripled their coverage of murders. This distortion of reality results, of course, in a general perception that we are in the midst of a crime wave.

Myth 3: Serious violent crime is found throughout the age structure. Crime is mainly a problem of male youths. Violent criminal behaviors peak at age 17 and by age 24 it is one-half the rate. Young males have always posed a special crime problem. There are some differences now, however. Most significant, young males and the gangs to which they often belong now have much greater firepower. Alienated and angry youth once used clubs, knives, brass knuckles, and fists but now they use Uzis, AK47s, and "streetsweepers." The result is that since 1985, the murder rate for 18–24 year-olds has risen 65 percent while the rate for 14–17 year-olds has increased 165 percent.

The frightening demographic fact is that between now and the year 2005, the number of teenagers in the U.S. will grow by 23 percent. During the next ten years, black teenagers will increase by 28 percent and the Hispanic teenage population will grow by about 50 percent. The obvious prediction is that violent crime will increase dramatically over this period.

Myth 4: The most dangerous place in America is in the streets where strangers threaten, hit, stab, or shoot each other. The streets in our urban places are dangerous, as rival gangs fight, and drive-by shootings occur. But, statistically, the most dangerous place is in your own home, or when you are with a boyfriend or girlfriend, family member, or acquaintance.

Myth 5: Violent criminals are born with certain predispositions toward violence. Criminals are not born with a criminal gene. If crime were just a function of biology, then we would expect crime rates to be more or less the same for all social categories, times, and places. In fact, violent crime rates vary considerably by social class, race, unemployment, poverty, geographical place, and other social variables. Research on these variables is the special contribution of sociology to the understanding of criminal behavior.

Let's elaborate on these social variables because these have so much to do with solutions. Here is what we know about these social variables:

1. The more people in poverty, the higher the rate of street crime.

2. The higher the unemployment rate in an area, the higher the crime rate. Sociologist William J. Wilson says that black and white youths at age 11 are equally likely to commit violent crimes

but by their late 20s, blacks are four times more likely to be violent offenders. However, when blacks and whites in their late 20s are employed, they differ hardly at all in violent behavior.

3. The greater the racial segregation in an area, the higher the crime rate. Sociologist Doug Massey argues that urban poverty and urban crime are the consequences of extremely high levels of black residential segregation and racial discrimination. Massey says,

"Take a group of people, segregate them, cut off their capital and guess what? The neighborhoods go downhill. There's no other outcome possible."

As these neighborhoods go downhill and economic opportunities evaporate, crime rates go up.

4. The greater the family instability, the higher the probability of crimes by juveniles. Research is sketchy, but it appears that the following conditions are related to delinquent behaviors: (a) intense parental conflict; (b) lack of parental supervision; (c) parental neglect and abuse; and (d) failure of parents to discipline their children.

5. The greater the inequality in a neighborhood, city, region, or society, the higher the crime rate. In other words, the greater the disparities between rich and poor, the greater the probability of crime. Of all the industrialized nations, the U.S. has the greatest degree of inequality. For example, one percent of Americans own 40 percent of all the wealth. At the other extreme, $14 1/2$ percent of all Americans live below the poverty line and 5 percent of all Americans live below *one-half* of the poverty line.

When these social variables converge, they interact to increase crime rates. Thus, there is a relatively high probability of criminal behavior—violent criminal behavior—among young, black, impoverished males in inner cities where poverty, unemployment, and racial segregation are concentrated. There are about 5 million of these high-risk young men. In addition, we have other problem people. What do we do? How do we create a safer America?

To oversimplify a difficult and contentious debate, there are two answers —the conservative and progressive answers. The conservative answer has been to get tough with criminals. This involves mandatory sentences, longer sentences, putting more people in prison, and greater use of the death penalty. This strategy has accelerated with laws such as "three strikes and you're out (actually in)," and the passage of expensive prison building programs to house the new prisoners.

In my view, this approach is wrongheaded. Of course, some individuals must be put in prison to protect the members of society. Our policies, however, indiscriminately put too many people in prison at too high a cost. Here are some facts about prisons:

1. Our current incarceration rate is 455 per 100,000 (in 1971 it was 96 per 100,000). The rate in Japan and the Netherlands is one-tenth ours. Currently, there are 1.2 million Americans in prisons and jails (equivalent to the population of Philadelphia).

2. The cost is prohibitive, taking huge amounts of money that could be spent on other programs. It costs about $60,000 to build a prison cell and $20,000 to keep a prisoner for a year. Currently the overall cost of prisons and jails (federal, state, and local) is $29 billion annually. The willingness to spend for punishment reduces money that could be

spent to alleviate other social problems. For example, eight years ago Texas spent $7 dollars on education for every dollar spent on prisons. Now the ratio is 4 to 1. Meanwhile, Texas ranks 37th among the states in per pupil spending.

3. As mentioned earlier, violent crimes tend to occur in the teenage years with a rapid drop off afterwards. Often, for example, imprisonment under "3 strikes and you're out" laws gives life imprisonment to many who are in the twilight of their criminal careers. We, and they, would be better off if we found alternatives to prison for them.

4. Prisons do not rehabilitate. Actually, prisons have the opposite effect. The prison experience tends to increase the likelihood of further criminal behavior. Prisons are overcrowded, mean, gloomy, brutal places that change people, but usually for the worse, not the better. Moreover, prisoners usually believe that their confinement is unjust because of the bias in the criminal justice system toward the poor and racial minorities. Finally, prisoners do not ever pay their debt to society. Rather they are forever stigmatized as "ex-cons" and, therefore, considered unreliable and dangerous by their neighbors, employers, fellow workers, and acquaintances. Also, they are harassed by the police as "likely suspects." The result is that they are often driven into a deviant subculture and eventually caught—about two-thirds are arrested within three years of leaving prison.

Progressives argue that conservative crime control measures are fundamentally flawed because they are "after the fact" solutions. Like a janitor mopping up the floor while the sink continues to overflow; he or she may even redouble the effort with some success but the source of the flooding has not been addressed. If I might mix metaphors here (although keeping with the aquatic theme), the obvious place to begin the attack on crime is *upstream*, before the criminal has been formed and the crimes have been committed.

We must concentrate our efforts on high-risk individuals before they become criminals (in particular, impoverished young inner city males). These prevention proposals take time, are very costly, and out-of-favor politically but they are the only realistic solutions to reduce violent street crime.

The problem with the conservative "after the fact" crime fighting proposals is that while promoting criminal justice, these programs dismantle social justice. Thus, they enhance a criminogenic climate. During the Reagan years, for example, $51 billion dollars were removed from various poverty programs. Now, under the "Contract for America" the Republicans in Congress propose to reduce subsidized housing, to eliminate nutrition programs through WIC (Women, Infants, and Children), to let the states take care of subsidized school lunches, and to eliminate welfare for unmarried mothers under 18 who do not live with their parents or a responsible guardian.

Progressives argue that we abandon these children at our own peril. The current Republican proposals forsake the 26 percent of American children under six who live in poverty including 54 percent of all African American children and 44 percent of all Latino children under the age of six. Will we be safer as these millions of children in poverty grow to physical maturity?

Before I address specific solutions, I want to emphasize that sociologists examine the structural reasons for crime.

This focus on factors outside the individual does not excuse criminal behavior, it tries to understand how certain structural factors *increase* the proportion of people who choose criminal options.

Knowing what we know about crime, the implications for policy are clear. These proposals, as you will note, are easy to suggest but they are very difficult to implement. I will divide my proposals into immediate actions to deal with crime now and long-term preventive measure:

Measures to protect society immediately:

1. The first step is to protect society from predatory sociopaths. This does not mean imprisoning more people. We should, rather, only imprison the truly dangerous. The criminal law should be redrawn so that the list of crimes reflects the real dangers that individuals pose to society. Since prison does more harm than good, we should provide reasonable alternatives such as house arrest, half-way houses, boot camps, electronic surveillance, job corps, and drug/alcohol treatment.

2. We must reduce the number of handguns and assault weapons by enacting and vigorously enforcing stringent gun controls at the federal level. The United States is an armed camp with 210 million guns in circulation. Jeffrey Reiman has put it this way:

> "Trying to fight crime while allowing such easy access to guns is like trying to teach a child to walk and tripping him each time he stands up. In its most charitable light, it is hypocrisy. Less charitably, it is complicity in murder."

3. We must make a special effort to get guns out of the hands of juveniles. Research by James Wright and his colleagues at Tulane University found that juveniles are much more likely to have guns for protection than for status and power. They suggest that we must restore order in the inner cities so that fewer young people do not feel the need to provide their own protection. They argue that a perceived sense of security by youth can be accomplished if there is a greater emphasis on community policing, more cooperation between police departments and inner city residents, and greater investment by businesses, banks, and cities in the inner city.

4. We must reinvent the criminal justice system so that it commands the respect of youth and adults. The obvious unfairness by race and social class must be addressed. Some laws are unfair. For example, the federal law requires a five-year, no-parole sentence for possession of five grams of crack cocaine, worth about $400. However, it takes 100 times as much powder cocaine—500 grams, worth $10,000—and a selling conviction to get the same sentence. Is this fair? Of course not. Is it racist? It is racist since crack is primarily used by African Americans while powder cocaine is more likely used by whites. There are also differences by race and social class in arrest patterns, plea bargain arrangements, sentencing, parole, and imposition of the death penalty. These differences provide convincing evidence that the poor and racial minorities are discriminated against in the criminal justice system. As long as the criminal justice system is perceived as unfair by the disadvantaged, that system will not exert any moral authority over them.

5. We must rehabilitate as many criminals as possible. Prisons should be more humane. Prisoners should leave prison with vocational skills useful in the real world. Prisoners should leave

prison literate and with a high school degree. And, society should formally adopt the concept of "forgiveness" saying to ex-prisoners, in effect, you have been punished for your crime, we want you to begin a new life with a "clean" record.

6. We must legalize the production and sale of "illicit drugs" and treat addiction as a medical problem rather than a criminal problem. If drugs were legalized or decriminalized, crimes would be reduced in several ways: (a) By eliminating drug use as a criminal problem, we would have 1.12 million *fewer* arrests each year. (b) There would be many *fewer* prisoners (currently about 60 percent of all federal prisoners and 25 percent of all state prisoners are incarcerated for drug offenses). (c) Money now spent on the drug war ($31 billion annually, not counting prison construction) could be spent for other crime control programs such as police patrols, treatment of drug users, and job programs. (d) Drugs could be regulated and taxed, generating revenues of about $5 billion a year. (e) It would end the illicit drug trade that provides tremendous profits to organized crime, violent gangs, and other traffickers. (f) It would eliminate considerable corruption of the police and other authorities. (g) There would be many fewer homicides. Somewhere between one-fourth and one-half of the killings in the inner cities are drug-related. (h) The lower cost of purchasing drugs reduces the need to commit crimes to pay for drug habits.

Long-term preventive measures to reduce violent crime:

1. The link between poverty and street crime is indisputable. In the long run, reducing poverty will be the most effective crime fighting tool. Thus, as a society, we need to intensify our efforts to break the cycle of poverty.

This means providing a universal and comprehensive health care system, low-cost housing, job training, and decent compensation for work. There must be pay equity for women. And, there must be an unwavering commitment to eradicate institutional sexism and racism. Among other benefits, such a strategy will strengthen families and give children resources, positive role models, and hope.

2. Families must be strengthened. Single-parent families and the working poor need subsidized child care, flexible work schedules, and leave for maternity and family emergencies at a reasonable proportion of their wages. Adolescent parents need the resources to stay in school. They need job training. We need to increase the commitment to family planning. This means providing contraceptives and birth control counseling to adolescents. This means using federal funds to pay for legal abortions when they are requested by poor women.

3. There must be a societal commitment to full and decent employment. Meaningful work at decent pay integrates individuals into society. It is a source of positive identity. Employed parents are respected by their children. Good paying jobs provide hope for the future. They also are essential to keep families together.

4. There must be a societal commitment to education. This requires two different programs. The first is to help at-risk children, beginning at an early age. As it is now, when poor children start school, they are already behind. As Sylvia Ann Hewlett has said:

> "At age five, poor children are often less alert, less curious, and less effective at interacting with their peers than are more privileged youngsters."

This means that they are doomed to be underachievers. To overcome this we need intervention programs that prepare children for school. Research shows that Head Start and other programs can raise IQ scores significantly. There are two problems with Head Start, however. First, the current funding only covers 40 percent of eligible youngsters. And second, the positive effects from the Head Start program are sometimes short-lived because the children then attend schools that are poorly staffed, overcrowded, and ill-equipped.

This brings us to the second education program to help at-risk children. The government must equalize the resources of school districts, rather than the current situation where the wealth of school districts determines the amount spent per pupil. Actually, equalization is not the answer. I believe that there should be special commitment to invest *extra* resources in at-risk children. If we do, we will have a safer society in the long run.

These proposals seem laughable in the current political climate, where politicians—Republicans *and* Democrats—try to outdo each other in their toughness on crime and their disdain for preven-tive programs. They are wrong, however, and society is going to pay in higher crime rates in the future. I am convinced that the political agenda of the conservatives is absolutely heading us in the wrong direction—toward more violent crime rather than less.

The proposals that I have suggested are based on what we sociologists know about crime. They should be taken seriously, but they are not. The proposals are also based on the assumption that if we can give at-risk young people hope, they will become a part of the community rather than alienated from it. My premise is this: Everyone needs a dream. Without a dream, we become apathetic. Without a dream, we become fatalistic. Without a dream, and the hope of attaining it, society becomes our enemy. Many young people act in antisocial ways because they have lost their dream. These troubled and troublesome people are society's creations because we have not given them the opportunity to achieve their dreams —instead society has structured the situation so that they will fail. Until they feel that they have a stake in society, they will fail, and so will we.

POSTSCRIPT

Is Incapacitation the Answer to the Crime Problem?

Many have complained that America has become lax on crime. Reynolds backs this statement up with statistics showing the dramatic drop in the average expected number of days in prison for serious crimes from 22.5 days in 1954 to 5.5 days in 1974. Since the number of crimes has increased more than fourfold during the time that expected days in prison shrank a similar amount, it is easy to assume that the declining punishment produced the increasing crime. During this period, however, many other changes occurred in the United States that would affect the crime rate, so the relationship of imprisonment to crime reduction may not be as clear as Reynolds's statistics suggest. Nevertheless, it is generally agreed that some people need to be deterred from crime. The real debate is whether or not current policies overemphasize imprisonment and underemphasize alternative crime reduction strategies, as Eitzen maintains. But are Eitzen's proposals of breaking the cycle of poverty, strengthening the family, improving employment opportunities and wages, and improving education for the poor feasible? Society is already trying to do these things, but success is elusive. Some of Eitzen's other suggestions, such as legalizing drugs and imposing tighter bans on guns, will confront tough opposition. Is it realistic, therefore, to emphasize imprisonment?

In *Crime in America* (Simon & Schuster, 1971), former attorney general Ramsey Clark takes a position that is in many ways similar to Eitzen's. Hans Zeisel, in *The Limits of Law Enforcement* (University of Chicago Press, 1983), argues that the criminal justice system can do little to effectively reduce crime. He emphasizes increasing protection from crime and attacking its root causes, which he believes lie in the conditions of poverty. The importance of the community in crime control is brought out by Robert J. Bursik, Jr., and Harold G. Grasmick in *Neighborhoods and Crime: The Dimensions of Effective Community Control* (Free Press, 1993). In a similar vein, Robert J. Sampson and John H. Laub show the importance of informal social control at home and at school in restraining juvenile delinquency in *Crime in the Making: Pathways and Turning Points Through Life* (Harvard University Press, 1993). On the other side, Andrew Von Hirsch's *Doing Justice* (Hill & Wang, 1976) is critical of Eitzen's philosophy, and Mark Tunick provides a defense of the use of punishment for retribution in *Punishment: Theory and Practice* (University of California Press, 1992).

The issue of deterrence is hotly debated by Ernest van den Haag and John P. Conrad in their book on the ultimate in deterrence punishment, *The Death*

Penalty: A Debate (Plenum Press, 1983). Graeme Newman presents an extreme position on punishment—advocating electric shocks and whippings—in *Just and Painful: A Case for the Corporal Punishment of Criminals* (Macmillan, 1983). A history of punishment choices other than prison is presented in *Alternatives to Prison: Punishment, Custody and the Community* (Sage Publications, 1990). Norval Morris and Michael Tonry advocate establishing a range of alternatives to prison in *Between Prison and Probation: Intermediate Punishments in a Rational Sentencing System* (Oxford University Press, 1993). Ulla V. Bondeson analyzes probation and other alternatives to imprisonment in *Alternatives to Imprisonment: Intentions and Reality* (Westview, 1994). She finds that lenient treatments produce lower recidivism rates. For a thorough and historical examination of parole, see Jonathan Simon, *Poor Discipline: Parole and the Social Control of the Underclass, 1890–1990* (University of Chicago Press, 1993). Many observers are appalled by the conditions in current American prisons. Nils Christie, a Norwegian criminologist, severely criticizes American prisons in *Crime Control as Industry: Towards Gulags, Western Style* (Routledge, 1993). Human Rights Watch has produced a report that is highly critical of the widespread abuse of human rights, which its investigations found in American prisons. Wilbert Rideau and Ron Wikberg's *Life Sentences: Rage and Survival Behind Bars* (Random House, 1992) presents a sympathetic insider's view of prison life that might soften the tough sentencing view of many.

PART 6

The Future: Population/ Environment/Society

Can a world with limited resources support an unlimited population? This question has taken on new dimensions as we approach the start of a new century. Technology has increased enormously in the last 100 years, as have worldwide population growth and new forms of pollution that threaten to undermine the world's fragile ecological support system. Will technology itself be the key to controlling or accommodating an increased population growth along with the resulting increase in waste production? All nations have a stake in the health of the planet and the world economy. Is America in a political and economic position to meet these global challenges?

- Does Population and Economic Growth Threaten Humanity?

- Are Standards of Living in the United States Improving?

ISSUE 19

Does Population and Economic Growth Threaten Humanity?

YES: Lester R. Brown, from'"Nature's Limits," in Lester R. Brown et al., *State of the World 1995* (W. W. Norton, 1995)

NO: Julian L. Simon, from "The State of Humanity: Steadily Improving," *Cato Policy Report* (September/October 1995)

ISSUE SUMMARY

YES: Lester R. Brown, president of the Worldwatch Institute, argues that the environment is deteriorating and that nature's limits are being exceeded due to economic and population growth.

NO: Julian L. Simon, a professor of economics and business administration, asserts that "all aspects of material human welfare are improving in the aggregate," so population and economic growth are benefiting, not threatening, humanity.

Much of the literature on socioeconomic development in the 1960s was premised on the assumption of inevitable material progress for all. It largely ignored the impacts of development on the environment and presumed that the availability of raw materials would not be a problem. The belief was that all societies would get richer because all societies were investing in new equipment and technologies that would increase productivity and wealth. Theorists recognized that some poor countries were having trouble developing, but they blamed those problems on the deficiencies of the values and attitudes of those countries and on inefficient organizations.

Nevertheless, progress was thought possible even in the least developed countries. If certain social and psychological defects could be overcome by a modernizing elite, and if 10 percent of the gross national product could be devoted to capital formation for at least three decades, then poor countries would take off into self-sustained growth, just as industrial societies had done decades earlier. See Walt W. Rostow's *The Stages of Economic Growth* (Cambridge University Press, 1960) for a review of this. After take-off, growth would be self-sustaining and would continue for the foreseeable future.

In the late 1960s and early 1970s an intellectual revolution occurred. Environmentalists had criticized the growth paradigm throughout the 1960s, but they were not taken very seriously at first. By the end of the 1960s, however, marine scientist Rachel Carson's book *Silent Spring* (Alfred A. Knopf, 1962) had worked its way into the public's consciousness. Carson's book traced the noticeable loss of birds to the use of pesticides. Her book made the middle and upper classes in the United States realize that pollution affected complex ecological systems in ways that put even the wealthy at risk.

In 1968 Paul Ehrlich, a professor of population studies, published *The Population Bomb* (Ballantine Books), which stated that overpopulation was the major problem facing mankind. This meant that population had to be controlled or the human race might cause the collapse of the global ecosystem and its own destruction. Ehrlich explained why he thought the death of the world was imminent:

> Because the human population of the planet is about five times too large, and we're managing to support all these people—at today's level of misery—only by spending our capital, burning our fossil fuels, dispersing our mineral resources and turning our fresh water into salt water. We have not only overpopulated but overstretched our environment. We are poisoning the ecological systems of the earth—systems upon which we are ultimately dependent for all of our food, for all of our oxygen and for all of our waste disposal.

In 1973 *The Limits to Growth* (Universe) by Donella H. Meadows et al. was published. It presented a dynamic systems computer model for world economic, demographic, and environmental trends. When the computer model projected trends into the future, it predicted that the world would experience ecological collapse and population die-off unless population growth and economic activity were greatly reduced. This study was both attacked and defended, and the debate about the health of the world has been heated ever since.

Let us examine the population growth rates past, present, and future. At about A.D. 0, the world had about one-quarter billion people. It took about 1,650 years to double this number to one-half billion and 200 years to double the world population again to 1 billion by 1850. The next doubling took only about 80 years, and the last doubling took about 45 years (from 2 billion in 1930 to about 4 billion in 1975). The world population may double again to 8 billion sometime between 2010 and 2020. Is population growth and the increased economic activity that it requires diminishing the carrying capacity of the planet and jeopardizing the prospects for future generations?

In the following selections, Lester R. Brown answers this question affirmatively and argues that we need to control population growth and to quickly reverse the dangerous deterioration of the environment that is occurring throughout the world. Julian L. Simon, currently the major proponent of the optimistic view of further economic development without serious environmental consequences, argues that the environment is becoming more beneficent for human beings because pollution is decreasing, resources are becoming more available and inexpensive, people are living longer, and population growth has largely positive economic and social impacts.

YES

Lester R. Brown

NATURE'S LIMITS

In the mid-nineties, evidence that the world is on an economic path that is environmentally unsustainable can be seen in shrinking fish catches, falling water tables, declining bird populations, record heat waves, and dwindling grain stocks, to name just a few.

The world fish catch, which climbed more than fourfold during 40 years, is no longer rising, apparently because oceanic fisheries cannot sustain a greater catch. The failure to coordinate population policy with earlier carrying capacity assessments of fisheries means the world now faces a declining seafood supply per person and rising seafood prices for decades to come.

Concern over water scarcity is rising in many areas. A prolonged drought in northern China, for example, and the associated water shortages have raised questions about the suitability of Beijing as the national capital and renewed discussion of a 1,400-kilometer (860-mile), canal that would bring water from the south to the water-deficient north. Although the cost of building this enormous conduit—comparable to bringing water from the Mississippi River to Washington, D.C.—was initially estimated at $5 billion, the total could ultimately be several times larger. Among other things, it will challenge engineers because it must cross 219 rivers and streams, including the Huang He (Yellow River), en route to Beijing.

Although collapsing fisheries and water scarcity attract attention because of their immediate economic effects, the decline of bird populations may be a more revealing indicator of the earth's health. Recently compiled data by Bird-Life International of Cambridge, England, show populations dropping on every continent. Of 9,600 species, only 3,000 are holding their own; the other 6,600 are in decline. Of these, the populations of some 1,000 species have dropped to the point where they are threatened with extinction. The precise reasons for this vary, but they include deforestation, particularly in the tropics; drainage of wetlands for farming and residential construction; air and water pollution; acid rain; and, for some species, hunting.

After two decades of steadily rising global average temperature, including the highest on record in 1990, the June 1991 eruption of Mount Pinatubo in the Philippines gave the world a brief respite from global warming. The explosion ejected vast amounts of sulfate aerosols into the upper atmosphere, which quickly spread around the globe. Once there, the aerosols reflected a minute amount of incoming sunlight back into space, enough to exert a cooling effect. By early 1994, however, almost all the aerosols had settled out, clearing the way for a resumption of the warming trend.

Evidence of new temperature highs was not long in coming. A premonsoon heat wave in central India lasted several weeks with temperatures up to 46 degrees Celsius (115 degrees Fahrenheit), taking a heavy toll on humans and livestock in the region. For the western United States, hundreds of new records were set, creating hot dry conditions that led to a near record number of forest fires....

On the food front, developments were particularly disturbing. Even though in 1994 the United States returned to production all the grainland that had been idled under commodity supply management programs, global food security declined further as the world's projected carryover grain stocks from the 1994 harvest dropped to the lowest level in 20 years. A combination of spreading water shortages, declining fertilizer use, and cropland losses, particularly in Asia, led to another harvest shortfall and the drawdown in stocks.

Thus in various ways, nature's limits are beginning to impose themselves on the human agenda, initially at the local level, but also at the global level. Some of these, such as the yield of oceanic fisheries or spreading water scarcity, are near-term. Others, such as the limited capacity of the atmosphere to absorb excessive emissions of carbon without disrupting climate, will manifest themselves over the longer term.

THREE IMMINENT LIMITS

One of the key questions that emerged as the world prepared for the Cairo conference was, How many people can the earth support? Closely related was, What exactly will limit the growth in human numbers? Will it be the scarcity of water, life-threatening levels of pollution, food scarcity, or some other limiting condition? After considering all the possible constraints, it appears that it is the supply of food that will determine the earth's population carrying capacity. Three of the earth's natural limits are already slowing the growth in the world food production: the sustainable yield of oceanic fisheries, the amount of fresh water produced by the hydrological cycle, and the amount of fertilizer that existing crop varieties can effectively use.

More than 20 years have passed since a marine biologist at the U.N. Food and Agriculture Organization (FAO) estimated that oceanic fisheries could not sustain an annual yield of more than 100 million tons. In 1989, the world fish catch, including that from inland waters and fish farming, reached exactly that number, an amount equal to world production of beef and poultry combined. During the following four years, it has fluctuated between 97 million and 99 million tons, dropping the fish catch per person 8 percent in four years. Recent FAO reports indicate that all 17 oceanic fisheries are now being fished at or beyond capacity. With the total catch unlikely to rise much above 100 million tons, the decline in the seafood supply per person of the last few years will continue indefinitely —or at least until the World Population Plan of Action succeeds in stabilizing population.

A combination of pollution and over harvesting is killing many inland seas and coastal estuaries. The Aral Sea, for instance, once yielded 44,000 tons of fish per year; the wholesale diversion of river water to irrigation has shrunk that body of water, raising its salt content and making the salt in effect a pollutant. All 24 species of fish that were once fished there commercially are believed to be extinct. In the Caspian Sea, the famous sturgeon harvest has been reduced to perhaps 1 percent of the level of 50 years ago through pollution and overfishing.

The Black Sea, which is the dumping point for the Danube, Dniester, and Dnieper Rivers, is the repository for chemical and organic pollutants for half of Europe. Of the nearly 30 species that once supported commercial fisheries there, only 5 remain. During the last decade the total catch has dropped from nearly 700,000 tons to 100,000 tons—a result of pollution, overharvesting, and the accidental introduction of destructive alien species of fish.

The U.S. Chesapeake Bay, once one of the world's most productive estuaries, is deteriorating rapidly from a lethal combination of pollution, overharvesting, and —for oysters—disease. Formerly a major source of this delicacy, the bay's annual harvest has dropped from nearly 100,000 tons of edible oysters (roughly 1 million tons in the shell) around the turn of the century to less than 1,000 tons in 1993.

With land-based food stocks, limits on production are being imposed by the amount of fresh water supplied by the hydrological cycle. Today, two thirds of all the water extracted from rivers and underground aquifers is used for irrigation. In parts of the world where all available water is now being used, such as the southwestern United States or large areas of northern China, satisfying future growth in residential and industrial demand will come at the expense of agriculture.

Although there are innumerable opportunities for increasing irrigation efficiency, only limited potential exists to expand freshwater supplies for irrigation. For example, roughly one fifth of U.S. irrigated land is watered by drawing down underground aquifers. A recent study of India found that water tables are now falling in several states, including much of the Punjab (India's breadbasket), Haryana, Uttar Pradesh, Gujurat, and Tamil Nadu—states that together contain some 250 million people. The drop ranges from less than one meter to several meters a year.

In many parts of the world, the diversion of water to nonfarm uses is also reducing water for irrigation. In the western United States, for instance, the future water demands of rapidly growing Las Vegas will almost certainly be satisfied by diverting water from irrigation. Similarly in China, most cities suffer from severe water shortages, and many of them will meet their future needs by taking water away from irrigation.

The physiological limit on the amount of fertilizer that current crop varieties can use is an even broader threat to world food expansion. In countries where fertilizer use is already heavy, applying more nutrients has little or no effect on yield. This helps explain why fertilizer use is no longer increasing in major food-producing regions, such as North America, Western Europe, and East Asia. During the last several decades, scientists were remarkably successful in increasing the responsiveness of wheat, rice, and corn varieties to ever heavier applications of fertilizer, but in recent years their efforts have met with little success.

Worldwide fertilizer use increased tenfold between 1950 and 1989, when it peaked and then began to decline. During the following four years it fell some 15 percent, with the decline concentrated in the former Soviet Union following the withdrawal of subsidies. In the United States, fertilizer use peaked in the early eighties and has declined roughly one tenth since then. With China, the other leading food producer, the peak seems to be occurring roughly a decade later. Some countries, such as Argentina and Vietnam, can still substantially expand their use of fertilizer, but the major food-producing countries are close to the limit with existing grain varieties.

For nearly four decades, steadily rising fertilizer use was the engine driving the record growth in world food output. The generation of farmers on the land in 1950 was the first in history to double the production of food. By 1984, they had outstripped population growth enough to raise per capita grain output an unprecedented 40 percent. But when the use of fertilizer began to slow in the late eighties, so did the growth in food output.

The era of substituting fertilizer for land came to a halt in 1990. (See Figure 1.) If future food output gains cannot come from using large additional amounts of fertilizer, where will they come from? The graph of fertilizer use and grainland area per person may capture the human dilemma as the twenty-first century approaches more clearly than any other picture could. The world has quietly and with little fanfare entered a new era, one fraught with uncertainty over how to feed the projected massive growth in world population.

Figure 1

World Fertilizer Use and Grassland Area Per Person, 1950–94

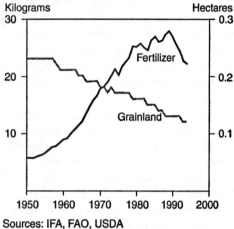

Sources: IFA, FAO, USDA

Unless plant breeders can develop strains of wheat, rice, and corn that are much more responsive to fertilizer, the world may not be able to restore the rapid growth in grain output needed to keep up with population. Either science will have to come up with a new method of rapidly expanding food production, or population levels and dietary patterns will be forced to adjust to much tighter food supplies. With the prospect of no growth in ocean-based food supplies and of much slower growth in land-based food supplies, the world is facing a future far different from the recent past.

THE ECONOMIC EFFECTS

The depletion of natural capital—of forests, rangelands, topsoil, underground aquifers, and fish stocks—and the pollution of air and water have reached the point in many countries where the economic effects are becoming highly visible, including a loss of output, of jobs, and of exports. Some countries have lost entire industries.

As the global demand for seafood overruns the sustainable yield of fisheries or as pollution destroys their productivity, for instance, fisheries collapse—raising seafood prices, eliminating jobs, and shrinking the economy. The economic wreckage left in the wake of these collapses can be seen around the world: Fishing villages that once lined the Aral Sea are now ghost towns. In Newfoundland, the collapse of the cod and haddock fishery has left 33,000 fishers and fish-processing workers unemployed, crippling the province's economy. And in New England, families who for generations have made their living from the sea are selling their trawlers and searching for other jobs.

Even as fisheries are being destroyed, the world demand for seafood is rising. Seafood was once a cheap source of protein, something that people ate because they could not afford meat. In 1960, a kilogram of seafood cost only half as much as a kilogram of beef. In recent years, that margin has narrowed and disappeared as seafood prices have risen above beef. During the last decade the world price of seafood, in real terms, has risen nearly 4 percent a year....

In some economies, overcutting forests has done even more economic damage than overfishing. The clear-cutting of tropical hardwood forests by lumber companies has almost completely destroyed this valuable resource in some developing countries, devastating their economies. Côte d'Ivoire, for example, enjoyed a phenomenal economic expansion in the sixties and seventies as its rich tropical hardwood forests yielded export earnings of $300 million a year. It became a development model for the rest of Africa, but as in many other countries that did not practice sustainable forestry, clear-cutting decimated its forests; exports dropped to $30 million a year in the early nineties. The loss of this major source of employment and export earnings, coupled with declining prices for other export commodities and other economic setbacks, led to a steady decline of the economy. Within just half a generation—from 1980 to 1994—income per person fell by half.

Similar forest destruction in other tropical countries, such as Nigeria and the Philippines, also led to industry collapse and to job, income, and export losses. Nigeria was once a major exporter of logs; by 1988, the nation was spending $100 million to bring in forest products. In the Philippines, exports peaked at $217 million per year in the early seventies, disappearing entirely by the early nineties.

As noted earlier, in many farming areas the claims on underground water supplies now exceed aquifer recharge rates. For farmers in northern India, where wheat and rice are double-cropped, the rate at which the water table is falling —more than a meter per year in some areas—may soon force a shift to less intensive cropping practices. Most likely this will mean a replacement of rice with a less water-demanding, lower-yielding staple crop, such as sorghum or millet. Although this may arrest the fall in the water table, it is not a welcome development in a country whose population is expanding by 17 million per year and is projected to reach a billion within the next six years.

In the agricultural regions surrounding Beijing, farmers no longer have access to reservoir water. They must now either drill their own wells and pursue the falling water table downward or switch to less intensive rain-fed farming. With some 300 cities in China reportedly now short of water, and 100 of them seriously short, similar adjustments will undoubtedly be made by farmers in the agricultural belts surrounding countless other Chinese cities....

In the absence of a dramatic new technological advance in agriculture comparable to the discovery of fertilizer or the hybridization of corn, there is now a real possibility that grain production could continue to lag and that prices could begin to rise in the years ahead, following those of seafood upward. The unfortunate reality is that with carryover stocks at such a low level, the world is now only one poor harvest away from chaos in world grain markets.

The collision between continuously expanding human demands and nature's various limits affects not only the world food supply but also overall economic growth. A 1993 study published by the World Bank notes that environmental damage takes many forms, including land degradation, pollution damage, the loss of biological diversity, deforestation, and soil erosion. Using a dozen or so examples, the two authors—both economists—show that the annual costs to countries of various forms of environmental damage can range from less than 1 percent to as much as 15 percent of gross national product. If the data were available to calculate all the economic costs of environmental degradation in its many forms, they would undoubtedly show an enormous loss. The authors observe: "If you asked any economist at the World Bank today if the environment is important to the country they work on, they would say 'Yes.' A few years ago, they wouldn't have said that."

The crossing of sustainable yield thresholds in sectors such as forestry and fishing and in aquifers, combined with the slowdown in the growth in world grain production, directly affects the performance of the world economy. To begin with, these primary producing sectors play a unique role in the global economy. If the growth in production of food from both land- and ocean-based sources falls far behind growth in demand, the resulting rise in prices could destabilize some national economies.

Economic growth, peaking at 5.2 percent a year in the sixties, dropped to 3.4 percent in the seventies and to 2.9 percent in the eighties. Thus far, during the nineties, it has averaged 1.4 percent, which means that the per capita output of food, energy, housing, and the other goods and services that determine living standards has declined by roughly 0.3 percent a year. (See Table 1.)

Several trends are contributing to slower economic growth, such as a near saturation of markets in some advanced industrial societies for basic consumer goods—automobiles and household appliances, for example. In some developing countries, burdensome external debt has slowed growth, and in Eastern Europe economic reforms have taken a toll. But also included among the reasons for slower world economic growth is the lack of growth in the fishing and farming sectors. Indeed, the 1994 fish catch was an estimated 3 percent smaller than in 1990, while the grain harvest was down nearly 2 percent. In addition, the economic uncertainty and, in some cases, instability associated with colliding with limits undermines confidence in the future. The bottom line is slower economic growth.

Although projections by the International Monetary Fund show economic

Table 1

World Economic Growth by Decade, Total and Per Person

Decade	Annual Growth	Annual Growth Per Person
	(percent)	
1950–60	4.9	3.1
1960–70	5.2	3.2
1970–80	3.4	1.6
1980–90	2.9	1.1
1990–94 (prel.)	1.4	−0.3

Source: Worldwatch Institute

growth accelerating in the years immediately ahead, these could be derailed by the instability associated with food scarcity. The nineties could turn out to be the first decade since the Great Depression when income per person for the world as a whole actually declines. Incomes fell in some 53 countries containing more than 800 million people during the eighties, many of them in Africa. But that incomes might fall for the entire world during the nineties has not been anticipated in any long-range economic projection.

UNSUSTAINABILITY FEEDS INSTABILITY

... The ecological symptoms of unsustainability include shrinking forests, thinning soils, falling aquifers, collapsing fisheries, expanding deserts, and rising global temperatures. The economic symptoms include economic decline, falling incomes, rising unemployment, price instability, and a loss of investor confidence. The political and social symptoms include hunger and malnutrition, and, in extreme cases, mass starvation; environmental and economic refugees; social conflicts along ethnic, tribal, and religious lines; and riots and insurgencies. As stresses build on political systems, governments weaken, losing their capacity to govern and to provide basic services, such as police protection. At this point, the nation-state disintegrates, replaced by a feudal social structure governed by local warlords, as in Somalia, now a nation-state in name only.

One of the difficulties in dealing with the complex relationship between humans and natural systems is that once rising demand for seafood or firewood crosses the sustainable yield threshold of a fishery or forest, future growth is often maintained only by consuming the resource base itself. This combination of continuously rising demand and a shrinking resource base can lead from stability to instability and to collapse almost overnight.

When sustainable yield thresholds are crossed, the traditional responses proposed by economists no longer work. One common reaction to scarcity, for instance, is to invest more in production. Thus the key to alleviating seafood scarcity is to invest more in fishing trawlers. But in today's world this only exacerbates the scarcity, hastening the collapse of the fishery. Similarly, as food prices rise, there is a temptation to spend more on irrigation. But where water tables are already falling, investing in more wells simply accelerates the depletion of the aquifer and the eventual decline in irrigation.

Once the demand on a particular system reaches a limit, the resulting scarcity sometimes spills over to intensify pressure on other systems. As seafood became scarce, for example, many expected that fish farming would take up the slack. But maintaining the historical growth in seafood supplies of 2 million tons per year over the last four decades by turning to aquaculture, where 2 kilograms of grain are needed to produce 1 kilogram of fish, requires 4 million tons of additional grain a year for fish raised in cages or ponds. Growth in the seafood harvest, which once relied primarily on spending more on diesel fuel to exploit ever more distant fisheries, now depends on expenditures on grain as more fish are produced in marine feedlots. With grain supplies tightening, the feed may not be available to sustain rapid growth in aquacultural output.

Some effects of crossing sustainable yield thresholds are indirect. If excessive demand for forest and livestock products leads to deforestation and rangeland degradation, the amount of rainfall runoff increases and the amount retained and absorbed for aquifer recharge decreases. Thus, excessive demand for timber and livestock products can reduce aquifer yields.

As another example of an indirect effect, when carbon emissions exceed carbon fixation, as is happening with the massive burning of fossil fuels, the level of carbon dioxide in the atmosphere rises, altering the earth's heat balance. The principal effect is to trap heat, raising temperatures. This in turn affects all the ecosystems on which humans depend, from estuaries to rangelands....

The bottom line of the growing instability between human societies and the natural systems on which they depend is political instability. This in itself is beginning to make economic development and agricultural progress difficult, if not impossible, in many countries. In some countries, the crossing of thresholds has international repercussions. When the growth in demand for food in a country as large as China begins to outstrip domestic productive capacity, the economic effects can spread far beyond national borders, altering the food supply/demand balance for the entire world.

THE CHINA FACTOR

The breathtaking pace of economic expansion in China promises to push demands on some of the earth's natural support systems beyond their sustainable yields.... When Western Europe, North America, and Japan industrialized during the century's third quarter, establishing the foundations of the modern consumer economy, they were home to some 340 million, 190 million, and 100 million people, respectively. By contrast, China, which is entering the same stage, has a population of 1.2 billion and an economy that is expanding much faster than the others did earlier. Given recent rates of economic growth, the World Bank projects that by 2002, greater China (which includes Hong Kong and Taiwan) will overtake the United States and become the world's largest economy.

We have no yardstick by which to assess the effect of this on demand for the earth's basic resources—simply because consumption levels have never risen so rapidly for so many people. Yet a sense of the potential effects on at least the world food economy is beginning to emerge. The escalating demand for food in China —where 14 million people are added each year and where the incomes of 1.2 billion people are rising at a record rate—could convert the world grain market from a buyer's to a seller's market, reversing the historical decline in grain prices.

The prospect of a massive grain deficit in a country that has essentially been self-sufficient comes on the heels of four decades of agricultural progress—progress that was particularly impressive following the agricultural reforms of 1978. These transferred land from production teams to individual families, unleashing energies that boosted the country's grain production by half—from 200 million tons in 1977 to more than 300 million tons in 1984. This put China ahead of the United States as the world's leading grain producer and raised output from the subsistence level of roughly 200 kilograms per person to nearly 300 kilograms.

On the demand side, China is projected to add 490 million people between 1990 and 2030, swelling its population to 1.6 billion—the equivalent of adding another Beijing every year for the next 40 years. Because its population is so large, even a slow rate of growth means huge absolute increases. Meanwhile, from 1991 to 1994, the economy expanded by a phenomenal 40 percent—an unprecedented rise in incomes for such a large number of people.

As incomes rise, people diversify their diets, shifting from overwhelming dependence on a starchy staple, such as rice, to more meat, milk, and eggs. When the economic reforms were launched in 1978, only 7 percent of grain was being used for animal feed; by 1990, that share had risen to some 20 percent, most of it used to produce pork. Now, demand for beef and poultry is also climbing. More meat means more grain—2 kilograms of grain are needed for each kilogram of poultry, 4 for pork, and 7 for each kilogram of beef added in the feedlot.…

With the cultivated area declining inexorably, China's ability to feed itself now rests entirely on raising the productivity of its cropland. Rice yields in China, which have been rising toward those in Japan, are starting to level off, suggesting that the potential for lifting them further is limited to the potential gain of 20–25 percent associated with the forthcoming new variety mentioned earlier.

With wheat, China's other food staple, the rise in yield is also slowing. In the early eighties, China's wheat yield per hectare surged past that of the United States and has remained well above it, at roughly 3 tons per hectare.…

Taking all these factors into account, it now appears likely that China's grain production will fall by at least one fifth between 1990 and 2030 (0.5 percent a year). This compares with a 33-percent decline in Japan since its peak year of 1960 (a fall of roughly 1 percent a year), a 31-percent decline in South Korea since its peak in 1977 (1.9 percent a year), and a 19-percent decline in Taiwan, also from a peak in 1977 (1.2 percent a year). Seen against this backdrop, the estimated decline of the one fifth by 2030 in China may, if anything, be conservative.

The resulting grain deficit is huge—many times the 28 million tons of Japan, currently the world's largest grain importer. In 1990, China produced 329 million tons of grain and consumed 335 million tons, with the difference covered by net imports of just 6 million tons. Allowing only for the projected population increase, China's demand for grain would increase to 479 million tons in 2030. In other words, even if China's booming economy produces no gains in the consumption of meat, eggs, and beer, a 20-percent drop in grain production to 263 million tons would leave a shortfall of 216 million tons—more than the world's entire 1993 grain exports of 200 million tons.

But even this is understating the problem, for China's newly affluent millions will of course not be content to forgo eating more livestock products. If grain consumption per person were to rise to 400 kilograms (the current level in Taiwan and one half the U.S. level), total consumption would climb to a staggering 641 million tons and the import deficit would reach 378 million tons.

... Who could supply grain on this scale? The answer: no one. Since 1980, annual world grain exports have averaged roughly 200 million tons, close to half of which comes from the United States. But the United States, with a projected addition of 95 million people during the next four decades, is simultaneously facing growth in grain demand and losses of cropland and irrigation water to nonfarm uses. As a result, the U.S. exportable surplus may not increase much, if at all.

At the same time, huge deficits are projected for other parts of the world. Africa, notably, is expected to need 250 million tons of grain by 2030—10 times what it currently imports. The Indian subcontinent is likely to rack up a deficit several times larger than its present one. Scores of countries with rapid population growth—among them Iran, Egypt, Ethiopia, Nigeria, and Mexico—will find themselves facing huge food deficits in the years ahead. In these circumstances, the vast deficit projected for China will set up a fierce competition for limited exportable supplies, driving world grain prices far above familiar levels....

Acute food scarcity and the associated political instability could bring the Chinese economic miracle to a premature end. At a minimum, this prospective deficit in China will force other governments—however reluctantly—to reassess painstakingly their national population carrying capacity and the closely related questions of population and consumption policies.

The bottom line is that when China turns to world markets on an ongoing basis, its food scarcity will become everyone's scarcity. Its shortages of cropland and water will become the world's shortages. Its failure to check population growth soon enough will affect the entire world.

It will probably not be in the devastation of poverty-stricken Somalia or Haiti but in the booming economy of China that we will see the inevitable collision between expanding human demand for food and the limits of some of the earth's most basic natural systems. The shock waves from this collision will reverberate throughout the world economy with consequences we can only begin to foresee.

NO

Julian L. Simon

THE STATE OF HUMANITY: STEADILY IMPROVING

The 1980 *Global 2000 Report to the President* began by stating that "if present trends continue, the world in 2000 will be more crowded, more polluted, less stable ecologically, and more vulnerable to disruption than the world we live in now." In the Introduction to *The Resourceful Earth,* which I edited in 1984 with the late Herman Kahn, we rewrote that passage, stating, "If present trends continue, the world in 2000 will be *less crowded* (though more populated), *less polluted, more stable ecologically,* and *less vulnerable to resource-supply disruption* that the world we live in now."

The years have been kind to our forecasts—or more important, the years have been good for humanity. The benign trends we then observed have continued. Our species is better off in just about every measurable material way. And there is stronger reason than ever to believe that progressive trends will continue past the year 2000, past the year 2100, and indefinitely.

When we widen our scope beyond such physical matters as natural resources and the environment—to mortality, the standard of living, slavery and freedom, housing, and the like—we find that the trends pertaining to economic welfare are heartening also. Please notice that this benign assessment does not imply that there will not be increases in *some* troubles—AIDS at present, for example, and other diseases in the future, as well as social and political upheavals. New problems always will arise. But the assessment refers to broad aggregate measures of effects upon people rather than the bad phenomena themselves—life expectancy rather than AIDS, skin cancers (or even better, lifetime healthy days) rather than a hole in the ozone layer (if that is indeed a problem), and agriculture rather than global warming.

We have seen extraordinary progress for the human enterprise, especially in the past two centuries. Yet many people believe that conditions of life are generally worse than in the past, rather than better. We must therefore begin by discussing that perception, because it affects a reader's reaction to the facts. Pessimism about the environment and resources is so universal that it needs no documentation. The comparison one chooses is always crucial. A premise of *The State of Humanity* is that it usually makes sense to compare

From Julian L. Simon, "The State of Humanity: Steadily Improving," *Cato Policy Report* (September/October 1995).

our present state of affairs with *how it was before*. That is the comparison that is usually relevant for policy purposes because it measures our progress....

THE PATH OF MATERIAL HUMAN WELFARE

Let us distinguish three types of economic change: 1) Change that is *mainly absolute* rather than *relative*. An example is health improvement that benefits everyone worldwide. 2) Change that is *mainly relative* but also has an important overall effect. An example is a productivity improvement, due to people working smarter in one country, that allows that country to greatly increase its exports to the benefit of both exporters and importers but causes problems for some other exporting countries. 3) Change that is *wholly relative*. An example is a change in the price charged by one trading partner to another, or in the terms of trade between raw materials and consumer goods, or the dollar-yen exchange rate; in such zero-sum situations there is no on-balance change for bad or good. It is only the third category in which one finds bad news, and indeed bad news is inevitable for one party or the other.

This is my central assertion: Almost every absolute change, and the absolute component of almost every economic and social change or trend, points in a positive direction, as long as we view the matter over a reasonably long period of time. That is, all aspects of material human welfare are improving in the aggregate.

For proper understanding of the important aspects of an economy, we should look at the long-run movement. But short-run comparisons—between the sexes, age groups, races, political groups, which are usually purely relative—make more news.

Let's start with the longest and deepest trends. Surprising though they may be, these trends represent the uncontroversial settled findings of the economists and other experts who work in these fields.

LENGTH OF LIFE

The most important and amazing demographic fact—the greatest human achievement in history, in my view—is the decrease in the world's death rate. It took thousands of years to increase life expectancy at birth from just over 20 years to the high 20s. Then in just the past two centuries, the length of life one could expect for a newborn in the advanced countries jumped from less than 30 years to perhaps 75 years.

Starting in the 1950s, well after World War II, length of life in the poor countries leaped upward by perhaps 15 or even 20 years because of advances in agriculture, sanitation, and medicine. (China excelled in this respect before developing its economy, which is exceptional.)

The extraordinary decline in child mortality is an important element in increased life expectancy, for which every parent must give fervent thanks. But contrary to common belief, in the rich countries such as the United States the gains in life expectancy among the oldest cohorts have been particularly large in recent years. For example, among American males aged 65 to 74, mortality fell 26 percent from 1970 to 1988, and among females of that age, mortality fell 29 percent and 21 percent from 1960 and 1970 to 1988, respectively (*Statistical Abstract of the United States*, 1990, p. 75).

The decrease in the death rate is the root cause of there being a much larger world population nowadays than in former times. In the 19th century, the planet Earth could sustain only 1 billion people. Ten thousand years ago, only 4 million could keep themselves alive. Now, more than 5 billion people are living longer and more healthily than ever before, on average. This increase in the world's population represents humanity's victory against death.

The trends in health are more complex. The decline in mortality is the most important overall indicator of health, of course. But whether keeping more people alive to older ages is accompanied by better or poorer health, on average, in those older years is in doubt.

AGRICULTURAL LABOR FORCE

The best single measure of a country's standard of living is the proportion of the labor force devoted to agriculture. When everyone must work at farming, as was the case only two centuries ago, there can be little production of nonagricultural goods. In the advanced countries there has been an astonishing decline over the centuries in the proportion of the population working in agriculture, now only about 1 person in 50. That shift has enabled consumption per person to multiply by a factor of 20 or 40.

RAW MATERIALS

People have since antiquity worried about running out of natural resources —flint, game animals, what-have-you. Yet, amazingly, all the historical evidence shows that raw materials—all of them —have become less scarce rather than more. It is beyond any doubt that natural resource scarcity—as measured by the economically meaningful indicator of cost or price—has been decreasing rather than increasing in the long run for all raw materials, with only temporary and local exceptions. And there is no reason why this trend should not continue forever. The trend toward greater availability includes the most counterintuitive case of all—oil.

Food is an especially important resource. The evidence is particularly strong that the trend in nutrition is benign despite rising population. The long-run price of food is down sharply, even relative to consumer products, as a result of increased productivity. And per person food consumption is up over the last 30 years. The increase of height in the West is another mark of improved nutrition.

(Africa's food production per person is down, but in the 1990s, few people any longer claim that Africa's suffering has anything to do with a shortage of land or water or sun. Hunger in Africa clearly stems from civil wars and government interference with agriculture, which periodic droughts have made more murderous.)

Only one important resource has shown a trend of increasing scarcity rather than increasing abundance. It is the most important and valuable resource of all—human beings. Certainly, there are more people on earth now than ever before. But if we measure the scarcity of people the same way that we measure the scarcity of other economic goods—by how much we must pay to obtain their services—we see that wages and salaries have been going up all over the world, in poor countries as well as in rich countries. The amount that one must pay to obtain the services of a barber or a professor has risen in India, just as the price of a barber or professor has risen in the United States over the decades. That increase in the price of people's services is a clear indication that people are becoming more scarce even though there are more of us.

THE STANDARD OF LIVING

The data show unmistakably how the standard of living has increased in the world and in the United States through the recent centuries and decades, right up through the 1980s. Aggregate data always bring forth the question: But are not the gains mainly by the rich classes, and the expense of the poor? For a portion of U.S. history, income distribution did widen (though this is hardly proof that the rich were exploiting the poor). But there has been little or no such tendency during, say, the 20th century. And a widening gap does not negate the fact of a rising absolute standard of living for the poor. Nor is there evidence that an increasing proportion of the population lives below some fixed absolute poverty line. There have been extraordinary gains by the poor in America in consumption during this century, as well as a high standard of living by any historical and cross-national standards.

A related question concerns possible exploitation by the rich countries that might cause misery for the poor countries. But the distribution of the most important element of "real wealth"—life expectancy—has narrowed between rich and poor countries (as well as between the rich and poor segments of populations within countries) over previous decades—to wit, the extraordinary reduction in the gap between the mortality rate of China and those of the rich countries since World War II. The reduction in the gap between literacy rates and other measures of amount of education in rich and poor countries corroborates this con-vergence. The convergence in economic productivity in the rich countries, along with general growth, dovetails with the other measures of income distribution. Data on the *absolute* gap between yearly incomes of the rich and poor countries are beside the point; widening is inevitable if all get rich at the same proportional rate, and the absolute gap can increase even if the poor improve their incomes at a faster proportional rate than the rich. Here one should notice that increased life expectancy among the poor relative to the rich reduces the gap in lifetime income, which is a more meaningful measure than yearly income.

CLEANLINESS OF THE ENVIRONMENT

Ask an average roomful of people if our environment is becoming dirtier or cleaner, and most will say "dirtier." Yet the air in the United States and in other rich countries is irrefutably safer to breathe now than in decades past; the quantities of pollutants—especially particulates, which are the main threat to health—have been declining. And water quality has improved; the proportion of monitoring sites in the United States with water of good drinkability has increased since data collection began in 1961. More generally, the environment is increasingly healthy, with every prospect that this trend will continue.

When considering the state of the environment, we should think first of the terrible pollutions that were banished in the past century or so—the typhoid that polluted such rivers as the Hudson, smallpox that humanity has finally pursued to the ends of the earth and just about eradicated, the dysentery that distressed and killed people all over the world as it still does in India, the plagues and other epidemics that trouble us much less than in generations past, or not at all. Not only are we in the rich countries free of malaria (largely due to our intensive occupation of the land), but even the mosquitoes that do no more than cause itches with their bites are so absent from many urban areas that people no longer need screens for their homes and can have garden parties at dusk. It is a mark of our extraordinary success that these are no longer even thought of as pollutions.

The root cause of these victorious campaigns against the harshest pollutions was the nexus of increased technical capacity and increased affluence—wealth being the capacity to deal effectively with one's surroundings.

I am not saying that all is well everywhere, and I do not predict that all will be rosy in the future. Children are hungry, and sick people live out lives of physical or intellectual poverty and lack of opportunity; irrational war (not even for economic gain) or some new pollution may finish us off. For most relevant economic matters, however, the aggregate trends are improving.

CAN ALL THIS GOOD NEWS BE TRUE?

Readers of articles like this often ask, "But what about the other side's data?" There are no other data. Test for yourself the assertion that the physical conditions of humanity have gotten better. Pick up the U.S. Census Bureau's *Statistical Abstract of the United States* and *Historical Statistics of the United States* at the nearest library and consult the data on the measures of human welfare that depend on physical resources, for the United States or for the world as a whole. See the index for such topics as pollution, life expectancy, and the price indexes, plus the prices of the individual natural resources. While you're at it, check the amount of space per person in our homes and the presence of such amenities as inside toilets and telephones. You will find "official" data showing that just about every single measure of the quality of life shows improvement rather than the deterioration that the doomsayers claim has occurred.

WHAT IS THE MECHANISM THAT PRODUCES PROGRESS RATHER THAN INCREASING MISERY?

How can it be that economic welfare grows over time along with population, instead of humanity's being reduced to misery and poverty as population grows and we use more and more resources? We need some theory to explain this controversion of common sense.

The process operates as follows: More people and increased income cause problems in the short run—shortages and pollutions. Short-run scarcity raises prices and pollution causes outcries. Those problems present opportunity and prompt the search for solutions. In a free society solutions are eventually found, though many people seek and fail to find solutions at cost to themselves. In the long run the new developments leave us better off than if the problems had not arisen. This theory fits the facts of history.

Technology exists now to produce in virtually inexhaustible quantities just about all the products made by nature—foodstuffs, oil, even pearls and diamonds—and make them cheaper in most cases than the cost of gathering them in their natural state. And the standard of living of commoners is higher today than that of royalty only two centuries ago—especially their health and life expectancy, and their mobility to all parts of the world.

The extent to which the political-social-economic system provides personal freedom from government coercion is a crucial element in the economics of resources and population. Skilled persons require an appropriate social and economic framework that provides incentives for working hard and taking risks, enabling their talents to flower and come to fruition. The key elements of such a framework are economic liberty, respect for property, and fair and sensible rules of the market that are enforced equally for all.

We have in our hands now—actually, in our libraries—the technology to feed, clothe, and supply energy to an ever-growing population for the next 7 billion years. Most amazing is that most of this specific body of knowledge was developed within just the past two centuries or so, though it rests, of course, on basic knowledge that had accumulated for millennia.

Indeed, the last necessary additions to this body of technology—nuclear fission and space travel—occurred decades ago. Even if no new knowledge were ever gained after those advances, we would be able to go on increasing our population forever, while improving our standard of living and our control over our environment. The discovery of genetic manipulation certainly enhances our powers greatly, but even without it we could have continued our progress forever.

CONCLUSION

Progress toward a more abundant material life does not come like manna from heaven, however. My message certainly is not one of complacency. The ultimate resource is people—especially skilled, spirited, and hopeful young people endowed with liberty—who will exert their wills and imaginations for their own benefit and inevitably benefit the rest of us as well.

POSTSCRIPT

Does Population and Economic Growth Threaten Humanity?

This debate cannot be resolved because the future is indeterminate. The key issue of the debate is whether or not future technological improvements can continue to overcome the law of diminishing returns on investments and increasing costs for nonrenewable resources and environmentally benign waste disposal. Brown shows that some of nature's limits have been exceeded and that present consumption is harming the environment, depleting resources, and endangering future consumption. If Simon is right that mankind will solve environmental problems when it becomes necessary for survival, then, according to Brown, it is time to act because present trends are seriously threatening mankind. Brown presents these ideas more fully in *Full House: Reassessing the Earth's Population Carrying Capacity*, coauthored with Hal Kane (W. W. Norton, 1994) and *Who Will Feed China? Wake-Up Call for a Small Planet* (W. W. Norton, 1995). Simon asserts that the pessimists always underestimate humankind's ability to adapt to environmental problems. Although the pessimists can cite a long list of environmental problems, Simon is confident that they will be taken care of by human effort and inventiveness. He expects necessity to give birth to inventions because technological developments will reap substantial economic rewards as resources become scarce. Simon's thesis is supported by Charles Maurice and Charles W. Smith with 10 major historical examples in *The Doomsday Myth: Ten Thousand Years of Economic Crisis* (Hoover Institution Press, 1985).

Publications by some of the prominent optimists on the availability of resources and the health of the environment include Julian L. Simon, *The Ultimate Resource* (Princeton University Press, 1981); Julian L. Simon and Herman Kahn, eds., *The Resourceful Earth: A Response to Global 2000* (Basil Blackwell, 1984); Dixy Lee Ray and Lou Guzzo, *Environmental Overkill* (Regnery Gateway, 1993); Ronald Bailey, *Eco-Scam: The False Prophets of Ecological Doom* (St. Martin's Press, 1993); Ronald Bailey, ed., *The True State of the Planet* (Free Press, 1995); and Gregg Easterbrook, *A Moment on the Earth: The Coming Age of Environmental Optimism* (Viking, 1995). Publications by some of the prominent pessimists include *The Global 2000 Report to the President* (Government Printing Office, 1980); William Catton, *Overshoot* (University of Illinois Press, 1980); Kingsley Davis and Mikhail S. Bernstam, eds., *Resources, Environment, and Population* (Oxford University Press, 1991); Paul R. Ehrlich and Anne H. Ehrlich, *Healing the Planet* (Addison Wesley, 1991); Al Gore, *Earth in the Balance* (Houghton Mifflin, 1992); Donella H. Meadows, Dennis L. Meadows, and Jorgen Randers, *Beyond the Limits* (Chelsea Green, 1992); Paul Hawken,

The Ecology of Commerce: A Declaration of Sustainability (HarperCollins, 1993); A. J. Michael, *Planetary Overload: Global Environmental Change and the Health of the Human Species* (Cambridge University Press, 1993); John Bellamy Foster, *The Vulnerable Planet: A Short Economic History of the Environment* (Monthly Review Press, 1994); and Eric Chivian et al., eds., *Critical Condition: Human Health and the Environment: A Report by Physicians for Social Responsibility* (MIT Press, 1993). Allan Schnaiberg and Kenneth Alan Gould examine the economic forces that are destroying the environment and show why it is hard for society to act more in concert with the environment in *Environment and Society: The Enduring Conflict* (St. Martin's Press, 1994). For a balanced review of both sides of the debate, see Barry B. Hughes, *World Futures: A Critical Analysis of Alternatives* (Johns Hopkins University Press, 1985). For a debate between a pessimist and an optimist, see Norman Myers and Julian L. Simon, *Scarcity or Abundance? A Debate on the Environment* (W. W. Norton, 1994).

ISSUE 20

Are Standards of Living in the United States Improving?

YES: W. Michael Cox and Richard Alm, from "The Good Old Days Are Now," *Reason* (December 1995)

NO: Beth A. Rubin, from *Shifts in the Social Contract: Understanding Change in American Society* (Pine Forge Press, 1996)

ISSUE SUMMARY

YES: Economist and banker W. Michael Cox and business journalist Richard Alm contend that U.S. living standards are improving. On average, they argue, Americans consume more, live better, live longer and healthier, achieve a higher net worth, enjoy more leisure time, and have more income per capita today than in 1970.

NO: Sociology professor Beth A. Rubin claims that Americans have not only lost income on average over the past 25 years, but they have also increasingly experienced insecurity and anxiety in their jobs and instability in their family relationships.

After World War II the United States emerged as the most powerful nation in the world. In part, this was because of the cumulative economic costs of two world wars for Germany, Great Britain, Japan, and the Soviet Union. America escaped the physical devastation that these nations suffered, and its economy boomed during and after the wars. With its unequalled prosperity and power, the United States assumed international leadership in armaments, investments, and aid.

Today that prosperity in terms of per capita income is equaled or surpassed by Japan and many European countries, and that leadership is in question. Over the past three decades, Japan, Germany, Taiwan, South Korea, China, and other countries in Europe and Asia have made enormous economic strides, while America has been stuck in first gear. American stores have been flooded with foreign-made goods—from shoes and textiles to cars and television sets. America has gone from winner to loser in many market competitions, resulting in large trade deficits.

Because of recent, painful restructuring and downsizing, America now competes more equally with other industrial countries. American business is doing well, but workers are suffering. American workers have been laid off as industries have downsized or moved part of their operations offshore where they can operate more cheaply than in the United States. The government, in the meantime, has continued to spend more than it receives in revenue, and America's national debt (the total of its accumulated annual budget deficits) is now more than $5 trillion. Many Americans worry that future generations will be burdened with debts that will drive the nation deeper into economic malaise.

Despite some signs of economic strength, Americans are anxious. Despite an endless array of new technological toys and gadgets, most Americans do not perceive life today as being better than it was a few decades ago. Visual signs of declining standards of living confront Americans in some of the grim aspects of daily life, particularly in its urban centers: homeless people sprawled on sidewalks, streets lined with boarded-up buildings, crumbling schools with metal detectors at the doors and peeling paint in the classrooms, bridges with chunks of concrete falling off them, and housing projects taken over by drug dealers. Declining standards of living are suggested by the massive layoffs by many large corporations and the government. Statistical signs of declining standards of living are found in the decline in real wages and in the median income.

The above factors deal with material standards of living. But it has often been said that money does not buy happiness. In fact, many studies show that once people have enough money to satisfy their basic material needs, additional increments of wealth are not correlated with increasing happiness. Surveys indicate that family, relationships, and meaningful activities are the keys to happiness. What are indicators in these areas telling us? Since 1960 divorce rates have shot upward, fertility rates have plummeted downward, and the time parents devote to children has declined about 10 hours per week. On the other hand, these trends bottomed out in the mid-1980s, and family values are staging a small comeback. Furthermore, Robert Wuthnow, in *Sharing the Journey: Support Groups and America's New Quest for Community* (Free Press, 1994), reveals that more and more Americans participate in small groups and are thereby connecting with God and with other people in the process of dealing with their problems.

So where do we stand? Is the quality of life in America improving? W. Michael Cox and Richard Alm admit that average wages have declined slightly, but they assert that those smaller wages buy more than the slightly larger wages of several decades ago. They also observe that since more people are working, per capita income is increasing. And the fact that Americans are living healthier and longer leads them to conclude that the quality of life is improving. Beth A. Rubin argues that Americans are victims of the changes taking place in the economy, especially the shrinking commitment of employers to employees. The employers gain flexibility, while the employees, even professionals, lose security. She also sees trouble on the home front and concludes that the quality of life is suffering.

YES   W. Michael Cox and Richard Alm

THE GOOD OLD DAYS ARE NOW

Draw a six-inch line on a piece of paper. Make a dot at the right end, and label it *Knowledge*. Make another dot two inches from the line's other end. Label that point *Ignorance*. What's to the left of that dot might be called *Mythology*. It's what we think we know but what isn't really so.

Often the biggest stumbling block to accurate perceptions of our world is getting beyond the glib notions that nearly everyone takes for granted. We spend an awful lot of time stumbling about in the realm of mythology:

- U.S. living standards are falling, and Americans aren't as well off as they were 25 years ago.
- These days, it requires two workers for a typical family to maintain a middle-class lifestyle.
- Today's children are likely to become the first generation that won't live as well as their parents.
- The United States, once the world's undisputed leader, is falling behind as other nations grow faster.

These are the myths that plague discussion of what's happening to U.S. living standards. They have been repeated so often, and by such respected authorities, that few Americans even question the proposition that the economy is failing them. The message pours out of Washington, where Labor Secretary Robert Reich frets that American workers are getting stiffed by greedy corporations. It's the central theme of leading academics and think tanks, including Ray Marshall at the University of Texas, Frank Levy at the Massachusetts Institute of Technology, and the Progressive Policy Institute in Washington, D.C. Downward mobility has emerged as a staple of big-city newsrooms, where hard-luck stories make good copy.

Anecdotes, of course, can only illustrate, not prove. In good times and bad, individuals and families will move up and down in the social pecking order for a variety of reasons. Making the case, then, for slipping American living standards demands broad-based evidence. More often than not, the negativists point to falling real wages as their smoking gun.

And the trends do seem decidedly grim: After adjusting for inflation, average hourly wages rose by 2.1 percent a year from 1953 to 1973. After that, wages stagnated and then began a long slide, with an average annual decline of 0.8 percent since 1978. If Americans are making less, it stands to reason they're not going to be able to maintain their living standards.

The pessimists bolster their argument with other trends that seem to show lost dynamism: lackluster economic growth, less-than-stellar productivity gains, widening trade deficits, fewer manufacturing jobs, an inability to match the growth rates of Asia's fast-growing nations. All told, these statistics make for a rather bleak view of the U.S. economy. To make matters worse, the country seems plagued by crime, pollution, insecurity, homelessness, cynicism, and a host of other social pathologies always in a downward spiral toward deeper crisis.

In a society that's addicted to hand-wringing, in a country that accentuates the negative, all this gets plenty of repetition. There are problems in these United States—no doubt about it—but the conclusion that we're not living as well as we once did is pure mythology. There's abundant evidence, easily obtained but largely ignored, showing that economic progress is still on track in the United States. Today's Americans aren't orphans of history. Far from it, they are experiencing what previous generations worked so hard to achieve—rising living standards.

In fact, Americans never had it so good.

CONSUMING CONFIDENCE

At best, real wages and the other evidence of a faltering economy are indirect barometers of living standards. It's curious that the declinists spend so much time examining a bunch of proxies but can spare so little energy for direct measures of what's been happening to Americans' well-being. . . .

Living standards are best measured by what we *consume*, not by our earnings or income. Looked at this way, the available numbers don't lend any support to the view that the country isn't doing as well as it once did. Comparisons to the early 1970s are particularly relevant. After all, no one doubts that Americans are living better today than they did a century ago, or even 50 years ago. The past quarter century is when the declinists contend the country's living standards started to slip.

But many numbers say it isn't so. On average, for instance, Americans now live in bigger and better houses. From 1970 to 1992, a typical new home increased in size by the equivalent of two 15-foot by 20-foot rooms. While home ownership rates have remained roughly constant over the past two decades, the average age at which Americans buy their first home has moved by roughly three years —from 27.9 in 1970 to 31.0 in 1992. Doomsayers, of course, have been quick to chalk this up to deteriorating economic conditions, ignoring the marked change in Americans' lifestyles. The median age at which we first marry (an event that often precedes home buying) has increased from 21.5 in 1970 to 24.7 in 1992—again roughly three years. And nearly 12 percent more of us today also decide never to marry. Add to this the fact that the average number of children per family has declined—from 1.09 in 1970 to 0.67 today—and the story clearly changes from deteriorating economic conditions to lifestyle changes.

Then there are the homes themselves. New houses are much more likely to have central air conditioning and garages. About 45 percent of homes now have dishwashers, up from 26 percent two decades ago. Clothes washers were in three-quarters of homes in 1990, up from less than two-thirds in 1970. At the same time, households with dryers jumped from 45 percent to almost 70 percent. The average number of televisions in a household rose from 1.4 in 1970 to 2.1 in 1990. Comparing 1970 and 1990, the typical U.S. family owned 4.5 times more in audio and video equipment, 50 percent more in kitchen appliances, and 30 percent more in furniture. For fun and games, the household has twice as much gear for sports and hobbies.

Among those 15 years and older, passenger vehicles per 100,000 people increased from 61,400 in 1970 to 73,000 in 1991. Americans are enjoying more luxuries, too. The average amount spent on jewelry and watches, after adjusting for higher prices, more than doubled from 1970 to 1991. Per capita spending on overseas travel and tourism is three times greater than in the early 1970s.

Of course, we could be paying for our consumption by depleting our savings. The evidence, however, suggests it isn't so. Although Americans may not set aside as much as people in many other countries, the average American still has managed to gain net worth. Median real wealth per capita rose by 2 percent a year from 1970 to 1990. The Dow Jones Industrial Average jumped sixfold since the early 1970s. The nation has had the best of two worlds: consuming more in the present and setting aside more for the future—not a bad standard for "better off."

No catalog of higher living standards would be complete without products that didn't even exist for past generations. Twenty years ago, only a lucky few could show movies at home. Now, two of every three households own video-cassette recorders. When Elvis was king of rock 'n' roll, records succumbed to warps and scratches. Today's practically unbreakable compact discs offer concert-hall quality sound. Microwave ovens, answering machines, food processors, camcorders, home computers, exercise equipment, cable TV, Rollerblades, fax machines, and soft contact lenses are staples of the 1990s lifestyles. As important, many products from computers to clothing, have been getting higher in quality even as they drop in price.

A decade ago, most motorists had to search out a pay telephone to make a call. Now, cellular technology has put a phone in millions of cars. Companies served 11 million subscribers in 1992, up from 92,000 in 1984. The past 20 years brought many medical breakthroughs—new drugs, new treatments, new diagnostic tools—to enhance and prolong our lives. Today's cars go farther on a gallon of gas. They've been improved with anti-lock brakes, airbags, fuel injectors, turbochargers, cruise control, and sound systems that outperform even the best home stereos of 1970. Today's youth may gripe, but they're already benefiting from products their parents didn't get until later in life. What's more, there's a huge inventory of even more world-shaking technologies that will create new waves of convenient, innovative consumer products.

The first test of national well-being, the one that makes the most common sense, should be the material facts of life. If the average consumer owns more of everything, plus the bonus of new products, then it's hard to fathom how a nation could have lost ground over the past 20 years. (*See Table 1.*)

WISTFUL AS WE WORK?

At least some declinists will concede that Americans have more material goods than ever, but they contend that it's only because we're working harder. The two-income family, with both husband and wife holding jobs, is all that keeps the country from the consequences of the weakening of the economy.

What conclusion could be more backward? Both adults have always worked. Running a household entails a daunting list of chores—cooking, cleaning, gardening, child care, shopping, washing and ironing, financial management, ferrying family members to ballet lessons and soccer practice. The average work-week of yesterday's housewife, the stay-at-home mom of the 1950s, was 52 hours, a more exhausting schedule than the 39.8 hours typically put in at the office.

The idea that people at home don't work isn't just insulting to women, who do most of the housework. It also misses how specialization contributes to higher and higher living standards. At one time, both adults worked exclusively at home. The man constructed buildings, tilled the land, raised livestock. The woman prepared meals, preserved food, looked after the children. Living standards rarely rose above the subsistence level.

Over time, household tasks were turned over to the market. At first, only one adult went to work outside the home, gaining specialized skills and earning an income that allowed the family to buy what it didn't have the time, energy, or ability to make at home.

When men went to work outside the home, living standards rose. Why do we insist that the same transition for women results in a squeezing of the household's possibilities? What's good for the gander is good for the goose. It's more efficient for workers to spend time earning money doing what they do best on the job and then pay others to perform at least some household chores. It makes no sense to suggest that the economic rules flip-flop when a second adult takes a job. Working women make families better off.

As the United States grows richer, tasks once done by family members continue to move out of the home and into the market. To the extent they can afford it, households hire professionals to clean, paint, tend the yard, figure taxes, care for clothing, and perform other responsibilities once assigned to family members. In getting their daily bread, Americans are finding ways to ease the burden of cooking at home. In 1993, restaurants received 43 percent of the country's spending on food, a big gain from the 33 percent of 1972. Eating out, once an occasional luxury, has become a way of life. And, even when we eat at home, we often rely more on market goods—heat-and-serve products, microwave meals, and carry-out items.

The data show that home production—the market of all housework and related chores—fell steadily from 45 percent of GNP at the end of World War II to 33 percent in 1973. Since then, it has drifted slightly lower, and it's likely to continue a gradual ebbing. Turning to the marketplace for many of the time-consuming, dull chores of maintaining a household frees time for more valuable

Table 1

Living Standards Compared 1970 and 1990

	1970	1990
Average size of a new home (square feet)	1,500	2,080
New homes with central air conditioning	34%	76%
People using computers	<100,000	75.9 million
Households with color TV	33.9%	96.1%
Households with cable TV	4 million	55 million
Households with VCRs	0	67 million
Households with two or more vehicles	29.3%	54%
Median household net worth (real)	$24,217	$48,887
Housing units lacking complete plumbing	6.9%	1.1%
Homes lacking a telephone	13%	5.2%
Households owning a microwave oven	<1%	78.8%
Heart transplant procedures	<10	2,125*
Average work week	37.1 hours	34.5 hours
Average daily time working in the home	3.9 hours	3.5 hours
Work time to buy gas for 100-mile trip	49 minutes	31 minutes*
Annual paid vacation and paid holidays	15.5 days	22.5 days
Number of people retired from work	13.3 million	25.3 million
Women in the work force	31.5%	56.6%
Recreational boats owned	8.8 million	16 million
Manufacturers' shipments of RVs	30,300	226,500
Adult softball teams	29,000	188,000
Recreational golfers	11.2 million	27.8 million
Attendance at symphonies and orchestras	12.7 million	43.6 million
Americans taking cruises	0.5 million	3.6 million
Americans finishing high school	51.9%	77.7%
Americans finishing four years of college	13.5%	24.4%
Employee benefits as a share of payroll	29.3%	40.2%**
Life expectancy at birth (years)	70.8	75.4
Death rate by natural causes (per 100,000)	714.3	520.2
Accidental death rate	56.2	34.9
Index of pollution	100.0	34.1

*figures are for 1991
**figures are for 1992

pursuits. A job is one of them. Another is the pursuit of pleasure.

KILLING TIME

In the 1990s, Americans aren't just enjoying the plenty of bigger houses, better cars, and more electronics. As people get wealthier, they are likely to want more time off work, trading higher income for additional leisure. Today's lickety-split lifestyles leave many people breathless, but there's plenty of evidence that a typical American spends less time than ever at work—either at home or on the job. (*See Table 2.*)

Additional free time comes from the confluence of several trends. Americans

Table 2

Less Work, More Leisure

Activity	1870	1950	1973	1990
Age starting work (avg.)	13	17.6	18.5	19.1
Life expectancy (years)	43.5	67.2	70.6	75.0
Retirement age (avg.)	death	68.5	64.0	63.6
Years on job	30.5	49.6	45.5	44.5
Retirement (years)	0	0	6.6	11.4
Annual hours worked	3,069	1,903	1,743	1,562
Annual hours home work	1,825	1,544	1,391	1,278
Lifetime Hours				
Working at job	93,604	94,389	79,307	69,509
Working at home	61,594	81,474	67,151	59,800
Waking leisure	99,016	216,854	266,129	308,368

Today's workers may feel pressed for time, but as a nation, we start to work later in life and work fewer hours than earlier generations. In 1870, Americans could expect to spend 39 percent of their waking hours at leisure. Now, the time we spend in childhood vacations, evenings, holidays, and retirement adds up to 70 percent of our waking hours.

are starting work later in life. On average, the age of initial employment has been pushed back seven months in the past 20 years. Once at work, Americans are putting in fewer hours because of shorter weeks, more holidays, and longer vacations. In the past two decades, there's been a gain of the equivalent of 23 days off a year. At home, Americans on average are devoting 18 minutes less a day to chores. Over the course of a year, that adds up to an extra four days of leisure. Toward the end of life, Americans are retiring earlier and living longer. As a result, a typical retirement grew by four years since 1973.

When it's all added up, the results are mind-boggling: Workers have added the equivalent of nearly five years of waking leisure to their lives since 1973. The typical employee spends less than a third of all non-sleeping hours on the job—that's better than any generation in U.S. history.

There's indirect confirmation that Americans have more free time these days: We're participating in more recreational activities and spending more money on leisure activities. Ownership rates more than doubled for vacation homes and rose 50 percent for recreational boats. Pleasure trips per capita rose from 1.5 a year in 1980 to 1.8 in 1991. Americans took 4.4 million cruises in 1994, compared with 500,000 in 1970 and 1.4 million as recently as 1980.

Increased leisure has fueled a sports boom. Attendance at National Football League games rose from 10 million in 1970 to 15 million in 1994. A fan backlash over [1994's] strike is keeping baseball attendance down, but hockey, basketball, golf, car racing, and other sports are drawing bigger crowds—in person and on television.

Participatory sports are booming, too. From 1970 to 1991, Americans who play golf regularly doubled to 11 percent of the population. In 1970, a quarter of Americans bowled; now, a third of them do. Even after adjusting for population growth, the number of adult softball teams jumped sixfold in two decades. Growing up, few of us ever imagined rock climbing, bungee jumping, or Rollerblading. These are now regular activities for millions of Americans.

Cultural activities haven't been shortchanged. Per capita attendance at symphonies and operas doubled from 1970 to 1991. Movies, pop-music concerts, and television fare are proliferating. We're even buying more books: Annual sales rose from 6.6 per person in 1974 to 8.1 in 1991. The much-bemoaned overcrowding of national parks bespeaks the arrival of a great democracy in free time, with the masses enjoying what was once possible for only a privileged few.

Money tells the same story. Total recreational spending, adjusted for inflation, jumped from $91.3 billion in 1970 to $257.3 billion in 1990, an average annual gain of 9.1 percent that well outstrips population growth of 1 percent a year. During the 1980s alone, outlays rose from $1.2 billion to $4.1 billion for recreational vehicles, $2.7 billion to $7.6 billion for pleasure boats, and $17 billion to $44 billion for sporting goods. Over the past 20 years, money allocated to recreation increased from 5 percent of consumer spending to nearly 8 percent.

One of the advantages of statistics is they reduce subjectivity. In polls, Americans will swear life is more hectic than it used to be, that there's not enough time anymore. What's crowding their lives, though, isn't necessarily more work and more chores. It is the relentless chasing after the myriad leisure opportunities of a society that has more free time and more money to spend.

REAL INTANGIBLES

The preferences of richer countries extend beyond additional consumption and leisure. The better off a country is, the more citizens will value non-material aspects of living standards: better health and safety, more pleasant working conditions, a cleaner environment. All of us could add other considerations we regard as important.

Intangibles, by their very nature, aren't as easy to count as televisions sets or hours of work. Yet, there are some numbers that counter fears that the United States is losing ground in most of what might be loosely called the quality of life.

In fact, longevity may be the most important measure of well-being in a modern society. The data show that an average American's life expectancy at birth has risen decade after decade. As might be expected, the biggest gains came in the first half of the 20th century, but the upward trend continues into the 1990s. Over the past 10 years, the life expectancy increased by more than one year and eight months.

What's more, the populace reports that it feels healthier. Surveys by the U.S. Department of Health and Human Services show a steady drop in the proportion of Americans who rate their health as "fair or poor"—from 12.2 percent in 1975 to 9.3 percent in 1991. Infant mortality rates fell from 20 deaths per 1,000 live births in 1970 to fewer than nine in 1991. The death rate from natural causes fell by 27 percent from 1970 to 1990, with most of the progress coming in combatting diseases of the heart. The portion of the adult population with high cholesterol fell sharply over the past two decades. What once was fatal can in many cases now be treated. Heart, liver, and lung transplants, experimental to theoretical in the early 1970s, are increasingly common today.

But the country isn't just healthier; in many respects, it's also safer. Accidental deaths have declined in every category, especially since 1970. In 1991, 88,000

Americans died in accidents, the lowest figure since 1972. Highway deaths totaled 43,500 in 1991, the best since 1962. Even more encouraging, the death rate per 100 million miles traveled on the nation's roads fell from 3.0 in 1975 to 1.8 in 1990. The incidence of death from crashes of scheduled airliners is just a fraction of what it was 20 years ago. Safety at work is improving, too. Accidental deaths on the job have declined steadily since at least 1945. Job-related injuries are well below what they were in previous decades.

Americans are also making progress on improving the environment. Levels of such major air pollutants as particulate matter, sulfur oxides, volatile organic compounds, carbon monoxide, and lead hit their peaks in 1970 or before. Levels of nitrogen oxides have been declining since 1980. Overall, air quality is better now than at any time since data collection began in 1940. Water quality has improved since the 1960s, when authorities banned fishing in Lake Erie and fires erupted on the polluted Cuyahoga River as it passed through Cleveland. The U.S. Geological Survey, examining trends since 1980, found that fecal coliform bacteria and phosphorus have decreased substantially in many parts of the country. Other indicators of water quality—dissolved oxygen, dissolved solids, nitrate, and suspended sediments—haven't been getting any worse....

WAGE DISCRIMINATION

A wealth of data makes a case for rising U.S. living standards. Even so, there's the pesky problem of the falling real wages the declinists bring up so often. Common sense seems to dictate that smaller paychecks are simply incompatible with a society being better off.

The data on rising consumption, plus additional leisure, suggest that the decline in real wages isn't the best indicator of what's happening to the country's economic prospects.

And, it turns out, there are better ways to show how the typical American is doing. The most straightforward alternative to real hourly wages is per capita income. One of its virtues is simplicity: divide total output by the number of people. This computation isn't skewed by changes in the way we work, the way we live, how we're paid, or what we produce. When we look at per capita personal income, the historical trend shows no monumental sign of a decline during the post–World War II era. It rose by an annual average of 1.7 percent since 1974, compared with 2.0 percent in the 1950s and 1960s.

Statistics on average hourly wages suffer from one glaring omission—fringe benefits. Over the past two decades, as tax rates and income have risen, these non-wage benefits have surged. Workers have chosen to take more compensation in the form of additional health care, contributions to retirement savings, or employee assistance programs. Overall, non-monetary benefits as a percentage of payroll increased by a third since 1970. Compared with a generation ago, more employers are providing eye care, dental benefits, paid maternity leave, and stock-purchase plans. Today's more progressive companies are starting to offer day care and paternity leave—both unheard of in the early 1970s.

When fringe benefits are included, there is indeed a slowdown in the *rate* of growth for total compensation in the past 20 years. But even so, the average American worker is still better off than his counterpart in the early 1970s, with a total gain of almost 15 percent.

Part of this relates to a change in the distribution of wages throughout the economy. Since 1973, the gap has widened between income and compensation. This trend tells us that the share of income paid for production and nonsupervisory work is declining, while the share paid elsewhere—to professionals, supervisors, managers, and owners—is growing.

One explanation appears to be the rising return to human capital. In an increasingly information- and service-oriented economy, business capital has come to encompass not just plant and machinery, but, more and more, intellectual capital as well.... [T]he workers reaping most of the economic gains have been those at the higher end of the education spectrum. The income premium to education is substantial and has grown markedly over the past two decades. In 1992, college graduates made an average of 82 percent more than high school graduates, up from only 43 percent in 1972. The really big returns to education these days come with advanced degrees—Ph.D.s, M.D.s, J.D.s, M.B.A.s, etc. In 1972, people with advanced degrees made 72 percent more income than high school graduates. By 1992, they made 2.5 times more. Today, high school dropouts earn scarcely half as much as high school grads, and the split is growing....

Per capita income and total compensation don't exhibit the downturn that's so unsettling in the statistics for real wages. To the contrary, they maintain an upward thrust up through the most recent data. More to the point, these measures of earning power square with the other evidence showing that Americans are better off than they used to be....

* * *

There's plenty of good, hard data refuting the notion that American living standards are in decline. We're enjoying more of almost all material goods. We're taking more leisure. We're healthier. We're making gains on other measure of well-being. We're making daily life easier by paying others to do what we once did for ourselves. We've got no reason to be alarmed by the evolution of two-income households, or the faster growth rates of other countries....

To be sure, economic changes are coming fast and furious. Many of us grew up in an era where workers could take a job and expect to keep it until retirement. Those entering the labor force today might have as many as four different jobs during their lifetimes—and three of them haven't been invented yet. In addition, there's an unsettling shift from a national economy to an international one, and all the new Information Age technology that changes the way we live and work. Transitions are hard on humans. The arrival of the Industrial Revolution created similar upheavals, though. Over time, people will get used to the new environment, make the necessary adjustments, and look back to wonder how they could have lived in the previous age.

The United States has its economic problems, no doubt about it. Budget deficits are too big. Too many people are still poor. Workers need skills to match today's technology—and tomorrow's. So, with real problems at hand, we shouldn't spend our time on phony ones. Being distracted by the myth of declining living standards isn't getting us anywhere. The evidence is overwhelming. On average, Americans are better off than ever before.

NO

Beth A. Rubin

SHIFTS IN THE SOCIAL CONTRACT: UNDERSTANDING CHANGE IN AMERICAN SOCIETY

SOCIAL CHANGE IN THE TWENTIETH CENTURY

Workers who once felt relatively immune from unemployment are discovering that a college degree and a big paycheck are no guarantee against it. Consider the example of IBM, which has long offered many of its workers essentially lifetime employment. In April 1993, in response to declining business conditions, IBM laid off 7,700 workers. Many of these workers were well-paid professionals in their 50s who thought they were at the zenith of their careers. Unlike many blue-collar workers, none of them had ever had to cope with layoffs and employment insecurity. This security was, after all, why they have invested in good educations at colleges and universities. Now, these well-educated, highly skilled, and highly paid workers—who were accustomed to a high standard of living—meet in support/prayer group meetings to discuss their lost careers, provide emotional support for one another, and develop strategies for job hunting and survival. Such support is necessary. In Dutchess County, New York, where three huge IBM plants are located, social service workers report an increase in drinking and family violence (*New York Times* editorial (The Rise of the Losing Class, Louis Uchitelle, November 20, 1994) claimed that the changing economy was linking the white-collar, skilled, college-educated workers with blue-collar, unskilled, high school educated workers through a shared experience of "uncertainty, insecurity, and anxiety about their jobs and incomes."

Surprisingly, unemployment and layoffs were occurring in a period characterized by economic recovery. But this recovery was an unusual one. Despite economic growth in the early 1990s, economic inequality (the gap between the rich and poor) continued to grow. While inequality has been increasing since the late 1970s, for perhaps the first time in America's history economists were faced with the puzzle of falling *median income* (the income level that half the population is above and half below) at the time of increased economic growth (*New York Times*, October 9, 1994)....

Turmoil is not, of course, confined to the United States. Economic insecurity is so great internationally that the International Labor Organization calls it a "global crisis." One out of three workers in the world's labor force is either unemployed or earning insufficient wages to allow a decent standard of living (*Times-Picayune*, March 7, 1994). Persistent long-term joblessness affects both industrial countries like the United States and developing countries like Mexico.

Global economic hardship has a number of consequences. It can increase competition for resources, engender political conflicts, and foster immigration. Former Secretary of State Lawrence Eagleburger called the current period one of global revolution (*Los Angeles Times*, February 18, 1993). Unchecked, such instability can lead to massive economic depression and even war. In fact, the 1990s provide evidence of such. As the countries that once constituted the Soviet Union struggle to redefine themselves, hatred, ethnic conflict, and bloodshed have often filled the gap left by a once strong centralized government....

Clearly the United States, along with most other countries in the world, is undergoing massive social change. Such change is related to a systematic transformation in the basis of social relations and social institutions (such as the economy, the government, the family).... *[C]ontemporary American society is changing from a social world characterized by long-term, stable relationships to one characterized by short-term, temporary relationships.* This social change alters the *social contract* that underpins society....

This shift results from changes in the economy. Specifically, economic relationships are changing to emphasize flexibility rather than stability in the use of resources. In a larger context the relationships among countries are growing increasingly complex. The result is a kaleidoscope of economic and social changes....

For over 200 years, a central part of American culture has been the belief in the American Dream. When people talk about the American Dream, they are talking about a belief in a society characterized by political and religious freedom in which anyone, regardless of family background, ethnicity, or race, can "make it." By *making it*, we mean that people can—by virtue of education, hard work, luck, and motivation—have a good job, a home, a happy family, and leisure time. Moreover, they can have these in a social climate free from oppression....

This dream continues to motivate people from all over the world. Waves of immigrants continue to come to the United States seeking the same mobility and opportunity that earlier generations sought. Achieving these goals, however, has grown increasingly difficult since the paths to upward mobility have altered.

Accord in the Post–World War II Era

By the beginning of the twentieth century, America was on its way to becoming one of the richest, most successful countries in the world. During the two and half decades following World War II, America was, in many ways, at its zenith. No country appeared richer, more powerful, more sure of itself. The American Dream seemed a reality for unprecedented numbers of Americans. For both blue-collar industrial workers (such as assembly line workers in automobile or electronics plants) and white-collar businessman (such as managers of Dow chemical or Metropolitan Life), upward mobility, comfort, and security appeared to be the norm. Secure workers married, had children, and bought houses. Those who were excluded from this expanding middle class, particularly African-Americans, placed demands on the government for civil rights and equal opportunities. The government responded with a variety of social programs. American culture also reflected the optimism of this period of expansion and growth....

The expansion of the economy provided a certain lifestyle to thousands of American workers. My father-in-law left the army after World War II with a high school degree and got a job with the telephone company. He moved to Santa Barbara, California, and was able to buy a house for $12,000. That house today would cost at least 20 times as much, something a worker with only a high school education is unlikely to have. However, the postwar economy provided him (as it did so many Americans) with a welter of opportunities, such as to marry and raise a family in economic comfort....

Many women who had filled in for absent male workers during World War II returned home, and men filled the jobs in their stead. Those jobs, however, paid well enough to allow a single income to provide for a family. Thus, although later generations of white, middle-class women would fight for the right for equal employment, postwar affluence freed many working-class women from participating in the paid labor force. The breadwinner-homemaker model of families that had dominated the middle class was now

a possibility for large portions of the working class as well. In 1940, 70% of families were male breadwinner–female homemaker families. For the next 25 years, more than half of all families conformed to this norm....

End of a Century, End of an Era

While not everyone's experience of life in America during the years 1947–1970 was upbeat, this period was generally one of economic growth, stable work, a liberal and interventionist state, and an increasingly exploratory culture. Once the stability and growth of the economy faltered, however, so too did stability and growth in other institutions. Clearly, the way social life was organized in the period after World War II is extremely different from the way social life is organized at the end of the twentieth century....

For a variety of reasons... the growth of the American economy slowed in the early 1970s. Increased international economic competition and failure to upgrade existing production techniques, among other factors, led to declining business success. As a result, employers experimented with a variety of strategies to maintain their prior economic dominance. All their efforts centered on decreasing the expenses involved in production and finding ways to compete more effectively. The less it costs to produce goods, the more profit businesses can make. Paying workers less, decreasing the number of workers hired, replacing workers with computers, robots, and automated assembly lines, moving to regions of the country and world where production was cheaper—all were ways in which American businesses tried to recoup declining profits.

Moreover, unlike in the decades following World War II, during the 1970s and 1980s other nations were competing successfully with the United States. Whereas American cars, for instance, used to dominate the automobile market, Japanese and German cars now outsold American cars. The increased economic strength of business in other countries also created more economic activity at a *global* level.

The efforts on the part of American business to succeed in the face of newly emerging international economic competitors have changed the national economy and workplace in a number of ways.

• Whereas our economic base previously came from manufacturing (e.g., cars, steel, electronics), it now comes increasingly from services (e.g., education, medical and financial services). This shift in the industrial base of the economy has, like other changes, had enormous consequences for workers and the workplace. Many service-sector jobs (such as restaurant and cleaning services) pay far less than manufacturing jobs. Those that pay well require *at least* a college education. Thus, this change results in fewer opportunities for the non-college-educated.

• Fewer and fewer workers are in jobs in which there is the possibility for continuous movement up a career ladder in a single firm. Like the IBM workers mentioned earlier, more and more workers are finding that jobs they thought they would have for a lifetime, or at least decades, are now part-time and temporary. In their efforts to create greater flexibility in the use of workers, technology, and resources, employers are replacing full-time jobs with temporary or part-time jobs, regardless of the skill or education associated with the occupation. Part-time workers are much cheaper since they receive not only lower wages but also few nonwage benefits such as health and disability insurance, paid vacations, and so forth.

• In manufacturing, roughly 75–80% of the workers used to be unionized (other industry groups such as trucking, mining, and construction had almost as many). Unions provide workers with high wages, benefits, and job security, and they provide employers with a well-disciplined work force. However, unions also create limitations for employers; they do not allow employers to fire workers when business conditions decline, for example. Thus, to increase the flexibility of the work force, employers have sought to rid their workplaces of unions, and so fewer and fewer workers have the economic and job stability that unions provide.

In summary, most of the changes in the economy and the workplace have resulted in far more insecurity and instability for workers. In addition, the paths to upward mobility have changed and have become unclear, and so many workers find themselves unsure of their future....

In addition to economic and political changes, major changes have occurred in another major institution—the family. The nuclear, breadwinner–homemaker family in which husband and wife raise their own biological offspring—once the dominant family form—is now a minority....

The increased divorce rate means that many families are now *blended*. That is, families are increasingly composed of biological parents, stepparents, children from multiple marriages, and so on. Similarly, more and more people in their 20s, instead of forming their own marriages and households, are "returning to the nest" (moving home to live with parents)....

As the question of responsibility has become more important in the context of the family, the same thing has happened in the context of government. Whereas in post–World War II years the government was actively involved in solving problems of poverty, inadequate housing and job and business regulation, in more recent decades it has withdrawn substantially from these commitments. Additionally, with the loss of the Vietnam War and the end of the cold war in the early 1990s, the American government has played an uncertain and vacillating role in international conflicts....

A second factor contributing to the withdrawal of the government from problem solving at home and intervention abroad is the reduction in resources available to the government to finance solutions. A combination of economic and demographic changes (more elderly and more young people, fewer people at high-paying jobs) has decreased the tax base. Moreover, the increasing national debt absorbs any economic surplus that could be used to finance social programs....

FROM INDUSTRIAL ECONOMY TO FLEXIBLE ECONOMY

When I graduated from high school in the Washington, D.C., area in 1972, I went to college, but my old boyfriend Ricky didn't. He looked for a good, unionized factory job. He knew he could make good money and maybe buy a little house in the same neighborhood his parents and sister Sara lived in. His sister didn't go to college, either. She had a job as a typist in a big office building outside the Beltway, in the Maryland suburbs. At the same time, my best friend's father was some sort of researcher. He worked in a big firm located in nearby Bethesda, Maryland, in which he had started out at the bottom and worked his way into one of the nice offices with huge windows. The occupants of those offices had expense accounts, three-martini lunches, and wives at home raising kids like us in well-heeled suburbs.

Now, the factory is gone, and Ricky is trying to figure out how he can keep paying his mortgage on one third of his old salary. The factory moved to Mexico and now employs young Mexican women. The home office is still in Bethesda, Maryland, but it employs only half the number of men it did 20 years ago. Most of the jobs have been taken over by computers or are done on a consulting basis. The only job Ricky could find was as a security guard for one of the new hotels that have opened up in the Washington, D.C. area.

The typewriter Sara used is also gone. When her office switched to computers, Sara had to learn how to use the new system. She thought that when she did, perhaps she could move into a better paying job, but that didn't happen. She still spends all her time typing, but now, instead of getting together with the other "girls in the pool" between typing letters, she sits alone all day in an office with a computer. During her breaks she sometimes logs into a computer bulletin board on the Internet. There, she pretends that she is a famous artist with an international reputation. Nobody knows differently; nobody will ever meet the face behind the computer identity.

My best friend's father doesn't work in Bethesda anymore, either. His office moved to Japan, and he travels back and forth now doing consulting work. He has also learned how to speak Japanese, German, and a little bit of Thai. He travels a lot and misses his family.

Neither Ricky nor his sister votes; they don't see what difference it makes. Sara is divorced and raising two children on her own. She isn't sure how to answer any of the questions her children ask; so they've stopped asking the questions. Ricky drinks too much and worries about losing his house; he blames his problems on welfare cheats and homosexuals. Neither brother nor sister really understands why nothing worked out the way they thought it would, the way it did for their parents.

The difficulty comes in seeing how large-scale social changes are affecting their day-to-day lives; but that's what is happening. From 1972, when they graduated from high school, to 1994 the *economy* —that is, the set of institutions and relationships that produces and distributes goods and services—has changed dramatically....

Bad Jobs: Statically Flexible Workers

Evidence suggest that the majority of workers in the flexible workplace are not in the relatively stable core but are working in an expanded secondary labor market characterized by the *instability* of jobs (Mingione, 1991; Colclough and Tolbert, 1992). This expanded sector is characterized by strategies of static flexibility (or *numerical flexibility*) rather than a dynamically flexible production process. *Static flexibility* refers to the organization of employment around labor demand. Employers attempt to reorganize the labor process so that they have to pay workers only for specific jobs or for short periods of time. Consider the typical secretary, for example. She (about 99% of all clerical workers are female)

may be very busy at some times, but under the usual employment contract (8 hours a day, 5 days a week) she may also have long periods when there is very little work to do. Under these conditions, an employer will be paying a worker just to sit around. However, reorganizing the workplace around statically flexible workers might mean that an office does not have a full-time clerical worker but instead uses part-time or temporary clerical workers as needed. This scenario is most feasible where the skills of the statically flexible workers are minimal and interchangeable. In the labor–capital accord era, employers used this strategy only with relatively unskilled workers. In the flexible economy, however, skilled, well-educated workers are used in the same way (Colclough and Tolbert, 1992; Harvey, 1989). In fact, Belous finds that more than half of all temporary workers are employed in technical, sales, and administrative support occupations (1989, p. 28). His research also shows that "at least 17% of the temporary work force is employed in occupations that are managerial, professional, technical or skilled blue collar" (Belous, 1989, p. 29). Those occupations may well include accountants, architects, engineers, financial advisors, lawyers, and doctors, just to name a few....

Displacement At the extreme, computerization and automation eliminate jobs. More jobs have been lost to subcontracting than to technology; but technology —in combination with industrial shifts, mergers, and general downsizing—has led to a massive displacement of workers. *Displacement* is the loss of jobs for reasons that are completely independent of how well workers have worked. A worker who is habitually late and is subsequently fired leaves an opening that will probably be filled. But a worker who is out of a job because the factory moves to Mexico has been displaced.

Well-paid blue-collar workers who had benefited from the labor–capital accord constituted the majority of displaced workers in the 1970s. In the 1980s, white-collar financial, professional, and managerial workers were also displaced. Using a broad definition of displacement, evidence suggests that "displacement rates have increased by 20% to 40% since the early 1970s" (Doeringer, 1991, p. 49). Displaced workers suffer far more than the pain and economic costs of immediate job loss. Workers who cannot find equivalent jobs right away often experience permanent wage reductions and repeated job instability. Additional problems may include loss of houses, breakup of families, increased rates of alcoholism, illness, and even homelessness.

In the film *Roger and Me*, Michael Moore interviews a woman who has been displaced from her job in the auto industry. Since there were few alternative sources of employment, she resorted to selling rabbits "for pets or meat" (the title of his next movie). In one particularly chilling sequence she calmly skins a rabbit while talking about how General Motors hurt her by closing the plant, leaving her with no option but the one so gruesomely depicted in the film. While all workers do not end up selling bunnies as future stew meat, they do end up strapped for work. In their study of displaced electronics workers in Indiana, Perrucci, Perrucci, Targ, and Targ (1988) found that in addition to lost income, a diminished community tax base, and other economic indicators, the displaced workers evinced "high levels of alienation and distrust of the groups and institutions that comprise the social fabric in the community and at the national level" (p. 123).

The displacement process is one factor that has enabled the creation of a numerically flexible labor force. Workers who have been displaced from a job because of industrial restructuring or downsizing are in very vulnerable positions. When an automobile plant closes, what happens to the 50-year-old who worked in the autobody painting department for the last 30 years? There are no other automobile plants in town for him to get a comparable job. And the sector of the economy that is expanding—services—is unlikely to provide him with a job comparable to the one he's been displaced from. He doesn't have the skills or experience to obtain one of the better paid, more secure jobs in the expanding financial and business sector. The types of jobs to which he will have access (security guard, janitor) are likely to be far less lucrative. Displaced workers may be unable to find any job at all and thus join the ranks of the structurally unemployed.

Workers who are displaced have a variety of strategies for coping. Some of the more skilled and privileged displaced workers are able to start their own businesses. The local paper often has stories of people who have turned their labor market adversity into an opportunity. For example, one woman who had been displaced from an administrative position used the skills and contacts she had gained on the job to develop her own temporary employment agency, a business that has relatively low start-up costs. But not all displaced workers have these opportunities. Some fall back on behaviors that are particularly destructive (like alcoholism and substance abuse).

Contingent Work One member of my family, Peter, worked in the banking industry for years, developing and using new computer software for the bank's information systems. Over the years Pete's job seemed to develop along the lines of flexibly specialized workers. He continually upgraded and used skills to improve the bank's communications network as part of an ongoing process, and he was rewarded handsomely for this work. When the bank merged with another bank, Pete played a central role in restructuring their communication network. Despite massive layoffs, his skills assured him of his position until his boss—and then he—were fired. For 3 years thereafter, despite an impressive array of skills and an equally impressive resume, he was unable to find another full-time job. Instead he has turned to temporary work. Corporations hire him to do a single job; when he completes the job, he has to look for more work.

Pete is not alone in this experience; he represents part of the new and expanding *contingent labor force*. The contingent labor force includes both part-time and temporary workers—some voluntarily contingent and some involuntarily so. Contingent workers receive lower pay, no fringe benefits, and little occupational protection. Their work is contingent on labor demand, and their security is up for grabs. Most would rather work full-time if they could. Research shows that since 1970, involuntary part-time work has grown 121% (Callaghan and Hartman, 1991, p. 4). It is no wonder that it is involuntary, given these conditions. Part-time workers are six times more likely to work for minimum wage than full-time workers. Additionally, the Internal Revenue Service has estimated that up to 38% of employers deliberately misclas-sify their workers as independent contractors rather than full-time workers to avoid paying unemployment compensation and social security tax (duRivage, 1992, p. 87). duRivage also finds that only one in six contingent workers is covered by a pension plan.

The involuntary, part-time work force is growing more rapidly than the full-time work force and is becoming a permanent part of the modern workplace (Callaghan and Hartman, 1991). Recent estimates suggest that contingent workers represent 25–30% of the work force and appear most often in the retail trades and in services, which are low-productivity, low-wage jobs (Callaghan and Hartman, 1991). Women make up roughly two thirds of the contingent work force. Black men in temporary, blue-collar manual work constitute the second largest category of contingent workers (duRivage, 1992). One report indicated that "displaced white-collar workers are told up front that any job they get in any company should not be expected to last longer than three to five years—if they are lucky and stay on their toes" (*Times-Picayune*, October 9, 1994).

In contrast to earlier periods, high levels of what economists call *human capital* (e.g., education, training, and skills) no longer ensure status as a primary worker as firms increasingly hire consultants, accountants, marketing researchers, lawyers and technical help on a temporary, as-needed basis. The firm of the future is likely to include very few permanent workers and to subcontract out for the rest of its workers, from the low-skill janitorial and cafeteria staff to the highly skilled workers.

Reliance on a contingent labor force has two major advantages for employ-ers. First, it dramatically decreases labor costs. On average, part-time workers earn 60% of the hourly wages of full-time workers (Belous, 1989; duRivage, 1992, p. 87). Most receive neither pensions, health benefits, fringe benefits, nor unemployment insurance. When banks hire Peter on a contingent basis to do work similar to what he had been doing, they get the same work from him as they used to. Now, however, they do not have to pay for the generous benefits workers at his level usually receive.

Second, reliance on contingent workers also allows employers to use workers only as they need them, rather than maintain a stable work force during, for example, periods of slack demand. Ironically, though, there is evidence that employers are not using contingent workers solely in response to shifting demand conditions (i.e., hiring extra sales workers during the holiday season). Rather, they are using contingent workers on a permanent basis (Belous, 1989; Callaghan and Hartman, 1991; duRivage, 1992)....

Conclusions

Industrial transformation has eliminated many of the good—that is, stable and well-paid—jobs held by workers with only a high school diploma. Now, increasing numbers of jobs require a college education. Moreover, they require complex interpersonal skills and computer literacy, something that schools often fail to provide to all students. These differences pose dilemmas for young entrants into the labor market. Students in wealthy school districts have access to a quality of education, both in content and in resources, that can provide them with the human capital necessary to compete in the future workplace. For many more students, however, particularly those in in-

ner cities or economically depressed rural areas—in fact, all communities that lack sufficient tax monies to maintain and upgrade existing schools—the education is of a quality that leaves them increasingly unprepared for the twenty-first century. Those students who are unable to acquire the necessary skills are likely to fall into the secondary labor market. Unfortunately, given the increasingly rapid pace of knowledge growth, initial deficiencies will be even harder for those students to overcome than they were in earlier periods.

The nature of the flexible economy is such that many workers can no longer anticipate long-term employment relationships with a single employer or a small number of firms over the course of their working lives. Instead of anticipating a relatively predictable career path, more and more workers are becoming contingent workers or homeworkers. The shift to flexible employment threatens the well-being of workers in a number of ways. Workers lose access to stable health care, for instance. Correspondingly, low pay associated with the secondary labor market makes health benefits purchased from private providers harder to afford.

Flexible work arrangements also result in loss of access to retirement and other benefits. This problem is exacerbated by the anticipated increased burden on the social security system as the population ages and fewer labor-market entrants support it. Moreover, lower paid workers contribute less in taxes, reducing government's resources for providing health and retirement benefits.

The flexible workplace is less an actual place than ever before. Workers go to a job, but they are less and less likely to have a "place of work." Likewise, the job ladders they used to climb are broken. Now, they may be confronted with an endless effort to upgrade skills and hustle up jobs, just to pay the rent. Finally, work in modern society has been a major source of identity. Without a stable workplace, what will provide the bond that links people to society? What will replace the social contract that used to be formed within the workplace?

POSTSCRIPT

Are Standards of Living in the United States Improving?

Cox and Alm label as a myth the statement "U.S. living standards are falling, and Americans aren't as well off as they were 25 years ago." They are aware that many indicators seem to support this idea. They even acknowledge that wages have declined 0.8 percent per year on average since 1978. Nevertheless, they conclude that "Americans never had it so good." They support this conclusion by showing that Americans have more living space, more appliances, more leisure time, and almost five more years of life now than they did in 1970. However, Cox and Alm do not discuss the quality of family life and personal relations, which Rubin maintains are highly correlated with happiness, and they omit many other indicators, such as crime rates and measures of anxiety and stress. Rubin focuses on family life and job insecurity and denies that "Americans never had it so good."

The pessimists dominate the literature on the direction of change in the overall quality of life. America's economic difficulties are analyzed by Jeffrey Madrick in *The End of Affluence: The Causes and Consequences of America's Economic Dilemma* (Random House, 1996). Two recent works are extremely pessimistic about job opportunities. Jeremy Rifkin, in *The End of Work: The Decline of the Global Labor Force and the Dawn of the Post-Market Era* (Putnam, 1995), presents a picture that is more bleak than that of Rubin. Stanley Aronowitz and William DiFazio, in *The Jobless Future: Sci-Tech and the Dogma of Work* (University of Minnesota Press, 1994), focus on the relentless expansion of technology, which displaces workers. For a sensitive and astute description of the impacts of layoffs on men's identities and lives, see Kathryn Marie Dudley, *The End of the Line: Lost Jobs, New Lives in Postindustrial America* (University of Chicago Press, 1994). For a close-up look at the lives of America's suburban middle class today, see Katherine S. Newman's *Declining Fortunes: The Withering of the American Dream* (Basic Books, 1993). As her title suggests, she portrays the current generation of young adults as worse off than the previous generation. Barbara Ehrenreich also describes the hardships of the middle class in *Fear of Falling: The Inner Life of the Middle Class* (Harper Perennial, 1990). A very different interpretation of the American dream is provided by Robert J. Samuelson in *The Good Life and Its Discontents: The American Dream in the Age of Entitlements* (Times Books, 1996). He argues that the economy is doing quite well and life has improved but that Americans have exaggerated expectations so their dreams have failed and they feel that they are losing ground.

CONTRIBUTORS
TO THIS VOLUME

EDITORS

KURT FINSTERBUSCH is a professor of sociology at the University of Maryland at College Park. He received a B.A. in history from Princeton University in 1957, a B.D. from Grace Theological Seminary in 1960, and a Ph.D. in sociology from Columbia University in 1969. He is the author of *Understanding Social Impacts* (Sage Publications, 1980), and he is the coauthor, with Annabelle Bender Motz, of *Social Research for Policy Decisions* (Wadsworth, 1980) and, with Jerald Hage, of *Organizational Change as a Development Strategy* (Lynne Rienner, 1987). He is the editor of *Annual Editions: Sociology* (Dushkin Publishing Group/Brown & Benchmark Publishers) and coeditor, with Janet S. Schwartz, of *Sources: Notable Selections in Sociology*, 2d ed. (Dushkin Publishing Group/Brown & Benchmark Publishers, 1996).

GEORGE McKENNA is a professor of political science and the chair of the Department of Political Science at City College, City University of New York, where he has been teaching since 1963. He received a B.A. from the University of Chicago in 1959, an M.A. from the University of Massachusetts in 1962, and a Ph.D. from Fordham University in 1967. He has written numerous articles in the fields of American government and political theory, and his publications include *American Populism* (Putnam, 1974) and *American Politics: Ideals and Realities* (McGraw-Hill, 1976). He is coeditor, with Stanley Feingold of *Taking Sides: Clashing Views on Controversial Political Issues* (Dushkin Publishing Group/Brown & Benchmark Publishers), now in its ninth edition, and he is the author of the textbook *The Drama of Democracy: American Government and Politics*, 2d ed. (Dushkin Publishing Group, 1994).

STAFF

Mimi Egan   Publisher
David Dean   List Manager
David Brackley   Developmental Editor
Brenda S. Filley   Production Manager
Libra Ann Cusack   Typesetting Supervisor
Juliana Arbo   Typesetter
Lara Johnson   Graphics
Diane Barker   Proofreader
Richard Tietjen   Systems Manager

AUTHORS

RICHARD ALM is a business writer for the *Dallas Morning News.*

EDWARD BANFIELD is a professor emeritus of urban studies in the Department of Faculty Arts and Sciences at Harvard University. He is the author of *The Unheavenly City Revisited: A Revision of the Unheavenly City* (Scott, Foresman, 1974).

JOHN C. BERG is a professor at Suffolk University.

JEFFREY M. BERRY is a professor of political science at Tufts University in Medford, Massachusetts. He is the author of *The Interest Group Society,* 2d ed. (Scott, Foresman, 1989) and coauthor, with Kent E. Portney and Ken Thomson, of *The Rebirth of Urban Democracy* (Brookings Institution, 1993).

PETER BRIMELOW is a senior editor for *Forbes* and *National Review* magazines. He is also the author of *The Patriot Game* (Hoover Institution Press, 1986).

LESTER R. BROWN is the founder, president, and senior researcher at the Worldwatch Institute in Washington, D.C. His publications include *Building a Sustainable Society* (W. W. Norton, 1981), and his *State of the World* reports remain his most highly regarded and popular works.

WILLIAM H. CHAFE is an Alice Mary Baldwin Professor at Duke University. He is the author of *The Unfinished Journey: America Since World War II,* 3d ed. (Oxford University Press, 1995).

JOHN E. CHUBB is a senior fellow in the Governmental Studies Program at the Brookings Institution in Washington, D.C., and a partner in the Edison Project in Knoxville, Tennessee. His publications include *Politics, Markets, and America's Schools* (Brookings Institution, 1990), coauthored with Terry M. Moe.

DAVID T. COURTWRIGHT is a professor of history and the chair of the Department of History and Philosophy at the University of North Florida in Jacksonville, Florida. His publications include *Dark Paradise: Opiate Addiction in America Before 1940* (Harvard University Press, 1982).

W. MICHAEL COX is vice president and economic adviser at the Federal Reserve Bank of Dallas.

JOHN J. DiIULIO, JR., is an associate professor of politics and public affairs at Princeton University in Princeton, New Jersey. His publications include *No Escape: The Future of American Corrections* (Basic Books, 1991).

D. STANLEY EITZEN is a professor emeritus of sociology at Colorado State University in Fort Collins, Colorado, where he has taught criminology, social problems, and the sociology of sport. His publications include *Society's Problems: Sources and Consequences* (Allyn & Bacon, 1989).

ERNEST ERBER is affiliated with the American Planning Association in Washington, D.C., which is involved in urban and rural development.

MILTON FRIEDMAN is a senior research fellow at the Stanford University Hoover Institution on War, Revolution, and Peace. He was the recipient of the 1976 Nobel Prize in economic science. He and his wife, **ROSE FRIEDMAN,** who also writes on economic topics, have coauthored several publications, including *Tyranny of the Status Quo* (Harcourt Brace Jovanovich, 1984).

FRANCIS FUKUYAMA, a former deputy director of the U.S. State Department's policy planning staff, is a consultant for the RAND Corporation in Santa Monica, California. He is the author of *The End of History and the Last Man* (Free Press, 1992).

GEORGE GILDER is a senior fellow of the Hudson Institute in Indianapolis, Indiana. He is also a contributing editor for *Forbes* magazine and the author of several books, including *Microcosm: Into the Quantum Era of Economics and Technology* (Simon & Schuster, 1989).

BILL HONIG is the superintendent of public instruction for California's State Department of Education in Sacramento.

CARL F. HOROWITZ is a policy analyst at the Heritage Foundation in Washington, D.C. He has also held an academic appointment at Virginia Polytechnic Institute and State University.

PETER KIM is the director of research services and consumer behavior at J. Walter Thompson North America.

JONATHAN KOZOL is a social commentator who writes on the problems of the American education system. His publications include *Savage Inequalities: Children in America's Schools* (Harper-Perennial, 1991).

EVERETT C. LADD is a professor of political science at the University of Connecticut and the president and executive director of the University of Connecticut's Roper Center for Public Opinion Research.

MARTIN A. LEE is cofounder of Fairness and Accuracy in Reporting (FAIR) in New York City, an organization that promotes free speech and a free press for U.S. citizens. He is also the publisher of FAIR's journal *Extra!*

MYRON MAGNET is a senior fellow of the Manhattan Institute for Policy Research in New York City.

H. JOACHIM MAITRE is a professor of journalism and of international relations at Boston University in Boston, Massachusetts, and the director of Boston University's Center for Defense Journalism.

TERRY M. MOE is a professor of political science at Stanford University in Stanford, California. His research interests focus on American political institutions, and he has written extensively on public bureaucracy, the presidency, interest groups, and the educational system. His publications include *Politics, Markets, and America's Schools* (Brookings Institution, 1990), coauthored with John E. Chubb.

RICHARD D. MOHR is a professor of philosophy at the University of Illinois, Urbana. His research interests focus on ancient philosophy and on gays in contemporary social life. His publications include *A More Perfect Union: Why Straight Americans Must Stand Up for Gay Rights* (Beacon Press, 1994).

CHARLES MURRAY is a Bradley Fellow at the American Enterprise Institute. He is the author of *Losing Ground* (Basic Books, 1986) and *In Pursuit of Happiness and Good Government* (ICS Press, 1994).

ETHAN A. NADELMANN is an assistant professor of politics and public affairs in the Woodrow Wilson School of Public and International Affairs at Princeton University in Princeton, New Jersey. He is also an assistant editor of the *Journal of Drug Issues* and a contributing editor of the *International Journal on Drug Policy*.

JAMES PATTERSON is chairman of J. Walter Thompson North America.

DAVID POPENOE is a professor of sociology and an associate dean for the social sciences at Rutgers–The State University in New Brunswick, New Jersey. He is the author of *Disturbing the Nest: Sweden and the Decline of Families in Modern Societies* (Aldine de Gruyter, 1988).

ARCH PUDDINGTON is a senior scholar at Freedom House, a New York research and human rights organization. He writes frequently on American race relations.

MARK ROBERT RANK is a sociologist and coeditor, with Edward L. Kain, of *Diversity and Change in Families: Patterns, Prospects, Policies* (Prentice Hall, 1994).

JEFFREY REIMAN is the William Fraser McDowell Professor of Philosophy at American University in Washington, D.C. He is the author of over 40 articles and numerous books on moral, political, and legal philosophy, including *Justice and Modern Moral Philosophy* (Yale University Press, 1992).

MORGAN O. REYNOLDS, a visiting scholar for the U.S. Congress Joint Economic Committee, is a professor of economics at Texas A & M University in College Station, Texas, and a senior fellow of the National Center for Policy Analysis in Dallas, Texas. He has published over 50 articles in academic journals, and he is the author of *Economics of Labor* (South-Western, 1994).

KATIE ROIPHE is a doctoral candidate in English literature at Princeton University in Princeton, New Jersey, and the author of *The Morning After: Sex, Fear and Feminism on Campus* (Little, Brown, 1993).

BETH A. RUBIN is an associate professor in the Department of Sociology at Tulane University.

WILLIAM RYAN is a professor in the Department of Psychology at Boston College in Chestnut Hill, Massachusetts, and a consultant in the fields of mental health, community planning, and social problems. His publications include *Distress in the City* (UPB, 1969).

ROBERT SHEAFFER is a consulting editor for *Skeptical Inquirer* and the author of *Resentment Against Achievement: Understanding the Assault Upon Ability* (Prometheus Books, 1988).

JULIAN L. SIMON is a professor of economics and business administration in the College of Business and Management at the University of Maryland at College Park. His publications include *The Ultimate Resource*, 2d ed. (Princeton University Press, 1994).

NORMAN SOLOMON is a media critic whose news analyses and articles have been published in numerous magazines and newspapers. His publications include *Killing Our Own: The Disaster of America's Experience With Atomic Radiation* (Delacorte Press, 1982), coauthored with Harvey Wasserman.

JUDITH STACEY is a professor in the Department of Sociology at the University of California, Davis. She is the author of *Patriarchy and Socialist Revolution in China* (University of California Press, 1983).

ROBIN WARSHAW is a freelance journalist based in Pennsauken, New Jersey.

ROGER WILKINS is an editorial board member of *Nation* and a professor of history at George Mason University.

INDEX

abortion, 94, 124, 222, 336; feminism and, 70, 71, 74, 75

accountability, lack of, school choice and, 276

acquaintance rape. *See* date rape

adoption, 252; homosexuals and, 100, 106

affirmative action, 14, 15, 43; controversy over, 174–187

Aid to Families with Dependent Children (AFDC), 250, 258, 260, 261

Against Our Will (Brownmiller), 84, 89

Agnew, Spiro, 27, 29, 30

agriculture, and controversy over environmental issues, 344–359

AIDS, 29, 120, 303, 309, 354; poverty and, 166, 167, 168–169

air quality: and controversy over environmental issues, 344–359; health and, 297–298

alcohol. *See* drugs

Alm, Richard, on U.S. standards of living, 364–372

ambiguity, moral, 14–15

aquifers, 346, 348, 349, 350

arrest, imprisonment and, 324, 325, 335

Asia, immigrants from, 47, 51

assault, 322, 323, 328, 331–337

Aston-Martin, 138–139

baby boomers, 119, 313

Baldwin, James, 182, 186

Banfield, Edward, 142, 143; on the poor, 158–162

Bennett, William, 185, 328

Berg, John C., on big business's influence on government, 212–219

Berkshire Paper Company, 135–137

Berry, Jeffrey M., on big business's influence on government, 220–227

big business, controversy over influence of, on government, 212–227

bilingual education, 43, 50–51, 52–52, 177

biodiversity, loss of, 344, 349

Blackmun, Harry, 174, 178

blacks, and controversy over affirmative action, 174–187

blaming the victim, date rape and, 84–85

Blankenhorn, David, 121, 122, 123

blended families, 118, 376–377

boot camp, for youthful offenders, 328, 335

Brazil, 42, 235, 236

breadwinner-homemaker model of families, 375, 376–377

Brimelow, Peter, 44–45; on immigration, 38–43

Britain, 245, 331; legalization of drugs in, 304, 306, 312, 314, 315

Brown, Lester R., on population and economic growth, 344–353

Brownmiller, Susan, 84, 89

Buchanan, Patrick, 29, 44, 45, 121, 124

burglary, 322, 323, 327

Bush, George, 27, 52, 194, 215, 217, 225

Canada, 42, 236, 238, 302, 331, 348

capital punishment, 14, 15

capitalism, 132, 139–140, 143, 213; controversy over role of government in, 232–246

Capone, Al, 302, 303, 305

carbon emissions, 345, 351

carrying capacity of the earth, and controversy over environmental issues, 344–359

Carter, Jimmy, 33, 203, 214

centrally planned economies, 241, 242

Chafe, William H., on feminism, 67–77

children: and controversy over preservation of traditional families, 114–126; and controversy over school choice, 268–277; poor, in the South Bronx, 163–170; sex and, 15–16. *See also* families

China, 242, 308, 312; environmental issues in, 344, 346, 348–349, 351–353, 355

Chubb, John E.: on school choice, 268–273; reaction to views of, 274–277

cigarette smoking, health and, 297–298. *See also* drugs

cities: and controversy over homelessness, 192–205; poverty in, 163–170; street crime in, 284–289

citizen groups, influence of, on Congress, 220–227

civil rights: and controversy over affirmative action, 174–187: homosexuals and, 107–109

Clinton, Bill, 20, 21, 22–23, 121, 122, 125, 180, 181, 250, 256

cocaine. *See* drugs

colleges, date rape and, 85–86, 88

communitarian individualism, 116–122, 125

community action, 161–162

Congress, controversy over influence of big business on, 212–227

consumer interest groups, 220–227

consumer protection, 242–243, 245

contingent workers, 380–381

controlled legalization, of drugs, 312–313, 315, 316

conviction, imprisonment and, 324, 325, 327

Courtwright, David T., on legalizing drugs, 310–318

Cox, W. Michael, on U.S. standards of living, 364–372

creationism, 14, 15, 62

crime: controversy over, 284–289; and controversy over legalizing drugs, 302–318; and controversy over prisons, 322–337; homelessness and, 195; immigrants and, 48; poverty and, 158

date rape, controversy over, 82–94
death penalty, 333, 335
death rate, decrease in global, 355–356
Declaration of Independence, 5–6
decriminalization, of marijuana, 317, 336
deforestation, 344, 348, 349, 350, 351
Democrats, media and, 22–23
denial, affirmative action and, 183–184
deterrence, prison as, 327, 329
Dilulio, John J., on street crime versus white-collar crime, 284–289
displaced workers, 378–379
distribution of wealth, controversy over, 132–154
divorce, 14, 149, 115, 119, 122, 123, 125–126, 251, 261, 376–377
Dole, Bob, 180, 183, 184, 186
"domestic partner" legislation, 103–104, 106
drugs, controversy over legalization of, 302–318, 336

economic growth: controversy over environmental issues and, 344–359; immigration and, 42
economic inequality: controversy over, 132–154; and controversy over homelessness, 195–205
economic theory of crime, 322–323
editor, news, as ideological gatekeeper, 23–25
education: and controversy over affirmative action, 174–187; and controversy over school choice, 268–277, human capital and, 372, 380, 381; of immigrants, 39–40; single-sex, 63
effective schools, 269, 271
Egypt, 236, 352
Eighteenth Amendment, to the Constitution, 303, 309
Eisenhower, Dwight, 8, 213
Eitzen, D. Stanley, on incapacitation as the answer to the crime problem, 331–337
electronic monitoring, of criminals, 328, 335
Elshtain, Jean Bethke, 121, 122, 125
employment discrimination: and controversy over affirmative action, 174–187; homosexuals and, 100, 106, 107
English as a Second Language, 53
entrepreneurs, 138, 235
environmental interest groups, 220–227
environmental issues, 297–298; and economic growth, controversy over, 344–359; and standards of living, 365, 370, 371
Environmental Protection Agency, 243–244
Equal Rights Amendment (ERA), 70, 74, 75, 77, 104, 222
Erber, Ernest, on government and capitalism, 232–238
Estrich, Susan, 90, 91

Etzioni, Amitai, 122, 124
expressive individualism, 116–117
Exxon, 213, 215

families: controversy over homeless, 192–205; controversy over preservation of traditional, 114–126; and controversy over welfare, 250–264; decline of, 13–14, 167–168, 333, 336; multiproblem, 159–160; standards of living and, 376–377
family values, immigrants and, 44–53
Federal Register, 242–243
Federal Reserve Board, 217, 234
Feminine Mystique, The (Friedan), 68–70
feminism, 49, 121, 123, 124, 125; controversy over, 60–77; date rape and, 88–94
fertilizer, 345, 346–347
fishing industry, environmental industry and, 344–353
flexible economy, 337–382
food additives, health and, 297–298
food stamps, 166, 241, 250, 258
Ford, Gerald, 33, 203
Frankel, Max, 23–24
Friedan, Betty, 68, 69, 71
Friedman, Milton, 21; and Rose, on government and capitalism, 239–246
fringe benefits, standards of living and, 371, 381
Fukuyama, Francis, on immigration, 44–53
fundamentalism, religious, 8, 121

Galston, William, 121, 122
Gans, Herbert, 28, 159
Garn–St. Germain Depository Institutions Act of 1982, 218, 219
gays. See homosexuality
General Motors, 213, 215
genes, criminality and, 332–333
Germany, 240, 245, 331, 376
Gigot, Paul, 44, 52
Gilbert, Neil, 88–89
Gilder, George, on economic inequality, 132–143
Gingrich, Newt, 184, 186
global warming, 344–345, 350, 354
government: controversy over influence of big business on, 212–227; controversy over role of, in capitalist economy, 232–246
Gramm, Phil, 180, 186
Granata, Anthony, 316–317
Great Depression, 204, 350

Hayes, Robert, 193–194
health care, consumer protection and, 296–297
health, standards of living and, 370, 372
heroin. See drugs
Hersh, Seymour, 30–31
homelessness, controversy over, 192–205
homosexuality, 14, 15, 71, 73, 124–125; controversy over, 98–110

Hong Kong, 305, 351
Honig, Bill, on school choice, 274–277
Horowitz, Carl F., on social acceptance of homosexuality, 105–110
"hostile speech" codes, on college campuses, 60–61
housing discrimination, homosexuals and, 100, 107–109
housing, standards of living and, 365–366, 368
human capital, 372, 380, 381
hunger, poverty and, 258–259

IBM (International Business Machines), 213, 215, 373, 376
immigration, 177, 284, 307; controversy over 38–53; income inequality and, 133, 134–135, 140, 150
India, 41, 236, 242, 305, 345, 346, 348, 358
indictment, imprisonment and, 324, 325
individualism: moral decline and, 10–12; traditional families and, 116–117
Industrial Revolution, 233, 236, 372
inheritance, wealth and, 137–138
instability, environmental, 350–351
institutional model, of Congress, 212, 213–214
intangible assets, standards of living and, 370–371
interest groups, controversy over influence of, on Congress, 212–227
International Monetary Fund, 349–350
Iran, 41, 305, 311–312, 352
Iran-contra scandal, media and, 30–32
issue networks, 223–227

Japan, 233, 236, 240, 245, 308, 333, 351, 352, 376, 377
Jencks, Christopher, 134, 143
Jim Crow laws, 5, 36
job ladders, 381–382
Johnson, Lyndon, 33, 117, 176, 241

Kelley, Nick, 135–137
Keynes, John Maynard, 139, 234, 236
Kim, Peter, on moral decline in America, 13–16
Kinsley, Michael, 25, 26, 29
Kleber, Herbert, 311, 312
Koss, Mary P., 82, 84
Kozol, Jonathan: on homelessness, 199–205; on the poor, 163–170
Kristol, Irving, 132, 143

Ladd, Everett C., on moral decline in America, 4–16
laissez-faire, 235, 238
Landrigan, Philip, 293–294
Latinos, immigration and, 47–49, 50–51, 52–53
law, homosexuality and, 105–110
Lee, Martin A., on bias in the media, 27–33
legalization of drugs, controversy over, 302–318, 336

leisure, standards of living and, 368–370, 371, 372
lesbians. See homosexuality
Levin, Michael, 62, 63
liberal bias, controversy over, in the media, 20–33
liberal feminism, 70–72, 77
life expectancy, increase in, 355–356, 366, 370
Lipset, Seymour Martin, 6–7
Losordo, Douglas, 22–23
luxuries, standards of living and, 336–367

MacKinnon, Catharine, 92, 93
Magnet, Myron, on homelessness, 192–198
magnet schools, 268, 276
Maitre, H. Joachim, on bias in the media, 20–26
manufacturing economy, decline of, 376, 377–382
Marable, Manning, 215–216
marijuana. See drugs
market, and controversy over role of government in capitalism, 232–238
market institutions, schools as, 270–271, 274
marriage, 115, 117–188, 120, 124, 125–126, 167; homosexual, 104, 106; open, 74; work ethic and, 141–143
Marxism, 62, 66, 233, 234
Marxist theory, of Congress, 214, 219
media: controversy over liberal bias in, 20–33; feminism and, 73–74; homosexuality and, 106
Medicaid, 137, 203, 241, 250, 261
mental illness: and controversy over homelessness, 192–205; homosexuality as, 99
Mexico, 236, 238, 352
Meyerson, Adam, 29–30
military, homosexuals in, 100, 106
Moe, Terry M.: on school choice, 268–273; reaction to views of, 274–277
Mohr, Richard D., on social acceptance of homosexuality, 98–104
moonshine, 315–316
moral decline, controversy over myth of, 4–16
Moynihan, Daniel Patrick, 122, 124
multiculturalism, 40, 43, 50, 51
multiproblem families, 159–160
murder, 322, 323, 328, 331–337
Murray, Charles, 122, 123, 126, 204–205; on welfare, 250–256

Nadelmann, Ethan A., on legalizing drugs, 302–309
Nader, Ralph, 222, 243, 296
National Gay and Lesbian Task Force, 99, 106
National Institute of Justice, 328, 329
National Longitudinal Survey of Youth (NLSY), 254, 255
National Organization for Women (NOW), 70, 71, 74
natural resources, increase in, 356–357
negative information, suppression of, by the media, 22–23
Netherlands, 331, 332, 333

Neuhaus, Richard John, 6, 24
New Deal, 23, 241
new familism, 119–120, 124
New York Times, 23–25, 26, 28, 194
Nietzsche, Friedrich, 50, 65–66
Nigeria, 41, 348, 352
Nixon, Richard, 27, 29, 30–31, 33, 176
nonmarital births, 114, 122, 126, 195, 334; welfare and, 251–255, 257
nuclear family, 46, 115, 117–118, 120
Nuclear Regulatory Commission, 223–224
numeric flexibility, jobs and, 378, 379

objectivity, lack of, in the media, 25–26
occupational safety and health, 290–298
O'Neill, Eugene, 312–313
opium, 305–306, 312, 315
organized crime, 331, 336

part-time workers, 376, 380
patent medicines, 305–306
patriarchy, 61, 72
Patterson, James, on moral decline in America, 13–16
Philippines, 344–345, 348
pluralist model, of Congress, 212–213, 218
political action committees (PACs), controversy over influence of, on Congress, 212–227
politicians, and the media, 27–33
Popenoe, David, 121, 122, 125; on traditional families, 114–120
population growth, and controversy over environmental issues, 344–359
pornography, 14, 15, 63
poverty, 48, 122, 275, 277, 285, 286, 287; controversy over cause of, 158–170; and controversy over economic inequality, 132–154; and controversy over homelessness, 192–205; and controversy over welfare, 250–264; crime and, 332–333, 334, 336
predatory criminals, street crime and, 284–289
premarital sex, 14, 15
price, role of, in the market, 239–240
prisons, controversy over effectiveness of, 322–337
privatization: of prisons, 327, 329; of public education, 274–277; of social responsibility, 16
professional detachment, lack of, in the media, 25–26
Prohibition, and controversy over legalization of drugs, 302–318
property crimes, 322, 328
prosecution, imprisonment and, 324, 325, 327
Puddington, Arch, on affirmative action, 174–179

Quayle, Dan, and family values, 121–126
queerbashing, 99–100, 110

quotas, racial, and controversy over affirmative action, 174–187

race, and controversy over affirmative action, 174–187
radical feminism, 70, 72–74, 77
Rank, Mark Robert, on welfare, 257–264
rape, 322, 323, 328, 331–337; controversy over date, 82–94
Rather, Dan, 20, 21, 26
Reagan, Ronald, 22, 27, 29, 30–33, 52, 194, 203, 205, 218, 222–223, 233, 292, 310, 311, 334
rehabilitation, prison and, 334, 335–336
Reiman, Jeffrey, on street crime versus white-collar crime, 290–298
religion: homosexuality and, 101–102; Latinos and, 48–49; media and, 23, 25; moral decline and, 6–8, 14; poverty and, 164, 169; violent crime and, 331–332
reverse discrimination, controversy over affirmative action as, 174–187
Reynolds, Morgan O., on incapacitation as the answer to the crime problem, 322–330
robbery, 322, 323, 328, 331–337
Roiphe, Katie, on date rape, 88–94
Roosevelt, Franklin, 33, 204, 242
Rossi, Alice, 68, 69
Rothman, Stanley, 8, 23
Rubin, Beth A., on U.S. standards of living, 373–382
Russia, 233, 242, 306, 308
Ryan, William, on economic inequality, 144–153

savings and loan industry, bailout of, 213, 214–216, 217–219
scandals, political, media and, 30–32
school choice, controversy over, 268–277
secondary labor market, 378, 381
sentencing, imprisonment and, 325, 333, 335
sex, children and, 15–16
sexual harassment, 88, 93
sexual revolution, 49, 120
Sheaffer, Robert, on feminism, 60–66
Simon, Julian L., 44, 50; on population and economic growth, 354–359
single-parent families, 49, 118, 122, 124, 142, 196, 286, 288, 337
Smith, Adam, 132, 233, 234, 239, 240–241, 245
Smith, Ted, 21–22
social contract, shifts in U.S., 373–380
social mobility, 149–151
Social Security, 137, 241
socialism, 132, 241
socialist feminism, 70, 74, 77
sodomy laws, 102, 103, 108, 110
soil degradation, and controversy over environmental issues, 344–359
Solomon, Norman, on bias in the media, 27–33
Somalia, 350, 352

Sontag, Susan, 92–93
South Bronx, poverty in, 163–170
South Korea, 236, 352
specialization, standards of living and, 367–368
sports, standards of living and, 369–370
Sprague, Peter, 138–139
Stacey, Judith, on traditional families, 121–126
standards of living, 357, 358–359; controversy
     over improving U.S., 364–382; income
     inequality and, 145–146
Stein, Andrew, 203–204
Steinfels, Peter, 24–25
stepfamilies, 118, 376–377
stereotypes, of homosexuals, 98–99
street crime, 284–289, 336
substance abuse, 114, 122; and controversy over
     homelessness, 192–205. See also drugs
Supreme Court, 25, 307, 326, 329; affirmative
     action and, 174, 175, 176, 178
sustainable development, and controversy over
     environmental issues, 344–359
Sweden, 235, 238

Taiwan, 236, 351, 352
taxes, on legalized drugs, 315–317, 336
technology, standards of living and, 358–359, 366,
     378–379
temporary workers, 376, 378, 380
Thailand, 305, 312
theft, 322, 323
Third World, controversy over immigration from,
     38–53
"three strikes and you're out" law, crime and, 333,
     334
Tocqueville, Alexis de, 10, 45–46
traditional families, controversy over preservation
     of, 114–126

Ulster, ethnic issues in, 41–42
underclass: and controversy over homelessness,
     192–205; street crime and, 284–289

unemployment, crime and, 332–333
Union of Concerned Scientists, 223–224
unions, labor, 376, 377

verbal coercion, date rape and, 91, 93
violent crime, controversy over prison and,
     322–337

wage discrimination, standards of living and,
     371–372
Warren, Earl, 326, 329
Warshaw, Robin, on date rape, 82–87, 94
Washington Post, 26, 29, 31, 32, 180, 184, 203,
     291
water quality, and controversy over environmental
     issues, 344–359
Watergate scandal, Nixon and, 30–32
wealth, controversy over distribution of, 132–154,
     357. See also standards of living
weapons, crime and, 332, 335
welfare, 158, 160, 162, 166, 185, 195, 199, 241,
     285, 286, 334; controversy over, 250–264
white-collar crime, 290–298, 331
white-collar workers, 379, 380
Whitehead, Barbara Dafoe, 121, 122, 124–125,
     251
Wilkins, Roger, 32; on affirmative action, 180–187
Willis, Ellen, 72–73
Wilson, Charles E., 213, 215
Wilson, William Julius, 285, 322–323
women: and controversy over date rape, 82–94;
     and controversy over feminism, 60–77
Women's Equity Action League (WEAL), 70, 71
work: prisoners and, 328, 329; standards of living
     and, 367–368; welfare and, 259–260, 262
work ethic, decline of, 14, 236, 374
workplace, occupational health and safety and,
     290–298, 370–371

Zabian, Michael, 135, 137, 138